INDEXES

compiled by

ALAN H. SOMMERSTEIN

Aris & Phillips Ltd – Warminster – England

ISBNs
085668 750 2   clothbound
085668 751 0   limpbound

British Library Cataloguing-in-Publication Data
A catalogue record of this book is available from the British Library

Contents

Preface

This volume, comprising comprehensive indexes to the preceding eleven volumes, completes the series *The Comedies of Aristophanes*. I am happy to dedicate it to Adrian Phillips in recognition of his sixtieth birthday, of the constant support which he and his family have given me over the twenty-four years during which I have been working on the series, and of a publishing endeavour that has deservedly made Aris & Phillips a household name among scholars and students of Greek and Roman antiquity throughout the English-reading world.

ALAN H. SOMMERSTEIN
Nottingham, August 2002

Index to Volumes 1-11

This index is divided into three sections.

Index I (Texts and Passages) includes all ancient texts, or passages thereof, outside the eleven surviving comedies of Aristophanes, that are significantly discussed in the introductions, commentaries or Addenda.

Index II (Persons) includes all persons mentioned in the plays or significantly discussed in the introductions, commentaries or Addenda, regardless of whether they are real, mythical or fictitious or of whether they are human or superhuman; it also includes all *dramatis personae*, speaking or silent, even if they are of subhuman status (e.g. birds, frogs, kitchen utensils). Numbers in parentheses following a person's name are those of his/her entry/entries in *PA* and/or *LGPN* ii (separated by a comma; if there is no comma, the reference is to *LGPN* ii only, unless otherwise stated)[1]. For Athenians, the father's name and (if living as a citizen after 508/7 BC) the deme affiliation are given, where known or plausibly inferable; for other historical ancient Greeks, the place of origin. **Boldface** is used for the headings of entries for persons who are *dramatis personae*, and also to refer to the sections of a play during which a character is present on stage; *italics* are used for the headings of entries for gods, heroes and mythical or fictitious persons. For historical persons whose adult life did not overlap Ar.'s (that is, roughly, those who died before 430 BC or who were born after 400 BC), a lower-case Roman numeral or numerals in parentheses denotes the century or centuries in which they were active; dates are BC unless a superscript [p] is added. Persons of the same name are listed, as nearly as possible, in chronological sequence.

Index III (General) includes all proper names not included in Indexes I-II and a selective listing of other subjects. The following classes of entries are grouped under collective headings:

---

[1] Where a number is given in square brackets, it indicates that in my opinion the register entry in question conflates two or more distinct persons. For a few persons with strong links to Athens who do not appear in *LGPN* ii (usually because they are known to have had citizenship of another state) the *LGPN* number is replaced by the number of their entry in M.J. Osborne and S.G. Byrne, *The Foreign Residents of Athens* (Leuven 1996), prefixed by F. One or two distinguished long-time residents of Athens appear not to have qualified for either register; the most notable of these is Aristotle.

animals [mammals, reptiles, amphibians]
Athens, places and buildings (ancient)
Athens, places and buildings (modern)
Athens, political and legal institutions
Attica, demes and localities (ancient)
Attica, localities (modern)
birds
clothing
crustaceans and molluscs
diseases and ailments
fish
food
footwear
insects and arachnids
meat
medical treatment
metre
military life
music
musical instruments
sport
stars and constellations
trees

References are normally to lines of the text; except in Index I, "n" is added where the subject of an entry is mentioned only in the commentary, and "d" where the reference is to a bracketed stage-direction; throughout, an asterisk indicates that the user should also refer to the Addenda. References to the Introductions are by page and are prefixed by "p".

Plays are abbreviated as follows:
Acharnians
Knights
Clouds
Wasps
Peace
Birds
Lysistrata
Thesmophoriazusae
Frogs
Ecclesiazusae
Wealth

Index I: Texts and Passages

This index is designed to include all those references in these volumes to ancient texts and passages, outside the eleven surviving comedies of Aristophanes, which might conceivably be of interest to a student of the texts in question.

The works of each author (likewise collections of inscriptions, papyri, etc.) are listed in alphabetical order, except in the case of the Old and New Testaments and the Epic Cycle. For Aeschylus, Sophocles and Euripides there are two alphabetical sequences, first of preserved plays, then of fragmentary ones. No attempt is made to distinguish between genuine and spurious works. Where the customary system of reference has changed since earlier volumes were published, the most up-to-date system is used here, with equivalents in previous systems added in square brackets where necessary..

References to the Introductions are to pages (in the form "C p3" or "W p.xv"); in references to the text, apparatus, or translation, or Addenda thereto, the line number is followed by "t"; all other references are to the Commentary. An asterisk indicates that the user should also refer to the Addenda.

Where a passage referred to in one place is included within a passage referred to elsewhere, the references are sometimes consolidated by the use of parentheses; thus the entry for Aeschylus, Eumenides "85(1-)2" includes references both to vv.851-2 and to v.852 alone.

ACHAEUS
Aethon fr. 11: F 184
Athla fr. 4: C 1012-4
Momus fr. 29: W 1081, P 357
Philoctetes fr. 37 B 364

ACHILLES TATIUS
Leucippe & Cleitophon 2.38.2: E 524
    5.5: L 770-1

ACUSILAUS
FGrH 2 F 6b [fr. 1 D-K]: B 693, 1193
    F 18: We p8

AELIAN
Nature of Animals 2.1: B 1137
    2.8: P 841
    3.2: T 416-7

    3.23: B 1355-7
    4.42: B 249
    5.21: B 102-3
    5.38: B 739
    6.43: T 100
    7.16: F 886
    7.17: B 299-300
    8.12: We 690
    9.33: We 710
    12.4: B 516
    12.28: B 739
    16.5: B 471
Varia Historia 1.27: P 395, B 1556, L 490
    2.8: W 1501, P 784, T 169, F 86
    2.25: K 660-1
    6.1: B 1551, E 734
    9.24: W 1259
    11.12: We 995

12.15: T 426
12.35: K 123, P 1070
13.4: F 85
13.12: B 997, T 273
13.15: F 991
14.15: A 854, T 949
14.20: W 1259
fr. 44: T p10
fr. 99: We p12

AELIUS DIONYSIUS
α98: W 807t*

AENEAS TACTICUS
7.14: E 6
16.16: E 6
24.15: T 1202, We 1157
26.13-14: E 6
27.2: E 6

AESCHINES
1 passim: E 365
1.(1-)2: We 31, 910, 914
1.19: We 21
1.19-20: K 877
1.23: T 379, E 128, We 382-3
1.28-32: K 877, T 819-820
1.30: E 400-2
1.42: E 672
1.52: C 349
1.53: We 1037
1.62: L 435-6, E 1023-4
1.65: L 435-6
1.66: L 435-6
1.74: E 617*
1.75: E 932
1.80-85: F 423*
1.84: K 901*
1.87: K 877
1.95: E 672
1.97: L 150-1
1.104: L 1139-40
1.111: E 103
1.120: E 617*
1.129: F 678
1.134: K 877
1.137: We 155
1.170-1: T 345
1.173: C p3, C 876
1.182: E 1104

1.190: We 423, 425
2 passim: L 1231-5
2.11: F 833-4
2.15: L 1139-40, We 382-3
2.49: F 833-4
2.76: T 805, F 678
2.78: L 397
2.79: L 331, F 1510-4
2.98: F 833-4
2.133: A 216*, K 1370
2.152: We 382-3
2.157: We 1
2.168: K 1370*
2.180: A 704*
2.183: A 704*, E 677
3.13: E 290
3.111: F 587
3.124-8: L 1129-32
3.125: E 444
3.137: T 861
3.138-9: We 550
3.152: C 353-4
3.154: B 1361
3.155: C 353-4
3.158: F 139-140, E 1087
3.159: C 353-4
3.160: K 656, F 833-4
3.161: We 377-385
3.166: E 356
3.171-2: A 704*, F 680-1
3.173: E 77
3.175-6: C 353-4
3.177-187: B 1274-5
3.179: F p21
3.187: A p24, F 367
3.194: E 248
3.212: W 523
3.224: We 875
3.251: C 845
3.252: F 685, 953

AESCHYLUS
Agamemnon 16-17: C 721
    28: L 1240
    40-257: F 914-5
    56: B 745
    74-82: C 1417
    104: F 1276
    108-111: F 1276
    109: F 1126

113-120: F 1289
116: F 1276
135: F 1291-2
245: L 217
258: F 1126
351: L 1124
369-402: C 1458-61
376: L 276
390-3: We 862
493-4: We 21
495: E 291
503-537: B 1706-19
508: We 771
515: We 1110
525-6: B 1240
565-6: W 500*
609: L 1198
619: F 1126
659: F 666
717-736: F 1431
783ff: F 963
978-980: F 814-829
1014-7: F 814-829
1022-4: We p8
1041: F 531
1042-5: W 1309
1050-1: B 199, F 93
1072-9: W 392
1081: W 875, T 489, 748
1118: L 240
1131-2: We 632
1216: B 1196
1228: B 1204
1236: L 240
1257: P 933, P 1011
1315: L 706-717
1343: F 1214
1345: F 1214, We 935
1386-7: We 1175
1439: T 941
1444-5: F 207
1456-67: P 865
1482-8: We 130-197
1555-9: F 790
1636 : E 238
1640-1: C 1300
1650-73: C 642
1671: F 935
Choephori: C 534
1-5: F 1124-76 passim

3b-c West: F 1142-3
6-7: F 1126-8
18-19: F 1126
20: F 312-5
106: T 888
123a [165]: F 1126, We 1110
124-8: F 1126
147-8: F 1462
238: A 1184
244-5: We 1175
267-8: E 829
490: L 742
583-4: F 1126
631-8: L 299-300
640: F 1284-95
660-1: T 1066
727-9: We 1161
750: A 478
826: B 313
866-8: F 792
900-2: F 830
919: L 43
942: L 240
962: F 1284-95
994: F 470ff*, 475
1036: We 772
1048-50: L 812
1054: F 472
1063-4: F 1126
1073: We 1175
Eumenides 18: We 9
19: B 516
24: T 991
29: We 9
38: C 1417
39: We 39
48-51: P 811
57-59: T 521-3
62: We 11
63: E p23
67: We 424
69-70: L 812
117: E p23
130: T 1096
140: E p23
183: L 1259
186-190: We 859
214: T 973
217: B 1734
229-231: E 285-310

231/244: E p23
246-7: F 472
269-272: F 145-153
292-8: F 659
292-3: L 347
347-353: L 812
352: We 770/1
360-7: F 814-829
365-7: L 812
387-8: F 814-829
500: We 424
529-532: F 814-829, We 245
538-548: F 145-153
640ff: C 904-6
656: P 969
685-690: L 678
700-3: F 378
725: We 93-94
741: F 685
746: W 523*
759-760: We 1175
778-1047: F 951
82(7-)8: B 1538, L 1198, T 414-5
843: F 1284-95
85(1-)2: K 732*, P 638
853-869: F 378
861: F 935
868: F 204, We 93-94
869: F 1448
903-915: F 378
973: K 410
984-7: L 1289
992-5: F 378
1005: F 1525
1008-9: F 1462
1011: A 75, B 123, L 481
1012-3: F 1530
1021-47 F 1528-33
1031: C 300-1
1043: B 222, T 129-130
1047: B 222, T 129-130
Persae: F p10, F 1026-9
1-139: F 914-5
1: W 220
23: K 159
65-113: T 101-129
112: F 442
155ff: F 963
184: L 1315t*
201-2: F 1340

222: F 1462
324: K 159
347: F 378
395: T 1041
428: W 1085
448: L 2
499: K 156, We 771
578: B 1338
631-2: F 1028
651: F 1029
656: F 1029
664: F 1029
672: F 1029
673: F 1029
681: F 1029
742: C 1458-61
864-7: F 814-829
880-2: F 814-829
979: A 92*
1029: K 567*
1031-2: T 945
1067: F 1029
1070-1: F 1029
1074-5: F 1029
Prometheus Bound: B 1494-1552, We p5
59: K 759*
64-65: We 942-3
125-6: B 1182-3
132: F 1438
283/397: E p23
308: K 759*
461: L 1248
547-9: B 686-7
622: W 873
678: E 80
709-710: B 941-4
756: We 124
766: B 1713
806: We 727
828: W 873
909: We 124
941-2: P 201, We 1170
950: L 1100
954: We 1170
966: We 1170
975: B 1547
983: We 1170
99(3-)4: P 320, B 1745
996: We 124
Seven against Thebes: F 1021

2: E 109
42-48: L 188, 195-7
62-64: E 109
95-96: K 31
103: B 1716
130: W 1532-3
202: L 126
210: T 765
252: F 607
269: L 240
385-6: F 963
495-6: P 1224-5
541: F 929
603: W 918
652-4: E 109
744-753: F 1185
758-762: E 109
817: E 868
855-6: K 546
991: F 1167-8
Suppliants 1-175: F 914-5
26: We 1175
62: L 770-1
154: T 856-7
234ff: F 963
304: E 80
370: E 81
463: T 773
480-9: L 1139-40
506: L 1139-40
558: F 442
559: T 856-7
676-7: L 700-1, F 1361-2
699: E 81
701-9: F 145-153
719-720: T 856-7
745: T 856-7
751-2: P 1125
779-782: W 324
868: F 442
871: F 1438
1039: P 456

Award of the Arms fr. 174: A 883
Bassarai: T 134-5
fr. 25b: E 1068-9
Carians fr. 99: F 1122
Edonians: T 134-5, F 605-673*
fr. 57.10: We 476t
fr. 60: B 276

fr. 61: T 136, F 46
Epigonoi fr. 55: We 1175
Glaucus of Potniae: fr. 36 F 1528
fr. 38: F 1403
Iphigeneia: F 1269-70
Laius fr. 122: F 1190
Lycurgus: T 134-5
Memnon: F 963, 1291-2
fr. 127: F 963
Myrmidons: F 911-2, 924-7, 929, 963, 1041
fr. 131: F 992
fr. 132: F 1264-5
fr. 132b: F 911-2
fr. 132c: F 911-2, 992
fr. 133: B 1256
fr. 134: P 1177, B 800, F 933
fr. 138: F 924-7, E 392-3
fr. 139: W 1259*, B 807
fr. 140: B 1420
Mysians fr. 143: F 1383
Nereids fr. 150: B 952
Netfishers fr. 46a.18-20 [464.18-20 M]:
P 296-8
fr. 47a.818-820: F 1251-60*
Niobe fr. 154a: F 911-2
fr. 160: B 1246-8
fr. 161: F 1392
fr. 162: C 1468
Palamedes fr. 181a: F 1451
fr. 182: F 1451
fr. 182a: F 1451
Penelope: T 547-8
Pentheus: T 996, F 605-673*
Philoctetes fr. 249: F 1383
Phineus fr. 258: P 811
Phrygians: F 911-2
Priestesses fr. 87: F 1273-4
Prometheus Unbound: B 1182-3, We pp5-6
Psychagogoi: B 1553-64
fr. 273: B 1553-4, F 1266
fr. 273a: B 1553-5
Psychostasia: F 963, 1365
fr. 280: P 831
Sisyphus the Runaway fr. 227: F 840
Sisyphus the Stone-Roller fr. 233: P 73
Sphinx fr. 236: F 1286
Telephus (?) fr. 238: F 1269-70
Theoroi fr. 78a.29-31 [17.29-31 M]: P 879-
880, T 647-8
Toxotides fr. 243: E 49

Thracian Women fr. 84: F 1294
Women of Salamis: F 1041
Xantriai: T 996
Youths: T 134-5
fr. 281a.10 [530.10 Mette]: C 903
fr. 282: F 1291-2
fr. 300: T 856-7
fr. 309: A 87
fr. 322: We 1063
fr. 373: T 921-2
fr. 383: T 973
fr. 384: We 1161
fr. 388: W 804, L 64, F 366
fr. dub. 468: F 844

AESOP
Fables (ed. Perry) 1: B 651-3
    2: B 571
    3: W 1448, P 133, L 694-5
    101: B 571
    223: P 1078
    255: K 1038*
    447: B 471

AGATHON
fr. 6: T 29, F 83
fr. 8: T 29, F 83
fr. 11: T 29, F 83
fr. 12: T 29, F 83
fr. 14: T 148
fr. 27: B 636-7

ALCAEUS (lyric poet)
fr. 6.13-14: P 1301*
fr. 34: L 1300, E 1068-9
fr. 38a: F 137-8
fr. 42.13: F 1060
fr. 141.3-4: W 1232-5
fr. 298.6: F 666
fr. 307: B 769-784
fr. 308: F 1266
fr. 326: W 29
fr. 332: We 644
fr. 345: B 1410-2
fr. 346: T 743
fr. 357: A 1072
fr. 364: We 437, 549
fr. 374: E 952-975
fr. 428: P 1298-9

ALCAEUS (comic dramatist)
Pasiphaë: We p1

ALCIPHRON
Letters 2.3.11: K 852-7
    2.37.2: T 80, 299
    3.10.3: L 985
    3.12.3: K 1246*
    3.40: We 535
    4.2.5: E 372, We 22

ALCMAEON
A5 D-K: C 163
A6 D-K: C 163

ALCMAN
PMG 1: B 919
PMG 1.7: F 1060
PMG 1.43-59: L 1296-1315
PMG 1.46: L 1315t*
PMG 1.100-1: F 207
PMG 3.68: E 973-4
PMG 26: B 299-300
PMG 89: B 777-8, T 43-50
PMG 145: K 1287
PMG 148: B 1553

ALEXIS
Ancylion: W 1397
Apeglaukomenos fr. 15: A 1211, E 821-2
    fr. 16: P 395
    fr. 18: L 560
Asclepiocleides fr. 24: We p12
Asotodidaskalos fr. 25: E 867-8
Dorkis fr. 57: E 102, We 176
    fr. 59: We 1132
Galatea: We 290-321
Gynaikokratia: E p8
    fr. 42: A p16*
Homoia fr. 168: We 999
Hypnos fr. 243 [241 K]: B 1529
Hypobolimaios fr. 246: We 1132
Isostasion fr. 103.10-12: E 907, We 513
Kouris fr. 112: E 663-4
    fr. 113.5 [108.5 K]: C 853
Kybernetes fr. 121 [116 K]: P 395
Lebes fr. 133: E 818
Linus fr. 140: F 62
Odysseus Hyphainon fr. 160: W 1253-5*
Olynthioi fr. 167 [162 K]: A 1116

Opora: P 523*
Orchestris fr. 172: We 324
Pamphile fr. 175: E 1092
Pannychis fr. 178 [172 K]: W 838, P 123
  fr. 179: B 1148*, E 154
Parasitos fr. 184 [179 K]: A p25
Phaedo or Phaedrias: L 355
Philousa fr. 255: We 149
Ponera fr. 193: E 1174
Pyraunos fr. 206: K 1246*
Tarantinoi fr. 223.16: E 22-23
  fr. 224 [222 K]: B 1716
Thrason fr. 96: E 119-120
fr. 281: E 1092
fr. 285 [283 K]: W 80
fr. 287: F 218-9
fr. 332 [331 K]: L 184

AL-MUBASHIR
Life of Zeno p.33 Rosenthal: B 1073*

AMEIPSIAS
Apokottabizontes fr. 2: T 728, F 1345
  fr. 3: L 48, E 929
Connus: C p2
  fr. 7: We 1128
  fr. 9: B 1282, We 942-3
Revellers: B p.1
fr. 23: F 808, We 869
fr. 26: We 884

AMMONIUS
On Similar & Different Words 17: F 378

AMPHIS
Gynaikokratia: E p8
Ialemos fr. 20: L 673
  fr. 22: L 560
Kouris fr. 23: We p6
Opora: P 523*

ANACREON
PMG 346 fr. 11.18: L 344-5
  357.3: T 992-3
  358 [fr. 13 Page]: B 1098-1101
  372 [fr. 27 Page]: A 850
  378 [fr. 33 Page]: B 1372-4
  379 [fr. 34 Page]: B 572-5
  381(b) [fr. 36(b) Page]: P 1298-9
  388 [fr. 43 Page]: A 850

426: We 1002

ANANIUS
fr. 1 West: F 659
frr. 2-3 West: F 659

ANAXAGORAS
A38 D-K: B 1005
A42.3 D-K: C 264
A84 D-K: C 376-8
A91 D-K: T 856-7

ANAXANDRIDES
Gerontomania fr. 9: E 922, We 149

ANAXILAS
Auletes fr. 3: E 154

ANAXIMANDER
A11 D-K: C 1280-1
A23 D-K: C 404-7
fr. 1 D-K: C 1292

ANAXIMENES
A7 D-K: C 404-7
A20 D-K: C 264

ANDOCIDES
1 *passim*: We p18
1.2: E 1064-5
1.11: E 835
1.13: K 242-3*
1.16: F 1512
1.17-22: C 109, W 1268-9
1.17: W 662
1.27: A 88, K 958, C 353-4, W 1187, P 395,
    446, B 289, 1556, L 489, T 605
1.35: C 64
1.36: W 690, P 395, B 1556, L 489, 490,
    T 277-8
1.43: A 220, P 395, 452, B 1556, L 489,
    846, F 620, 629, We 824, 875
1.44: E 1064-5, We 382-3
1.45: B 766-7, E 444
1.47-68: C 109, W 1268-9
1.47: W 1301-2*, L 103
1.52-53: K 242-3*
1.67-68: K 242-3*
1.73-80: W 917, L 581, F p21, F 686-705
1.77-79: B 790

7.67.6: F 140
7.731.6: E 1073
9.357: We 586
9.588.5-6: K 571
11.22.2: E 909
11.42.5-6: E 1073
11.196.1: E 1072
11.408: E 878, We 1064
12.22.8: L 673
12.161: T 1172

ANTIGONUS OF CARYSTUS
Wonders 23 Giannini: B 299-300*

ANTIPHANES
Aeolus fr. 19: F 1081
    fr. 20 [19 K]: A 1002
Aphrodisios fr. 55: E 1-18, We 515
Asclepius fr. 47: We p12
Birth of Aphrodite fr. 57 [55 K]: P 1244,
    B 523
Boeotia fr. 59 [58 K]: W 1056-7
Boutalion fr. 69.14-15: We 594
Cleophanes fr. 120: T 1114
Cyclops: We 290-321
Dodonis fr. 91: T 163
Ganymede fr. 75 [74 K]: W 21
Halieuomene fr. 27: A 893-4*
Hautou Erôn fr. 51 [49 K]: P 1178
Hydria fr. 210: E 877-1111
Knoithideus fr. 122 [124 K]: W 21
Korinthia fr. 124 [126 K]: A 793, We 305
Leukadia fr. 137: E 137
Minos fr. 156: We 544
Neottis fr. 166: We 253
Omphale fr. 174: We 815
    fr. 175: We 884
Parekdidomene fr. 185: We 1004
Philothebaios fr. 216.20-22: E 126-7
Philotis fr. 221: E 292
Poiesis fr. 189.22: E 372, We 22
Skleriai fr. 196: T 1114, E 707-8
Skythes fr. 197: E 691-2
Timon fr. 204: We 138
fr. 225: F 942, We 253
fr. 233.4 [236.4 K]: W 838, P 250

fr. 259: We p7
fr. 288 [296 K]: W 83, B 194
fr. 293.3: T 1195

ANTIPHON (orator)
1 *passim*: T 430, 561
1.10: F 616
2.2.5: E 544
2.4.7: We 6-7
5.11: F 587
5.13: B 1455
5.17: E 1064-5
5.40: P 452, L 846, F 620, We 875
5.51: F 685
5.69-70: W 1, P 364
5.82-84: P 968
5.88: L 186
6.11: B 1403*, F 1036-7
6.13: B 1407
6.34: B 474
6.49: F 1505
fr. 1: K 448*
frr.21-24: B 1569
fr. 23: B 1021
fr. 30: B 1021
fr. 57: W 98, B 102-3
fr. 65: W 421, B 1701

ANTIPHON (sophist)[2]
fr. 10 D-K: F 634
fr. 13 D-K: B 1005
fr. 45 D-K: B 1553

ANTONINUS LIBERALIS
19: F 1356
29: P 1078

APOLLODORUS OF ATHENS
FGrH 244 F 35: T p1, F p8
    F 75: We p8
    F 108: F 798

APOLLODORUS OF CARYSTUS
Hekyra fr. 8: P 1146

---

2   I separate Antiphon "the sophist" from Antiphon "the orator" merely for clarity; it should not be taken to imply any opinion on the question whether the two are or are not the same person.

APOLLODORUS OF CARYSTUS *or*
    GELA[3]
fr. 13: E 316-7

[APOLLODORUS] (mythographer)
1.6.(1-)2: W 1038*, B 553
1.7.1: B 686
1.7.8-9: F 194
2.1.2: E 80
2.5.12: F 289-296, 468
3.4.3: L 1282, F 215-6
3.9.2: L 785
3.12.6: F 464
3.14.1: T 318-9
Epitome 1.4: E 1021
    1.9: F 1211-3

APOLLONIUS RHODIUS
1.153-5: We 210
1.164-171: F 1402
1.916-921: P 277-8
1.1207-1357: K 67
3.117-126: W 295-6
3.1342: B 1500
4.264-5: C 398
4.662-671: F 1340
4.866-879: C 1068
4.871: K 1095
4.1705: B 870

APOLLOPHANES
Cretans fr. 5: A 802
    fr. 6: We p12

APOSTOLIUS
10.97: E 630
13.31 [= *com. adesp.* 12 K]: K 523
14.14: B 1556
17.68: A 846

APPENDIX PLANUDEA
242.1: W 27
261: L 553

APULEIUS
Apologia 24: F 991

ARAROS

Campylion fr. 8: W 1522

ARCHESTRATUS
SH 150 [fr. 19 Brandt]: L 560
SH 154.14: We 912
SH 176.1-9 [fr. 45.1-9 Brandt]: K 361
SH 192.17-18 [fr. 62.17-18 Brandt]: P 252,
    T 1192

ARCHILOCHUS
fr. 5: P 1298-9, 1301, E 670-1
fr. 41: B 299-300*
fr. 66: E 906
fr. 107: W 1032, P 755
fr. 109: P 603t
fr. 119: E 963-4
frr. 172-181: B 51-3
fr. 187: A 120-1*
fr. 196a.21 West (D): T 60-62, E 316-7, 971
fr. 196a.23-24 West (D): B 161
fr. 196a.39-41 West (D): P 1078
fr. 213: F 704
fr. spur. 324: A 1234
fr. spur. 331: K 1277*

ARCHIPPUS
Fishes: E p8, We p7
fr. 23 [25 K]: B p.2
fr. 27: B p.2, T 295-311
fr. 28: P 804, B p.2, B 151
fr. 31: E 252
Rhinon: We p7
Wealth frr. 37-39: We p7
fr. 48 [45 K]: W 44
fr. 50 [2 Dem.]: B 161
fr. 60 [53 K]: B 1553

ARETHAS
on Plato Lysis 206e: F 970

ARISTEIDES
Orationes 3.154: E p31, We p25
    3.365: F p9
    34.28: L 751
    47.11: We 669-670
    48.31: We 625
    48.35: We 669-670
    48.46: We 669-670

---

3. This fragment is ascribed by the quoting author simply to "Apollodorus" without distinguishing between these two contemporary and homonymous comic dramatists.

49.19: B 1552

ARISTIDES QUINTILIANUS
2.101: T 124-5

ARISTOCRITUS
FGrH 493 F 5: W 846, P 864

ARISTODEMUS
FGrH 104 F 16: P 603t

ARISTOMENES
Admetus: We p1
Dionysos Asketes fr. 13: F p11
Porters: K p2

ARISTONOUS
Paean 10-11: We 213

ARISTOPHANES
Aeolosicon: F 499, E 867-8, We p1, p22,
    pp23-24, p26
fr. 3: E 818, 821-2, We 862
fr. 6: We p24
fr. 8: We p22
fr. 9: We p22
fr. 10: We p22
fr. 11: F 62
Amphiaraus: W p.xv, T p2, F p1, We p1
    fr. 17 [18 K]: C 661
    fr. 21: We 701-2
    fr. 26: T 861
Anagyrus fr. 41: F 148, E 907
    fr. 53: A p4*
    fr. 58: A p4*, C p2*
Babylonians: A p2*, A 377-8, 630,
    W 1018-29, 1284-91, B p.1
fr. 84: P 395, B 1556, L 490
Banqueters: A p2*, C 528-531, W 1018-29,
    B p.1
    fr. 205 [198 K]: W 44, L 372, F 833-4,
        1422, E 1032
    fr. 207 [200 K]: A 967
    fr. 209: F 293, We 594
    fr. 210: E 1032
    fr. 211: We 995
    fr. 214: T 556
    fr. 225 [216 K]: W 911, P 344
    fr. 227: B 998
    fr. 228 [219 K]: K 839-840, B 1423

fr. 229 [218 K]: C 528-9
fr. 232: B 1432
fr. 233: A 255t*
fr. 234: C 1484-5*
fr. 235: T 161-2*
fr. 236: L 1061-4
fr. 240 [229 K]: A 575, W 823
fr. 244 [554 K]: A 716, 1422
Clouds I: C pp2-4, P p.xix
    fr. 392: C p4*, T p4, T 451, F 839,
        1491-2
    fr. 394: F 1056-7
Cocalus: T p11, We p1, p22
    fr. 364: L 196, 197, E 1119, 1123,
        We p22, We 1021
    fr. 365: L 381, We p22
    fr. 370: We 149
Daedalus fr. 191: E 8
    fr. 192 [188 K]: C 326
    fr. 193 [185 K]: C 661
    fr. 194 [186 K]: C 661
Danaids fr. 256: P 923, We 1197
    fr. 258: E 544
    fr. 264: A p4*
    fr. 265: A p4*
    fr. 271 [261 K]: W 1245-7
Dionysus Shipwrecked: F p11
Dramas test. iv K-A [fr. 290 K]: A p4
Dramas/Centaur fr. 282: A p4*
    fr. 284: A p4*
Dramas/Niobus fr. 295 [291 K]: C 104,
    W 1408, B 1296
Dramas/(?) fr. 299: F 798
Farmers fr. 101: B 481-521
    fr. 102 [100 K]: K 6
    fr. 103 [101 K]: K 963
    fr. 109: L 1173
    fr. 110: L 1173
    fr. 111: B 131-2, L 1173, We 615
    fr. 112: L 1173, We 773
    fr. 116 [112 K]: C 1001
    fr. 117: F 1302
Gerytades fr. 156 [149 K]: A p25,
    B 1372-1409, F p9, F 146, 153,
    1302, E 330
    fr. 157: F 366
    fr. 158 [151 K]: W 1313, F p9
    fr. 160 [CGFP 74.16ff]: A p25, P 174,
        E 891
    fr. 178 [169 K]: A p25, T 29, F 83

fr. 179: We 179
see also fr. 596
Heroes fr. 314: E 686-7
Islands fr. 402: P 530-8, 1149, E 1172
fr. 403 [388 K]: C 326, B 296
fr. 409: B 440-1
Lemnian Women: E p10
fr. 373: T 605
fr. 374: E p10
fr. 375: E p10
fr. 376: E p10
fr. 380 [364 K]: W 195, P 1005, L 36,
E 1170
Merchant Ships: W 1038
fr. 416: K 908*
fr. 420: P p.xx
fr. 422 [407 K]: A 122, K 1374
fr. 425: L 1168-9
fr. 437: P 215
Old Age: We p7
fr. 135: L 645
fr. 136: E 252
fr. 144: F 1480
fr. 149: K 129*
Peace II: P pp.xix-xx, We p7, p29
fr. 305: P p.xx, L 1173
fr. 306: P p.xx
fr. 307 : P p.xx
fr. 308 [694 K]: K 963, P p.xx
fr. 309: P p.xx
Phoenissae: We p29
Preview: W p.xv*, B p.1, T p2, F p1, We p1
fr. 477: B 1552, We 782
Seasons fr. 577 [567 K]: K 1312
fr. 578: B 873, L 388
fr. 581: P p.xx, E 1172
fr. 582 [571 K] W 1183-4, P 928,
B 822-3, L 63
fr. 583: F 501
Skenas Katalambanousai fr. 484: T 861
fr. 488: T p4
Storks fr. 444 [430 K]: C 1365, W 1222,
1225, P 1154, L 632, E 938-945
fr. 450: F 710-3
fr. 453: F 1302
fr. 454: E 254, We 665
fr. 455: We 84
Tagenistae fr. 504: F 1462
fr. 505: T 840-1
fr. 506: F 52-53, 1114

fr. 521: B 76
Telemessians fr. 550: K 1053*
fr. 551: E 647, We 314-5
fr. 552 [539 K]: C 104, W 1408, B 1296
Thesmophoriazusae II: A p3*, P p.xix,
T p11
fr. 331: T 299
fr. 333 [318 K]: W 510, P 811, T p11,
fr. 334: B 1256, T p11, F 48
fr. 332: L 530-1, T p11, T 220, F 711-2,
E 65, 125, 732, 929, We 1064
fr. 336: T p11
fr. 337: T p11
fr. 338: T p11
fr. 341: T p11
fr. 344: T p11
fr. 345: T p11
fr. 346: T p11, We p24
fr. 347: T p11
fr. 348: L 1279, T p11, T 301, F 334-5
fr. 350: L 629, F 258-9
fr. 351: T p11
fr. 355: T p11
fr. 358: L 621, T p11
Triphales fr. 561: L 947
fr. 568 [557 K]: C 1001
Wealth I: P p.xix, We p7, pp26-31, We 115
fr. 458: We p27
fr. 459: F 1094-6, We p7, p27, p30
fr. 460: We p27
fr. 461: We p27
fr. 462: We p27
fr. 465: We p27
fr. 590.44-51 [CGFP 56.44-51]: W p.xv
fr. 591.43-46 [CGFP 63.43-46]: W 462,
B 281-2, T 168, F 1488-9
fr. 591.55 [CGFP 63.55]: C 595
fr. 591.70-71: B 126
fr. 591.84-86 [CGFP 63.85-87]: A p25
fr. 592.16-28: L 109, 159, E 45, 916
fr. 592.29-30: T 491-2, E 225
fr. 595 [CGFP 294k]: A p25, T p4
fr. 596: T p4, F 944*
fr. 598: F 82
fr. 608: L 443, F 293
fr. 624 [611 K]: W 1215, F 938
fr. 625: F 578
fr. 633: F 4
fr. 645: C 1005-8t*
fr. 655: F 733

fr. 673: P 1081t*
fr. 682: T p4
fr. 689: K 908*
fr. 692: B 11
fr. 695: E 652
fr. 715: T 204, 491-2, E 150, 225
fr. 723: P 803, F 151
fr. 914: F 1285
fr. dub. 925: We 1151
fr. dub. 926 [fr. 63 K]: K 1281, W 1280,
    P 883, E 120
fr. dub. 928: We 149
fr. dub. 939: E 284

ARISTOPHON
Philonides fr. 13: L 184
Pythagoristes fr. 10: F 942, We 253
    fr. 11: B 572-5

ARISTOTLE
de Anima 431b5-6: E 6
Athenaion Politeia 2.2: We 147
    6.1: We 147
    9.1: We 147, 908
    11.2: We p18
    16.7: We p6
    18: L 632
    18.1: W 1410
    19.1: W 502, L 619
    19.3: L 665
    19.4: L 1150-6
    19.5: B 832, L 1150-6
    19.6: L 1150-6
    24.3: W 662, E 304-5
    27.3: E 304-5
    28.1-3: P 684
    28.3: L 536, T 805, F 141, E 252
    28.5: F 541
    29.2: E 396-7
    29.3: F 967
    29.4: E 396-7
    32.1: T p3
    33.2: B 126
    34.1: T 805, F p6, F 678
    34.3: L 577-8, F 367, 965, 967, E 97
    34.5: W 157
    39-40: We 1146
    40.1-2: F 367
    40.2: T 78-79, 943, E 202-3, We 550
    40.3: We p18

41.3: E 102, 183-4, 301, We 171, 176
42.1: W 578
43.4-6: We 171
43.4: A 19
43.5: K 855, W 1042*, We 923
43.6: L 981, 1139-40, We 382-3
44.1: P 906, T 373
44.2-3: E 87
44.4: C 584-5, B 800
45.1: T 78-79, We 476t
45.4: E 396-7
48.1: K 248*, 774
50.2: T 1195, E 614
51.1: W 1407
51.3: K 407*
52.1: F 772, We 524, 932
53.3: E 982-4
53.7: K 1370
54.2: K 442
54.3: T 432
55.3: W 388, B 1527
55.5: L 186
56.3: A 392
56.6: C 845, We 278
57.2: We 278
57.4: L 602
58.2-3: We 278
59.1-6: E 290, We 278
59.3: We 168, 923
59.7: E 290
61.1: K 912-3, T 837
61.4: B 799
62.2: We 171
63-66: E 290, 681, We 277
63.4: E 683, We 277
65.2: We 278
66.1: We 278
66.3: E 303
67.1: W 595
68.2: E 296, We 278
69.1: F 685
69.2: W 106
Eudemian Ethics 1231a17: C 686*, W 84,
    F 934
de Generatione Animalium 749a35-b3:
    B 695
    750b3ff: B 695
    785b18: F 730
Historia Animalium 490a7-13: B 1296
    493a27: L 413

502a19-23: K 416
522b2-5: E 404, We 719
538a27: C 170
542b24-25: B 1594
544b4: B 303
557b25-31: B 590
559b21-560a18: B 695
564b1-3: B 102-3
571a14: W 1087*
592b23-25: B 303
593a12: B 299-300*
597a23: B 710
597b1-3: B 1137
599a31: C 170
608a28-31: T 416-7
609a15-16: B 1083
613a22: B 1083
613b17-24: B 768
614a10-28: B 1083
614b35-615a3: B 266
615a19: B 568
615b23-24: B 1355-7
616a14-19: B 251, F 1309-12
616b4ff: B 887t*
de Incessu Animalium 705b34: We 1129
Mechanica 851a38-b6: F 1220
de Mel.,Xen.,Gorgia 980b1-3: T 5-21*
Metaphysics 993b15: C 969-971*
    1050a19: We 602
Meteorologica 362a23: A 876-7
Mirabilia 834a12-22: We 586
Nicomachean Ethics 1098a18: B 1417
    1100b32: F 179
    1106a14-1109b26: We 245
    1106b36-1107a3: We 245
    1107b8-14: We 245
    1111a9-10: F 886
    1119b22-1122a17: We 245
    1123a24: W 57
    1123b6-8: B 1678, E 629
    1148b32: A 255t*
    1156a27: F 944
    1159b29-32: We 345
    1160a18: E 1023-4
    1170b11: F 944
de Partibus Animalium 686b4-11: P 789*
    687b18-19: K 546
Poetics: F p15
    1447a16: T 156
    1448a6: A 854, T 949, We 602

1448a27: A p24
1448a31-32: W 57
1449a19-21: F 1005
1449a21-27: C 642
1449b7-9: A p8, K 537
1451b19-23: T 29, F 83
1452b19-20: F 1119
1453a33-35: F 141
1453a36-39: B 15-16
1454b23: F 86
1454b25: L 139
1455a22-34: T 149-150
1455a26: F 86
1456a26-30: T 29, F 83, E 729/730,
    We 321/2
1458a(18-)21: W 1313, F p9
1458b31: K 1281, W 1280, P 883,
    We 1005
1461b30-32: B 672*
Politics 1252b5-9: We 461-3
    1253b20-22: We 6-7
    1255a21-35: We 461-3
    1256b26-1258a14: We 188-9
    1257b14-17: We 287
    1258a38-b2: We 1063
    1258b2-8: C 1294-5
    1259b1-3: E p8
    1260a8-13: E p8
    1260b27-1269a28 E p16
    1261b38-1262a14: E 643
    1263a26-39: E p19
    1263a35-37: E p16
    1266a31-36: E p16
    1266a37-1267b13: We p18
    1267a2-17: W 959, E 608, We 565
    1267b3-5: E 608
    1269b24: E p8
    1274b9-10: E p16
    1275a23-32: We 917
    1298b26-33: A 755
    1305a3-7; We p18
    1306b2: We 476
    1309a14-20: We p18
    1311b30-34: F 953
    1313b33: E p8
    1313a40: F 494
    1316a29-32: K 1044
    1323a29: T 1009-14
    1335b4-16: F 942
    1340a36: We 602

Problems 863b19-28: F 1280
  887b38-888a22: We 873
  890b7-26: P 542, L 444
  922b10-28: We 321/2
  950a4: F 934
  951a20-952a16: F 685
  953b4: E 663-4
Rhetoric 1374a11-15: E 663-4
  1375b31-34: F p10
  1383a5: T 930-1
  1384a34: W 447
  1385a9-13: T 930-1, We 476
  1389a9-11: We 1066
  1389b2-12: We 1066
  1391a14-19: W 1309
  1400a9-14: W 1187
  1400b20: E 202-3, We 550
  1402a19ff: C 112-5
  1405a19-20 : B 284, F 428, E 810
  1407b2-4: We 816
  1409b25-30: B 1385, F 366
  1416a28-35: T 451
  1419a2-5: B 521
  1419a26-30: L 421
Rhetorica ad Alexandrum 1437b13-16:
  E 173-4
de Sensu 444b12: B 590
Topics 115b22-25: B 1529
  117b17-19: E 1073
  145a22-25: T 556*
fr. 67: A 710, W 592
  227: W 146
  386: L 397
  394: L 664
  504: We 41-43
  513: B 1463
  542: L 1140
  544: P 623
  583: W 1259
  591: C 398
  611.37: We 287
  627: T p4
  630: F 404-6

ARISTOTLE, COMMENTATORS ON
  (*CAG*)
xxi.2 p.106.32: E 825

ARISTOXENUS
Harmonics p.34.15ff Meibom: F 1323

ARRIAN
Anabasis 1.25.6: F 683-4
  7.14.8: C 621*

ARTEMIDORUS
Onirocritica 1.37: W 51
  1.80: F 67, E 470, We 295
  3.3: P 1056

ASCLEPIADES
FGrH 12 F 1: F 1403

ASTYDAMAS II
Hector fr. 1h.10: E 729/730, We 321/2
Hermes fr. 3.3-4: W 616*

ATHENAEUS
1.3a: F 943
1.3d: K 656
1.4d: B 1695-6
1.5b: E 1169-75
1.5f-7a: W 84, F 934
1.7a: We 290-321
1.16b-c: P 1060, B 1705, We 1110
1.20e: F 896
1.28e-29e: L 196, E 1119, We 1021
1.32d-e: F 204
1.32f: E 1139
1.33c: F 204
2.44f: K 348-9
2.63e-64b: E 1092
2.64b: L 1078
3.73d: L 537
3.79e: P 1169
3.84a: W 1056-7
3.96a: A 793
3.98f: T 1114
3.109b: E 851
3.116a: E 851
4.130d: We 253
4.146f: E 1169-75
4.171c-e: C 1198
4.174f: F 1302-3
5.181b: F 849
5.215c: E 74
5.217a: T 29, F 83
5.218b: F 429
5.219a: B 968
5.220b: F 934, 970

5.220b-c: K 1281
6.251a: E 71
6.260b: F 651
6.267e-270a: We p6
6.269f-270a: C 521-3*
7.285b: A 640
7.325a: We 594
8.338b-d: W 1410
8.347d: F 1040
9.391e-f: L 723-5
9.397c-d: A 63
9.400c: K 1225
9.409b: P 969
10.426b-427a: We 1132
10.427e: T 401-4*
10.430d-431b: We 1132
10.437c-d: F 218-9
10.453b: W 22-23
11.461c: C 315, B 1490-3
11.464d: B 1299
11.484f-486a: P 916
11.487d-f: B 523
12.512b-c: K 967
12.515c: K 1384
12.516d: P 123
12.524f-526d: T 163, E 883
12.534c: K 967
12.551d: B 1372-1409
12.554c-e: E 907
13.555d-556a: L 593
13.565f: T 1114
13.569f: A 527
13.573b-c: E 883
13.580d: F 1302-3
13.585c: We 1206
13.585d: L 1199
13.592a: P 523*
13.592c-d: We 179
13.596f: A 1093*
13.602d: L 1162-3
13.604d-f: F 148
13.612a: E 302
14.614d: F 651
14.620e-621b: E 883
14.638e: K 1225
14.644f: We 999
14.646f: P 869
14.647d-e: We 677
14.653f: P p.xx
14.654b-c: C 109

15.685c-692f: E 841-2
15.687a: E 302
15.688e: L 944
15.689c: W 1056t*

ATHENION
Samothracians fr. 1.18: P 1040, B 518-9,
    We 1130-1

AUGUSTINE
*City of God*18.9: E p28*

AXIONICUS
Tyrrhenos fr. 1.4: T 1114

BABRIUS
19: K 1068
32: A 255*
50: K 1068
106: K 1068

BACCHYLIDES
3.85: F 1483
3.96-98: P 830
5.60: W 1031*
5.104-135: F 863-4
12.140: C 335
15.7: T 101-129
18 *passim*: We 290-321
18.27-30: E 1021
18.55: L 299-300
20 *passim*: B 1731-6
fr. 4.69-70 [3.6-8 Jebb]: A 279, T 246
fr. 4.80 : T 1041
fr. 20a : L 344-5, F 194
fr. 20b.50: T 969
fr. 44: F 38
fr. 66: F 38

BION
1.75: L 602, E 538

CALLIAS
Atalantas fr. 4: B 153-4
Cyclopes fr. 8: T 163
fr. 9: B 603
*Pedetai*fr. 14: B 151
fr. 15 [12 K]: W 61, F 1491-2
fr. 17 [13 K]: W 1221, B 31
fr. 20 [14 K]: C 332, B 521

fr. 35 [28 K]: W 1489
fr. 36 [29 K]: C 1383
fr. 38: We 307-8

CALLIMACHUS
Epigrams 31.6 Pf.: T 1009-14
Hymn (2) to Apollo 1: We 213
  59: B 870
Hymn (3) to Artemis 13: C 271
  69: T 246
  173-4: L 447
  189-199: W 369
Hymn (5) to Athena 132-3: B 1653
Hymn (6) to Demeter 108: W 844
  124: B 994
fr. 64.11-14: E 1068-9
fr. 194.101: F 804
fr. 196.43: E 284
fr. 199: L 1078
fr. 203.58: T 1009-14
fr. 215: F 1198-1247
fr. 227.5-7: T 94
fr. 254: P 603-4
fr. 260.66: F 1296-7
fr. 414: B 304
fr. 607: P 363
fr. 638: K 1172

CANTHARUS
Tereus: B 15-16
  fr. 6: T 1185, E 903
  fr. 8: F 854
  fr. 10: T 647-8, E 470

CATULLUS
45.8-9: K 639
58.5: L 739-740
61.119-143: P 1339
64.305-383: B 1734
88.8: E 470, We 295
105.2: P 637

CEPHISODORUS
Amazons: E p10
Antilais: E p10
Trophonius fr. 4: L 45

CHAEREMON
Dionysus fr. 6: We 21

CHARICLEIDES
Halysis fr. 1: We 594

CHIONIDES
Beggars fr. 4: F 1302

CHOERILUS
fr. 2 Bernabé: F 1299-1300*

CICERO
ad Atticum 5.10.3: W 1431
  16.2.4: P 637
de Legibus 2.37: W 9
de Natura Deorum: 1.10 C 219, B 1730
in Pisonem 19: F 420
Tusculan Disputations: 1.41 W 1431
  5.64: B 1001-9
  5.108: We 1151
in Verrem 2.5.135: P 1306

CINESIAS
PMG 774 [fr. 1 Page]: B 1372-1409

CLEARCHUS OF SOLI
fr. 68 Wehrli: E 1029
fr. 109 Wehrli [72 Müller]: E 1101

CLEMENT OF ALEXANDRIA
Paedagogus 2.1.3: B 277
  3.4.30: B 277
Protrepticus 2.30.4: We 84
Stromateis 1.21.105: We p11
  7.3.23.6: L 754-5

COLUMELLA
de Re Rustica 2.10.24-25: K 606
  4.23: P 1147
  7.8.3-4: F 559
  9.15.5-6: W 456-460
  10.235-6: F 303
  11.2.61: P 1147

COMICA ADESPOTA
fr. 63: E 867-8
fr. 101.12-13: E 1123, We 1132
fr. 119 [64 K]: P 395, B 1556, L 490
fr. 123: L p2*, F 1422
fr. 173 [Et.Gen. λ34]: B 126
fr. 283: E 97
fr. 338 [24 K]: B 11

fr. 213 [200 K]: K 526-8*, 1225,
F 13-15
fr. 214 [203 K]: W 1301, L 270
fr. 215 [202 K]: C 103
Satyrs: K p2
Seasons fr. 276: F 1327-8
fr. 279 [259 K]: C 666
fr. 281 [263 K]: W 1187
fr. 283 [262 K]: A 846, K 1304, C 551,
W 1007, P 681, T 840
fr. 290: F 1065
fr. 294: L 1190
Seriphioi fr. 223 [208 K]: W 1309
fr. 227 [212 K]: C 686, W 74
fr. 228 [217A Edm.]: K 231-3*, P 395
fr. 229: E p31, We 953
Thrattai fr. 73 [71 K]: A 530
fr. 77: We 307-8
fr. 81: B 285, F 428, 501, E 810,
We 168
fr. 299: T 401-4
fr. 329: F 943
fr. 335: B 530, L 1164
fr. 339: K 129*
fr. 342 [307 K]: A p25, K 527, T p4
fr. 344: F 1380
fr. 346: P 741, F 62
fr. 348: P 395
fr. 349 [317 K]: K 534
fr. 357: F 295
fr. 360: T 395
fr. 367: F 186
fr. 382: F 494
fr. 397: E 829
fr. 406: T 921-2
fr. 460: T 163
fr. 462 [334 K]: W 151

CRITIAS
Peirithous: F p10, p12, F 142
fr. 1: F 464, 1244*
fr. 4.4 : T 1054
Rhadamanthys: F p10
Sisyphus fr. 19 [fr. 25 D-K]: C 1421-2, F p10
Tennes: F p10
fr. 21: We 50
fr. 37 D-K: K 849, P 662, L 106
fr. eleg. 6.13 West: L 426

CROBYLUS
Pseudhypobolimaios fr. 5: L 304
fr. 7: We 305

CTESIAS
FGrH 688 F 1.23-28: B 1021
F 13-14 (33-34): F p6
F 14: E 293
F 15 (47-51): F p5, p6
F 60: B 1553

DEAD SEA SCROLLS
1QS VI 25-27: E 665

DEINARCHUS
1.12: We 948
1.15: A 704*
1.38: F 965, E 97
1.(38-)39: E 248
1.60: K 442
1.76: E 248
2.14: We 382-3
2.16: T 331-351
2.17: K 442

[DEMADES]
On the Twelve Years: 12 E 720

DEMETRIUS OF PHALERUM
FGrH 228 F 5: E 738

DEMOCRITUS OF ABDERA
A1 D-K: C 380
A83 D-K: C 380
A93 D-K: C 376-8, 404-7
fr. 9 D-K: W 589
fr. 24 D-K: We 437
fr. 167 D-K: C 380

DEMOCRITUS OF EPHESUS
FGrH 267 F 1: K 967, C 912

DEMON
FGrH 327 F 16: We 1002
F 19: F 439, E 828

DEMOSTHENES
3.31-33: W 682-718
3.36: B 540-3*
4.1: T 383-4, E 151-2

4.5: P 1118
4.11: E 1105
4.24: We 173
4.26: B 799
5.1: T 386, E 176
6.30: K 348-9, C 417
7.45: P 669
9.1: T 386, E 176
10.37: K 925-6*
10.75: E 239
12.10: E p4, We p3
13.24: T 426
14.3: T 386, E 176
14.19: E 825, We 195
16.2: T 386, E 176
17.30: T 432
18 passim: We p18
18.1: K 763, B 866-7, E 171-2
18.6: C 1187
18.7: C 941
18.28: F 141
18.41: We 377-385
18.107: L 1139-40, We 382-3
18.120-1: W 1489, B 1072, 1274-5
18.127: F 464
18.129-131: E 77
18.129: K 394*, W 897, We 276
18.130: F 289-296
18.133: We 875
18.136: F 790
18.137: We 948
18.143: K 852-3, E 296-7
18.169-170: E 377
18.170: T 379
18.171-2: We 800
18.175: E 509-510
18.179: T 432
18.180: F p8
18.196: A 915
18.219: E 248
18.248: E 396-7
18.251: E 248
18.259(-260): C 254-262, W 9, B 873,
     L 388
18.262: F 778
18.300: L 1162-3
18.322: We 377-385
19 passim: L 1231-5
19.39: We 17
19.46: K 348-9, C 417

19.70: T 331-351
19.71: T 349
19.86: F 651
19.113: We 948
19.124: E 1026
19.125: F 651
19.128: P 714*
19.158: A 66*
19.191: F 1512, E 644-5
19.229: F 1068
19.237: F 1084
19.246(-7): F p8, F 55
19.249: F 1084
19.265: K 179*
19.272: L 751
19.273: B 284
19.277-280: E 71
19.281: W 9
19.290: E 428
19.337: F 778
20.52: E 195, 729
20.58: E 729
20.59-60: E 202-3, We 550
20.107: L 980*
20.135: F 1086
20.158: P 969
21.13: B 1403*
21.14: T 544-5, We 948
21.17: B 1403, E 808, 1160
21.21: We 483
21.32: L 602
21.33: We 21
21.44: We 373
21.45: We 910
21.47: W 1418
21.51: K 1320
21.71: T 31
21.99: W 568-9
21.103: K 979*
21.117: A 285
21.149: T 339-340
21.158: We 1013-4
21.167: We 948
21.174: B 147, F 1071
21.186-8: W 568-9
21.191: We 118
21.198: We 948
21.205: E 677
21.216: B 946
22.44: E 825, We 195

23.51: F 1167-8
23.68: L 186
23.97: T 331-351
23.130: K 281*
23.136: K 281*
23.206: W 567
24.12: We 382-3
24.21: We p19
24.23: B 1288
24.27: We p19
24.29: T 943
24.26-31: C 398*, We p16
24.45: E 183-4
24.105: K 394*, B 1625
24.112: K 442
24.113-4: F 772
24.114: B 1625, F 1200, E 1101
24.120: K 301-2
24.127: K 442
24.128: K 301-2
24.134: We 177, 1193
24.135: F 367, E 102, We 176
24.136: We 1193
24.144: K 248*, E 1064-5
24.147: K 248*
24.149-151: We p18
24.210: We 192
25.11: F 1032
25.40: K 862*, 1017
25.46: We 1156
25.64: K 862*
25.71: W 769*
25.80: F 733
26.5: K 1227
27 passim: W 578
27.7: K 925-6
27.9: E 252
29.20: E 1026
29.22: E 560-1
32.29: W 1042, E 1064-5
33.15: W 524
34.23-24: C 1041
34.39: E 547, We 982-3
35.9: We 869
35.29-30: W 659
35.48: K 912-3, T 837
36.29: W 233, L 259
36.43: E 366
37.40ff: F 616
39.2-4: B 765, F 418

39.8: K 912-3, T 837
39.17: F 1466, E 982-4
39.22: B 494
40.22: We 174
41.27: We 529
43.51: B 1661-2
43.57: C 1425-6
43.62: B 474
43.66: B 1233, L 645
43.69-70: P 1135t*
44.4: E 757
45.4: F 1466, E 982-4
45.27: T 345
45.74: We 768-9
47.11-12: W 1287
47.34-35: W 69
47.43: T 78-79
47.55: T 515
47.60: E 675
47.64: F 1133
47.70: F 587
48.24: B 544
48.56: B 14, E 251, We 12
49.6-10: W 964
49.37-38: E 560-1
49.67: We 1024
50.34: C 912
52.9: K 941-2*
53.15: F 995
53.20: P 1146*, L 908
54 passim: E 663-4
54.4: F 94-95, E 640
54.8-9: W 1418, B 1046-7
54.9: K 697t*
54.14: E 1037-97
54.39: B 1529, F 366*, We 597
56.7: We 1156
57 passim: C 1219
57.10: We 254
57.20: C 1372
57.34: A 896, W 659
57.45: W 712
57.54: B 765, F 418
57.(67-)68: W 1397, E 1115
57.70: W 523
58.1-2: We 31
58.6: W 1284-91
58.11: We 923
58.19: E 1023-4
58.21: E 1023-4

58.27: K 1227
58.65: E 668
58.67: B 126
58.70: P 1113
59.1-14: We 31
59.21-23: F 157
59.22: We 536
59.(29-)32: We 149, 1003
59.33(-34): L 907, T 489, 491-2, We 1003
59.35-39: A 524-5*
59.35: We 1003
59.37: We 1003
59.40: E 1023-4, We 1003
59.41: We 168
59.45: E 1023-4
59.46-47: We 1003
59.52: W 1108, 1109
59.64-66: We 168
59.65(-66): E 1064-5, We 168
59.67: E 617*
59.76: C 303-4, F 216-7
59.89: E 183-4
59.92: F 694
59.104: F 694
59.106: F 694
59.114: T 575, We 306
59.124: F 616
60.8: We 385
60.31: B 558-9
Prooemia 5.1: T 386, E 176
  6.1: T 386, E 176
  13: T 383-4
  44.1: T 386, E 176

DICAEARCHUS
fr. 83 Wehrli: We 1082
fr. 89 Wehrli: C 1365

DICAEOGENES
Medea: E 1-18

DIDYMUS
on Demosthenes 11.22: We 290-321

DIO CHRYSOSTOM
2.59: F 372-382
3.63: B 9t
6.20: T 1092
31.121: F 16
59.5: A 424*

DIODORUS SICULUS
1.79.5: We 147
1.88.3: E 1068-9
1.96.4-5: F 1032
1.97.3: F 186
2.51.2: F 937
2.56.4: T 18
3.57.2: B 971
3.64.5-6: L 1282, F 215-6
4.3.3: L 1
4.12.3-7: F 38, 902
4.25.1: F 1033
4.26.1: F 504
4.33.1: F 38
4.43: P 277-8
4.59.3: F 966
4.59.5: E 1021
5.76.3-4: W 369
5.77.3: F 1032
11.58.2-3: K 84
11.63.1: L 1137-44
11.64.1: L 1137-44
12.3-4: T 446
12.7: A 603, B 284
12.10.3: C 332, B 521
12.22.2: P 1047
12.31.1: F 608
12.36.2: B 997
12.39: P 605
12.40.6: P 603t
13.6-7: B 1073*
13.27.6: E 259-260
13.52-53: T 805, F p6, F 678
13.52.3: L 1163
13.64.3: F 541
13.64.5-7: L 104
13.65.1(-2): B 1406, L 1170
13.66: F 541
13.72-73: F 1023-4
13.95.1: E 246
13.97-100: F p2
13.100.2: F 1072
13.100.3: F p4, F 49-50, 1072
13.100.6: F p3, F 1463-5
13.101-2: F p2
13.101.2-4: F p3, F 541, E 202-3, We 550
13.103.4: T p1, F p8
13.104.1-2: F p3
13.104.4: F p6

13.105.3-4: F 1422
13.107.4: L 1170
13.108.1: F p6, p22, E p1
14.19.5: E p1
14.81.2-82.1: E p5
14.81.4: E 201
14.82.1-3: E p2, E 193
14.83.2: We p4
14.84.2: We p4
14.91.2: We p1
14.92.1: E p3
14.92.2: We 173
14.94.2-4: E 202-3, We 550
14.109.1-3: We 550
15.2.3: We 178
15.29.7: We 180
15.66: L 1141
15.74.1-4: We 550
16.23ff: B 553
16.31.6: F 608
16.93.7: T 491-2
17.15: We 377-385
20.11.3-4: W 1086
20.41: W 1035, P 758, E 77
20.100.7: F 608
34.2.13: E 259-260

DIOGENES OF APOLLONIA
A5 D-K: C 380*
A16 D-K: C 376-8
A16a D-K: C 264
A18 D-K: C 272
A19 D-K: C 229, 232-3, 627
A20 D-K: C 229-230
A33 D-K: C 232-3
fr. 4 D-K: C 229

DIOGENES OF ATHENS (tragic dramatist)
Semele fr. 1: T 1175

DIOGENES LAERTIUS
1.42: W 1410
2.9: C 376-8
2.12: A 703
2.26: L 593
2.27: C 412-7t
4.59: T 414-5
5.1: We p9
5.16: W 386
5.33: W 386

6.46: L 673
6.51: We 203, 312, 885
8.46: C 219, B 1730, F 520
9.31-32: C 380*
9.45: C 380
10.90: C 380*

DIOGENIANUS
2.72: C 730*

DIONYSIUS (comic dramatist)
Sozousa fr. 5: T 743

DIONYSIUS CHALCUS
fr. 4.3 West: K 546

DIONYSIUS OF HALICARNASSUS
Demosthenes 43: T 163
Lysias 12: K 281*
29-30: We 550
32: F 965, E 97

DIONYSIUS (writer on fowling)
Ixeuticon 2.11: We 912

DIOPHANTUS (comic dramatist)
Metoikizomenos fr. 1: T 741-2

DIOSCORIDES
1.116: E 355
2.82.2: We 267
4.164-5: E 405
5.154: T 504

DIPHILUS
Kitharoidos fr. 51: T 556
Paiderastai fr. 57: E 137
Peliades fr. 64.2: E 252
fr. 91: K 414

DURIS
FGrH 76 F 14: L 1190
F 17: W 1035, P 758, E 77
F 70: L 1190

ECPHANTIDES
fr. 3 [2 K]: W 57
fr. 4: T 990
fr. 5 [4 K]: W 1187

EMPEDOCLES
A49 D-K: T 5-21*
fr. 35 D-K: B 700
fr. 43 D-K: C 614
fr. 84.12 D-K: T 5-21*
fr. 100 D-K: C 570
fr. 128.2 D-K: B 586*

EPHIPPUS
Cydon fr. 13.2: E 45
Geryones fr. 3: L 757, E 137, 1172

EPHORUS
FGrH 70 F 19: E 828
   F 20: L 381
   F 31b: B 188-9
   F 73: E 201
   F 74: E 201
   F 119: F 685
   F 134: F 1266
   F 183: We 1002
   F 196: P 603-4

EPIC CYCLE and other early epics
   (ed. Davies in Epicorum Graecorum
   Fragmenta)
Epigonoi fr. 1 : P 1270
   fr. 3: We 41-43
Cypria epit.: F 963, We 210
   fr. 13: L 118, We 210
   fr. 14: We 210
Little Iliad epit.: T 101-129
   fr. 2 : K 1056*
   fr. 6 : P 724
   fr. 9: E 1029
   fr. 19: L 155-6
   fr. 20: We 69-70
Nostoi fr. 6: K 1321

Alcmeonis fr. 7: We p6
Danais fr. 3: L 558
Naupactia fr. 10a-c: We p8

EPICA ADESPOTA
4.17 Powell: P 603-4

EPICHARMUS
Alcyoneus fr. 5: We 83
Busiris fr. 21: F 62*
Heracles and the Girdle fr. 76: P 73

Hope or Wealth fr. 34: We p7
   fr. 35: We p7
   fr. 37: We p7
   fr. 148: W 1253-5*
   fr. 170: C p2*
   fr. 245: P 832-3*
   fr. 265: P 832-3*

EPICRATES
Amazons fr. 1: E p10
Antilais: E p10
   fr. 3: K 532-3*, We 179
   fr. 4: F 1302
Chorus fr. 8: L 217
Dyspratos fr. 5.4: F 544
   fr. 10.29: We 617-8

"EPIMENIDES"
fr. 5 D-K: B 695

EPINICUS
Hypoballomenai fr. 2: W 616*

ERATOSTHENES
Catasterisms 13: T 17
   15: P 832-3*, T 1011-2
   17: P 832-3*, T 1011-2
fr. 91 Strecker: F 798

ERIPHUS
Meliboea fr. 3: E 1170
Peltastes fr. 6: We 149

ETYMOLOGICUM MAGNUM
118.56-119.2: F 418
200.37-42: B 530, L 1164
304.30-31: We 689
367.21: E 943
533.21-22: T 94
597.56-598.5: We 1142
756.56-757.8: We 1037

EUBULUS
Amaltheia fr. 6 [7 K]: K 895, B 534,
   E 1171, We 30, 925
   fr. 7: We 1129
Anasozomenoi fr. 8: E 102, We 176
Ancylion: W 1397
   fr. 2: B 494-8, T 795, F 393
Antiope fr. 9: B 1407

Bellerophon fr. 15 [16 K]: P 1244
Cercopes fr. 52 : T 485
   fr. 53: We 149
Chrysilla fr. 115.9: T 547-8
Echo fr. 34 [35 K]: A 893-4*, P 1014
Graces fr. 114.4: F 708-9
Ion fr. 36 [37 K]: A 893-4*, P 1014
Kybeutai fr. 56.5: T 902
Laconians fr. 61: L 465
Nannion fr. 67.9: We 1044t
Nurses fr. 109: E 1170
Olbia fr. 74: K 979*
Orthannes: E 916
   fr. 75: B 1529, E 1-18, 842, We 515
Pamphilus fr. 81: E 821-2
Procris fr. 89.2-3: L 729, F 543
Semele fr. 93: W 1253-5*, E 663-4,
   We 1044t
Sphingokarion: We 1
Stephanopolides fr. 98: K 1286t*
fr. 117: E 652
fr. 118.7: T 200
fr. 123: E 867-8
fr. 127: T 239
fr. dub. 148 [150 K]: P 1149, E 554

EUPHANES
Muses fr. 1: A 348, C 325, E 22-23

EUPHORION
fr. 82 Powell: P 363
fr. 121 Powell: T 1142

EUPHRON
Synepheboi fr. 9: We 1

EUPOLIS
Astrateutoi fr. 35 [31 K]: P 395*, B 1556,
   L 490
   fr. 43 [41 K]: P 804, B 151
   fr. 45: T 861
Autolycus: W 1301-2*
   fr. 48 [42 K]: A p27, P p.xvii, E p28
   fr. 50 [44 K]: C 109, W 1268-9
   fr. 52: T 633
   fr. 53: T 633
   fr. 54: L 229, E 265
   fr. 55: E 1106*
   fr. 58: L 270
   fr. 60 [52 K]: A p25

fr. 61 [53 K]: W 1301*, L 270
fr. 62 [54 K]: P p.xvii
Baptai fr. 79 [70 K]: W 83
fr. 80: F 417
fr. 89 [78 K]: A p25, K p4, K 1225,
   C p2*, C 554, P 767
fr. 90 [80 K]: W 687
fr. 96: We 884
Cities fr. 220: B 1297
fr. 222 [209 K]: C 686, W 74*
fr. 223: B 1467
fr. 224: F 1512
fr. 225 [211 K]: P 1031
fr. 227 [213 K]: W 98
fr. 231 [212 K]: P 1046
fr. 232 [215 K]: W 1301*, L 270
fr. 235 [218 K]: C 351
fr. 237: F 970
fr. 238: B 471
fr. 246: B 879
fr. 248 [234 K]: A 595
fr. 249 [235 K]: A 605, C 686*, W 84
fr. 252 [238 K]: A 846, K 1304, C 551,
   W 1007, P 681, T 840
fr. 253 [239 K]: C 103
fr. 255: B 17-18
Demes: F pp9-10
   fr. 99 [*CGFP* 92]: A p28, A 854,
   C 553*, F pp9-10
   fr. 99.1-34: F p10
   fr. 99.5-8 [*CGFP* 92.5-8]: W 1183-4,
   P 928, B 822-3, L 63, T 949, We 602
   fr. 99.9 [*CGFP* 92.9]: W 1183-4, P 928,
   B 822-3, L 63
   fr. 99.24: F 418
   fr. 99.28: L 577-8
   fr. 99.30-32 [*CGFP* 92.30-32]: C 553*,
   580, E 792
   fr. 99.33 [*CGFP* 92.33]: K 1288-9
   fr. 99.56-57: F p9
   fr. 99.64-65: F p9
   fr. 99.79-119: F p9
   fr. 99.112: We 942-3
   fr. 100 [*CGFP* 93]: C 553
   fr. 101 [*CGFP* 94]: C 553
   fr. 103: L 391
   fr. 104 [100 K]: W 1070, B 1569, F p9
   fr. 105: F p9
   fr. 106: F p9, E 105
   fr. 107: B 1569

fr. 108: F p9
fr. 112 [103 K]: C 1001
fr. 113: L 391, 397
fr. 116 [95 K]: K 1377
fr. 130: F 798
fr. 139: T 861
Flatterers: W 1301-2*, P p.xv, F 428, E 810
fr. 160: F 1068, E 606
fr. 171 [158 K]: A 716, F 1422, E 103
fr. 172 [159 K]: W 1318
fr. 172.11-16 [159.11-16 K]: W 1221
fr. 174 [161 K]: W 510
fr. 178 [164 K]: P 804, B 151
fr. 179 [166 K]: A 702, 1167-8
fr. 180 [165 K]: C 104, W 1408, B 1296
Friends fr. 295 [273 K]: W 1301*
Golden Race: B p.2
fr. 301 [281 K]: W 844
fr. 316 [290 K]: K 75
fr. 318: F 1036-7
Helots: K 1225
fr. 147 [138 K]: K 1225
Maricas: K p4, C p2, C 552-6*, L p4,
     T 840, F 570
fr. 192 [CGFP 95]: C 554
fr. 192.29: L p4
fr. 192.48: E 624
fr. 192.98-99 L p4
fr. 192.102: T 491-2, E 225
fr. 192.117-121: L p4
fr. 192.170: A 774*
fr. 193 [181 K]: K 6, L p4, F 570
fr. 194: B 1440-1, We 338
fr. 195 [182 K]: P 395, B 1556, L 490
fr. 196: L 835
fr. 208 [193 K]: C 554
fr. 209: C 555*
New Moons: A p32
Prospaltioi fr. 261 [244 K]: W 57
fr. 264: K 1085*, B 988
Taxiarchs: P 348, F p11, F 197ff
fr. 259 [250 K]: P 788
fr. 259.72: B 1297
fr. 268: L 804, F p11
fr. 269: F p11
fr. 270: E 413
fr. 272: T 163, F p11
fr. 274: F p11
fr. 282: B 153-4
fr. 334: T 730

fr. 340: E 845
fr. 342: T 21t
fr. 352 [CGFP 100]: A 88, T 605
fr. 372: F 1400
fr. 392 [357 K]: A p24, P 603-4
fr. 385: F 1451
fr. 395 [361 K]: C 178
fr. 406: E 934

EURIPIDES (see also under Critias)
Alcestis: W 1238-9, T p6
1-2: F 1309-12
1-8: B 516
3-4: We p8
98-100: E 1033
122-9: We p8
177-182: K 1250-2
252-7: L 606, F 137-8, 180ff, We 278
333: L 1315t*
343-5: T 137
367-8: A 893-4
393: E 915
405: T 179-180
436-7: B 546-7
442: B 546-7
443: F 137-8
521: A 396, T 120-1
570: T 969
591: B 1267
675: B 1244
691: C 1415, T 194
746/861: E p23
747-772: B 567, L 928
759: P 1154
856: T 179-180
862: W 750
866-7: W 752
923: We 770/1
939-949: L 865-9
Andromache: T p5, T 390-1, F p8
1-6: F 1309-12, 1383
56: W 1297-8, T 582-3
64: W 1297-8, T 582-3
85: E 238
167: L 381
189: L 276
252: F 1396
257-8: T 721-2
260: P 1020
266-7: E 1110

269-272: L 369
327: L 276
353: T 392-4, E 224
374-7: E p16
445-453: P 623, L 169, 629
468-470: B 718
627-631: L 155-6
630: T 392-4
841-850: F 121-134
863-4: K 1310*
911: E 238
921: F 750
930-953: L 891
943-953: L 369
950-1: T 414-5
952: T 392-4
1009-18: T 109-110
1085: We 772
1093: T 110
1100ff: We 227
1115: We 213
1129-36: C 988, F 153
1165: We 11
Bacchae 58: P 251, L 32
59: L 3, We 476t
64-104: T 101-129, F 323-353
66: T 991
84: T 991
112: F 1324
113-4: F 332-3
115: T 975, F 326, 1324
118: B 831
120-9: W 8, L 558, F 1309-12
123: L 1032
124-5: L 3
135-167: T 992
141: T 990
141ff: T 975, F 326
144-153: T 101-129, F 323-353
146: C 604
151-161; T 991
157: T 990
170: C 1154-70*
188-190: F 345-9
194: F 401-2
235-6: E 955
236: F 1045
252: F 1396
271: F 1396
284: F 22

306-8: C 604, F 1212
357: B 1045, T 853
370-402: T 101-129, F 323-353
406-8: T 856
41(4-)5: P 453, B 1320
434-656: F 605-673*
453ff: T 134-5, E 955
513: L 3
519-575: T 101-129, F 323-353
519-520: L 381, T 855
538-544: C 853
566: T 990
579: T 990
614: F 401-2
625: L 381
642: E 650
660-768: T 992
661-2: C 273
717-721; We 162
725: F 323-353
737-764; F 401-2
889: F 100
935-6: T 255-6
995-6: C 853
997-1001 T 680
1084-5: B 777-8, T 43-50
1090-1: We 758-9
1167: T 990
1236: B 831
1271-89: K 1232-52
1301-26; T 680
1325-6: T 672
1333-8: B 1522-3
1344-6: T 680
1379-80; A 176
Cyclops 11-12: F 204
63-72: T 992-3
110: W 10t
122: We 298
132: F 1448
156-172: T 961
169: L 847
182: W 1087*
235: W 897
239: F 1235
261: T 887t
325: We 298
328: E 327-356
386-7: K 605t*
424: F 844

433-4: B 527
443: T 120
502: E 952ff, 971
519-520: F 22
525: F 22
543: W 1208*
675-687: T 1218ff
Electra: C p2*, C 534
1: F 1383
17: B 1070-1
107-111: F 312-5
168: T 1158-9
178-180: T 1031
292: L 1300
432-441: F 1309-12
435-7: F 1317-8
439: F 1324
489-490: L 288
561: F 942
654: L 757
671: C 1468
691: L 240
748: B 1745
778: T 37
798-839; P 948-1018
811-2: P 973
930-7: E 727
971-2: We 11
1028: T 392-4
1125-6: L 757
1147-8: T 723
1241-2: E 1068-9
1246: We 11
1268-9: F 685
1302: We 11
1342-3: F 472
1347-53: E 1068-9
Hecuba 9: B 1702-3
68-72: F 1331-7
151-3: B 670
154-215: C 1154-70
159-161: C 718-9
269: L 1315t*
344-5: F 1352
428: B 1702-3
466-474: K 566
641: T 109-110
730: B 1135
753: T 936
823: C 1484-5

878: T 430
884: E 238
927: T 1122
1015: B 1241-2
1092: T 1018-9
1093: L 128
1109-11: T 1056-97
1196-1232: F 956
1267: B 276
1276: L 506
Helen: T p5, pp6-8, T 763-4, 848, 850, 855-
923 passim, 1011-2
1-3: T 855-7
16-17: T 859-860
17-21: T 860
22: T 862
34: T 14
49: T 866
52-53: T 864-5
56: T 868
68: T 871
71: T 903
72: T 905
175: L 742
205-211: L 1301
241: K 1310*
363: F 1334
330-385: E 285-310
385/515: E p23
411-3: T 877
416: T 910
422: T 910
460: T 874
461: T 878
466: T 886
549: T 904
554: T 910
557(-8): T 903, 905-6
561-6: T 907-912
569(-570): L 443, 700-1, T 858,
F 1361-2
584: T 14
729: F 179
800: T 888
858-860: F 604
1010: F 1448
1013-6: P 832-3
1034: T 765
1079-80: T 910
1095-6: B 623

1111-3: B 213-4, T p5
1126-31: F 666
1131: T 1050-1
1149: F 64
1165-8: W 389*
1181: B 1070-1
1189-90: T 903
1193: W 1297-8, T 582-3
1201: T 887t
1204: T 910
1258: L 191-2
1282: T 910
1346-50: L 3
1347: We 476t
1593-1614: T p6
1641: F 179
1666-9: L 1314
Heracleidae: We 385
70: We 385
73-110: B 406-433
94: T 179-180
167: L 372
218-9: F 142
777-783: T 1136-7
976-7: P 316-7
Heracles 23-25: F 187
29-30: A 905
179: B 576
181-3: F 38
216: T 723
240ff: T 721-2
364-374: F 38
372-3: F 902
510: F 1352
619: F 142
640: F 1323
926-9: P 948-1018, B 863
1042-71: T 660
1094: T 1106
1120: L 215
1169-70: F 142
1271-2: W 1032-5, P 755-8
1341-6: C 904-6, 1080-1, F 634, E p27
1397: W 332
Hippolytus II: F 1043, 1044
12: We 948
34: We 773
61-71: E 3
72: F 215-6
76: F 1273-4

88: W 1297-8, T 582-3
93-94: C 48
141-4: E 1068-9
167: T 1018-9
178: C 265
196: E 115
228-231: T 153
230: B 1267
306-8: E 105
310: F 57
317: F 355
325-335: T 936
345: K 16
362: F 1173
375-6: F 930-1
380: F 1173
385-7: F 1181
394: F 1173
429: E 125
451-8: E 779
480-1: E 238
503-4: F 759
605: T 936
612: T 275-6, 451, F 101-2, 1471
616-633: T 683, 787
627: T 392-4, E 224
675-7: T 715-6
683: F 587
742-751: C 271
752-7: F 1309-12
882-3: F 838
914-5: L 712-4
953(-5): F 52-53, 1032, We 1063
1082-3: T 735-8
1152: A 1069-70
1186: B 180t
1282: P 130
ad finem: E 1182
Ion: T p5, T 848, We 521
4: P 201, We 1170
76: T 110
91-93: We 9
105-8: B 525
154-181: B 525
164: F 229-233
220: T 110
228-9: We 227
233: T 110
245: T 110
251: A 398-9

294: P 251, L 32
344ff: C 531
419-420: We 227
515-6: F 604
522: B 893*
534-6: We 41-43
589-590: W 1076, L 1082
616-7: T 430
714-8: F 1212
736-7: B 1451
739: L 288
890: T 902
936-941: L 721
943: F 1448
951ff: C 531
1074-86: F 371
1075: F 442
1150-1: T 1066
1196-8: B 525*
1305: E 868
1309-10: We 39
1445: C 265
1486-7: T 741-2
1529: F 825
1571: We 773
1575-88: L 582
Iph. Aul.: F 1309-12, 1400
1-48: F 946-7, 1206-8
49-114: F 946-7, 1206-8
151: F 827
231ff: F 933
239: A 547
247-252: A 547
342: We 192
385: We 192
505: B 1451
905: E 1034
1139: F 1396
1259: K 567*
1387-90: P 865
1400: We 461-3
1403: P 868*
1532ff: We 647
1540-1: We 647
1563-9: P 948-1018
1578-1629: We 647
1601: We 660-1
Iph. Taur.: T p5, T 848, F p8
1-2: F 1232-3
28-29: T 1218ff*

111: T 778
150-2: F 1331-7
165: W 1116t*
410: F 1438
430-4: F 1438
466: A 485t*
512: A 396, T 120-1
585-7: E 1056-7
701: T 936
843: F 1352
953-4: F 22
976: We 39
1032: E 238
1068: T 936
1089ff: F 1309-12
1104-5: F 207
1120: F 1323
1143ff: T 1031
1252-7: We 9
1294-1301: T 1218ff
1450-7: L 447
1568-9: B 863
ad finem: E 1182
Medea 1: F 1382
4: K 1310*
21-22: A 309
54-55: F 178
92: F 804
187-8: F 804
190-203: C 1358*
207-9: T 101-129
265-6: L 369
278: F 1002-3
298(-9): T 1106, 1130-1
384ff: T 430
408-9: L 369
422: E 238
440: F 1352
523-5: F 999-1000
625: We 114
709-710: P 1113
1074-5: T 735-8
1081-9: L 1124
1172: E 1068-9
1179-80: We 758-9
1208: F 309-319
1209: L 372
1242-50: A 485*, 483-8*
1332: T 392-4
1349: P 629*

Orestes: F p8
140-151: W 318-9, T 660
162: We 39
176: B 695*
181-6: W 318-9, T 660
279: F 304
318: We 424
329: We 39
397: F 64
632-5: F 942
852-956: E 372
903: F 838
904: T 120-1
917-930: We 162
1050: T 1122
1087: C 265
1154: B 1451
1204: L 1124
1368-1502: F 1331-63, E 1098-1111
1373: F 1352-5
1376-7: B 349-351
1381: F 1352-5
1389: P 1011
1390: F 1352-5
1391: F 1352-5
1415: F 1352-5
1480: L 1032
1604: F 355
1635-7: L 1314
1683-90: L 1314
ad finem: E 1182
Phoenissae 1-3: E 1-18
13-22: F 1185
26-27: F 1192
109-110: F 1361-2
155: E 338
210: B 952
263: E 338
272: A 396, T 120-1
297: We 203
347-8: P 843, L 378
494: L 1100
606: A 905
631: W 875, T 748, We 1114
802: C 273
807-810: F 1337
823-4: T 138
890: T 765
1018-32: F 1337
1018: F 1352-5

1054: F 1352-5
1067: C 1154-70*
1115: E 80
1124-7: F 1403
1179: T 778
1202: P 868*
1214: E 288
1265-6: T 1031
1271: T 1018-9
1296: L 198
1333: A 1069-70
1337: T 1018-9
1357: B 1241-2
1552: T 1018-9
ad finem: E 1182
Rhesus: F 1206-8
36-37: E 1068-9
119: F 792
217: T 1202, We 1157
306-8: F 963
383-4: F 963
564/674: E p23
590: E 338
675-6: A 281-2, C 1508
921-2: B 670
943-4: F 1032
972: B 276
Supplices 1ff: E p23
32: F 1334
42: E p23
51-53: W 727
59: W 727
180-3: T 149-150
187: P 623, L 169, 629
240-3: W 225
271-4: W 727
392: F 451
419-420: L 57
447: B 829-831
473-5: E 109
532-6: P 832-3
619: F 451
640: B 1241-2
741-3: W 1309
744-9: T 735-8
782-797: W 727
822-3: B 718
971-6: W 392
980-1030: C 1484-5
990-1030: W 317-333

1202: P 1224-5
Troades: T 769-770
4-6: T 109-110
60: B 1241-2
89-90: B 1242t
306-461: We 425
308: W 1326, B 1720
314: P 1332, B 1736
325: T 981-2t*
342: T 981-2t*
351: We 425
419: F 1438
421: We 312
454: F 1438
457: We 425
511: C 595
542-555: T 101-129
545-7: T 981-2t*
551-4: T 114-5
651-2: L 891
803: C 457-475
814: T 109-110
886: C 377
948-950: C 1080-1, E 779
969-1032: F 956
1026: A 849*, T 838
1223: E 538
1256ff: C 1484-5
1307-9: W 727
1320: F 1352

Aeolus: C 1371, T 406, F 850, 1081*, We p24
fr. 17: P 114-123
fr. 18: P 119
fr. 19: F 1475
fr. 28: T 177-8
Alcmene fr. 88: F 93
Alcmeon fr. 66: K 1302*
Alexandros: T 769-770
fr. 42: F 100
Andromeda: P 832-3*, T pl, p5, pp6-8, T 848, 850, 1011-1135 *passim*, F 52-53
fr. 114: T 1065-9
fr. 115: T 1070-2
fr. 116: T p6
fr. 117: T 1015
fr. 118: T 1018-20
fr. 120: T 1022-3

fr. 122: T 1029-40, 1047-55
fr. 123: T 1101-2
fr. 124: T 1098-1100
fr. 125: T 1105-6
fr. 127: T 1058, 1110
fr. 128: T 1107-8
fr. 132: T 1115
fr. 139: T 1128-9
fr. 144: F 105
Antigone fr. 157: F 1182
fr. 170: F 1391
Antiope fr. 221: F 1314
Archelaus: F 1206-8
fr. 228: T 856-7, F 1206-8
fr. 235: We 203
fr. 248: We 437
fr. 2 Austin/Harder: T 1122, F 1206-8
see also fr. 846
Auge: F 1080
fr. 266: F 1080
Bellerophon: P 146-8
fr. 286: P 105, T 451, F 889-891
fr. 306: A 427, P 76
fr. 307: A 427, P 154-172
fr. 308: A 427, W 757
fr. 310: K 1249*
fr. 312: P 722
Chrysippus fr. 839: C 265, T 11ff, 15, F 892
Cresphontes fr. 453.10: F 359
fr. 457: W 447
Cretans fr. 471: F 1356
fr. 472: F 1356
fr. 472e Kannicht/CCL: F 850
Cretan Women: A 433
fr. 464: T 430
fr. 465: W 763
Danaë: F 1206-8
fr. 322: L 43
Dictys: F 1206-8
Erechtheus fr. 363: L 1135
fr. 369: A 279, F 943
fr. 369d Kannicht [370 Nauck]: T 120
fr. 370.107-8 Kannicht [65.107-8 Austin]: P 832-3*
fr. 370.116 Kannicht [65.116 Austin]: T 1018-9
Hippolytus I: T 153, F 1043, 1044
fr. 429: L 253
fr. 443: C 265
Hypsipyle: F 1305-22 *passim*

fr. 752: C 604, F 1211-3
fr. 755: F 1327-8
fr. 763: F 64
fr. 765: F 1320-1
fr. 769: F 1305-6
fr. 1 ii 9 Bond: F 1305-6
fr. 1 ii 11-12 Bond: F 1313-6
fr. 1 iii 7 Bond: F 1323
fr. 7.5 Bond: F 1309-12
fr. 60.102ff Bond: F 1319
fr. 64.65 Bond: F 1319
fr. 64.101 Bond: T 120
fr. 64.152 Bond: F 1322
Ino: A 434, W 1414
fr. 409: E 508
Melanippe (Captive): T 547*, F p8
fr. 493: T 392-4
fr. 660 Mette: T 785-845*, E 446-9*
Melanippe (Wise): T 547*, F 1245
fr. 481: F 1244
fr. 483: L 1124-7, E 110
fr. 484: L 1126-7*, T 11ff, 15
fr. 485: T 547*
fr. 487: C 265, T 272, F 100, 311, 892
Meleager: F 863-4
fr. 515: F 1238-41
fr. 516: F 1238-41
fr. 522: B 829-831
fr. 523: F 1316
fr. 530: F 1402
fr. 531: F 1402
Oedipus fr. 544: L 253
Oeneus: A 418-9
fr. 565: F 72
fr. 566.2: P 699
fr. 568: A 472
Palamedes: T p6, T 769-770, 776-784, 848
fr. 578: T 769-770, F 1451
Peleus: F 863-4
fr. 623: C 1154-70*
Phaethon 111: L 539
163 [fr. 777 Nauck]: We 1151
164-7 [fr. 776 Nauck]: We p7
221-3: L 1198, T 414-5
248-250: W 846, P 864
Philoctetes: A 424, P 146-8, T 93
fr. 788: F 282
Phoenix fr. 804: T 413
fr. 812: A 421

Phrixus A and *B* fr. 819 (*B*): F 1225-6
fr. 833: F 1082
Pleisthenes fr. 628: B 1232
Polyidus fr. 638: F 1082, 1477
Protesilaus fr. 653: E p16
Scyrians fr. 682: T 406
Stheneboea: P 140*, F 1043
fr. 661: F 1217-9
fr. 663: W 1074
fr. 664: T 401-4*, F 1043, 1044
fr. 665: W 111-2, F 1044
fr. 669.4: P 126*
fr. 671.1: K 1249*
Syleus: P 741*
Telephus: A 326*, 430*, 472, 504*, 524-5*, 659-662*, C 922, P 146-8, T p6, T 93, 466ff, 472, 473, 689ff, 693-5, 700-1, 717, F 855, 1400
fr. 696: F 1383
fr. 698: A 440-1
fr. 699: L 706-717
fr. 700: K 1240
fr. 703: A 497-8
fr. 704: A 430
fr. 705a Nauck-Snell: A 1174-89
fr. 706: A 318, 593
fr. 707: A 446
fr. 708: A 540
fr. 708a Nauck-Snell: A 541
fr. 709: A 543
fr. 710: A 555-6
fr. 711: T 518-9
fr. 712: A 577*
fr. 713: K 813, We 601
fr. 717: A 454
fr. 722: C 891
fr. 727: P 528
Temenidae fr. 730: L 32
Theseus fr. 382: F 1314
fr. 385: W 303-316 (312)
fr. 386: W 303-316 (314)
Thyestes fr. 396: A 433
fr. 397: P 699:
fr. 846: F 1206-8
fr. 858: A 119
fr. 877: C 265, T 11ff, 14, F 311, 892
fr. 883: L 706-717
fr. 885: F 840
fr. 908b Nauck-Snell: C 570*
fr. 912.4: C 274

fr. 918: A 659-662*
fr. 919: C 265, F 892
fr. 925: T 17
fr. 941: C 265, T 11ff, 14, F 341, 892
fr. 968: F 293
fr. 1011: C 30
fr. 1023: T 11ff, 15

EUSEBIUS
Chronicle year 1563: A 849
    year 1566: K 537

EUSTATHIUS
on Iliad 9.529: L 1243
    11.104-5: B 1738-40
    11.724 [pp.880.63-881.1]: F 194
    13.637: 1490
    23.123: P p.xx
on Odyssey 4.708: L 173
    7.120: P p.xx
    14.159 [p.1756.24-25]: B 865
    14.435: T 977
    20.105: L 643

FESTUS (ed. Lindsay)
de verborum signif. p.318.23-24: E 1101t*
    p.410.17-21: L 723-5

FIRMICUS MATERNUS
Error of Profane Religions 22: We 327

FULGENTIUS
Mitologiae 3.9: We 287

GALEN (ed. Kühn)
iii 871 [de usu partium 11.8]: F 548
xi 807.2-3: We 720
xii 141.7: E 405
xiv 478: T 504
xix 445: We 267

GELLIUS, AULUS
1.6.2: L 1039
3.16: T 741-2
5.10: A 710
6.16.5: F 475
15.20.6: L 593
15.20.9: F 85

GORGIAS
Encomium of Helen 8-10: F p15*
    13: E 571
fr. 6 D-K: B 636-7
fr. 11a.30 D-K: F 1451
fr. 23 D-K: T 1129
fr. 24 D-K: F 1021

HARPOCRATION
α235: L 644-5
ε35: We 1175
δ13: W 389
ι9: E 201
κ4: E 128
λ28: L 378
ν1: We 179
ν18: B 1656
ο25: We 594
ξ2: We 173
φ5: F 733
φ16: We 177

HECATAEUS
FGrH 1 F 27: F 187

HELIODORUS
Aethiopica 10.31.3: L 1083

HELLANICUS
FGrH 4 F 19: P 832-3
    F 63: B 1021
    F 99: L 785
    F 109: W 1043, P 422, We 417
    F 131: K 67
    F 172: F 720, E 815
FGrH 323a (Atthis) F 25: F 33

HELLENICA OXYRHYNCHIA
6.1: K 648*, E 444
6.2: E 195-6, 202-3, 208, 444, We 550
7.2: E 71, 195-6, 248
15.1: E 201

HENIOCHUS
Trochilos fr. 4: A 854, T 949, We 602
fr. 5.8: P 879-880

HERACLITUS (philosopher)
A16 D-K: C 627
fr. 34 D-K: K 1119-20*

fr. 48 D-K: We 33-34
fr. 92 D-K: P 1095
fr. 94 D-K: C 1292

HERACLITUS (Homeric allegorist)
Homeric Problems 52.8-12: F 204

HERACLITUS (paradoxographer)
On Incredible Stories 34: E 77

HERMIPPUS
Artopolides: C 552, 556, T 840, F 570
    fr. 7 [9 K]: P 395, B 1556
    fr. 9: T 840, We 1024
    fr. 12: T 840
Cercopes fr. 36 [35 K]: K 1268, B 1406
Fates fr. 43: B 1073, F 320
    fr. 48: B 523
Phormophoroi fr. 63: W 433, 838, P 150,
    T 935, F 204, We 521
fr. 77: L 196, F 1150, E 1119, 1139,
    We 807, 1021
fr. iamb. 3 West: B 1149-51
fr. iamb. 5 West: W 1169

HERODAS
1.76: L 365
2 *passim*: W 1309
3.95-97: F 1510-4, We 276
4.19-20: T 773
4.78: C 870, F 619, We 312
4.79-90: We 669-670
5.45: T 239
5.59-62: We 276
5.65-79: B 760, L 331, F 1510-4
6 *passim*: E 45, 916
6.19: L 109
6.97: E 1179
8 *passim*: F 1331-63
8.79: B 1379
12.1: C 763, W 1341

HERODIAN
1.426.11-12: A 1055t*

HERODOTUS
1.14.3: We 287
1.16-22: We 1002
1.30.2: E 571
1.34: A 1072

1.60(.4): B 1678, 1720t*, E 629
1.61.1: L 417
1.82.1: W 466
1.82.8: B 1282, L 279-280
1.86.2: L 238, We 681
1.94.3: L 908
1.113: F 1190
1.114.2: A 92
1.114.3: E 1090
1.131: P 411
1.132.1: P 952
1.133.1: A 85-86
1.141.4: We 1002
1.143.1: We 1002
1.143.3: A 104
1.147.2: L 582
1.155.4: B 994
1.159.3: B 525
1.170.2: B 172*
1.173.5: B 1289
1.178-181: B 552
1.178.3-179.3: B 1125-31
1.193.4-5: B 590*
1.202.4: K 1088, B 145
1.216(.1): E p16, E 987
1.216.4: L 191-2
2.2: C 398
2.13-14: T 856
2.22: T 856-7
2.35.3: E 222, We 1198
2.38.3: L 1199
2.46.1: F 230
2.51: P 277-8
2.57.2: T 856-7
2.64.1: L 912, T 489
2.64.2: L 754-5
2.69.2: A 75, C 768
2.75-76: B 1296
2.77.2: P 1254, T 856-7
2.84: E 364
2.96: L 45
2.104.2: T 856-7
2.104.3: B 507
2.112-120: T 850
2.127: B 1130
2.130.1: L 238, We 681
2.134.3-4: B 471
2.136.4: B 1145
2.141.5: F 840
3.15.4: K 83

3.57.4: K 197, 199
3.61-88: F p6
3.101: T 489
3.102.3: B 1559-60
3.131: W 1432, B 584, We 408
3.135.3: L 1113
3.136.1: B 598
4.32: P 1270
4.42-3: B 710
4.45.3: L 908
4.46.3: B 941-4
4.49.2: B 1529
4.79.4: L 832
4.94.2: E 1090
4.99-100: T 1218ff*
4.104: E p16, E 987
4.113: W 500*
4.120.2: B 1013-4
4.132.3: B 349-351
4.150-163: We 925
4.178-180: L 347
4.180.5: E p16
4.189.3: L 240
5.1-2: B 484
5.6: E 987
5.18.4: C 974
5.25: K 371
5.35.4: E 338
5.49.3: W 1087
5.55-56: L 632
5.61.2: A 709
5.62.2: W 502, L 619, 665
5.63: L 1150-6
5.64.2: B 832, L 1150-6
5.65.1-2: L 1150-6
5.71: K 445-6
5.92β.3: K 1037, T 514, F 1431
5.92η.2-3: P 891
5.93.2: E 338
5.97.2: W 708, E 1132-3
5.99.1: We 1002
6.34.2: B 188-9
6.35.1: C 1407*
6.50: C 1356
6.61.3-5: L 1314
6.69.3: W 389*
6.69.5: T 741-2
6.71.2: L 77
6.73.2: C 1356
6.74.1: E 338

6.79-80: T 721-2
6.87: K 560, B 868
6.105: C 67
6.105.3: L 721
6.108: F 694
6.114: F 1296-7
6.125: T 263
6.127.1: P 344
6.129.2: F 896
6.131.2: K 1037, C 64, T 514, F 1431
6.134-136: T p10
6.134.1: T 101-2
6.136: F 1086
6.138.4: L 299-300
7.2-4: F p5, p6
7.6(.2): W 490, B 1074-5
7.6.3: W 1410, F 1033
7.28.2: C 1041
7.61.1: W 1087
7.83.2: B 278
7.86-87: B 278
7.99: L 675, T 1200
7.110: E 987
7.111.2: B 276
7.113.1: We 283
7.113.2: L 191-2, We 1181
7.117: A 709
7.123.1: B 824
7.128.1: We 283
7.133: K 1362, F 574, We 431
7.141.3: K 1040, 1189
7.144: K 1350-3
7.153.2: T 101-2
7.153.4: T 131
7.175-238: L 1254
7.187.2: E 424, We 986
7.197: C 257
7.200.2: L 1129-32
7.201: W 361, L 1129-32
7.226: W 1084
7.229.1: F 192
8.1-21: L 1251
8.20.2: K 123, P 1070, B 962
8.23.1: B 1204
8.41.2-3: L 601, 759
8.44.2: B 123, L 481
8.46.2-3: L 582
8.47: A 214, W 1206-7
8.52-53: L 318
8.52.2: W 490, B 1074-5

8.53.2: W 1079
8.55: T 318-9
8.59: L 1000
8.68-69: L 675, T 1200
8.77(.1): K 123, 197, P 1070, B 962
8.87-88: L 675, T 1200
8.93.2: L 675
8.96.2: K 123, P 1070, B 962
8.98.2: W 1203-4
8.101-3: T 1200
8.111.3: We 437
8.135: B 982
8.138.2-3: We 287
9.7α.2: K 1253
9.13.2: W 1079
9.28.6: L 1143
9.37(.2): K 394*, 1049
9.42-43: B 1522-3
9.43: K 123, B 962
9.54.1: P 623, L 169
9.64.2: L 1137-44
9.73.2: A 322
9.99.3: W 361
9.105: B 798
9.116.3: T 489
9.122: B 836

HESIOD
Shield 134: B 883
188-190: F 902
292: P 1197t*
Theogony 52-62: L 1248
78: F 674
116: C 424, B 691
116-8: B 470
116-123 B 693
124: E 105
124-5: B 1193
126-8: B 701-2
154ff: T 11-18
184-6: B 824-5, F 825
21(1-)2: F 1335, We 549
233-8: B 1230
265-6: B 1230
287: K 416
295-332: F 473
31(1-)2: K 416, W 1032-5, P 755-8
321: P 1065
337ff: C 271, B 691
399: T 110

409-411: F 1361-2
440: T 1033
450-2: L 700-1
521-616: B 1494-1552, We p21
535-557: We 1128
545: B 689
551-612: We 87
590-612: T 786, E 224
594ff: W 1116t*
600-7: L 1039, T 787
720: B 693
742-4: B 695
756: We 549
759: We 549
821ff: K 511
824-830: W 1032-5, P 755-8
825: F 473
837: W 1032-5, P 755-8
869-880: K 511, C 336
886-900: We p16
915-7: L 1248
921-3: B 1654
924: We p16
969-973: T 299, We p5
Works & Days: F 1034
3: We 130-197
41: We 544
42-105: B 971, We 87
45: B 434t*
94-95: E 14-15
109-201: We 50
109-119: We p6
111: B 586
122-6: We p6
143-155: F 730
160: F 1060
166-173: W 640
190-3: We 50
259: C 903
302-4: W 1116t*
375: E 238
384: B 710
448-451: B 710
486: F 1380
504-560: P 1127-90*
568: B 15-16
568-9: B 714, T 1
582-596: P 1127-90*, 1159
582-3: B 1095-6
586-8: W 1032, P 755

596: T 743, We 1132
598: P 832-3
619-629: B 711
650-9: We 1162
800-1: B 718
fr. 1.6-7: B 1485-6
23a.26: F 1361-2
31.3: L 139
50: We p8
51: We p8
52: We p8
59: We p8
60: We p8
72-76: L 785
151: B 941-4
153: K 416
163: P 832-3*
294: E 80
310: B 977
338: W 725-6
fr. dub. 343.12: L 347
343.18: K 1177, L 1273t*

HESYCHIUS
α7241: We 953
β466: A 255t*
β889: L 397
δ599: L 1061-4
δ743: E 634
δ1881: E 1029
ε1992: L 1314
ε5413: E 943
ε6402: B 865
ε7077: T 299, We p5
ε7567: W 1191
θ787: E 34t
ι501: T 395
κ646: P 123
κ673: L 1314
κ2225: C 350
κ2242: P 1067, We 912
κ2267: B 1296*
κ2652: E 647, We 314-5
κ2913: W 1245-7
κ3098: T 624
κ3213: T 620
κ3517: L 664
κ3522: L 982
κ3795: T 620
κ4087: T 730

λ126: B 1563
λ251: E 77
λ871-4: L 299-300
λ1022: B 1242
λ1392: L 664t
μ278: K 129*
μ1560: T 392t
μ1904: T 100
ο1785: F 1144-5
ο1793-4: F 1144-5
π513: T 395
π566: E 904
π2674: L 173
σ2136: T 1197
χ2913: L 1237

HIERONYMUS OF RHODES
fr. 32 Wehrli: A 322
fr. 44 Wehrli: L 593
fr. 45 Wehrli: L 593

HIPPARCHUS [comic dramatist]
Anasozomenoi fr. 1: F 938

HIPPIAS
fr. 21 D-K: B 1005

HIPPIATRICA BEROLINENSIA
119 (p.379.24 Oder-Hoppe): P 1077

HIPPOCRATES OF CHIOS
A3 D-K: B 1005

HIPPOCRATIC CORPUS
Acute Diseases 5: P 1068-9
    6: F 943
    18: F 943
    65-68: F 1280
Airs, Waters, Places C 332
    1: K 815
    8: C 1280-1
    10: B 14, E 251, We 12
    18: B 941-4
Ancient Medicine 20: E 571
Coan Prognoses 489 [v 696 L]: C 1276
Cutting Up the Foetus 4: E 528-9
Diet 1.35.7: W 1489
    2.54.2: T 616
    2.55.1: E 355
Diseases 2.50.5: F 942

2.52.3: F 942
Epidemiae: C 332
  3.17.2: B 14, E 251, We 12
Nature of the Child 13.2: L 82
Nature of Man 1: C 332*
Sacred Disease 4: C 749*
  18: C 833, P 66, L 397
Setting Joints 33.38-40: F 940ff
  46: E 10
  48: E 10
  50.36-39: F 940ff, 942
Superfetation 31: F 753
Women's Conditions 1.77: T 504
  2.143: C 1075*
  2.144: E 906
  2.145: E 906

HIPPONAX
fr. 3a: P 402, We 1139-40
fr. 5: F 733
frr. 6-10: K 1405, F 733
fr. 6.2: F 621-2
fr. 17: E 8
fr. 25.6: A 872
fr. 32: B 904-953*
fr. 34: B 904-953*
fr. 36: We p6
fr. 70.8: L 1168-9
fr. 84.17: F 339
fr. 104.(47-)49: K 1405, B 971, F 733
fr. 120: L 361

HIPPYS
FGrH 554 F 7: C 398

HOMER
Batrachomyomachia 116-7: B 194t*
Iliad 1.4-5: F 1291-2
  1.14-15: B 893
  1.28: B 893
  1.39-41: W 556
  1.131: L 1252
  1.135-9: We 468-470
  1.248: C 1057
  1.317: B 191-3
  1.356: P 1123
  1.358: C 1068
  1.396: C 1068
  1.450: B 623
  1.462-3: P 1110

1.464: P 1089
1.528: B 929
1.611: B 950
2.159: T 1067
2.202: C 419
2.246: C 1057
2.661-3: B 1242
2.729: We p8
2.731-2: We 639
3.15: P 1273-4
3.64: F 483
3.103-4: B 971
3.135: B 359-360, 401-2
3.150: C 1057
3.247: P 1094
3.273-4: P 973
3.299: B 461t
3.336-7: F 1038
4.1-4: B 1757
4.75-78: B 1710
4.90-91: K 163
4.111: B 1112
4.194: We p8
4.214: P 443
4.219: We p8
4.293: C 1057
4.446-9: P 1273-4
4.450: P 1276
4.485: P 1328
4.515: L 347
4.521: L 1015
5.201-3: C 67*
5.289: A 964, P 241
5.306: W 1495
5.343: F 634
5.385-391: F 1149
5.387: P 990
5.452-3: F 924
5.593: P 255, L 1015
5.734: L 645
5.778: P 1067
5.859-861: F 634
5.895: F 634
5.900: F 634
5.902-3: P 1185, E 404, We 719
6.130-7: L 1282, F 215-6
6.146-9: B 685
6.155-197: A 427, F 1043
6.206-210: P 1301*
6.213: B 359-360

6.298-300: T 101-129
6.344: B 1204
6.460: T 605
6.492: L 513
7.126: C 1057
7.239: A 964
7.452: T 109-110
8.141: K 200
8.203: F 666
8.367-8: F 111
8.397-425: B 1199-1261
8.398: B 575
8.399: B 1204
8.423: B 1204
8.556: B 778t
9.63-64: P 1097-8
9.96-133: P 1078
9.372-3: F 1474
9.447-484: A 421
9.468: We 660-1
9.485: L 1252
9.557: F 194
9.673: K 200
10.164: F 116
11.36: L 560, F 929
11.41-42: F 1038
11.185: B 575
11.416: L 1255-8
11.462: F 258-9
11.492-5: K 526-8
11.674: F 467
11.772-5: P 1110
12.23: F 1060
12.200-7: K 197
12.200-243: W 17
13.21: F 666
13.198: K 1017
13.474: L 1255-8
13.519-522 P 457
13.624: F 815
13.636-9: We 188-9
13.795: L 324
14.16-17: K 692
14.122: B 718
14.168: T 422-3
14.201: C 271, B 701-2
14.231: We 549
14.286-291 B 1181
15.4-219: We p21
15.39-40: P 844

15.80-83: F 401-2
15.237: B 516*
15.280: F 485
15.371: B 623
15.607: L 1255-8
16.112-129 F 933
16.114-8: F 828
16.137-8: F 1038
16.187: L 742
16.251: P 1089
16.259-267: L 475
16.267: P 1287
16.275-294: F 933, We 951
16.514-6: F 659
16.611: E 1165-6
16.617: E 1165-6
16.672: We 549
16.779: B 1500
17.20: L 1015
17.88: We 660-1
17.136: F 823
17.243: P 1089
17.602: F 935
17.727: P 1077t
17.755: B 295
18.2-34: E 392-3
18.55-60: C 1068
18.105-6: C 419
18.433: B 718
18.535: P 255
18.590-606: E 1165-6
19.79-80: E 589
19.89: P 1123
19.91-133: We p21
19.209-214: C 621*
19.249-268: L 203
19.305-8: C 621*
19.380-3: F 1038
20.34: F 1144-5
20.71-72: T 101-129
20.72: F 1144-5
20.78: A 964
20.168-9: L 1255-8
20.231-2: P 724
21.108: B 1678, E 629
21.172: B 20
21.194-7: L 381
21.441-457: B 516
21.470-513: T 101-129
21.573-8: L 1015

22.31: W 1032, P 755
22.75: L 363
22.78: We 168
22.119-121: E 603
22.140: P 1067
22.205: L 126
22.209-212: F 1365
23.88: W 295-6
23.141-153: We 937
23.144-9: B 569
23.257-897: We 1162
23.667(-675): W 1503, L 688-690
23.690: F 1268
24.24: P 402, We 1139-40
24.80-83: C 1068
24.88: B 689
24.97: T 1069
24.104: T 1069
24.109: F 1149
24.143-188: B 1199-1261
24.315-6: B 883
24.333-694: We 1159
24.366: B 695
24.525-6: F 634
Margites fr. 1.2 West: B 910
Odyssey 1.128-9: T 220
1.441: B 1112
3.9: P 1040, B 518-9, 975, We 1130-1
3.40: P 1040, B 518-9, 975, We 1130-1
3.177-9: K 561
3.278: C 401
3.332-341: P 1060, B 1705, We 1110
3.430-463: P 948-1018
3.446: P 973
3.450: B 222, L 240, T 129-130
3.456-461: P 1021, B 191-3, T 693-5,
   We 1128
3.461: P 1040, B 518-9, 975
4.73: We 815
4.121-136: E 89
4.242-258: W 351
4.435-443: W 1032, P 755
5.125-8: T 299, We p5
5.194ff: F 518
5.217: B 1678, E 629
5.274: P 832-3
5.381: F 666
5.463: We 771
5.482-7: K 605t*
5.488-490: B 841

6.57: P 120
6.76: L 1184, T 284
6.92: We 1061
6.107: B 1678, E 629
6.237: B 139
6.261: P 1089
6.304-7: E 89
7.137: P 1089
8.37: P 1306
8.264-5: B 925
8.426: F 1339
9-10 *passim*: We 290-321 *passim*
9.58: B 1500
9.65: F 184
9.112: B 1695-6
9.184: We 292
9.219-249: We 298
9.246-7: F 559
9.273-6: B 1695-6
9.288-293: F 134, We 297
9.311: We 297
9.319-333: We 301
9.344: We 297
9.366-7: W 184
9.374: We 297
9.375-397: We 301
9.424-463: W 181
9.460: W 186
9.500-536: F 299
10.234-6: We 302
10.318-396: We 312
10.501-2: P 124-5
10.513-4: F 137-8
10.515: F 470
10.527: B 971, 1559-60
10.528-9: B 1561
11 *passim*: B 1553-64
11.14: F 187
11.35-37: B 1561
11.235-259: L 139
11.250: L 139
11.298-300: L 1300
11.456: E 238
11.522: F 963
11.604: K 529
12.279: F 116
13.107: T 822
13.289: B 1678, E 629
13.437-8: We 298
14.417: W 1116t*

14.422-3: P 973
14.429: P 1040
14.434-6: P 1056
14.446: P 1056
15.20-23: E 1161
15.526: B 516
16.15-21: F 790
16.46-48: K 605t*
17.33-39: F 790
17.96-97: E 89
17.390-1: L 696-7
17.448: B 1045, T 853
17.541(-7): K 639, B 720
18.87: L 363
18.100: F 1089-90
18.338: B 1204
19.395-7: P 402, F 1149, We 1139-40
19.414-7: F 790
19.446: F 822
19.518-523: B 15-16
19.519(-520): B 682-3, F 682
19.538: K 197*, 204*
20.25-27: K 208, C 409
20.105-121: B 720, E 739
20.274: C 1057
20.353: T 11041
22.189-190: L 455
22.408: L 240, T 129-130
23.243-6: C 571
24.1-10: We 1159
24.71: We 660-1
24.508: B 1451

HOMER AND HESIOD, CONTEST OF
(ed. T.W. Allen)
passim: F p14*
107-8: P 1282-3

HOMERIC HYMNS
To Apollo 16: B 870
114: B 575
194: L 1279
395-6: We 213
440-2: B 1710
443: K 1016
490-501: F 398-9
493-4: F 1319
534-9: F 398-9
To Demeter 18: T 320
48: T 101-2

61: T 101-2
63: C 571
88: C 571
105-110: L 254-387
147: E 915
153: A 774
192-211: F 416-439
235-242: K 1095*
272: F 451
288-290: L 254-387
334ff: T 301, F 1500-27
352: B 686
473-9: F 398-9
474: A 774
486-9: T 299, We p5
To Hermes: F 1149
2: F 1266
19: We 1126
43-46: F 401-2
47-51: F 234
175: P 402, We 1139-40
194: P 1065
292: P 402, We 1139-40
294-7: K 639*
Minor Hymns 1.8-9: F 215-6
7: F 204
14.1: B 874-5
19.1: C 595
19.2: F 230
21.1-3: B 769-784, 771-2*, F 207
26.3-5: L 1282, F 215-6
27.15: L 1279
32.20: B 910
33: E 1068-9

HORACE
Ars Poetica 94: We 22
96: F 868
189-190: E 1111/2
281-4: A p26
340: E 77
Carmina 2.7.9-14: P 1298-9
3.10.3: E 962
3.11.17-18: W 1032-5, P 755-8
Epistulae 1.10.24: P 637
Epodes 5.45-46: C 749

HYGINUS
Fabulae 4: A 434, W 1414
105: T 769-770

186: T 547*
187: B 558-9
191: We 287
273: F 1319

HYPEREIDES
Against Athenogenes: W 433*
Against Philippides 3: L 632
For Euxenippus (7-)8: F 362, 367
29-30: F 367
For Lycophron 10: We 168
12: We 948-9
Funeral Speech 18: L 1129-32
fr. 114: F 651
fr. 171: E 890, We 1082

IAMBLICHUS
Life of Pythagoras 55: E 446-9
249: C 1484-5

IBYCUS
PMG 296 [fr. 15 Page]: L 155-6
PMG 300 [fr. 19 Page]: C 1051

IDOMENEUS
FGrH 338: F 2 F 289-296

INSCRIPTIONS
AD 19 [1964] B 72: E 825
Agora xv 1.27: F 934
xv 12.26: E 444
xv 38.78-82: E 290
xv 49.7: K 407
xvi 68: K 852-78
xvii 1.140: K 67
xvii 23.104-6: A 134
xvii 52: L 321
xxi F79: L 184
xxi F176: L 322
xxv 90-91: T 805, F 678
xxv 100: T 861
ATL A9: W 660, 707
A9.IV.126-173: W 700
CEG 93: L p5
483: F 84
485: F 84
501: F 84
511: F 84
512: F 84
527: F 84

539: F 84
559: F 1506
564: F 84
569: F 84
CIL iv 2360.3: E 470, We 295
iv 8512: E 470, We 295
Defix. 15: P 523*
89.a.6: C 1075
EMI 2: We p12
3: We p9
4: We p9
6: We p13
7: We p9
11: We p9
17: We 733-4
22: We p9
27: We 710
31: We p12
34: We p12
36: We p9
38: We 710
39: We p12, We 733-4
42: We p12, We 733-4
45: We 733-4
GDI 1884: We 986
Hesperia 6 (1937) 347-8: K 846
7 (1938) 3, lines 28-33: T 758
7 (1938) 5 no.1.86-91: P 374-5*
12 (1943) 1: C 557, F 73
43 (1974) 179-88, lines 18-23: K 407*
IC iv 41 V-VI: We 147
IG I^3 5: We 820, 1161
15.19: B 1021
19: P 170-2
21.56 [*SEG* x 14.58]: A 6
32.8-9: E 304-5
34.7: B 1021
35: L p5
35.11: P 1122-3
35.17: L 1012
37.15 [i^2 14.5]: K 763
37.25: A 66*
40.40: B 434-6
40.64-67: P 1046
41: P 1047
41.38 [i^2 42.23]: A 6
52.4: B 1040-1
52.A15-18: L 174, We 1193
52.B23-25: L 174, We 1193
61 [i^2 57]: K 1085, W 380, B 988

61.2 [i² 57.2]: A 603
61.34: B 289, T 605
61.51 [i² 57.51]: C 109, W 1268-9
62.5-7: B 1025
63: B 790
66.4 [SEG x 69, xiii 8]: K 969*
68.5: B 289, T 605
69.3-4: B 289, T 605
71.55-58: L 582
73.21-22 [i² 70.5]: A 603
75.4: W 240
76.15-16 [i² 90.15-16]: C 1425-6
76.20-21 [i² 90.20-21]: C 1425-6
78.37: We 820
78.47 [i² 76.47]: C 332, B 521
78.52: B 1541
78.53-54 [i² 76.53-54]: C 615-6
78.54-59: B 832
78.60: L 1012
79.1 [i² 81.1]: A 843
80.19: B 1541
82.20: E 304-5
82.30-32: F 131
91: L 391, T 372-9
97: T 372-9
101: T 372-9
102: B 1072, 1274-5, F 1196
104: T 372-9
110.6: B 798
113: E p4, We p3
117.30: L 421-2
127: L 582
131: F 764, E 834
131.5-7: K 786*
131.9-10: P 1084*
137: C 686*
145.2: W 401
161: P 170-2
182.9-11: W 658
252.4: L 645
254.4: W 753
255.B8-9: P 1060, B 1705, We 1110
287.5: W 459, B 822-3
297-299 [i² 237-9]: A 614, C 46
300.6 [i² 240.94]: A 855
301.2 [i² 241.102]: K 969*
301.25 [i² 241.110]: A 855
306.24: W 157
308.65: P 1008, B 168
322-324 [i² 261-3]: A 614, C 46

331.32-33: P 1008, B 168
349.58 [SEG xxiv 37]: A 614, C 46
351.19: T 1197
364.1-2: P 990
364.9: T 876
364.20: W 157
365.5 [i² 296.5]: K 129
365.30: K 567*
365.30-40 [i² 296.30-40]: C 1261,
    W 1501, P 782, T 169, F 86
372.2: B 1040-1
375: T 805, F 141
375.1: F 708-9
375.35: B 126
376: T 805, F 141
376.32: B 1040-1
377: T 805, F 141
387.2: W 401
391.7 [i² 311.8]: A 843
421-430: We 1
421.34-49: E 593, We 157
421.34: W 828, P 1138, T 280
421.35: W 828, P 1138, T 280
421.40: W 828, P 1138, T 280
421.173: W 1215
422: F 1512
422.204-5: K 242-3*
422.210-1 [SEG xiii 13.170-1]:
    K 242-3*
422.286: E 907
422.305: P 1263
426: F 1512
426.53 [SEG xiii 17.63]: K 242-3*
427.8: We 1
430: F 1512
435: L 751
469.9: W 1301
472.1-3: P 395, 1008, B 1556, L 490
472.11 [i² 370.9]: A 855
472.13 [i² 370.11]: A 855
474: L 722
474.1: L 262
475.65-67: F 173
475.251-6: F 173
475.272-285: F 173
476.33-45: F 173
511 [i² 400]: B 799
894: A 843*
895: B 1128*
958: F 1036-7

959: F 1036-7
964 [*Hesp.* 42 (1973) 173-5]: B 126
965 [i² 770]: C 985
967: F 1036-7
970 [ii² 3090]: A p25, We p29
1032.409: A 887*
1135: A 887*
1179 [i² 945]: P 832-3
1190.30 [i² 950.30]: W 234
1190.54 [i² 950.54]: T 1102-3
1330: L p5*
1361.2 [i² 1084.2]: P 1146, L 908
1401-3 [i² 924, 921, 923]: W 97-98
1405-6 [i² 926, 925]: W 97-98
IG ii² 1.41: F 367, E 102, We 176
1.61-62: B 1024-5
10: E 202-3, We 550
14: E p2
18: B 1372-1409, F 153, E 330, We 550
21: E 202-3, We 173, 550
24: E 202-3, We 550
29: E 248
34.36: E 208
40 Addenda: E 248
42.19-20: E 208
44.12: B 434-6
75.7: A 1028
111.37-39: T 78-79
145: E 825
276: We p12
333.11: E 729
337.33-45: B 1296, We 382-3
410.17-18: B 868
674.16: L 645
676.11-12: F 378
772: We p9
847.21: F 323-353
1006.12-13: F 16
1008.21: F 378
1028.10: F 323-353
1035.10: L 743, F 1080
1096: L 397
1138.25-27: E 825
1176.2-9: T 834
1182.20: B 872
1187.16-20: T 834
1227.5: We 819
1237.60-61: F 798
1243: L 285
1356: P 254, T 758, We 1128

1358 : P 374-5*, T 300
1361.4-7: T 758
1366.23-24: We 1142
1367.14: We 1142
1368.8: L 1
1368.101: L 1
1368.180: T 746
1388.74: W 1501
1496 A 84-85: We 1159
1496 A 88-89: We 1175
1496 A 115-6: We 1159
1496 A 118-9: We 1175
1496 A 134-5: We 627
1514.16: K 1406
1514.48: K 1406
1524.140: T 803
1525.13: T 803
1533.33: E 1101t*
1553.16: T 347, We 435-6
1556.30: A 568
1556.34-35: K 852-7*
1561.22: W 433
1561.32: F 1084
1570.78-79: L 435-6*
1576.5-6; K 852-7*
1594-1603: W 658
1602.17: K 407
1609.9: K 1309
1611.123: B 1204
1622.157: K 1309
1627.404: P 145
1627.429: P 145
1629.205: A 392
1641.28-30: E 677
1642.14-15: B 619
1642.16: A 388*
1656: E p2, We p2
1658-64: E p2, We p2
1672.31: B 1149-51
1672.59: We 1
1672.61: B 1149-51
1672.67: We 1
1672.100-5: We 982-3
1673.22: We 1
1698.6: A 1028
1740.24: A p25*
1927.110: C 64
1951.82-93: F 48
1951.99: E 366
2311.58: C 28

2316.56-57: C 28
2317.20: C 28
2318.8: K 520
2318.34: K 574
2318.81: C 1261, W 1501, P 782
2318.115: A p24, P 1
2318.196: A p25, p28, We p1
2318.201-3: We p30
2318.241: T p12
2319.82-83: C 64
2321: A p25
2325: A p24*, p26, p28, A 849
2325.9: F 86
2325.44: K 520
2325.52: K 537
2325.60: P 1
2325.65: F 14
2325.124: C 556, F 13
2325.126: C 553
2325.133: F 14
2325.140: T p12
2325.142: T p12
2325.253; C 64
2343: T 898
2346.23: We p12
2346.109: E 167
2409.21-22: E 428
2492.5-9: E 567
2370: A p25
2645: W 787, L 1105
2812: E 825
2933: L 285
3028: B 1372-1409, F 153, E 330
3091: F 1124
3177: L 397
3453: L p5
3483: F 378
4355: We p11
4473: We 639
4619: We p12
4791: B 872
4960+4961: We p11, We 411
4962: T 285, We p11, We 660
5055: L 397
5057: B 872
5075: L 397
5378: E 1
5765: A 1093, K 786
6217: C 1162*
7424: E 43

7702: E 43
7717: E 43
7879: We p12
8476: W 1371
11000: T 803
11365: T 803
12034: P 1146, L 908
12035: T 728, F 1345
12035a: T 728, F 1345
12037: B 657
12124: W 433
12508: E 1
12508a: E 1
12687: P 1146
12888: We p12
13019: W 433
13139: T 746
13142: T 746
IG iii[3], *see Defixiones*
IG iv² [1] 121: W 123 (*see also* under *EMI*)
122: W 123 (*see also* under *EMI*)
123: W 123
124: W 123
126.4: W 122
127.2-4: We p9
128.29-31: We p9
IG vii 537.18: W 234
585.iii.1: W 234
1138: L 6
1888 *I*6: P 62
2444.*I*b: L 6
2809: L 6
IG xii[1] 1032: A 1030, We 408
IG xii[2] 73: A 793
IG xii[3] 540: L 982
1347: B 868
IG xii[5] 647.16: E 652
IG xii[7] 115.11: P 890
237.15-20: P 1060
IG xii[8] 63a.13: E 644-5
IG xii[9] 56.437-8: We 22
245B.174: We 22
IGSK ii 205.23-25: We 678
ii 207.1-3: We 1126
IGUR 216.13: We p1
Inschr. Priene 174.8-10: P 1056, 1060,
B 1705, We 1110
364.4: P 1060, B 1705, We 1110
Inscr. Magn. 17.36-41: We 41-43
JHS 32 (1912) 270-6: F 970

Laws of Gortyn
v 7-9: C 1425-6
vi 24-25: C 1425-6
ix 16-17: C 1425-6
x 25-29: We 147
LSCG 119.4: E 782
LSS 76.4: E 782
77.6: E 782
129.4-6: E 782
ML 45: B 1040-2
84.17: A 1093
85: F 689
94: F 696
SEG i 375-6: K 763
xii 80: L p5
xii 100.64: B 284, F 428, E 810
xii 212: T 633
xiii 201: F 1506
xiv 65.3-4: P 414
xiv 529.15-17: P 151*
xvi 39e: L 6
xvi 126.15: K 362*, W 659
xvii 98: F 1506
xvii 146.5: P 62
xix 39.c.1: W 230
xix 149.145 W 232
xix 244: We 800
xxi 131.11-13: A 134
xxi 541: P 1122-3, T 300, 758, We 1126, 1138
xxiii 547.53: We 1159
xxiv 67.6: K 67
xxiv 223.4: W 433
xxiv 223.7: W 433
xxiv 371: L 6
xxv 226: W 123, We p11, We 411
xxv 240: L 321
xxvi 72: E 290
xxvi 1275: L 1
xxvii 27.437: C 1468
xxviii 225: We p11
xxix 86: E p4, We p3
xxx 203: T 373-4
xxx 908: We 1155
xxxi 60.65: L 645
xxxiii 167 e.ii.13: L 742t, E 369t
xxxiii 1039.82: T 773
xxxiv 103.21-25: T 834
xxxiv 122.37: P 1146*, L 908
xxxvii 1673: We 1157

xl 266: F 1144-5
xl 760-762: E 369
*SIG*³ 2: B 434-6
436: L 1129-32
527.15: W 846, P 864
714.28-31: We 1126
1002.3: P 1122-3
1004.30: P 1122-3
1004.32: We 1138
1010.5: P 1122-3
1013.3-4: B 518-9
1026.10: We 1138
1215: We 529
Stroud *Athenian Grain-Tax Law*: E 102*, We 176
Tod 113.42: We p3
121: K 901*
123: K 901*
124: K 901*
204: P 457, E 767
ZPE 62 (1986) 183-4: K 855*

ION OF CHIOS
Guards fr. trag. 44: F 1425
Omphale fr. trag. 29: F 560
Phoenix fr. trag. 41: F 706-7
FGrH 392 F 6: F p7, F 82
PMG 745 [fr. lyr. 6 Page]: P 836
fr. eleg. 27 West: E 948

IOPHON
Sack of Troy: C 1484-5*

ISAEUS
2.9: We 529
2.29-31: F 1412
2.36: L 613
3.19: E 560-1
3.30: B 496
5.(37-)38: E p3, p6
6 passim: W 1250
6.19: E 617*
6.21-26: B 765, F 418
6.42: F 1363
6.48-50: T 294
8 passim: A 1167-8
8.8: E 426, We 529
8.14: E 426
8.20: E 1115
9.18-19: E 1026*

10.10: E 1024-5
11.10-11: B 1561
fr. 21 Thalheim: K 1246*

ISOCRATES
4.24: W 1076, L 1082
4.34-36: L 582
4.56-63: We 385
4.57: T 331-351
4.68-70: L 678
4.100-2: B p.5
4.120: B 284
4.157: F 354-371
6.2: T 383-4, E 151-2
7.10: K 656
7.15: K 744
7.16: C 1187
7.45: K 1382
8.52: E 797-8
8.82: A 505, B 1361
8.94: B 540-3*
9.14-15: F 464
9.54-57: E p4, We p3
9.57: We 1175
9.68: E p4, We p3
10.63: L 1314
10.65: F 1045
12.5: F 907-8
12.63-65: B p.5
12.70: B p.5
12.94: F 694
12.166: L 582
12.190: L 582
12.227: B 1529
13.11: E 571
13.14: E 571
13.18: E 571
13.21: E 571
14.31: P 130
14.48: We 147
15.101-139: We 180
15.109-110: P 1020
15.15(5-)6: W 421, B 1701
15.287: E 672
15.314: W 1042, We 923
16 passim: E 848
16.2: E 603
16.7: L 995
16.40: F 1422
17.9: We 373

17.12: W 1042
17.14: E 1023-4
17.15: F 616
17.31-32: E 102, We 176
17.41: E 825
17.42: K 300-2*, T 78-79
17.43: E 366
17.52: W 1501, P 784
18.1: F 907-8
18.6: K 300-2*
18.9: We 370
18.23: E 202-3, 802, We 550
18.57: T 861
18.59-60: F 1065
20 passim: E 663-4
20.19: E 663-4

ISTROS
FGrH 334: F 16 E 128
    F 29: F 155

JOHN CHRYSOSTOM
Twelfth Homily on Ephesians
    (xi 92 Migne): B 721

JUBA
FGE 239: F 303

JULIAN
Orations 8.179d: B 874-5

JUVENAL
3.197-222: B 997
4.107: F 422-4
8.32: F 55
14.97: C 252

LACTANTIUS
on Statius' Thebaid 4.740: F 1319

LAMPROCLES
PMG 735 [fr. 1 Page]: C 967

LEUCIPPUS
A1 D-K: C 380*
A25 D-K: C 376-8

LEUCON
Ambassadors: W p.xv
Phrateres: P p.xv

fr. 3 [2 K]: P 804, B 151

LEXICON RHETORICUM
CANTABRIGIENSE
s.v. εἰσαγγελία: A p33
s.v. Λύκος: W 389

LIBANIUS
Declamationes 13.52: F 355
Epistulae 374.3: B 968
  754.3: B 968
Narrationes 8 Förster: P 1078
Orationes 1.9: A p17*
  17.8: F 991

LIVES OF LITERARY FIGURES
Aeschylus 1: F 886
  6: F 911-2
  11: F 1296-7
  12: F 868
Aesop G 124-142 Perry: W 1446-7
Aristophanes 35-39 K-A: F p21
  50-51 K-A: T p11
  56 K-A: We p1
Euripides 2: T p1, F p8, F 939, 944*, 953,
  1206-8
  3 [ll.55-59 Mér.]: F p8
  5: T 1
  6 [ll.92-96 Mér.]: F 944
  see also Papyri (*POxy* 1176)
Sophocles 4: K 522, T 164, We 953
  5: K 522
  7: F 82
  10: F p7
  12: P 699
  13: P 523*, F 73
  14: F p8

LIVY
23.11.5: We 21
34.27.4: L 1301

"LONGINUS"
On the Sublime 23.3: T 941

LONGUS
Daphnis and Chloe 3.13.4: K 634
  3.23: T 1092

LUCAN
Pharsalia 1.614-5: L 205

LUCIAN
Alexander 4: W 1043, P 422, We 417
Amores 53: F 991
Anacharsis 2: K 490
  24: F 775
Asinus 38: L 1189
Bis Accusatus 9: L 721
  12: F 464
  23: E 974
Calumniae non temere credendum 17-18:
  W 392
Contemplantes 19: L 1242
Demonax 17: L 417
  18: T 163
  49: B 441-3*
Demosthenis Encomium 24: We 602
  27: We p11
Dialogi Deorum 3.1: We 11
  18.1: We 11
Dialogi Meretricii 4.2: K 1246*
  8.3: T 561
Dialogi Mortuorum 1.1: F 366, We 597
  2.1: F 140
  11.2: F 464
Hermotimus 40-43: F 792
  84: K 1068
Icaromenippus 27: B 191-3
Juppiter Tragoedus 11: T 658
  42: A 263
Kataplous 7: We 597
  22: F 289ff, 294, We 425
Lexiphanes 8: F 566
  12: E 647, We 314-5
  13: T 427
de Luctu 4: F 464
  10: F 140
Menippus 8: F 464
de Morte Peregrini 9: C 1083, We 168
Navigium 42-43: We 884
Necyomantia, see *Menippus*
Nero 1: F 204
Nigrinus 1: B 301
de Parasito 55: F 715-6
Piscator 49: L 115
Pseudologistes 17: B 721, F 196
Quomodo historia conscribenda sit
  20: W 1309

34: B 1406
Rhetorum Praeceptor 9: K 348-9
   23: E 119-120
de Saltatione 21: L 748
   26: F 896
   45: F 499
Scytha 2: L 191-2
   11: L 1045
Somnium 6: L 748
Timon 12: P 637
Tyrannicida 5: F 790

LYCURGUS
Against Leocrates: F 953
   1-2: E 171-2
   3-8: We 910
   4: We 917
   17: F 378
   39: L 995
   40: T 903
   67: We 948
   94: F 145-153
   97: F 145-153
   101: We 948
   112: We 875
   113: F p10
   120-1: P 395, B 1556, L 490
   122: K 1227, L 602
   134: We 948
   149: We 914
fr. 10/11.2 Conomis: We 948-9

LYRICA ADESPOTA
PMG 848: B 680, 714, T 1
   851a,b: A 263-279*
   856: F 372-382
   862: We p5
   869: C 1358
   879: We 327
   884-890: B 1416
   885: T 299, We p5
   892: K 608*
   893:    A 980, W 1225, B 1416,
      L 632, 664t*, E 938-945
   894:    A 980, W 640, 1225, B 1416,
      E 938-945
   895:    A 980, W 1225, B 1416,
      L 632, E 938-945
   896:    A 980, W 1225, B 1416,
      L 664t*, E 938-945

898: L 1237
899: L 1237
903: T 528
907: B 1416, L 665
909: B 1697-9
911: W 1226-7
912a: W 1241
934: We 639
948: C 967
953: B 950
974: L 1001
985: C 398

LYRICA ALEXANDRINA ADESPOTA
   (ed. Powell)
fr. 34.1: We 530

LYSIAS
1 *passim*: C 1077
1.7: L 495, F 983-8*, E 211-2
1.9-14: T 482
1.12: E 721
1.14: E 732, We 1064
1.15-29: E 225
1.16-17: L 723-5
1.18-20: We p15
1.20: E 916
1.24: E 49
1.26: E 1056-7
1.38: E 675
1.40: E 675
1.41-42: E 560-1
1.49: We 168
2.1: F 598
2.4-6: L 678
2.11-16: We 385
2.17: W 1076, L 1082
2.59-66: E 202-3, We 550
3 *passim*: E 1037-97
3.6: T 903
4.9: E 1037-97
5.5: E 593
6.6: P 251
6.17(-18): C 830, W 377-8, F 320
6.29: P 908, T 936-7, E 782
6.51: W 831
7.4: P 395, B 1556, L 490
7.33: We 948
8.10: C 21*, We 157
9.4: K 1370*

9.15: K 1370*
10 passim: E 639-640
10.6-9: C 1466
10.16: K 394*
12.6: A 11, T 170
12.10: F 587
12.11: E 602
12.13: A 11, T 170
12.21: L 593
12.38: W 952-8
12.43: L 577-8, E 23
12.62-78: F 970
12.65: L 421
12.67: B 126, F 541
12.68-76: F p22, F 541
12.73: W 157
12.98: We 147
13.7-12: T 805, F 678
13.10: F p3
13.12: F p22
13.13-33: F p22
13.21: E 444
13.27: F 629
13.37: W 987-8
13.59: F 629
13.65: W 1042, We 923
13.70-72: F 689
13.73: F 689
13.80: E 208
14 passim: K 1370
14.25: F 417
14.25-28: L 723-5, E 932
14.27: E 672
14.38: F 1512, E 644-5
14.39: A 614*
15 passim: K 1370
15.5: We 174
15.6: K 225
16.13: K 1370, E p2, E 193
16.15: E 195-6, 202-3, We 550
16.18: K 580, W 466, E 632, 955
17.3: F 1466
17.5: C 134, E 1027, We 904
18.4-5: L 103
18.10: E 428
19 passim: E 201
19.19-20: E 825, We 550
19.25-26: C 1216, W 98, We 240
19.27: W 1214
19.38-41: E p3

19.40: We 180, 196
19.48: B 284, T 805, F 428, 678, E 810
19.51: E 1105
20.7: We 370
20.(10-)12: W 1302, F 689, E 77
20.24: K 301-2
20.31: We 831
20.34: W 568-9, We 382-3
21.1-4: F 153
21.3: L 654
21.4: E p10
21.5: K 560, B 868
21.20: B 1372-1409, F 153, E 330
22 passim: K 407*, E 424
22.2: T 78-79
22.3: We 914
22.16: K 407
22.18-22: We 910
23 passim: F 694
23.3: We 338
23.9-12: E 1023-4
24.6: E 593
24.10: E 571
24.13: We 948
24.19-20: K 744
24.22: We 948
25.9: W 1302, F 689
25.13: We 831
25.25: F 708-9
25.26: E 77
27.1: K 1359*, W 241, 1113, E 563
27.3-6: E 71
27.9: E 77
27.10: K 925-6*, F 419
28 passim: We p2, We 550
28.1: E 77, We 483, 910
28.3-4: E 197-8, We p2
28.5-8: We 550
28.6-7: We 567-570
28.9: We 381
29 passim: We p2, We 550
29.6: We 381
29.9: We p2
29.11-14: We 910
30.2: L 435-6
30.5: L 435-6
30.9-14: T 805, F p22, F 678, 1506
30.21: We 30
30.22: K 774*
30.26: F 1084

30.27-29: F 1084
30.28: A 603
30.31: F 1506
31.6: We 1151
31.26: F 362
31.31: E 444
31.34: E 239
32.13: C 1233
32.16: We 942-3
33 passim: We 550
fr. 1: F 1496-8
fr. 53: A 999, B 1372-1409, F 153, 366*,
    E 330
fr. 82: We 179
see also Papyri (POxy 1606)

LYSIPPUS
Bacchae fr. 6: C 332, B 521

MACHON (ed. Gow)
211-7: We 817
226-230: We 152
327-332: We 152
fr. XII : L 231
fr. XIV : T 728, F 1345
fr. XV : T 728, F 1345

MAGNES
Dionysus I and II: F p11

MARINUS
Life of Proclus 30: We 733-4

MARSYAS
FGrH 135 F 8: T 29, F 83

MARTIAL
3.82.12: K 59
11.11.6: T 633

MATRON
Attic Dinner 10-11: K 956, C 591, B 567

MELANIPPIDES
PMG 759: F 137-8

MELANTHIUS (tragic dramatist)
Medea: P 1012, 1014*

MELANTHIUS (historian)
FGrH 326 F 3: B 1073, F 320
    F 4: F 404-6, We 845

MELISSUS
fr. 7.2-6 D-K: F 634

MENANDER
Adelphoi II fr. 13: We 345
Arrhephoros fr. 69 [63 KT]: W 1489
Aspis: P 742, E 293, We p23
    2: W 87
    34: W 87
    106: W 87
    222: We 823
    269: F 991
    372-3: L 629
Chalkeia fr. 401: E 1123
Dis Exapaton: P 742
    103: We 322
Dyskolos: L 70, E p28, E 867-8
    1-49: T 977
    49/50: E 1111/2
    81ff: F 730
    81-87: P 743/742
    89: E 251, We 12
    93: E 143
    107: W 556
    153-166: We 335
    183-4: We p23
    194: F 598
    197: T 326
    204: F 604
    234-6: We 249
    247: W 163
    260-3: W 82
    291-3: We 483
    366: E 934
    384-9: E 110
    392/3: E 1111/2
    393ff: P 948-9, 1017, B 856
    401: B 1581-2
    407-418: W 82
    415: E 80
    427: We 963
    430-441: W 82
    432-4: L 2
    434: B 1469
    438: B 901-2
    450: T 285, We 660

453: We 963
455/6: E 1111/2
456-521: P 261, E 446-9
459: C 132
463: C 132
486/7: E 1111/2
488: P 1, We 305
498: C 132
499: K 1215
502: We 953
521/2: E 1111/2
533: E 10
550: We 821
557: P 536
586: K 1326
640: We 30
659: W 875, T 748, We 1114
665/6: E 1111/2
718-721: We 58
731: W 478
758: T 265
857: T 795
871-3: T 903
873/4: E 1111/2
873-9: E p31, We 958/9
880(-1): P 952, L 1242, T 1160-75, E 891
911-2: C 132
921: C 132
922-3: E 991
923-4: W 1215, F 938
925: We 963
926: We 963
946-953: E 1-18, We 515
947: E 14
950-3: E 1166-7
964: E 691-2, We 1194
965-7: F 1029
967: E 1146
968-9: L 1293
Encheiridion F 7 Arnott: We 332
Epikleros I or II fr. 130: We 321/2
Epitrepontes: C 531, T p12, E 293, We 1
169-171: A 982
229: E 80
325-333: L 139
328: E 80
335: P 1201
341-2: L 139
451ff: L 447

462: P 536
468: We 706
478: F 319
538-540: W 1353
860: We 322
874-5: F 604
887: F 598
952: We 30
1062-75: E p31
1064: We 30
1087-8: W 707
1088-9: W 708, E 1132-3
1100: We 30
1118-20: E p31
1122: E p31
1126-8: E p31
Georgos: C 684, L 70, T p12
41: We 322
46-52: W 277, L 987, F 1280
53: P 59
Hauton Penthôn fr. 74: We p7
Heros: L 70
2-3: We 276
Hippokomos fr. 194: E 744
Hypobolimaios fr. 373: E 867-8
Kolax 1: We 50
F 1: W 1, P 1060, B 866-7
F 4: T 1114
Leucadia 3 Arnott: We 322
Menagyrtes fr. 235 [275 KT]: T 743
Methe fr. 224.14: E 102, We 176
Misoumenos 555 Arnott: P 1146*
577 Arnott [177 Sandb]: We 706
607f Arn. [206f Sandb]: F 604
704 Arnott [303 Sandb]: L 683
715 Arnott [314 Sandb]: T 748, We 1114
989f Arn. [459f Sandb]: E 691-2, We 823, 1194
993f Arn. [463f Sandb]: E 1146
F 8: T 422-3
Naukleros fr. 246 [286 KT]: P 143
Orge fr. 265: E 652
Perikeiromene: A 849*, L 70
1ff: T 721-2
153ff: E 994-7
159-162: We 249
172ff: W 1
321-2: L 391
366: We 30

484: T 153
810ff: C 531
996: P 1017
1013-4: L 1173
Perinthia 18: P 241
   21: W 1
Phasma 43-44: L 391
Plokion fr. 296.13 [333.13 KT]: W 135
   fr. 300: E 867-8
   fr. 307 [343 KT]: T 741-2
Pseudherakles fr. 409 [451 KT]: B 1637
   fr. 412: We 17
Samia: E 867-8
   35-41: W 1353, T p12
   38-46: L 389, T 795
   46: L 409
   69: We 46
   192: W 163
   256: K 127, C 219, B 1730, F 520
   258: K 127, W 1353
   269: F 598
   309: T 748, We 1114
   311: K 821t
   348: E 934
   399-404: B 901-2
   444: T 748, We 1114
   509-513: We 338
   530: E 81
   596: E 81
   641-657: We 335
   674: We 660-1
   731: E 691-2, We 1194
   733-4: E 1146
   73(6-)7: B 787, L 1293
Sikyonios 135: W 163
   142: W 163
   150-271: E 372
   160: P 395
   187: F 886
   188: E 311, We 332
   418(-9): E 691-2, We 1194
   420: E 1146
Synepheboi fr. 348 [394 KT]: B 1490-3
Theophoroumene: E 867-8
   37-38 Arnott: W 7-8t*
   F 1.15: We 50
Thettale: C 749
Trophonios fr. 351 [397 KT]: B 1637
   fr. 421: E 1002
   fr. 432 [928 KT]: W 433

fr. 450 [679 KT]: L 43
fr. 482: We 1175
fr. 585 [902 KT]: F 425
fr. 652: E 891, We 1011
fr. 659: We 468-470
fr. 669 [785 KT]: F 187
fr. 798: E 867-8
fr. 815 [592 KT]: L 16
fr. 844.11 [620.11 KT]: B 358
fr. 862: We 332
fr. 884 [801 KT]: T 748, We 1114
fr. 901: E 867-8
fr. 908.6: We 689

MESOMEDES
Hymn to the Sun: T 43-50

METAGENES
Homer fr. 10: W 1301
   fr. 12 [11 K]: B 1297
Philothytes fr. 14 [13 K]: W 1221, B 31
   fr. 15: E 579
Thuriopersae: C 521-3*
   fr. 6: P 1314, B p.2

MIMNERMUS
fr. 12 West: C 571

MNESIMACHUS
Hippotrophos fr. 4.55: E 10
Philip fr. 9: W 508, B 734

MORSIMUS(?)
fr. 1 : P 1012

"MUSAEUS"
fr. 14 D-K: B 693

NEMESIANUS
Cynegetica 168: K 1026t

NEPOS
Alcibiades 8: F 1422
Timotheus 2.2: P 1020
   3.5: We 180

NEW TESTAMENT
Matthew 4.8: K 170
Mark 10.25: C 448
Luke 11.53: E 356

16.3: B 1432
Acts 16.16-39: W 1019-20

NICANDER
Alexipharmaca 91: We 1206
    186-194: F 126
    409: L 553
fr. 74.30: W 27

NICOCHARES
Galatea fr. 4: We 179, 290-321
Laconians: We p1
Lemnian Women: E p10
    fr. 15: E p10

NICOPHON
Adonis: We p1
Encheirogastores fr. 8: E 891
    fr. 11: E 634
Sirens: C 521-3*
    fr. 20.1-2: W 500*
    fr. 21 [13 K]: P 1314, B p.2

NICOSTRATUS (comic dramatist)
Anterosa fr. 3: B 603
Diabolos fr. 9 [10 K]: P 143
Habra fr. 1: E 292
Kline fr. 13 [15 K]: B 567, We 1142
Patriotai fr. 22: E 50
Wealth: We p8

OLD TESTAMENT
Genesis 1.2: B 693
    49.23: E 356
Leviticus 24.5-9: We 678
Deuteronomy 32.48-52: K 170
    34.1-4: K 170
Judges 8.2: F 92
2 Samuel 21.19: T 822
Isaiah 3.17: E 150
Proverbs 7.16: B 816

OLYMPIODORUS
Comm. on Pl. Phd. p.43.15-17: We 327
    p.111.14-19: We 327

OPHELION
Ialemos fr. 1: W 1522

OPPIAN
Halieutica 3.637-641: K 313

ORPHICA
Argonautica 13-14: B 694
Hymns 14.9: B 874-5
fr. (Kern) 32b.1: F 194
    37: F 311
    54: B 695
    57: B 695
    60: B 695
    66a: F 311
    68: F 311
    70: B 695
    127.3: B 696
    205-220: We 327
    222: F 155

OVID
Amores 1.6 *passim*: E 952-975
Ars Amatoria: 1.581 L 208
Metamorphoses 6.671-4: B 100-1
    7.159-293: K 1321
    8.391-402: F 1402
    9.285-323: P 1078
    11.85-193: We 287
    11.475: P 1306
    15.634-5: We 213
Tristia 2.406: We 1127

PANYASSIS
fr. 19a-e: F 499, We p8

PAPYRI
PBerol 21243: C 997*
PGM vii 186: L 23-24
    vii 191-2: A 1066*
    xxxvi 283-294 A 1066*
    xxxvi 284: C 1075
PHeid 182.a.4: K 191*
PLitLond 50: E 952-975*
POxy 413: E 952-975*
    466.21-24: E 259-260
    663: L 723-5
    1176 fr. 39 coll. i 21-ii 22: F 1491-2
    1176 fr. 39 coll. x-xiii: L 283
    1176 fr. 39 coll. xii-xiii: F 944
    1176 fr. 39 col. x 15ff: T 451
    1176 fr. 39 col. xv 28ff: T p4
    1176 fr. 39 col. xix 11ff: F p7

1176 fr. 39 col. xxi 2-25: F p8
1176 fr. 39 col. xxii: F 1336
1606.29-47: E 802, We 550
1606.118-124: E 802
1606.157-173: We 550
1801.45: K 635
2455.192-200: F 1319
2455.247-263: A 424
2455.267-8: F 1225-6
2455.270-3: F 1225-6
2457.25: F 1081
2457.25-26: T 406
2457.31-32: F 1081
2538 ii 23-28: F 418
2686: We 875
3013: B 15-16
ZPE 53 (1983) 1-25: E 924

PARIAN CHRONICLE
FGrH 239: A15 F 1033
    A43: W 1479
    A59: F 939
    A63: T p1, F p8
    A70: T p12

PARMENIDES
fr. 1.14 D-K: C 1292

PARTHENIUS
Peri erotikon pathematon 3: T 547-8

PAUSANIAS
1.1.2: E 1107
1.1.3: E 686, We 1175
1.1.5: C 52, L 2, T 130
1.2.4: F 313-4, 324
1.2.6: T 533
1.3.2: E p4, E 685, We p3
1.3.4: P 422, E 685
1.8.4: K 852-7*
1.9.4: F 694
1.14.7: B 881
1.15: L 679
1.15.1: K 297
1.15.4: K 846
1.17: L 679
1.17.2: K 1312
1.18.2: T 533
1.22.3: L 835
1.23.2-3: A 1093*

1.23.8: B 1128*
1.23.10: K 562*, L 804
1.24.6: F 929
1.24.7: L 759, We 185
1.27.2: L 439, T 318-9
1.27.3: L 642
1.28.2: L 751
1.28.4: L 721
1.30.2: W 1203-4, F 131
1.30.4: F 129
1.31.4: We 327
1.31.4-5: B 872
1.34.3: We 701-2
1.38.3: T 533
2.1.4: F 966
2.2.5: We 179
2.10.5: A 793
2.25.5-6: B 396
2.28.1: We 690
2.30.1: W 122, We p10
2.32.7: F 194
3.9.8: E 71, 248
3.13.2: F 378
3.14.6: L 1301
3.15.3: L 1314
3.17.1-3: L 1299
3.18.3: B 619*
3.18.6-19.6: L 1298
3.19.9: L 1314
3.20.9: L 186, 191-2
3.21.8: We 658
3.25.5: F 187
4.15.8: L 186
4.17.1: T p10
4.24.2: A 510-1
4.24.5: L 1137-44
4.27.4: P 1070
5.9.3: L 679
5.11.1(-2): B 510, We 185
5.14.1: P 1100
5.14.9: We 1161
5.15.3: We 586
5.24.9: L 186
6.6.1: L 679
6.10.4: B 292
6.17.9: F 1021
6.20.15-19: K 247
6.26.3: B 515
7.21.12: We 382
7.25.1: T 224

7.25.3: A 510-1
7.27.1: We 1157
7.27.11: We 658
8.7.2: L 191-2
8.31.1: F 378
8.31.3-4: L 254-387
8.45.7: F 1402
9.11.3: P 1078
9.39(.7): C 506-8, We 658
10.4.3: F 1212
10.9.2: A 214, W 1206-7
10.10.4: We p2
10.12.11: P 1070
10.29.1-2: F 186
10.36.8: K 560

PAUSANIAS THE ATTICIST
fr. 72 Erbse: L 1094

PEISANDER
fr. 7: C.1051

PERSIUS
1.59: We 287

PETRONIUS
Satyricon 25: T 480

PHANODEMUS
FGrH 325 F 11: F 218-9

PHERECRATES
Agathoi fr. 2: E 302
Agrioi fr. 6: A 16, P 951, B 766, 858
   fr. 10: E 739
   fr. 11: B 1296
   fr. 12: K 762
   fr. 15 [14 K]: W 1501, P 784
Automoloi fr. 22 [19 K]: P 473
Cheiron fr. 155 [145 K]: C 969-971, P 904,
   B 1372-1409, T 68, 100, F 153,
   1327-8, E 330
   fr. 158 [148 K]: P 1154
   fr. 159: E 920*
Corianno fr. 76: T 743, F 1343
   fr. 80: E 221
   fr. 84: E 579
Epilesmon fr. 62: L 560
Ipnos fr. 70 [64 K]: K 1375, F 505-511,
   E 302, 713

Krapataloi fr. 85: F p10
   fr. 86: F p10
   fr. 87: F p10
   fr. 92 [87 K]: W 875, T 748, We 1114
   fr. 100: P 749*, F p10, F 1004
   fr. 102: E 1160
   fr. 103: E 707-8
Leroi fr. 105: E 841-2
Metallês fr. 113.29: F 516*
   fr. 113.30: F 1150, We 807
   fr. 114: F 155
Myrmekanthropoi fr. 130: T 728, F 1345
Petale fr. 143: We 1011
   fr. 148 [139 K]: P 804, B 151
Tyrannis: E p9
   fr. 152: E p9
   fr. 164 [155 K]: A 716, F 1422
   fr. 186: We 1024
   fr. 193: L 158
   fr. 269: E p9, E 835
   fr. 271: We 307-8
   fr. 281: F 1190

PHERECYDES OF ATHENS
FGrH 3: F 10-12 T 1101
   F 21: T 855
   F 35: We p8
   F 90: P 832-3
   F 119: F 177

PHERECYDES OF SYROS
fr. 1 D-K: F 311
fr. 5 D-K : B 695

PHILEMON
Ephebos fr. 28: L 304
Moichos fr. 45: E 867-8
Pittokopoumenos fr. 66: E 821-2
Pterygion fr. 69: T 803
Sardion fr. 76: E 821-2
   fr. 117 [125 K]: P 1146
   fr. 136: L 304
   fr. 158 [188 K]: K 254, W 1310

PHILETAERUS
Asclepius fr. 1: B 603, We p12
   fr. 2: We p12
Kynagis fr. 6: F 965, E 97
   fr. 9: We 179, 1082

PHILIPPIDES
Ananeousa fr. 5.4: L 962, F 1280
Argyriou Aphanismos fr. 9.3-5: W 491

PHILO
de Opificio Mundi 45: B 971

PHILOCHORUS
FGrH 328 F 5: P 1168
F 9: E 743
F 35: B 33
F 46: E 825, We 195
F 67: L 439
F 105: L 439, T 533
F 106: T 533
F 117: L 1137-44
F 119: We 178
F 121: P 605
F 122: B 998
F 127: W 240
F 138: L 174
F 139: L 1163, T 805, F p6, F 678
F 141: F 720, E 815
F 148: E p5
F 149: E p3, E 71
F 151: P 1020
F 173: P 1168
F 202: A 220
F 203: P 145
F 208: F 1033
F 216: E 678
F 218: A 457, T 387, F 840

PHILOCLES
Pandionis: B 15-16, 281-2

PHILODEMUS
On Vices p.37 Jensen: E 647, We 314-5

PHILONIDES
Kothornoi fr. 6: F p1, F 541
Preview: W p.xv*, T p2
fr. dub. 17 [15 K]: A 688

PHILOSTEPHANUS OF CYRENE
fr. 31 Müller: T 427

PHILOSTRATUS THE ELDER
Epistulae 8: B 501
Heroicus 35.9 De Lannoy: T 746

66.20 De Lannoy: T 1009-14
Imagines 1.13: K 313
2.6.3: B 441-3*
Life of Apollonius 3.17: We p11
3.47: B 1553
4.22: F 16
4.25: E 909
6.11: F 868
6.39: B 971
7.24: L 759
8.19: C 506-8

PHILOSTRATUS THE YOUNGER
Imagines 13: We p11

PHILOXENUS OF CYTHERA
Cyclops: We p29, We 290-301 *passim*
PMG 818: We 290ff
PMG 819: We 290ff, 297
PMG 820: We 298
PMG 821: We 290ff
PMG 822: We 290ff, 297
PMG 823: We 290ff
PMG 824: E 1104, We 290ff

PHILOXENUS OF LEUCAS (?)
PMG 836: E 1169-75

PHILYLLIUS
Auge fr. 3: F 518
Plyntriai fr. 8 [9 K]: B 1569
fr. 22: We 179

PHOCYLIDES
fr. 12 Gentili-Prato: We 245

PHOCYLIDES, PSEUDO-
158: B 1432

PHOENICIDES
Misoumene fr. 2: P 1154

PHOTIUS
Bibliotheca 534a3-6: L 646-7
Lexicon α1197 Theodoridis: W 807t*
s.v. τρίτος ἀριστεροῦ: We 953

PHRYNICHUS (tragic dramatist)
Phoenissae fr. 9: W 220
fr. 13: W 273-280, 1518-37*

fr. 14: W 273-280
fr. (dub.) 17: W 1490

PHRYNICHUS (comic dramatist)
Epialtes fr. 4: B 1297
Monotropos: B p.1
    fr. 19 [18 K]: B 1549, L 808
    fr. 21 [20 K]: P 395, 1008, B 11
    fr. 22 [21 K]: B 997
    fr. 23 [22 K]: B 363
    fr. 27 [26 K]: B 1297*
Muses: F p1*, F 13
    fr. 32: F p1, p20, F 82
    fr. 33: F p1
    fr. 34: We 1024
Mystai: F p12
Poastriai fr. 43 [41 K]: B 1297
Revellers: B p.1
    fr. 16: F 1462
    fr. 17 [16 K]: B p.1, B 1569
Satyrs fr. 47 [45 K]: B 1463
    fr. 49 [47 K]: C 686*, W 84
Tragedians fr. 55 [53 K]: B 766
fr. 62 [59 K]: K p2, K 6
fr. 77: F 13

PHRYNICHUS (grammarian)
Eclogae 114: E 137
    268: A 920
Praeparatio Sophistica 21.6: E 838t

PHYLARCHUS
FGrH 81 F 18: We p11

PINDAR
Isthmians 1.60: We 1161
    2.23: A 216*
    2.26: B 572-5
    4.50: F 815
    5.1: T 320
    5.39-41: F 963
    8.25-27: F 464
    8.27-53: C 1067
Nemeans 1.37: B 950
    3.5: T 103
    3.20: A 654*
    3.80-83: K 1020, P 830
    4.93: A 710
    5.10: K 1253
    6.65: A 710

7.15: A 671
7.86-101: W 389*
7.105: F 439, E 828
8.1ff: T 990-4
10.18: T 973
10.44: B 1421
10.49-90: P 285
10.55-91: L 118
10.60-72: We 210
10.80-82: L 1300
11.1: P 348
11.6: W 846, P 864
Olympians 2.68-80: W 640
    2.71-75: F 155
    2.85: F 1483
    2.86-88: K 1051
    3.11-35: We 586
    4.20: B 1321-2*
    6.1-3: F 1004
    6.79: We 1161
    7.27-31: B 1242
    7.49: F 215-6
    8.31-34: T 109-110
    8.53: A 710
    9.26: F 1299-1300*
    9.30: E 76
    9.98: B 1421
    10.105: L 1015
    14.20-24: T 1056-97
Pythians 1.1(ff): B 218-9, T 315, 990-4
    1.5-12: B 777-8
    1.6-7: B 510
    2.10: We 1161
    2.78: K 1068
    3.8-44: We p8, p9
    3.55-58: We p8
    3.77-79: B 746, L 2
    4.19: B 719
    4.26: T 1067
    4.44: F 187
    4.184: F 1060
    4.260(-1): B 950, We 925
    5.55-59: We 925
    5.107: F 1483
    6.55: W 1116t*
    8.1(-4): B 1321-2*, L 1289, T 976
    8.7: T 102
    8.8-18: L 1289
    8.12: B 553
    8.17: B 553

8.20: T 102
8.56-60: W 389
8.63: T 110
9.8-9: We 925
9.18: B 831
9.63: K 1095*
9.69: We 925
10.53-54: P 830
11.10: T 103
12.11-17: T 1101
fr. 30: B 1734
70b.9: L 3
75.10: T 991
76: A 637-9, K 1323
85a: F 215-6
89a: K 1264-6
95: B 746
105a: B 926-7
105b: B 941-4
107b: E 1165-6
109: B 1321-2*, L 1289
123: T 103, 170
125: T 1217
129: F 155
135: P 990
139.6: P 1332, B 1734
169a.8: F 467
188: K 1287
189: W 308
249b: W 1032-5, P 755-8, F 473
fr. dub. 346b.4-5: F 289-296

PLATO (comic dramatist)
Adonis fr. 3: P 142, E 39
Ambassadors fr. 127: F 965, E 71
    fr. 130: E 71
    fr. 132 [124 K]: W 476-7, L 279-280
Cleophon: F p1, F 678
    fr. 57: F p1
    fr. 58: F p1
    fr. 59: F p1
    fr. 60: F p1
    fr. 61: T 805, F p1, F 680-1
Festivals fr. 29: T p4
    fr. 30 [31 K]: B 798
    fr. 36 [37 K]: P 73
Hai aph' hierôn fr. 9: L 114
    fr. 14: We 174
Hellas fr. 23: We 468-470
Hyperbolus: C 558, T 840, F 570

fr. 182 [166 K]: A 396, T 120-1, 808-9
fr. 183: F 678-9
fr. 185: T 840
Laconians fr. 69: F 854
    fr. 71 [69 K]: W 1217, 1219, F 514,
        518, 1302-3, E 883
    fr. 72: F p9
Laius fr. 65 [64 K]: A 598, B 819, We 179
Metics fr. 82: E 378
Miners fr. 113 [108 K]: P 1314, B p.2
Peisander fr. 103 [96 K]: C 248
    fr. 110 [103 + com. adesp. 66 K]:
        W 1270
Perialges fr. 114 [106 K]: C 109, W 506,
        1268-9, P 1008, T 1033
    fr. 116 [108 K]: B 1297
Persians fr. 137 [130 K]: P 1314, B p.2
Phaon: E pp7-8
    fr. 188: L 982, 1078, E 10, 845, 916,
        1092, We p11, We 168
    fr. 189: E 1092, 1169-75
    fr. 195: E p8
    fr. 196: We 179
Skeuai fr. 136: F p9
    fr. 140 [132 K]: P 804, B 151
    fr. 141: F 367
Sophists fr. 143 [134 K]: C 1261, W 1501
    fr. 144 [135 K]: B300
    fr. 148 [139 K]: W 157
Symmachia fr. 168 [153 K]: K 855
Syrphax fr. 176 [161 K]: P 1008, B 168
Victories fr. 85 [80 K]: B 1297
    fr. 86 [81 K]: P p.xvii
    fr. 199: E 1107
    fr. 200 [184 K]: B 1372-1409, 1379, F 153,
        1070-1, E 330
    fr. 201: E 248, We 176
    fr. 202: E 112-3
    fr. 214: We 884
    fr. 222: E 1146
    fr. 231: F 1380
    fr. 235: F 303
    fr. 238: We 177

PLATO (philosopher)
Alcibiades I: 108c-d We 190
    119a: C 876
    120a-b: B 1298
    123b: W 500
    132a: K 732

135e: B 1355-7
Apology 18b-d: A p7, C p3*, C 112-5, 188
19(b-)c: A p7, C p3*, C 112-5, 188,
E p15
20a: B 284, F 428, E 810
20b: C 876
20e: W 621
21a: C 104, W 1408, B 1296
22a: W 83
23(c-)d: A p7, C 112-5, 188, 247-8,
F 889-891, E 571
23e: F 1302
24b: C 247-8
24e: C 1174
26b: C p3
26b-27a: F 889-891
28e: E 571
29e: B 1555
30c: W 621
32b-c: F p2
33a-b: C 876
33e: C 1162*
34c-d: W 568-9
35e-38b: W 106
36d-37a: E 834
38b: E 1064-5
40c: We 434
41a: F 464, 1033
Charmides: C 178, B 1296
153d-154d: W 1025
155d: C 967, 992
158a: A 63, W 98
161e: T 556
163b: E 385, 617*
Cratylus 383a: F 1181
391c: C 659
396a-b: B 586t*
401d: W 846, B 864
403e: F 1462
409a: P 1031
409b-c: T 119
418b-d: E 215-228
Crito 54d: W 8
Euthydemus: F 771
272c: K 534
273a: W 1025
276a-277c: F 25-32
277d: C 254-262, W 8
277e: C 659
277e-278b: F 1181

291a: C 1260-1
292e: E 828
295d: K 534
297d-298e: F 25-32
300d: W 638
301d: E 253
302b-d: C 1468
303a: K 680
303b: C 213
Euthyphro: C p3
3a: W 846
3e-4e: C 1413-4
6b-c: K 566
7b-8b: E p27
Gorgias 447a: F 771
456b-c: C 332*
465b: E 737
466e: F 1374
469d: L 985
472a-b: B 126
473c: E 829
481d(-e): K 732, W 98
482b: W 83
482c-484c: C 1075
483a-d: C 902
487c: E 426
492e: F 1082
493d: W 526-7
494b: B 266
497c: C 140, We 845
501d-502d: F p15
501e-502a: B 1372-1409
502a: B 766
502b(-d): A p28, C 539, P 966, L 1050,
F 141, 598
513a: C 749
513c: A 285
514d: C 332*
514d-515b: W 1432, B 584, We 408
515e: W 476-7, B 1281, E 304-5
516d-e: K 1362, P 906, F 574, 1086,
We 431
522a: W 621
523b: W 640
523e: F 464
526b-d: F 464
Hipparchus 228c: W 1410
Hippias Major 282b-c: F 771
289a: E 1072
Hippias Minor 363a-d: F 771

363c: P 342
368c: T 556
Ion 530a: B 1581-2, We p12
530b: F 1034
533e: L 558
534a-b: P 830, F 1299-1300, E 974
536b: F 1033
540d-541c: F 1035-6
Laches 179c: C 686
180d-181a: B 142
183a: T 390-1
186c: W 959
187b: We 1
188d: W 959
196e-197a: L 1015
197c: A 566, P 304, T 841, F 1039
Laws 625b: F 113, 1356
625d: F 1356
631c: We p7
636b-c: L 621
638b: F 970
646a: C 1417
658a-d: A p28, P 966, L 1050, F 598
659a: F 141
666b: F 345-9
684d-e: We p18
700e-701a; F 141
701c: C 1273, W 1370
738c: B 619
739b-e: E p18, We 345
747c: C 1130, T 921-2
782c: F 1032
790d-e: W 8
800e: F 1302-3
806d-e: E 651
815a: C 988, F 153
815c: E 1068-9
817a-d: F p15
817b-c: A p28, P 966, L 1050, F 598
881d: C 1468
906e: E 756t
929c: C 845
953b: E 982-4
954a-b: C 499, L 1198, T 414-5, F 1363
Letters 7.326b: W 911
13.363a: L 150-1
Lysis: C 178
204a-b: W 1025
206e: W 295-6, We 816

207c: We 345
211e: P 788
Menexenus 235a-c: W 638
235e-236a: K 534
237b: W 1076, L 1082
237e: T 339-340
239b: We 385
245a: E p15
245e: E p15
249a: B 1361
Meno 71e: L 495, F 983-8*, E 211-2
76e: C 140
82b-85b: B 1001-9
85b: F 801
90c: E 252
92a-c: C 331
94c-d: A 710, C 686
Parmenides 126b: W 98
Phaedo 62a: A 860
69c: C 463-5*, F 145-153
79d: W 873t*
81a: C 463-5*, W 873t*
82a: P 1100
89b: E 955
95a: F 1034
96e: E p15
98e: W 83
107e: We 434
108c-115a: C 188
112b: B 695
112e-114b: F 137-8
115c: C 362, W 386
116d: C 362
117b: C 362, F 804
117e-118: F 126
118a: We p12
Phaedrus 227b: A 887*
227c-d: E 626
228d: E 891
229c-e: E 1029
241b: K 855*
247a: B 95
247b: T 1067
250b: C 140
250c: F 745
258e-259d: B 1095-6
259a: W 500*
261a: B 1555
262d: B 1095-6
267c: F 1181

268e: E 251, We 12
270c: We p9
274c: B 1296
276b: P 420, L 389
279c: We 345
Politicus: We 833
299b-c: C 332
308c-309b: L 574-586
Protagoras 310b: E 338
311b: We p9
312a: C 331
313a: B 1555
313c-d: We 1063
314c-316a: B 284, F 428, E 810
314c-e: K 127, C 219, 331, B 1730, F 520
314e-315c: C 815
315d-e: T 29, F 83
316d: F 1033
317b: We 114
318e-319a: C 419
319b: W 859
319c: E 143
322a-d: C 1421-2, B 172
323c-e: F 1112
325e-326c: F 729, We 190
327d: T 861
337a-c: F 1181, We 548
341e: F 970
342(b-)c: W 476-7, P 624, B 1012-3, 1281
347c-348a: C 1358*
Republic 1.328b: C 156, F 967
1.329a-b: W 551
1.329e-330a: A 542
1.332a-b: B 419-420
1.333d: P 1197t*
1.340a-b: C 156, F 967
1.343a-344c: C 902, 1038-40
1.344d: K 1091
1.352a: C 903
2.358e-359b: C 1421-2
2.363c: F 1033
2.363d: F 145-153
2.364e(-365a): F 1032, 1033
2.365d: L 577-8
2.369c-372c: We 903-5
2.370b: W 537t*
2.372a-d: E 606
2.372b: We 1133

2.372c: P 772, 1136-7, 1154
2.373c: E 737
2.375a: W 537t*
2.376e-3.398b: F p15, F 868, 1053
2.378a: F 338
2.378b-c: C 904-6
2.383c: F 868
3.390c: C 1080-1
3.391b: We 937
3.391c: C 1063
3.391c-e: C 1080-1
3.392a: W 1179
3.392d: T 156
3.396b: We 293
3.397a: We 293
3.400b: C 651
3.404d: W 911, We 149
3.405c: F 775
3.405d: We p9
3.416d: E p14, E 673-4
3.416e: E p14
4.420e: L 1190
4.424a: We 345
4.425c-e: E p13*
4.439e: K 1362
5.451a: E 486-8
5.451c: E p16
5.452a-d: E pp16-17
5.454b:. E 673-4
5.455c: E 843
5.455d: E p17
5.457a: E p17, E 678-9
5.457c-d: E p14, E 614
5.458c: E 673-4
5.458d-461c E p17
5.459c-460c: E 614
5.460b-d: E p13, E 635ff, 1042
5.461b: E 1104
5.461c-e: E p14, E 635ff
5.463b: E p14
5.463c-e: E p14, E 635ff, 643
5.464c: E p14
5.464d: E p14, E 656
5.464e-465a E 663-4
5.465a-b: E p14, E 635ff
5.466c: E 678-8
5.468a: E p14, E 678-9
5.468d: E p14, E 678-9
5.469b-c: We 461-3
5.469b-471c: E 678-9

5.470c-471b: P 1097-8
5.474e: T 31
5.479b(-c): W 21, B 1296*
6.488a: F 937
6.493d: E 1029
7.529(a-)b: C 172-3t*, W 1215
7.540b: W 640
8.556d: F 200
8.563b: F 952
8.566a: We p18
9.590b: We 203
9.592b: E p18
10.595e-608b: F p15
10.598b: T 156
10.615e: E 1090
10.621a: F 186
Sophist 252c: W 1019-20
Symposium 172c: T 29, F 83
173a: T 29, F 83, E 1181
174a: C 103, 837, B 1282, We 85,
    942-3
175e: W 1010
176b-c: A p26
176e: C 1358*, W 1219, F 514
177d: T 29, F 83
182d-183d: C 973-980
183a: We 297
183c: B 137-142
184a-185b: K 734
185c: A p26
186d: We p9
188a-b: C 332
189a-b: A p26
189c-193a: A p26
190b-d: A p7
190d: We 1129
191d: L 115
191e-192a: A p7
192a: A 79, K 167, 179, C 1093,
    L 524, T 173-4, E 104, 112-3
192b-193a: A p7
193a: E p15
193b: T 29, F 83
192e: A p8
193a-d: A p7, p26
198b: T 1102-3
198c: T 29, F 83
203a-e: A p8, E p3, We 437, 549
203d: We 297
205c-206a: A p8

209e: C 140
209e-210a: F 745
212c(-e): A p26, W 1254, We 1040
212e(-213b): L 603, F 393
213b: K 889
214a: C 417
215a-b: C p3, C 103*, W 1308, F 906
215e: W 8
217b-c: C 417
217c: F 518
218c-d: K 734
219e-220d: C 415-6
220a: C 417
220b: C 103, B 1553, We 942-3
220e-221c: C 353-4
221b: C 362
223b: We 1040
223c-d: A p26, C 417, T 795
Theaetetus 142a-b: E p15
142c: We 833
143e: C 103*, E 617
148e-151d: C 137*
149b-c: T 505
151b: We 114
151e: B 695
155e: C 140
161a: B 695
161c: K 416
166c: We 307-8
173d: L 577-8
174a(-c): C 171-3, W 828, P 1138,
    T 280
179d: A 932-4
Theages 128d-130e: C 156
Timaeus 23d: P 348, E 999
29c: E 1105t*
42b: P 832-3*
65d-e: F 711-2

PLATONIUS
On the Different Kinds of Comedy
27-28 Perusino: We p22
34-35 Perusino: We p24

PLAUTUS
Amphitruo: P 201, We 1170
863: We 1123
Asinaria 159: E 1106*
241-2: E 1106*
693-4: We 1011

Aulularia 561-8: B 901-2
Bacchides 70: T 633
  122: C 180, B 1009
Captivi 274-5: C 180, B 1009
Casina: L 70
Curculio 158-161: T 487
Menaechmi 348: K 1326
  903: C 33
Mercator 124: T 3
Mostellaria 404-5: T 422-3
Pseudolus 1331-end: L 1043-57, E 1148
Rudens 1418-22: L 1043-57, E 1148
Stichus 24-25: A 82
Trinummus 291: E 1073

PLINY THE ELDER
Nat. Hist. 7.53: B 1553
  8.120: F 937
  8.216: K 416
  10.35: B 358
  10.47: B 70-71
  11.147: W 8
  11.205: T 3
  12.15: W 1056-7
  13.5: L 944
  14.80: W 878, E 1174
  19.39: K 895
  19.135: F 942
  20.54-55: W 1172
  20.152-5: P 712
  20.196: T 486
  20.219: K 629-630
  21.93: K 422
  22.100-6: K 895
  22.146: T 486
  24.54-55: T 486
  28.25: W 625
  30.7: C 749
  31.114: F 711-2
  34.54: T 1142
  34.72: A 1093*
  34.76: L p5
  35.54: B 515
  35.75-77: We 385
  35.123: We 385
  35.129: E 685
  35.137: F 186
  35.195-8: F 713
  36.18: K 1169
  36.19: We 185

PLUTARCH
Agesilaus 3.1-3: L p2
  13.4: L 746
Agis 1.4: K 546
Alcibiades 13: K 1377, T 840, F 570
  16.1: B 816, L 560
  16.3: F 1431t
  17.5-6: B 997, T 273
  18: L 390-7
  18.2: T 841, F 1039
  21.9: A 566, P 304, T 841, F 1039
  23.7-9: L p2, F 1422
  32-33: F 1422
  33.1: F p10
  34.4: F 323-353
  34.7: F 1432
  35.5: We 172
  36.6-37.3: F 1422
  37.1: F 1512
  38.5-39.7: F 1422
Alexander 2.3: E 1104
Antony 33.4: P 788
  59.8: E 922
Aristeides 10.10: L 801, E 303
  20.1: L 801, E 303
  24.3: We p6
  26.5: W 523, E 644-5
Artaxerxes 2.4: F p5
  17.7: K 371
Camillus 19.10: F 323-353
Cimon 4.1: P 804
  4.7: P 804
  4.9: P 804
  8.3-5: B 1427
  8.5-7: K 1312
  8.8: E 1160
  13.6: L 1170
  13.8: C 1005
  15.8: L 1144
  16.1: K 407
  16.4(-5): A 510-1, L 1137-44
  16.7: L 1137-44
  16.9-10: L 1137-44
  18-19.1: T 446
  18.7: B 619
Comparisons:
  Lysander & Sulla 3.2: P 1189-90
Demetrius 23.5: We 1193
  26(.4): F 745, We 845

Demosthenes 9.4: B 194
   23.4-6: K 1017, We 377-385
Dion 58.2: P 252, T 1192
Lucullus 3.3: F 1220
Lycurgus 14-15: L 82
   15.12-13: E p16
   16.12: B 1282, L 279-280
   21.2: E 678
Lysander 9.2: F p6
   9.7: F 1512
   13.3-4: E 243
   14.4: F 694
   15.1: F p22
   18.7: F 1299-1300*
   28-29: E p2
   29.1: E 202-3, We 550
Moralia 8c: We 1024
   17a: F 1365
   22f-23a: F 508
   144a-b: L 397
   158a: We 544
   177a: F 85
   193f: We 594
   249e: F 1212
   256a-c: T 561
   280c: F 293
   290d: F 293, We 594
   291e: L 664
   312a: F 1238-41
   388e-389c: F 1212
   396e: We 602
   414e: W 1019-20
   473c: F 186
   505d-f: A 1093*
   559b: C p2*
   581d-e: W 98
   668c: F 934
   693e-f: F 621-2
   708f-709a: We 594
   715e: F 1021
   729f: P 960, B 959
   732f: W 1490, B 750, T 164, F 910
   747a: T 94
   753d: We 768-9
   779d: We 925
   802d: C 332, B 521
   803f: E 171-2
   812d: B 1293
   833a: W 1270
   833d-834b: K 327

   835f-836a: We 550
   841b: B 1296
   842a: We 1013-4
   842d: B 1463
   845b: E 22-23
   847a: K 852-7*
   848a-b: W 191
   862a: K 660-1
   931e: C 967
   953d: F 1212
   964c: T 504
   968a-b: T 100
   990b: E 524
   1045a: L 754-5
   1086e: F 1198-1247
   1087b: F 191
   1105b: F 155, 157
   1128b: F 934
   1132c-e: K 1287, F 1282, 1298
   1133a: K 1287
   1133b: C 969-971, T 68
   1133d: K 9
   1134b-d: K 1287
   1135b: K 9
   1141b: K 1287
   1141c: W 1410
Nicias 2.1: F 970
   4.2; W 52, B 593
   5: K 89
   6.1: W 523, E 644-5
   11: T 840, F 570
   12-13: L 390-7
   12.6: L 390-7
   13.1: W 52
   13.2: B 619, L 767ff
   13.7-8: B 997, T 273
   13.11: L 389, 398
   15.1: A 566, P 304, T 841, F 1039
   15.4: We 179
   16.8-9: B 639
   18.5: L 389
   18.6: K p3
   19.6: E 76
   23.7: P 1031
   29.2-4: F p7
   30.1-2: B 1440-1, We 338
Pelopidas 30.12: E 71
Pericles 8.5: A 710
   8.6: W: 652, E 171-2
   9.2-3: A p28*

11.1: A 710
11.2: K 852-3, E 296-7
11.5-6: K 262
13.10: A 63
13.15: W 98, B 1293
20: A 566, P 304, T 841, F 1039
22-23: C 859
23.4: P 1047
24.3: A 527
24.5: A 527
24.6: K 132
27.3-4: A 850
28.5: F 393
30.1: A 537
30.3: P 246, 483
31: P 605
32.1: A 527
32.2-5: K 1085, W 380, B 988
32.3: W 157
35.3: We p10
Phocion 10.1: W 476-7
Sertorius 11.8: K 647
Solon 4.1-4: F 378
8.4: C 52, L 2, T 130
18.6: We 908
19.4: P p.xx
20.3: E 890, We 1082
22.1: C 1444
24.3: W 897
29.6: W 1479
Sulla 13.3: E 1101t*
Themistocles 1.4: We 327
12.1: W 1086
13.2: K 639
15.4: W 1085
29.11: B 493
31.1: K 814
32.4: K 819
32.5-6: E 1107
Theseus 8.3: F 966
10.3: A 774
11.1: E 1021
24.5: K 963
36.2-3: K 1312
36.4: K 1312, We 62ı
Timoleon 26: W 480
fr. 178 Sandbach: F 155, 157

POLLUX
1.248: E 634

2.61: We p27
2.222: E 963-4
3.40: B 1738-40
3.55: E 738, 742
4.75-76: F 1302-3
4.102: L 82
4.128: T 1098
4.151: E 1150
6.9: E 907
6.17: E 634
6.19: T 557, We 1087
6.57: F 134
6.78: We 1142
7.40: F 711-2
7.77: T 730
7.88: E 74
7.121: F 854
7.153: T 1197
8.20: K 852-7*
8.52: F 362
8.121: W 389
8.124: A 171
9.101: E 825
9.107-9: B 1299, We 1037
9.112: K 855*
9.121: We 1129
10.45: B 1552
10.75: We 1087
10.80: E 744
10.153: T 1197
10.177: We 476

POLYAENUS
1.41.3: L 1137-44
6.2.1: E 6
7.22: P 69-71*
8.45: A 1093*

POLYBIUS
2.62.6-7: E 825, We 195
4.75.7: F 467
5.19.2-3: L 1298
8.28.7: E 1073
10.43-47: E 6

POLYZELUS
Demotyndareos: F 499
fr. 5: T 840

PORPHYRY
On Abstinence 2.6.2: P 1040
  2.9.3: P 960, B 959
Life of Pythagoras 17: B 570

POSEIDIPPUS
Choreuousai fr. 28.19: We 820
Hermaphroditus fr. 12 [11 K]: C 531

PRATINAS
PMG 708.5 [fr. 1.5 Page]: P 830

PRAXILLA
PMG 749 [fr. 3 Page]: W 1238-9
PMG 750: T 528
PMG 754: T 797-9

PRODICUS
fr. 2 D-K (Choice of Heracles): C 361*
fr. 4 D-K: C 361, B 692
fr. 5 D-K: F 22

PROLEGOMENA DE COMOEDIA (ed.
  Koster)
III 29ff: L 158
III 33-34: C 553, 556, F 13
III 38: C 531
XI a.ii.62-70: P 741
XIc (p.45.50): P 741*
XIIa (p.35.65): P 741*
XXVIII 20: W 1284-91
XXIXa 14-15: W 1284-91

PROPERTIUS
4.3.21: F 186

PROTAGORAS
A27 D-K: C 659, T p7
A28 D-K: C 659, T p7
fr. 1 D-K: F 1475
fr. 3 D-K: F 1112
fr. 6a D-K: C 112-5

PTOLEMY (astronomer)
Almagest i 205.15-21 Heiberg: B 997

QUINTILIAN
3.1.10: A 710
10.1.66: F 868

SALLUST
Historiae 4.3: F 1220

SANNYRION
Danaë fr. 8: F 303
  fr. 9: F 367
  fr. 10: T 902

SAPPHO
fr. 1.5ff: C 356, W 556
fr. 1.9-10: L 723-5
fr. 44.33: T 969
fr. 82: B 668, L 1061-4
fr. 94.5-7: K 1250-2*
fr. 105a: C 997*
fr. 110a: P 1339
fr. 111: P 1339
fr. 136: B 682-3
fr. 140: L 389
fr. 141.1: P 856-867
fr. 156: T 1217
fr. 163: E 973-4
fr. 168: L 389
fr. 168b: E 911-3

SATYRUS, see Papyri (POxy 1176)

SCHOLIA TO ARISTOPHANES
Acharnians 11: T 170
  22: E 378
  44: We 382-3
  61: W 506, P 1008
  67: A p26
  378: W 1284-91
  605: E 932
  548: E 686
  866: P 951
Knights 44: W 38
  400: F 357
  410: We 382-3
  772: E 1002
  1013: B 978
  1291: K 1288-9
Clouds Hypothesis I Dover : C pp3-4
  46: A 614
  48: A 614
  70: L 1190
  555: T 840
  800: A 614
  1372: W 1043

Wasps 88: K 51
675: F 134
718: We 178
787: L 1105
1169: W 1301
1178: W 1397
Peace Hypothesis II Holw.: P p.xx, We p28
130: W 1448
173: P 223/4t*, 261/2t*
741: F p11*
758: W 1035
1310: We 162
Birds 281: W 462, T 168
513: E 630
521: P 1084*
822: W 1183-4, P 928, L 63
1487: A 1167-8
1490: C 315
1541: K 51
Lysistrata 537: K 41
963: T p6
Thesmo. 190: T p1
Frogs Hypothesis I: F p21
53: T p1, T 1011-2
85: T 29
366: F 153, E 330
367: E 102, We 176
439: E 828
479: We 327
1087: F 131
Ecclesiazusae 193: E p5
Wealth Hypothesis III: We p1
1: E 729/730, We 321/2
115: We p27, p28, p30
119: We p27, p28, p30
173: We pp27-28, p30
178: E p4
179: We p28, p29
252/3: E 729/730, We 321/2
295: E 470
497: We p14
594-7: F 366
619: E 729/730, We 321/2
626/7: E 729/730, We 321/2
641: E 729/730, We 321/2
771: E 729/730, We 321/2
802: E 729/730, We 321/2
845: F 404-6
850: E 729/730, We 321/2
954: A p28

972: We p28
1042: E 729/730, We 321/2
1075: We 1002
1097: We 1170/1
1110: P 1060
1146: We p28, p30

SCHOLIA TO OTHER AUTHORS
Aeschines 1.52: C 350
Aeschylus *Eumenides* 13: B 188-9
Prometheus 167: We p16
Aratus 97: P 832-3
172: P 832-3*
Aristeides 3.444 Dindorf: C p2
Aristotle *Rhetoric* 1373b18: We 6-7
Clem. Alex. *Protrepticus* 11.14: T 1098
Demosthenes: 18.52 E 22-23
19.281: T 561
23.71: K 449*
24.136: We 1193
Euripides *Andromache* 445: T 390-1
IT Hypothesis: T 1218ff*
Medea Hypothesis: F 1400
Orestes 965: B 1695-6
Phoenissae 1173: P 69-71*
Rhesus Hypothesis B: F 1206-8
Homer *Iliad* 2.262: C 1264-5
Iliad 2.308-319: L 723-5
Iliad 6.252: E 982-6
Iliad 8.70: F 1365
Iliad 13.21: F 666
Iliad 16.134: W 615
Iliad 21.271: We 1005
Iliad 23.711: E 259-260
Lucian *Dial.Mer.* p.276.3-5 R: P 151
Lycophron 91: L 802-3
103 (Tzetzes): T 480
Pindar *Nem.* Hypothesis II: F 1319
Nem. 4.57: C 1063
Nem. 7.105: E 828
Olymp. 1.97: F 121-134
Olymp. 3.11-35: We 586
Olymp. 7.49a: C 1264-5
Olymp. 7.54: C 1264-5
Olymp. 9.1: B 1764
Olymp. 13.45c: W 480
Olymp. 13.159: K 561
Pyth. 7 inscr.: A 615, C 69
Plato *Apology* 23e: W 1301, L 270
Gorgias 473e: T 373

Republic 5.455c: T 285, We 660
Republic 5.479b-c: B 1296*
Republic 6.493d: E 1029
Theaetetus 160e: L 757
Sophocles *Oed.Col.* Hypothesis II: F 73
  Oed.Col. 1600: L 835
Theocritus 2.156: E 1101t*

SCRIPTORES HISTORIAE AUGUSTAE
Didius Julianus 7.10: We 382

SEMONIDES
fr. 7 *passim*: T 788, E 224
fr. 7.10: E 119-120
fr. 7.12-18: We 1015
fr. 7.49: E 609-610
fr. 7.(71-)76: A 120-1*, E 907
fr. 7.96-98: T 787
fr. 7.106-7: E 225
fr. 7.115: T 787
fr. 12: P 1100
fr. 13: T 1009-14
fr. 20.1: T 977
fr. 36: B 874-5

SENECA
Epistulae Morales 77.2: F 1220

SERVIUS
on *Virgil's Aeneid* 2.166: W 351
  10.315-6: We p9

SEXTUS EMPIRICUS
Against the Mathematicians 7.81: T 5-21*

SIMONIDES
PMG 507 [fr. 2 Page]: C 1356
PMG 508 [fr. 3 Page]: B 1594
PMG 512 [fr. 7 Page]: K 406
PMG 531 [fr. 26 Page]: L 1247-72
PMG 555: We 1161
PMG 563: F 194
PMG 592: F 295
PMG 627: We 327
fr. eleg. 9 West: P 736
epigr. 5 Page: F 230
epigr. 30 Page: C 602

SOLON
fr. 4.1-4: K 1175-6:

fr. 11: W p.xviii
fr. 11.5: W 859
fr. 13.1: L 1248
fr. 13.71-73: E 608, We 188-9
fr. 27.2: F 418
fr. 34.8-9: We p18

SOPHILUS
Encheiridion fr. 4: We 1132

SOPHOCLES
Ajax 1: We 312
  5-8: F 893
  19: E 71
  108-110: C 870
  29(2-)3: F 951, E 570
  536: E 255
  593: A 1096
  665: W 1160
  728: A 320
  742: F 340-1
  813-4: E 285-310
  814/866: E p23
  857: E 1
  895: We 853
  977: A 1184
  1146: We 1061
  1178: F 587
  1205: We 190
Antigone 2: B 1246-8
  47: F 116
  133: B 1763
  153-4: T 975, F 326
  162-3: W 29
  200: F 1167-8
  224: T 981-2t*
  30(8-)9: C 870, F 619, We 312
  508: T 544-5, We 948
  569: A 995-8, L 1173
  641-4: B 419-420
  678: L 450
  705: T 148
  707: T 544-5
  781ff: T 990-4
  844: F 442
  894: L 742
  1006-11: T 693-5
  1094: We 39
  1115: T 320
  1115ff: T 990-4

1119-21: F 323-353
1126-30: F 1212
1146-8: F 343
1154: F 323-353:
1155: B 1246-8
1311: We 853
Electra: C p2, C 534
278ff: C 621
491: F 294
622: L 369
648-654: We 134
674: P 933
698-756: W 1429
721-2: C 1300
1021-3: B 371
1058-62: B 1355-7
1142: F 340-1
1355: P 193
1361: W 1297-8, T 582-3
141(4-)5: F 1214, We 935
1485: We 853
Oedipus at Colonus 19: K 751
35: F 340-1
192-6: K 751
249: E 1168-78
311-4: L 676
318: L 706-717
340: L 43
409-411: F 1023-4
616-623: F 1023-4
668-678: B 1088-1101*
969-973: F 1185
1102: W 466
1104: W 466
1113-4: W 873
1333: F 750
1382: C 903
1456ff: C 292, B 1751
1606: B 1745
1631-7: A 309, F 754, We 753
1654-5: We 771
1695: C 992
Oedipus Tyrannus: T 168
22-24: W 29
82-83: We 21
157: F 483
186-7: T 1041
188: F 483
211: T 990
240: P 969

299: P 130
360: L 1113
362-7: E 1042
391: F 1286
42(2-)3: L 675, E 1106
457-460: E 1042
629: W 418
631ff: E 564
711-4: F 1185
718: F 1192
741: F 352-3
747: E 643t
791-3: E 1042
1034-6: F 1192
1048-53: T 101-2
1098-1109: T 977
1121-85: K 1232-52
1134-9: F 1190
1207-15: E 1042
1208(-10): L 675, E 1106
1256-7: E 1042
1288-9: E 1042
1403-7: T 941, E 1042
1468: L 706-717
1471: L 706-717
1475: L 706-717
1515ff: C 642
Philoctetes 4: F 1383
27-29: L 288
108-110: F 1474
133: T 1202, We 1157
216: B 1716
219: L 706-717
229: F 340-1
369: W 156
466: W 156
578: E 288
743: T 945
745: L 215
746: T 945
750: L 706-717
754: T 945
785(-793): L 215, 706-717, T 945
800: L 299-300
804: L 706-717
813: A 309, F 754, We 753
815: B 1715
843-8: T 660
931-3: E 563, We 33-34
936: E 110

fr. 778: L 475
fr. 884: B 510
fr. 885a: K 1248*
fr. 888: P 1126
fr. 959: F 215-6
fr. 1060: F 187
PMG 737(b): We p11

SOPHRON
fr. 68 Kaibel: W 1038*, 1039, E 639-640
fr. 70 Kaibel: W 1038*, E 639-640

SORANUS
5.2: E 528-9

SOSIBIUS
FGrH 595: F 23 F 849

SOSICRATES (comic dramatist)
Parakatatheke fr. 2: P 143

SOSICRATES (historian)
FGrH 461: F 3 B 521

SOSIPATER
Katapseudomenos fr. 1.14: E 867-8, We p24

SOSTRATUS
FGrH 23 F 3: F 1081

STEPHANUS OF BYZANTIUM
p.269.19 Meineke: P 1126

STESICHORUS
PMG 187: C 997*
PMG 192: T p6, T 850
PMG 193: T p6
PMG 194: We p8
PMG 210 [fr. 33 Page]: P 775-780
PMG 211 [fr. 34 Page]: P 797-802
PMG 212 [fr. 35 Page]: P 797-802
PMG 213: F 1451
PMG 242 [fr. 65 Page]: K 1172
S8.1 Page: B 924t

STOBAEUS
4.22.102: E 739
4.31.34: E 974

STRABO
3.2.7: F 475
3.2.9: We 727
7.3.12: P 1146, L 908
8.3.7: K 1057
8.5.1: F 187
8.6.11: B 1695-6
8.6.20: We 149
8.6.22: L 1170
8.7.1: L 285
8.7.4: F 666
8.7.5: B 1421
9.1.22: L 447
9.1.23: P 252, T 1192
9.2.13: F 666
9.3.7: L 1129-32
9.3.17: L 1129-32
9.5.17: A 793
10.5.1: F 713
10.5.5: B 870
13.1.12: L 982
14.1.35: B 1694

STRATTIS
Anthroporestes fr. 1: F 303
Atalantos fr. 4 [*CGFP* 74.8-11]: P 174, E 891
fr. 5 [4 K]: W 195
Cinesias fr. 17: B 1372-1409*, E 330
fr. 18 [19 K]: B 1372-1409, F 153, 1437, E 330
fr. 19 [16 K]: B 1569, F 153
fr. 20: We 550
Lemnomeda fr. 24: F 970
Macedonians fr. 27: We 149, 179
fr. 32 [31 K]: W 195
Myrmidons fr. 37 [36 K]: C 248
Troilus fr. 42: E 920
fr. 63: F 303
fr. 71: F 1309-28*
fr. 75: A 255*

SUDA
α1722: L 757
α1842: A p4*
α3737: T p12
αι60: L 1273t*, E p27
ε3657: C 553
ε3695: T p4, T 1
ζ33 B 1738-40

θ282: W 1479
κ2035: E 848
κ2340: B p.2
κ2578: K 41, L 537
κ2800: We 476t
λ60: E 154
λ139: W 1410
λ787: P 290
μ884: B 277
ν407: We p1
π253: F 1327-8
σ1273: T 1197
τ99: B 277
τ1174: We 476t
φ378: W 462, B 281-2, T 168
χ611: B 358
χ35: B 642
χ185: L 770-1
χ595: F 1299-1300*

SUETONIUS
Divus Iulius 51: We 1082

"SUSARION"
fr. 1.3-5: L 1039

SYNESIUS
Letters 106: K 895
    121: We 290ff, 298

TELECLEIDES
Amphictyones fr. 1: P 1314, B p.2
    fr. 7 [6 K]: K 1085, W 380, B 988
Apseudeis fr. 12 [11 K]: W 506, P 1008
Hesiods fr. 15 [14 K]: W 462, T 168
    fr. 16 [15 K]: W 1187
    fr. 19 [18 K]: W 325, B 1126
Prytaneis fr. 25 [22 K]: K 815
    fr. 29 [27 K]: W 83
    fr. 41 [39 K]: W 61, T p4, T 451, F 1491-2
    fr. 42 [40 K]: W 61, T p4, T 451, F 1491-2
    fr. 44 [41 K]: K 6
    fr. 50 [46 K]: B 17-18

TELESTES
PMG 810: T 1217

TERENCE
Adelphoe: W 1397, T 373-4, E 867-8
    803-4: We 345

Andria 166: We 22
Eunuchus: L 355, E 372
Heauton Timorumenos: W 1397, T 373-4,
    E 867-8
    626ff: C 531, We 521
    640: We 521
Hecyra: W 1397, L 70, 304, T 373-4,
    E 867-8
    400: C 531
Phormio: L 355
    220: C 870, F 619
    862: W 433*

TERPANDER
PMG 697 [fr. 1 Page]: C 595
fr. 5 Campbell [*PMG* 1027c]: E 1068-9

TERTULLIAN
de spectaculis 9: L 759

THEOCRITUS
2 *passim*: F 1331-63
2.79-80: B 139
2.94-103: E 916
2.143: T 813, E 104
3.52-53: E 962, We 297
4.63: E 1068-9
5.86: F 559
7.2: A 954
7.55: L 839
7.76: We 1034
7.106-8: F 621-2
7.132: A 954
7.134: P 1147
10.19: We p7
10.45: We 946
10.54: We 1004
11.14: We 1034
11.19-79: We 297
12.27-33: A 774
13: K 67
14.1: B 1581-2
15.40: A 582, K 693, P 474, F 925
15.48: T 921-2
15.87-89: E 119-120
15.102-5: P 1168
15.106-8: K 1095*
15.109: T 320
15.125-7: L 729, F 543
16.96: A 279

18 *passim*: B 1731-6
18.22-48: L 1314
18.22-23: L 1301
18.39: L 1301
18.58: P 1332, B 1734
20.10: K 1286
22.5-23: E 1068-9
24.111-2: F 957
25.4-6: We 1159
27.50: E 903
Epigrams 5.6: L 998

THEOGNIS
27-28: B 1362-3
85-86: W 447
335: We 245
432: We p9
457-460: E 323
602: E 909
667-682: W 29
702-712: F 177
1216: F 186

THEON OF SMYRNA
p.14.24 Hiller: F 355
p.59.7-10 Hiller: W 1410

THEOPHILUS
Neoptolemus fr. 6.3: P 142
Philaulos fr. 11: B 161

THEOPHRASTUS
Characters 2.3: K 908*
    5.9: B 1283, L 991, F 938
    6.3: C 540
    6.5: E 757
    6.9: E 818
    7.7: F 93
    9.2: W 82
    9.8: K 1091, F 710-3
    10.13: E 446-9
    14.5: T 485
    15.5: A 1049
    16.3: B 721, F 196, 304, E 792
    16.4: W 389*
    16.8: B 358
    16.10: We 1126
    17.2: A 1049
    18.4: T 414-5
    18.7: E 446-9

20.9: E 154
21.6: W 129-130
21.7: A 988, We 820
21.15: W 1215
24.5: E 1026
25.2: B 1501
27.14: F 957
28.3: L 229, E 265
de Causis Plantarum 6.7.6: F 204
Historia Plantarum 2.8.1-2: B 590
    3.7.3: F 859
    3.11.1-2: A 180
    3.16.1: F 859
    4.4.2: W 1056t*
    4.4.9: W 737
    4.10.4: F 244
    5.1.2: T 427
    5.2.4: We 943
    5.3.3: A 180
    5.7.1: K 1310
    5.7.3: K 1185*
    5.9.5: W 146
    6.2.3: W 1082
    6.3.1: K 898
    6.6.11: T 910
    6.8.3: T 910
    7.13: C 188
    9.8.3: F 943
    9.9.3: T 504
    9.11.5-11: E 405
    9.14.3: P 1077
    9.17.2: We 884
    9.19.2: F 1033
On Fire 72: W 146
On Odours 26: W 1056t*
    31: W 1056t*
On Stones 56: E 878, We 1064
    62: F 713
On Weather Signs 47: C 323*

THEOPOMPUS (comic dramatist)
Aphrodite fr. 5: We 179
Boys fr. 40 [39 K]: B 1569
Hedychares fr. 15: We 768-9
    fr. 16: E p15
Kapelides fr. 25 [24 K]: B 1405
Nemea fr. 33 [32 K]: A 985
Odysseus fr. 36: E 920
Peace fr. 10 [9 K]: C 661
Sirens fr. 51: E 943

Stratiotides: E pp9-10, p17
  fr. 56: E p9
  fr. 57: E p9
  fr. 58: E p9
Teisamenus: A 603*
  fr. 61 [60 K]: W 1221, B 31
fr. 70 [69 K]: C 1417

THEOPOMPUS (historian)
FGrH 115 F 30a: E 444
  F 75a: We 287
  F 88: L 1144
  F 93: A 7*
  F 94: A 6*
  F 104: B 879
  F 344: W 96, 804, F 366
  F 387: P 1047

THRASYMACHUS
fr. 1 D-K: E 515-2
fr. 3 D-K: B 879

THUCYDIDES
1.2,5: W 1076, L 1082
1.2.6: L 582
1.5-6: B 481-521
1.6.3: C 984, W 1267
1.12.4: L 582
1.31.1: P 477
1.35.3: P 477
1.40.5: P 622
1.44-45: P 990
1.45.2: L 1138, T 876
1.47.1: L 57
1.58.1: P 622
1.58.2: B 172*
1.67.2: A 653
1.67.4: A 533-4, P 609
1.70: B 471
1.70.2: W 859, F 1112, E 587
1.71.7: B 540-3*
1.77.6: P 623
1.93.2: K 814-6t*
1.93.3-7: K 815
1.93.5: B 1139
1.94.2: W 236-7
1.95: P 623
1.98.4: W 355
1.100.1: L 1144
1.101.1-2: P 622

1.101.2-3: L 1137-44
1.102.1: L 1143
1.102.3: L 1137-44
1.102.4-105: L 1137-44
1.103.4: L 1170
1.105.4: L 177, E 845
1.105.4-106: L 801, E 303
1.108.2-3: L 801, E 303
1.108.3: B 153-4
1.112.2(-4): L 1144, T 446, E 304-ͻ
1.112.5: B 556
1.114: C 213, P 622
1.114.3: P 1047
1.115.1: K 1388-9
1.115.2: F 459
1.115.4-5: A 100*
1.121.3: P 477
1.126(.11): K 445-6, 1312, T 224
1.128.1: A 510-1
1.131.1: W 236-7
1.138.4: K 84
1.138.5: K 819, W 500, B 493
1.139(.1): A 533-4, 538, P 609, 623
1.139.3: E 396-7
1.140-144: P 609
1.140.3: A 538
1.141-3: F 1463-5
1.144.2: P 624, B 1012-3
1.144.4: B 540-3*
2.2.4: B 631
2.6.2: E 338
2.8.4: P 214
2.12.1-3: P 435-6
2.13.6: A 72, L 177
2.13.7: L 1162-3
2.13.8: K 225
2.15.2: B 172*
2.15.4: F 216-7
2.15.5: P 843, L 328, 378
2.17.1: B 832, L 482
2.17.3: A 72
2.19-21: L 62-63
2.19.2-20.5: A p33
2.19.2: K 597
2.21.3: A p33, K 61, L 767ff
2.22.2: K 597
2.23.2:   C 1261, W 1501, P 782,
    T 169, 876, F 86
2.24.1: L 174
2.25: C 1261

2.27(.1): A 653, F 363
2.30: C 1261
2.31.3: P 246, 483
2.32: B 1427
2.34: B 395
2.36.1-2: B 540-3
2.38.2: W 520
2.39.1: B 38, 1012-3
2.40.1: E 571
2.40.2: B 44, 471
2.40.3: F 1112
2.40.4-5: E p20
2.43.1: K 732*
2.48.3: F 459
2.52.3: L 743, F 1080
2.54: K 61
2.56.4: We p10
2.56.6: P 242
2.59.2: P 213
2.62.3: B 540-3*
2.63: B 471
2.65.7: F 360
2.65.9: B 1584, E p11
2.67.1: B 1028
2.69: K 1070-1
2.69.1: B 1427
2.70: K 438
2.70.3: L 277-8
2.75.5: B 1248
2.79: P 395*, B 1556
2.80-81: A 604
2.81.5: E 875-6
2.83-92: L 804
2.84.3: E 835
2.91.2: P 555
2.93-94: A 918
2.94.1: E 6
2.96.1: B 1179
2.96.4: B 1529
2.101.3: A 156
2.103: K 562*
3.1.2: K 597
3.2.1: P 622
3.2.3: B 1021
3.7.1: K 562, L 804
3.15.1: T 647-8
3.16.2: P 625
3.17.4: A 162, B 1186
3.19: K 1070-1
3.19.1: K 924, W 660, E 825

3.19.2: K 132
3.22.7-8: E 6
3.26: A p32
3.34.2: A 100*
3.35-50: E 797-8
3.36-40: K 835
3.36: K 1030
3.36.6: F 569
3.37.3(-5): K 986, B 1038
3.38.2: K 834
3.38.4-7: F 1374-5
3.42.1: L 57
3.50.1: K 835
3.50.2: C 203, W 660
3.51: A 760, P 246
3.55.3: F 694
3.63.3: P 214
3.75: W 81
3.80.2: E 6
3.85.2: B 1427
3.86: W 924-5
3.87.4: A 510-1*
3.89(.1): A 510-1*, E 791
3.90.2: W 240
3.91.4: B 284
3.92-93: K 238
3.103.1-2: W 965
3.104.2: L 743, F 1080
3.115.2: W 240
4.9.2: W 965
4.15-22: P 215
4.16.1: E 424
4.22.2: P 217
4.25.5: F 121
4.27-28: K 1054, F 569
4.27.3: W 1183-4, P 928, B 822-3, L 63
4.28.4: T 232
4.28.5: W 1463
4.32.2: F 1074
4.38.4: C 186
4.39.2: K 1054, 1167, W 970
4.39.3: F 569
4.41.1: C 186
4.41.2-4: K 794-5, 1330, P 215, 219, 665, L 104, 1166
4.42-44: K 604
4.47.2: B 1463
4.50.2-3: A 647, K 478
4.52.1: C 584-5

4.53: W 81
4.53.2: P 625
4.53.3: B 1427
4.62.3: C 1292
4.65.3-4: K 1303
4.66.1: P 246, 483
4.67.2-5: E 845
4.69: P 246, L 1170
4.75: W 700, P 304
4.76-77: P 507
4.76.1-3: K 479
4.79: P 283-4
4.89-101: P 507
4.94.1: T 232
4.96.4-5: C 353-4, W 19
4.97.1: L 461
4.100: A 920
4.101.2: C 1001, T 273
4.101.5: B 1529
4.105.1: B 670
4.109.1: L 1170
4.109.2-3: B 1042
4.118.1: B 188-9
4.118.6: C 7
4.118.8: C 615-6, W 62, B 434-6
4.118.11: A 603
4.118.12: P p.xvi
4.119.1: C 615-6, L 1138
4.119.2: W 81
4.120-1: W 62
4.121.1: B 1274-5, F 393
4.122.3: W 62
4.125.1: We 249
4.126.4: B 1521
4.127.1: B 1521
4.129: W 81
4.129.2: L 563
4.133.2: W 210
4.135.1: B 842
5.1.2: B 1028
5.4(-5): K 1377, P 250
5.6.2(-4): A 156, L 563
5.8.1: B 1013-4
5.10: F 569
5.10.3: B 1013-4
5.10.5: B 1013-4
5.13-15: P 478
5.14.2: P 219
5.14.4: K 465
5.16.1: K 805-8, P 282, 681, 921

5.17.2: P p.xv, P 466, 481, L 1177
5.18.2: P 342, B 188-9
5.18.3: A 194, K 1388-9
5.18.4: L 513
5.18.7: P 466
5.18.9: B 632, L 169
5.19.1: C 615-6, P p.xv
5.19.2: A 566, C 332, W 240, 1183-4, P 304, 928, B 126, 521, T 841
5.20.1: T 67068
5.23.2: B 632, L 169
5.23.3: E 651
5.23.4: A 505
5.24.1: C 332, W 240, 1183-4, P 928, B 126, 521
5.26.3(-4): K 61, P 466, 993-4, 1049, B 188-9
5.28.2: K 465
5.28.3: P 475
5.29.3-4: P 1082
5.31.1-5: B 149
5.32.1: F 694
5.32.4: P 466, B 188-9
5.34.1: B 149
5.35.5: P 466
5.35.6-7: L 1166
5.39.2-3: P 466
5.40.3: K 465
5.42: P 466
5.43.2: W 44, 240, E 203
5.44-46: L 1010
5.45.4: A 171, E 791
5.47.8: A 308
5.47.10: B 632, L 169
5.54.3-4: P 414
5.56.1-3: L 513
5.56.3: L 1166
5.62: B 149
5.67.2: B 399
5.70: L 550
5.74.2: L 461
5.74.3: W 81
5.105.2: C 1075
5.105.4: P 623, L 169
5.114: B 186
5.116: B 186
6.1.1: B p.4
6.4.6: T 55
6.6.1: B p.4

6.7: B 399
6.8.1: W 924-5
6.9.1: L 57 -
6.13.1: E 296-7
6.14.1: P 906, E 396-7
6.15.2: K 1303
6.15.4: F 1432
6.18.7: B 44
6.20.1: T 386, E 176
6.24.3: B p.4
6.25.1: L 390-7
6.25.2: F 1356
6.26.1: L 390-7
6.26.2: K 1370*
6.27.1: P 924, L 1094, We 1153
6.29.3: L 390-7
6.30.1: L 390-7
6.31.2: B 879, F p2
6.31.3: A 162*, K 1370*
6.31.6: B p.4
6.34.2: K 1303
6.43: B 1204, L 394
6.50-51: B p.4
6.54-59: L 632
6.54.2(-3): A 1093, L 634
6.54.6-7: B 95
6.55.1: A 449
6.56.1: L 646
6.59.2: W 502, L 619
6.60.1: B 766-7, 1584
6.60.4: B 1074-5, L 619
6.61: B p.4, B 145-7
6.61.2: B 766-7
6.62.4: W 924-5, F 1235
6.63-71: B p.4, B 363
6.71: B 639
6.71.2: B p.5
6.74.2: B p.5
6.85.2: B 879
6.87.3: B 471, E 923
6.88.4: W 924-5, B p.4
6.88.6: K 1303, B 1576
6.88.9: B p.5
6.91.7: F 720
6.93.4: B p.5
6.95.1: E 791
6.97: B 639
6.101.6: T 841, F 1039
6.105.2: P 242, B p.5, B 1569
7.9: B 1369, L 563

7.11-15: K p3
7.18.3: L 513
7.19.5: L 57
7.27-30: L 563
7.27.2: A 158
7.27.5: F 720
7.28.1(-2): W 715, L 555-6, T 495
7.28.4: W 659, F 363
7.29-30: B 798
7.31.2: L 394
7.35.1: E 729
7.41-2: K 762
7.44.8: K 290-1
7.50.4: K p3
7.53.4: A 920
7.57.4-5: B 879
7.57.7: L 394
7.60.4: T 232
7.71.5: B 1013-4
8.1.1: L 767ff, F 1086, E 797-8
8.1.2: L 653
8.1.3: L 421, T 808-9
8.2: L p1
8.3.1: L 1168-9
8.3.2: F 364
8.4: L 421-2
8.5-6: L p3, L 1133
8.6.1: B 1028
8.7-10: T 647-8
8.9.2: B 126
8.12.2: L p2, p3
8.14: L p1
8.15.1: L p1, L 174, 653
8.16: L p1
8.17.3: L p1, L 57
8.18: L p3, L 1133
8.19.4: L p1
8.20.1: T 647-8
8.23: L p1
8.24.1: L p1
8.24.3: B 1694
8.25-27: L p1
8.25.1: W 1302, L 313, F 689
8.28.3-29.2: L p3
8.30.1: L 313
8.35.1: L p1
8.35.3-4: L 57
8.36.2-37.5: L p3, L 1133
8.38.3: P 835
8.41.3-43.1: L p2*, T 804

8.42: T p1
8.43.2-4: L p3
8.44.2: L p1
8.44.3: L 57
8.44.4: L p2*
8.45-47: L p2
8.45.2: K 1366-7, L p2
8.47-51: L 313, F 689
8.48.2-3: L p2*
8.49-56: P 395, B 1556, L 490
8.49: L p2*
8.50.5-51.2: L p2*
8.53-54.2: L p2, T p2, T 365, 1143-4
8.53.1: L p2
8.53.2-3: L p1, p2
8.54.3: L p3
8.54.4: L p3, L 577-8, T p3
8.56-59: T p3
8.56-57: L p2
8.57-59: L p3
8.60.1-2: T p3
8.61-2: L p2
8.63-68: P 395, B 1556, L 490
8.63.4: T 1143-4
8.64.2: B 798, L 103
8.65.2: W 1187, T p3, p4, T 419
8.65.2-66.5: T p3, T 1143-4
8.65.3: F 1466
8.66.5: T p4
8.67: T p3
8.67.3: F 1466
8.68.3: W 1302, F 689
8.68.4: F 541
8.69.1: L 555-6, T 495
8.69.3: L 1059
8.69.4: E 304-5
8.73-76: E 202-3, We 550
8.73.3:   W 1007, P 681, T 804, 840, F 570
8.73.4: L p3
8.73.5: F 1071, 1072
8.74.1: B 147, F 1071
8.74.2: F 1072
8.76.2: T 804
8.78: T p3
8.81-82: F 1422
8.81.1: E 202-3, We 550
8.82.2: F 1422
8.86.4: F 1422
8.86.9: F 1072

8.87: T p3
8.87.4: A 193
8.89-92: F 541
8.90-91: L p3
8.90.5: E 686
8.92: B 126
8.92.2: W 1302, F 689, E 845
8.95: T p3
8.96.2: W 715
8.96.5: W 859
8.97.1: F 1466
8.98.1: P 395, B 1556, L 490
8.99: T p3
8.102.1: E 6
8.103.3: L 539
8.104-106: T p2

TIBULLUS
2.3.15-16: F 559
2.4.22: E 962

TIMAEUS
FGrH 566 F 24: We 179
   F 48: W 1259
   F 102b: F 504

TIMOCLES
Heroes fr. 12: We 328
Konisalos fr. 22: We 1132
Orestautocleides: F 499
fr. 41: B 194

TIMOCREON
PMG 730: W 1259*
PMG 731 [fr. 5 Page]: A 532, K 610, T 299,
   We pp6-7
PMG 732: W 1259*
PMG 733 [fr. 7 Page]: W 1063-5, We 1002
PMG 734: W 1259*

TIMOTHEUS
PMG 791 (*Persians*): T 119, F 1336
PMG 791.5-6 [fr. 15.5-6 Page]: K 546
PMG 791.91 [fr. 15.91 Page]: L 173
PMG 791.155-6 [fr. 15.155-6 Page]:
   P 291, T 1179
PMG 799: E 1030

TRAGICA ADESPOTA
fr. 46: B 1147

fr. 51: E 110
fr. 61c: We 213
fr. 63: We 1127
fr. 123a: B 194
fr. 226a: E 829
fr. 408a: W 1490, B 70-71
fr. 588: F 1144-5
fr. 625.8/9: E 729/730, We 321/2

TYRTAEUS
fr. 10.21-30: L 1020, T 939
fr. 12.6: We 287

VALERIUS MAXIMUS
7.2.7: F 1431t

VIRGIL
Aeneid 3.90-91: We 213
    3.120: F 847
    5.772: F 847
    6.420: L 601
    6.591: F 230
    7.378-383: B 1461
    10.315-6: We p9
    12.766-9: We 943
Eclogues 4.61: T 741-2
Georgics 3.266-8: F 1403
    3.404-8: T 416-7

XENARCHUS
Boutalion fr. 1: E 1-18, 1092, We 515
Didymoi fr. 2: E 1123
Porphyra fr. 9: We 1132

XENOCLES
Licymnius fr. 2: C 1264-5

XENOPHANES
fr. 11 D-K: C 1080-1
fr. 16 D-K: F 730
fr. 21 D-K: P 697
fr. 22.3 D-K: P 1136-7, E 45
fr. 30 D-K: C 1280-1
fr. 32.24-25 D-K: F 634

XENOPHON
Agesilaus 1.24: F 494
Anabasis 1.1.1: F p6
    1.2.9: F 1356
    1.2.10: K 580

1.2.13: We 287
1.2.14: E 729
1.2.21: E p1
1.4.2: E p1
1.4.3: E p1
1.4.9: W 500
1.5.2: B 874-5, L 1061-4
1.5.8: W 1087
1.7.18: E 602
1.8.18: B 364
1.9.13: We 859
2.4.15: We 249
2.5.10: F 792
2.5.23: B 487
3.1.21: P 1118
3.2.9: K 640, B 720
3.2.12: K 660-1, L 1262
3.3.20: B 933
3.4.4: E 875-6
4.1.18: B 933
4.2.22: E 154
4.5.7-8: We 873
4.5.35: L 191-2
5.4.13: B 946
5.4.33-34: T 489
5.7.21: A 281-2, C 1508
5.8.4: E 1037-97
5.8.20: K 543
6.1.10: T 1175
6.5.11: We 1081
6.5.27: B 364
7.1.27: W 660, We 1192
7.3.21: E 744
7.8.4-5: C 408
7.8.6: C 21*, We 157
Athenaion Politeia 1.5: W 959
    1.10-12: F 952
    1.16-18: B 1422
    1.17: W 658
    1.18: W 554
    2.14: E 197-8, We 203
    2.18: T 85, We 800
    3.4: K 912-3, F 1065
    3.8: T 78-79
Cyropaedia 1.3.3: B 836
    1.4.19: K 290-1
    2.1.29: T 1211
    2.1.31: B 1186
    2.3.6: E 486-8
    4.4.3: B 1701-3*

7.1.29: K 271t*
7.5.6: B 383
7.5.67: B 836
8.1.34-38: K 1382*
8.8.19: L 1189
Hellenica 1.1.6-7: T p2
1.1.12: F 541
1.1.22: F 541
1.1.33: P 356
1.3.13: W 1183-4, P 928, B 822-3, L 63
1.4.12-20: F 1422
1.4.16: F 1457
1.4.20: T 1147
1.4.21: B 126, 1311, F 1512
1.5.3: F p6
1.5.6-7: F p4
1.5.(7-)8: F p4, We 172
1.5.16(-17): B 126, L p3, F 1422, 1431
1.5.20: F p3, p4
1.6.1: We 1193
1.6.16: F 1431
1.6.17: F p4
1.6.21: F p4
1.6.22(-23): F pp3-4
1.6.24-38: F p2
1.6.24: F 33
1.6.25: F p3
1.6.35: F 541, 1072
1.6.37: K 656
1.6.38: F p3, F 1463-5
1.7.1-34: F p2
1.7.1-2: F 1431
1.7.1: F 1512
1.7.2: B 126, F 417, 1196
1.7.4: F p3, F 541
1.7.5(-6): F 541, E 202-3, We 550
1.7.8: F p3, F 541
1.7.9: W 987-8
1.7.14-15: E 87
1.7.17: F 541
1.7.20(-21): K 1362, F 574, E 1089, We 431
1.7.22: B 1585-6, We 30
1.7.31: F p3, F 541
1.7.32: F 1072
1.7.34-35: E 797-8
1.7.34: B 126, E 1089, We 725
1.7.35: F 417
2.1.5: F p7, F 365

2.1.7: F p7, F 365
2.1.8-11: F p6
2.1.9: F p6
2.1.11-15: F 365
2.1.11: F p6
2.1.12: F p7, F 365
2.1.13: F p6
2.1.14: F p4, p6
2.1.16-21: F p3
2.1.16: F 1463-5
2.1.18: F 1463-5
2.1.20: F p4
2.1.25-26: F 1422
2.1.29: B 147, F 1071, 1512
2.1.30: B 1427
2.1.(31-)32: F 1512, E 644-5
2.2.2: F 1431, E 243
2.2.3: F p5
2.2.5: F 694
2.2.9: A 653
2.2.11: F p22
2.2.16-22: F 541
2.2.16: F p22
2.2.19-20: L 1177, F p5
2.3.2: A 11, W 157, T 170
2.3.15-56: F 541
2.3.15: F p10
2.3.23: L 985
2.3.24-34: F 970
2.3.27: F 419
2.3.31: F 541
2.3.36: F p10
2.3.40: W 1270*
2.3.42: E 202-3, We 550
2.3.47: T 263
2.3.55: We 57
2.3.56: L 856-7
2.4.1: E 802.
2.4.20-22: B 876, F 1437
2.4.21: C 1468
2.4.32: K 271t*
2.4.41: W 897
3.1.1: E p1
3.1.10-17: T 728, F 1345
3.2.24: E 791
3.2.25: B 149
3.3.3: K 1085, B 988
3.3.11: W 897
3.5.5: E p2
3.5.7-17: E 193

3.5.16: E p2, E 202-3, We 550
3.5.17-24: E p2
3.5.21: E 937
3.5.22: E 937
4.1.14: B 434-6
4.2.1: E 193
4.2.17: We p4
4.2.18-23: E 195, We p4
4.2.20: L 1262
4.2.23: E 199
4.3.17-23: E 195
4.4.1-6: E 199, 200
4.4.6: E p3, We p2
4.4.7-13: E p3
4.5.1: E p3, We p2
4.5.4: B 43
4.5.5: We p2
4.5.11-18: E 810, We p1, We 173
4.5.13: B 284, F 428
4.5.19: We p2
4.7.7: E 792
4.8.6: E 509-510
4.8.8: We 173
4.8.9-10: We p2
4.8.12-16: We p3
4.8.12: E 509-510, We p3
4.8.13: E p3, E 102, We 176
4.8.14: We p3
4.8.15: E p3
4.8.17-22: We p3
4.8.18: F 467
4.8.24: W 98, E p4, We 178
4.8.(24-)25: E p4, E 197, 202-3, We 550
4.8.(25-)30:   E 202-3, We p2, p3, We 172, 550
4.8.31-33: We p3
4.8.34: E p3
5.1.1-5: We p2
5.1.2: We 174
5.1.5-13: We p2
5.1.5: We 174
5.1.6: We p3
5.1.10: L 397, E p4
5.1.13-14: We p3
5.1.26: L 397, We 550 bis
5.1.28: E p4, We p3, We 550
5.1.30-34: We p3
5.1.31: E p4
5.2.9: E 338
5.4.20: E p2, We p2

5.4.34: E p2, We p2
6.2.6: F 1150, We 807
6.2.34: T 837
6.3.2-6: B 284, F 428
6.5.33: L 1137-44
7.1.24: L 524
Hiero 1.27: We 192
Hipparchicus 3.1: P 356, We 1181
    3.6-8: P 356
    3.11: B 799, B 1701-3*
    5.10: We 816
On Horsemanship: 1.1 K 242-3
    1.10: B 1701-3*
    1.14: B 1701-3*
    2.3: T 1211
    7.10: P 83-86*
    8.5: P 83-86*
    9.6(-7): P 83-86*, T 1211
    10.4: B 1701-3*
    10.5: B 1701-3*
    10.17: P 83-86*, B 1701-3*
    11.12: B 1701-3*
    12.1: P 1224-5
    12.6: B 1416
    12.9: We 513
On Hunting 1.2: L 785
    1.7: L 785
    4.6: F 893
    6.11-26: P 1178
    7.5: B 1204
    7.6: F 1359
    12.6-8: K 1382
Lakedaimonion Politeia 1.4: L 82
    1.5-9: E p16, E 613
    2.5-6: B 1282, L 279-280
    5.3: B 1282, L 279-280
    6.3: E p16
    11.3: B 1282, L 279-280, 1140
    13.8: L 1262
    14: P 623, 624, B 1012-3
Memorabilia 1.1.18: P 906
    1.2.12-39: C 876
    1.2.48: C 156
    1.2.49: C 845
    1.2.64: T 5
    1.6: W 1270
    1.6.2:   C 103, B 1282, 1553, We 942-3
    1.6.13: We 155
    2.1.4: B 1083

Index II: Persons

Abscondippides, see Apodrasippides

Academus, hero or god worshipped just outside Athens, C 1005n

Acalanthis, friend or servant of Alcmene, transformed into a polecat, P 1078

Acastus, king of Iolcus whose wife fell in love with Peleus, C 1063n

Accuser, W 1415-41

Aceso, daughter of Asclepius, We 639n, 660n

Acestor (474, 3), nicknamed "Sacas", tragic dramatist, W 1221, B 31-32, T p4

Achaeus of Eretria, tragic dramatist (v), F 184n

Acharneus, (invented?) eponymous hero of an Attic deme, A 322

Acharnians, see Chorus (a)

Achelous, river-god, L 381

Achilles, greatest hero of the Trojan War, A 430n, K 1056n, C 621n*, 1068n, W 741n, P 1123n, B 569n, 807n, 1420n, L 1252n, F p16, p19, p20, F 840n, 912, 922n, 924-7n, 963n, 1264-5, 1291-2n, 1365n, 1400, E 110n, 392-3n, We 583n, 937n, 951n, 1005n, 1162n

Aeschylus compared to, F 992 nickname for Cinesias, E 330n

Acoris, king of Egypt, E p4, We p3, We 178n

Actaeon, hunter torn in pieces by his hounds, F p8

Acusilaus of Argos, mythographer (vi/v), B 685-702n, 693n, 1193n

Adeimantus (202, 19), son of Leucolophides of Scambonidae, politician and general, F 1512, E 644-5n

Admetus, king of Pherae and husband of Alcestis, C 1415n, W 1238, L 1237n, T 194n

Adonis, mortal lover of Aphrodite, A 793n, P 420n, B 720n, L 389-396, E 39n

Adrastus, leader of the expedition of the Seven against Thebes, F 1021n

Aeacus, "keeper of the keys of Hades", F p10, p13, **465-478, 605-673,** 738n

Aegeus, father of Theseus, K 1067

Aegina, mother of Aeacus, F 464n

Aegisthus, lover of Clytaemestra, T p5, F 1126-8n, 1168n

Aegle, daughter of Asclepius, We 639n

Aegyptus, brother of Danaus, F 1206-8

Aeneas, son of Anchises and Aphrodite, a Trojan noble, E 1165-6n

Aeolosicon, title character of Ar.'s last play, We p24; *see also* Aeolus, Sicon

Aeolus, son of Hellen, T 547n, F 1244n

Aeolus, master of the winds, who married his sons and daughters to each other, A p4, F 499n, 864, 1081n, We p24

Aër, see Air

Aërope, wife of Atreus, A 433n

Aeschin(ad)es, a peasant, P 1154

Aeschines (337, 8), a boaster, W 325n, 459, 1220, 1243, B 821n, 823

Aeschines (69) of Perithoidae, hellenotamias in 418/7, B 822-3n

Aeschines (366, 84), son of Lysanias of Sphettus, author of Socratic dialogues, K 1281n, F 970n

Aeschines (354, 54), son of Atrometus of Cothocidae, actor and politician (iv), F 8n, 289-296n, 778n, 833-4n, We 155n

Aeschylus (442, 20), son of Euphorion of Eleusis, tragic dramatist (v), A p6, p12, p13, A 10*, K 401n, 522n, C 1365-7, 1458-61n, W 29n, P 749n*, B 750n, 807, 1121n, 1553n, L 188, T p1, T 134, 164n, 390-1n, F p4, p6, p9, p10, p13, pp14-18*, pp19-20, F 145-153n, 151-3n, 177n, 209-268n, 389-390n, 508n*, 686-7n, 758, 768-9, 771n, 778, 782, 783n, 786, 788-790*, 791n, 792, 794n, 797-801n, 803-4, 807-810, 814-829, **830-1481*,** 1485-90, **1500-33,** We p5

Aesimus (311, 1), politician, E 208

Aeson, father of Jason, K 1321n

Aesop, reputed author of animal fables (vi), W 566, 1259, 1401-5, 1446-8, P 129. B 471-5, 571n, 651-3, 968n, L 694-5n

Aether, see Sky

Agamemnon, leader of the Greek expedition to Troy, P 1123n, B 509, L 203n, T 560n, 689-758n, 788n, F p20, F 1126-68nn, 1140, 1141, 1172, 1212n, 1232-3n, 1270, 1284n, We 425n

Agariste (92, 2), daughter of Hippocrates of Alopece and mother of Pericles (vi/v), K 1037n, C 64n

Agariste (91, 1), wife of Alcmeonides, informant in the Mysteries affair, F 1512n

Agasias (11), son of Phanomachus of Lamptrae, voted against in an ostracism (v), K 855n*

Agathon (83, 2), son of Teisamenus, tragic dramatist, A p7, p25, A 408n, K 522n, C 178n, L 1222n, T p7, p8, p9, p11, T 29-70, 88-92, **95-265**, 390-1n, 574n, 1001n, 1160-1226n, F p8, F 46n, 71-88n, 83-85, 830n, 953n, E 1-18n, 65n, 167n, 722n

Agathos Daimon, see Good Spirit

Agaue, daughter of Cadmus and mother of Pentheus, T p5, We 424n

Agenor, father of Cadmus, F 1226

Agesilaus II, king of Sparta, E p2

Agis II, king of Sparta, L p2*, F p1, F 1023-4n, 1422n

Aglaurus, daughter of Cecrops, T 533

Agoracritus, *see* Sausage-seller name explained, K 1257-8

Agriculture (Georgia), goddess/ personific-ation, P p.xix

Agrius, brother of Oeneus, A 418-9n

Agyrrhius (179, 1) of Collytus, politician, A p28, F 367n, E 71n, 102-4*, 182n, 184-8*, 248n, 301n, We 171n, 176

Ahuramazda, supreme god of the Zoroastrian religion, P 411n

Aidos, see Honour

Air (Aër), god worshipped by Socrates, C 264, 626, 667, B 1193n

Ajax, leader of the Salaminians in the Trojan War, K 1056n, L 1237n, F

p16, F 828n, 1016-7n, 1041n, 1294, 1400n

Alcaeus of Mytilene, lyric poet (vii/vi), B 769-784n, T 162-3*, E 952-975n

Alcaeus (576, 3), son of Miccus, comic dramatist, We p1

Alcestis, wife of Admetus, who gave up her life to save his, K 1250-2n, C 1415n, L 606n

Alcibiades (600, 23), son of Cleinias of Scambonidae, politician and general, A 524-5n, 716, 846n*, 967n, 1303n, 1377n, C p2, W 44-46, 52n, 1187n, P 681n, B p4, B 44n, 145-7n, 619n, 766-7n, 1297n*, L p1-2*, L 390-7n, 513n, 560n, 723-5n, T pp2-4, T 647-8n, 840n, 1143-4n, F p3, p5*, p10, p17, p18, pp19-20, F 689n, 894n, 1422-32, 1457n, 1512n, E 103n, 202-3nn, We 550n, 1040n

Alcibiades jr. (598, 24), son of the above, F 417n, 1488-9n

Alcidamas of Elaea, sophist (iv), We 6-7n, 179n

Alcmaeon of Croton, natural philosopher (v), C 163n

Alcman of Sparta, lyric poet (vii), B 919n, L 1296-1315n, 1311n

Alcmene, mother of Heracles, C 1264-5n, P 1078n, B 558, 1242n, 1652n, L 254-387n*, F 58-60n, 531, 582, We 385n

Alexander III (the Great), king of Macedon (iv), C 621n*, W 392n, We 377-385n, 385n

Alexandros, see Paris

Alexis of Thurii, comic dramatist (iv/iii), We p12, We 290-321n

Alope, beloved of Poseidon, mother of Hippothoön, B 559

Althaea, mother of Meleager, F 863-4n

Amasis, king of Egypt (vi), We 178n

Amazons, female warriors, L 191-2n, 678-9, E 246n

Ambassadors, A 64-110

Amedocus, king of the Odrysians, We p3

Ameinias (670, 3), archon in 423/2, C 31n

Ameipsias (708, 1), comic dramatist, C p2, C 524n, B p1, F 14

Ammon (Amun), Egyptian god equated with Zeus, B 619n

Amorges, rebellious satrap in Caria, B 1028n

Amphiaraus, seer who joined the Seven against Thebes, F 1319n, We 658n, 701-2n

Amphidamas, ruler of Chalcis (viii/vii): sons of, We 1162n

Amphion, builder of the walls of Thebes, B 1247

and Zethus, the "twin gods" of Thebes, A 905n

Amphitheus, *see* Godschild

Amphitrite, sea-goddess, L 347n

Amphitryon, husband of Alcmene, B 558-9n, 1652n, L 254-387n*

Amun, *see* Ammon

Amynia, derogatory feminine name for Amynias, C 691

Amynias (737, 2), son of Pronapes of Prasiae(?), politician, C 686-692, W 74-76*, 325-6nn, 459n, 466, 1267, E 408n

Amynias, a creditor of Strepsiades, C 31, 1267-70n

Amynon (1), politician, reputedly a passive homosexual, E 365

Amyntor, father of Phoenix, A 421n

Anacreon of Teos, lyric poet (vi), T 137n, 161-3*

Anagyrus, eponymous hero of an Attic deme, A p4*, A 322n

Ananius of Euboea(?), iambic poet (vi), F 659n

Anapnoe, see Respiration

Anaxagoras of Clazomenae, philosopher (v), K 1085n, 1281n, C 376-8n, W 380n, P 1031n, B 988n, 1005n, T 856-7n

Anaxandrides of Rhodes(?), comic dramatist (iv), T p12

Anaxilas of Rhegium, founder of Sicilian Messene (vi/v), L 1141n

Anaximander of Miletus, philosopher (vi), C 404-7n, 1280-1n, 1292n

Anaximenes of Miletus, philosopher (vi), C 404-7n

Ancaeus, one of the hunters of the Calydonian Boar, F 1402n

Anchimolus, Spartan general (vi), L 1150-6n

Ancylion, father of Myrtia, W 1397

Andocides (828, 7), son of Leogoras of Cydathenaeum, politician, B 1293n, L 421-2n, T 805n, F 367n, 678n, E p3, p6, E 71n, 102n, 202n, 248n, We 176n, 1192n

Androcles (870, 49) of Pithus, politician (assassinated 411), A 88n, W 1187, T p3

Androcles, politician (after 403), W 1187n

Andromache, wife of Hector, L 520n

Andromeda, daughter of Cepheus, rescued by Perseus from a sea-monster, C 556n, P 832-3n*, T p6, pp7-8, p9, T 547-8n, 1007-81n, 1012-3, 1015-1134, F 53

Antalcidas, Spartan admiral, We p3, We 550n

Anteia, alternative name for Stheneboea (q.v.), F 1043n

Antigone, daughter of Oedipus, L 676n

Antileon, tyrant of Chalcis (vii-vi?), K 1044, W 1232-5n

Antilochus, son of Nestor, F 924-7n, E 392

Antimachus of Teos, epic poet (vi??), P 1270n

Antimachus (1106, 6), a former *choregos*, A 1150-73

Antimachus (8), reputedly a passive homosexual, A 1150n, C 1022

Antipater (1162, 2), archon 389/8, We p28

Antiphanes (1219, F7435), son of Stephanus, comic dramatist (iv), We p12, We 290-321n

Antiphates (1260=?1261, 15), son of Antisthenes of Cytherrus, naval war casualty *c.*406, E 366n

Antiphon (1304, 57), son of Sophilus of Rhamnus, rhetorician, sophist and politician, K 327n, 448n*, C p3*, W 421n, 1270(?)*, 1301(?)*, B 1005n, 1569n, 1701n, T 1143-4n, F 634n

Antiphon (1283, 5), son of Lys(id)onides, a rich man, W 1270(?)*, 1301(?)*

Antisthenes (1186, 1), banker, E 366n

Antisthenes (1184, −) of Cytherrus(?), a rich man, E 366-8, 806-8

Antisthenes (1194=1196=1197, 25), son of Antiphates of Cytherrus, (?)grandson of the preceding, E 366n

Antitheus of Gargettus, father of Critylla, T 898

Antitheus (1040a, 1) of Cydathenaeum(?), member of a religious guild, T 898n

Anytus (1324, 4), son of Anthemion of Euonymon, politician, F 967n, E p9, E 208n, 252n

Apaeole, see Fraud

Apelles of Colophon, painter (iv/iii), We 385n

Aphrodite, goddess, A 792-4, 988, P 40, 420n, 456, B 553n, 565, 696n, 881n, 1104n, L p4, L 208, 252, 389n, 551, 556, 723-5n, 749, 785n, 832, 833-4, 858, 898, 939, 1273-90n, 1279n, 1290, T 205n, 254, F 483n, 634n, 1045-7, E p28, E 8, 39n, 189, 190, 558, 722, 845n, 965, 973, 981, 999, 1008, 1136, We 1069

Apodrasippides ("Abscondippides"), patronymic assumed by Philocleon, W 185

Apollo, god, A 1212, K 229, 408n, 1015, 1024, 1047, 1072, 1081, 1233, 1240, 1248, 1270-3, 1318n, C 595-7, 603-4n, 1372n, W 158-161, 388n, 392n, 398-9n, 869-884, P 238, 422n, 453n, 555n, 1044n, B 61, 126n, 216-220, 263, 295, 516, 553n, 584, 716, 722, 769-784n, 772, 857n, 869n, 971n, 982, 1527n, 1710n, 1763, L 721n, 1281, 1287n, 1291, 1298, T 101-129n, 108-113, 128, 311, 315-6, 332-3n, 969, 972n, F 207n, 231, 503n, 659, 754, 1184, 1212n, 1319n, E p27, p28, E 39n, We p5, p8, p9, p13, p20, p21, We 8-12, 21n, 32, 39-47, 48-50n, 63, 81, 134n, 213-4, 215n, 287n, 327n, 358, 359, 438, 854, 1054n

Agyieus, pillar and altar of, W 804n, 875, T 489, 689-758n, 748, We 1114n

and Asclepius, We pp9-10, p11, p21, We 660n

sworn by, A 59, 101, K 14, 870, 942*, 1041, C 372, 388, 732, W 1366, P 16, 615, B 438, 470, 479, L 465, 917*, 938, 942, T 269, F 51, 508, 951, 1074, 1166, 1510, E 160, 631, 659, 680, We 987

Apollodorus (1378, 10), painter, We 385n

Apollodorus (1393, 40), son of Asclepiades, chronographer etc. (ii), F p8

Apollodorus of Tarsus, scholar (date unknown), F 320n

Apollonius, son of Chaeris(?), scholar (i?), F 1269-70n, 1435-66n

Araros (1575, 1) of Cydathenaeum, son of Ar., comic dramatist, A p3, p4, p28, T p11, p12, We p1, p24

Arcesilaus, name of four kings of Cyrene (vii-iv), We 925n

Archedemus (2326, 26) of Pelekes(?), politician, A p6, F 417-421, 431-3n, 588, 1196n

Archelaus, son of Temenus, founder of the Macedonian royal house, F 1206-8n, We 287n

Archelaus, king of Macedon, L 421-2, T 29n, 390-1n, F p8, F 83n, 85n, 953n, 1206-8n, 1299-1300n*, We 287n

Archemorus, see Opheltes

Archenomus (2376, 1), a man allegedly deserving death, F 1507

Archeptolemus (2384, 3), son of Hippodamus, of Agryle, politician, K 327*, 794, P 667n

Archer(s):
  (a) A 40-173
  (b) L p4, 387-460, E 261n
  (c) T pp7-8, p9, T 855-923n, 923, 929-946, 1001-7, 1015n, 1017, 1022, 1026-8, 1051, 1083-1201, 1208, 1210-25
  see also L 184n *and under* Ditylas, Pardocas, Sceblyas

Archestratus (2405, 10), banker, E 366n

Archilochus of Paros, iambic poet (vii), A p8*, P 1298-9n, B 1313-22n*

Archinus (2526, 15) of Coele, politician, F 367n, 368n, 967n

Archippus (2540, 5), comic dramatist, B p2, F p11, E p8, We p7

Archvillain (Miarotatos), assumed name and patronymic of Trygaeus, P 183-7

Ares, god of war, P 457, B 835, 1654n, L 344-5, F 634n, 1238-41n, We 328 nickname of Phormio, F p11

Arethas, cleric and scholar (ix/x^P), A p17, E 920n

Argus, hundred-eyed giant slain by Hermes, E 76n, 80

Argyrius ("Mr Cash"), nickname of Agyrrhius(?), E 186n*, We 176n

Arignotus (1612, 1), son of Automenes, citharode, K 1277-9*, W 1277-8

Ariobarzanes, satrap of Dascylium, We p3

Ariphrades (2201, 1), son of Automenes, comic dramatist(?), K 1277-9n, 1280-9, W 1280-3, P 883, E 846n, We 1005n

Ariphrades (2), noted for talking during Assembly meetings, E 129

Aristarchus of Samothrace, scholar (ii), A p16, F 186n, 970n, 1206-8n, 1269-70n, 1400n, 1413n, 1435-66n

Aristeides (1695, 32), son of Lysimachus of Alopece, politician (v), K 1325, F p9

Aristocrates (1904, 99), son of Scellias, general, B 125-6

Aristodemus (73), reputedly a former male prostitute, E 97n

Aristogeiton (1777, 9), son of Theotimus, tyrannicide (vi), A 980n, K 786n*, W 1225n, L 619n, 632n, 633, 634n, 664n, E 682n, 834n, 938-945n, 943n

Aristogeiton (1775, 4), son of Cydimachus, politician (iv), K 862n*, 1017n

Aristogenes (1781, 1), general, F p2

Aristomache, typical woman's name, T 806

Aristomenes (1992, 4), comic dramatist, A p2*, K p2, We p1

Ariston (2139, 10), speaker of Demosthenes 54, E 640n, 663-4n

Aristophanes of Aegina, father of Aristocleidas (v), A 654n*

Aristophanes (2090, 32), son of Philippus of Cydathenaeum, comic dramatist, A p2-16*, p28, pp32-33, A 377-382*, 502-3, 628-664*, 1154-5n*, K p4, K 509-550, 1253n, C pp2-4*, C 518-562*, W p.xv*, p.xviii*, W 1015-59*, 1284-91*, P 734-774, 775-818n*, B 590n, L 574-586n, T p6, p11, F p14*, p15, E 1-18n, 444n, We p1, pp21-24, p29, We 461-3n, 1061n

Aristophanes (2082, 2), son of Nicophemus, admiral and diplomat, C 1216n

Aristophanes of Byzantium, scholar (iii/ii), A p16, C 967n, B 1343n, F 151-3n

Aristoxenus, politician, We 175

Aristoxenus of Taras, musical theorist (iv), F 1323n

Aristotle of Stageirus, philosopher (iv), A p24, C 1294-5n, W 386n, T 156n, F p15*, F 141n, 404-6n, 1124n, E p8, p16, p19, We p9, We 461-3n

Aristyllus (2126, 2), reputedly a coprophiliac, E 647-650, We 314

Arms-dealer, P 1208-1264

Arsaces, *see* Artaxerxes II

Arsinoe, daughter of Leucippus, We p8

Artachaees, a gigantic Persian (v), A 709(?)

Artaxerxes I, king of Persia, A 61-124, 647-651, K 84n, 478, W 98n, F p6

Artaxerxes II, king of Persia, F pp5-6, E pp1-4, We p3, We 170, 178n, 550n

Artemis, goddess, K 660, 1406n, C 598-600, P 831n, 874n, B 515n, 870n, 871, L 435, 447, 645, 700-1n, 785n, 922, 949, 1262-72, 1280, 1287n, T 101-129n, 114-9, 320-1, 332-3n, 517, 569, 742, 970-3, 1175n, 1218ff.n*, 1274, F 1238-41n, 1358n, 1361-2n, E 90, 136, E 3n, We p9

Artemisia, queen of Halicarnassus (v), L 675, T 1200n

Artemisia, a bawd, Euripides disguised as, T p10, T 1056-97n*, 1160-1226*

Artemon of Teos, an extravagant debauchee (vi), A 850

Asclepiades of Myrleia, scholar (i), F 1269-70n

Asclepiodorus (2625a, 31), first known bearer of this name, We pp11-12

Asclepius, healing hero/god, W 123, B 1372-1409n, E p28, E 22-23n, 404-6n, We pp8-13, p14, p20, p21, p26, We 411, 621, 636, 639-640, 653, 658n, 659, 660n, 662n, 664, 669, 684-6, 687n, 690n, 695n, 696, 698, 700-1, 704-6, 708-712, 716-722, 723-732, 740-1, 742, 745-8

temple staff of, 668-671, 676-681, 687

Ascondas, Boeotian(?) pancratiast, W 1191, 1383-5

Ashurbanipal, king of Assyria (vii), B 1021n

Ashur-uballit II, last king of Assyria (vii), B1021n

Asopodorus (2671, 3), a very small man, B 17-18n

Aspasia of Miletus, mistress of Pericles, A 527, K 132n, F p2

Ass, see Donkey

Asterie, sister of Leto and mother of Hecate, F 1361-2n

Astyanax, son of Hector, We 69-70n

Astydamas (2649, 2), son of Astydamas, tragic dramatist (iv), F p9

Astydameia, see Hippolyte

Atalanta, huntress and long-time virgin, C 997n*, L 785n, F 863-4n

Athamas, husband of Ino, father of Phrixus and Helle, A 434n, C 257, W 1414n, F 1225-6n

Asychis, king of Egypt, B 1145n

Athena, goddess, A 547, K 301-2n, 445-6n, 581-594*, 656, 763, 1056n, 1090-5, 1168-89, 1203, C 300, 401n, 587n, 601-2, 967, 989, 1265, W 652n, 1086n, P 832-3n*, B 516, 827n, 828-831, 1052n, 1104n, 1114-5n*, 1536n, 1653, 1710n, L 174, 254-387n*, 262n, 263n, 302-4, 341-9, 381n, 439n, 443n, 454n, 632n, 642n, 643n, 645n, 722n, 751n, 759n, 760n, 1012n, 1126-7n*, 1273*, 1299, 1320-1, T p2, T 317-9, 1011-2n, 1136-47, F p13, F 378(?), 933n, 1080n, 1090n, 1530n, E p27, p28*, E 474-5n, 476, 999n, 1161n, We p16, We 185n, 772, 1175n, 1193
  forms of name, in tragedy, L 742n
  Parthenon statue of, K 1169n, P 605n
  Polias, priestess of, P 992n, L p5, L 1273*; *see also* Lysimache
  sworn by, P 218
  see also Victory

Athenaeus the Spartan, son of Pericleidas, L 1138n

Athenian Delegates, L 982ff.n, 1012n, **1082-1188, 1216-1321**

Athenian Women, L 65-253, 1273-1321, T 292-654
  see also Calonice, Chorus (g,h,k), Critylla, Garland-seller, Girl, Lysistrata, Mica, Myrrhine, Myrtia, Old Woman/Women, Wife, Woman/Women

Atlas, nickname given to dwarfish slaves, F 55n

Atreus, king of Mycenae and father of Agamemnon, A 433n, F 1270, We 130-197n

Auge, mother of Telephus, F 1080n

Autocleides (2709, 2), noted pederast (iv), F 499n

Autocles (2724, 18), son of Tolmaeus of Anaphlystus, general, W xvi

Autolycus (2748, 10), son of Lycon, athlete, W 1301n, I 270n

Automenes (2751, 4), father of Arignotus and Ariphrades, W 1275-6
  second son of (name unknown), actor, W 1279

Axiochus (1330, 5), son of Alcibiades of Scambonidae, exiled for sacrilege, F 1512n

Baby, L 845-908, 909

Bacchus, see Dionysus

Bacchylides of Ceos, lyric poet (v), F 1483n

Bacis, alleged source of numerous prophecies, K 123-4, 1003-4, P 1070-2, 1119, B 962, 970

Bamboozlers (Phenakes), gods of deception invoked by the Sausage-seller, K 634, We 508n

Basileia, see Princess

Basileides, reputedly a former male prostitute, E 97n

Battus of Thera, founder of Cyrene (vii), We 925

Bdelycleon, hero of *Wasps,* A p26, **W** pp.xvii-xviii*, W 40-41n, 67-70, 114-123, 134-5, **136-155*, 167-399, 400-436*, 456-798, 805-848, 851-1008, 1122-1264, 1352-9, 1360-1449,** 1462-73*, F 298n, E p31, We p10, We 278

Bearers of corpse, F 170-7

Beetle, P 1-49, 72-81, **82-181**, 720-4

Bellerophon, monster-slaying hero and rider of Pegasus, A 427-8, W 757n, P 76n, 105n, 109n, 126n, 136n, 140n*, 146-8n, 154-172n, T 401-4n*, F 1043n, 1051, 1217-9n

Bentley, Richard, scholar (xvii/xviii[P]), A p20

Bereskhethoi, see Follies

Better Argument, personification, A p6, K 1373n, C p4, C 112, 361n*, 882-6, **889-1104**, 1336-7, B p6*, F 1070-1nn, 1087-8n, We 578n

Birds, see Chorus (f)

Blaydes, Frederick H.M., scholar (xix[P]), A p20

Blepes, an old man in Menander's *Sikyonios,* E 311n, 372n, We 332n

Blepsidemus, a friend of Chremylus, E 311n, **We** p13, p20, p22, p23, p25, p26, We 22n, 223n, 321n, 332-4, **335-626**, 770/1n, 782n

Blepyrus, husband of Praxagora, F 345-9n, E p11, p12, p19, pp21-22*, pp24-25, p30, p32, E 74n, **311-477**, 504n, 511, **520-727**, 746n, 931n, 1015n, 1112-26n, 1113n, 1125-8, **1129-79**, We p19, We 22n, 332n, 1197n

Blockhead (Coalemus), god of stupidity honoured by the Sausage-seller, K 221, We 508n

Boeotian, see Theban

Bowl, see Kitchen Utensils

Boy(s):
  (a) K 732n, **1384-1408**
  (b) **W 230-414***, P p.xviii
  (c) son of Lamachus: P **1265-94**
  (d) son of Cleonymus: P **1265-1304**
  (e) servant to the Honest Man: **W e 823-958**

Brag, see Sellus

Brasidas, Spartan general, K 984n, 1331n, W p.xv, p.xvi, W 475, P p.xv, P 281-4, 640, 642n, B 1274n

Brazier, see Kitchen Utensils

Brideswoman, **A 1048-66**

Briseis, captive concubine of Achilles, P 1123n

Bromius, see Dionysus

Brunck, Richard F.P., scholar (xviii/xix[P]), A p20

Bupalus of Chios, sculptor and enemy of Hipponax (vi), L 361

Byrsine, comic distortion of name of Myrrhine wife of Hippias, K 449

Cabeiri, gods worshipped in various mystery-cults, P 277-8n

Cadmus, founder of Thebes, B 558-9n, T 680n, 855n, F 1021n, 1225

Calchas, seer to the expedition against Troy, F 1289n

Callias sr. (7825, 82), son of Hipponicus of Alopece, grandfather of Callias jr. (v), B 283, L 679n

Callias (7807, 20), archon in 456/5, C 969-971n*

Callias jr. (7826, 84), son of Hipponicus of Alopece, second priest at Eleusis, A 702n, 1167-8n, C 815n, B 283-6, L 270n, F p19, F 355n, 428-430, 431-3n, 501n, 1193n, E 810, We 168n

Callicles (7927=?7776=?7906, 13) of Acharnae, politician, a character in Plato's *Gorgias,* E 426n

Callicoön, see Cillicon

Calligeneia, goddess associated with Demeter, T p11-12, T 299

Callimachus (7992, 8), archon in 446/5, C 969-971n*

Callimachus (13), lyric poet or chorus-trainer, E 809

Callimedon (8030, 2), politician, E 102n, We 176n

Callimedon (8032, 3=7) "the Crayfish", son of Callicrates of Collytus, politician (iv), E 102n, We 176n

Callippides (16), tragic actor, C 64n

Callippides, proposed name for Strepsiades' son, C 64

Callisto, beloved of Zeus, raised to heaven as the Great Bear, P 832-3n*

Callistratus (8127, 3), producer for Ar., A p2*, p15*, p32, A 654n, C 528-9n, 531n, W 1018-29n, B p1, L p1

Callistratus (8129=8130=8157, 50), son of Callicrates of Aphidna, politician, E p4, E 71n, 102n, We 176n

Callistratus, scholar (iii/ii), A p16, F 790n, We 385n, 1110n

Calonice, a friend of Lysistrata, **L** p3, **L** 1n, **5-253***, **830-844**, E p23, E 509-510n

Calonicus, name of several Boeotians, **L** 6n

Calyce, one of the women in the Acropolis, **L** 322

Calypso, nymph who loved and detained Odysseus, F 518n

Cambyses, king of Persia (vi), 178n

Canace, daughter of Aeolus, who was raped by her brother, C 1371n, T 406n, F 850n, 1081n, 1475n, 1491-2n

Cannonus (8249, 2), son of Sibyrtius of Lamptrae, politician (v), E 1089

Cantharus, local hero at Peiraeus, P 145n

Cantharus (8247, 1), comic dramatist, A p24, P 1n, B 15-16n

Capaneus, one of the Seven against Thebes, C 1484-5n, P 69-71n*

Carcinus (8254, 1), son of Xenotimus of Thoricus, tragic dramatist and general, C 1261, **W** 1501-30, **1531-7**, P 781-796, F 86n

sons of, **W** **1500-37**, P 289n, 781-790, 863, E 1165-6n; *see also* Xenarchus, Xenocles, Xenotimus

Carcinus jr. (8253=8255, 2), son of Xenocles and grandson of the above, tragic dramatist, F p9, F 86n

Cardopion, character of low popular myth, W 1178

Carion, name of various slaves and freedmen (v-iv), We 1n

Carion, slave of Chremylus, F 271n, E p31, **We** pp12-13, pp22-23, pp24-25, p26, p30, **1-229**, **253-321**, 321/2n, 342n, 401n, 410-1n, 624, **626**, **627-770**, 770/1n, **782-801**, **802-958**, 964n, 1096/7n, **1097-1170**, 1172n, 1194-1209n, **1196-1209**

Carion, name of various comic slaves and cooks, We 1n

Carystion (8259a, –), made an Athenian citizen for services in Samian war, W 283n

Cassandra, daughter of Priam, B 1720n, T 101-129n, We 425n

Cassiepeia, mother of Andromeda, P 832-3n*, T 1011-2n

Castor and Pollux/Polydeuces (the Dioscuri, the Tyndaridae or "the Two Gods"), patron heroes/gods of Sparta, P 214, 285, **L** 81, 86, 90, 118n, 142, 983, 1095, 1171, 1174, 1300, E 1069, We 210n

Castor mentioned alone, L 206, 988

Cebriones, one of the Giants, B 553

Cecrops, an early king of Athens, K 1055, C 301, W 438, L 439n, T 533n, E p28*, We 773

Cedeides (3), dithyrambic poet, C 985

Celeus, Eleusinian hero, A 48, 55

Cephalus, great-grandfather of Odysseus, We 41-43n

Cephalus (8277, 5) of Collytus, politician, E 208n, 248-253, We 175n

Cepheus, father of Andromeda, P 832-3n*, T 1011-2n, 1022n, 1040n, 1056, 1113

Cephisodemus (8306, 1), father of Euathlus, A 705, 712

Cephisodorus (8341, 6), comic dramatist, A p2*, E p10

Cephisophon (50), musical assistant (?) to Euripides, A 395n, F 944*, 1408, 1452-3

Cerberus, watchdog of Hades, L 601n, F p9, F 111, 187n, 465-6n, 467, 468n, 473n, 504n

Cleon/Paphlagon compared to, K 416n, 1030, W 1031-5nn*, P 313, 754-8, F 569n

Cercope, courtesan (iv), We 1082n

Cercyon, wrestler killed by Theseus, father of Alope, B 558-9n

Chabas, name in use at Tanagra, W 234n

Chabes, a deceased ex-juryman, W 234, L 6n

Chabrias (15086, 2), son of Ctesippus of Aexone, general, We 173n

Chaereas (15091, 1):

son of, a frequent prosecutor, W 687

Chaereas (55), alleged to be of foreign birth, W 687n

Chaereas, a young man in Menander's *Aspis* and *Dyskolos,* E 51n

Chaerecrates (15131, 2) of Sphettus(?), brother of Chaerephon, C 156n, B 1296n

Chaeredemus (15125, 26), son of Euangelus of Coele, dedicator of a bronze Trojan Horse, B 1128n*

Chaeremon (10), tragic dramatist (iv), F p9

Chaerephon (15203, 21) of Sphettus(?), associate of Socrates, C 104*, 144-7, 156-8, 503-4, 831, 1465-6, **1497-1509, W 1388-1414***, B 1296, 1562-4, E 1073n, We 422n

Chaerestratus, name of characters in Menander's *Aspis* and *Epitrepontes,* E 51n

Chaeretades, husband of a member of the chorus, E 51

Cha(e)rippus, proposed name for Strepsiades' son, C 64, E 51n

Chaeris (F2470), piper, A 16*, 866, P 951-5, B 858*, 861n

Chaos, see Void

Chares (15286, 3), ambassador to Sparta in 446/5, A 603n

Chares. ruler of an unidentifiable territory on the fringes of Greece, A 604*

Charias (15324, 8), archon 415/4, We p28

Charinades, name of a member of the chorus, W 232; *see also* P 1142-58n, 1155, E 51n

Charippus (15464, 2), denounced for impiety in 415, C 64n

Charippus (6) of Phalerum, father of the next-mentioned, C 64n

Charippus (15467, 5), son of Charippus of Phalerum, a public arbitrator in the 320s (iv), C 64n

Charisius, a young man in Menander's *Epitrepontes,* E 51n

Charites, see Graces

Charitimides (15497, 1), general (v), E 293n

Charitimides, assumed male name of a member of the chorus, E 51n, 293

Charixene, courtesan (vi?), E 943

Charminus (15517, 1), general, T p1-2, T 804*

Charoeades (15529, 2), son of Euphiletus, general, W 965n

Charon, ferryman of the dead, L 606, F p11, p12, F 139-140, **180-270,** 1480n, We 278

Cheek (Mothon), god of impudence invoked by the Sausage-seller, K 635

Cheese-grater, see Kitchen Utensils

Cheiron, a wise and virtuous centaur, A 421n, L 1126-7n*, We p8

Chloe, see Demeter

Choerilus of Samos, epic poet, F 1299-1300n*

Choirion, see Pussy

Chorus:

(a) A p33, A 177-185, 200, 203, **204-1234,** P p.xviii, K 1408n, L 1320-1n, E 277-9n, We 1209n

(b) A 1234n, K pp3-4, 225-6, 242-6, **247-1408,** L 1320-1n, We 1209n

(c) C p3, C 252-3*, 265-322*, **323-1511,** F 892n, E p12, p28, We 1082n

(d) W 214-229, **230-1537**

(e) P p.xviii-xix*, P 296-300, **301-1359***, E 277-9n

(f) B 197-205, 227-264, **294-1765**

(g) P p.xviii, L pp4-5, L 247-8, **254-1042** (men), **319-1042*** (women), **1043-1321,** E p23, p25, We 1209n

(h) T 292-1231

(j) A 1234n, P p.xviii, L 1320-1n, F p10, p12, p13, p18, p19, F 156-8, 312-322, **323-1533**

(k) E pp23-25, p30, p32, E 24-29, **30-310*,** 478-1183

(l) A 1234n, K 1408n, L 1320-1n, E 277-9n, 729-730n*, **We** pp22-23, p25, We 223-6, 253-6, **257-1209**

Chorus, Subsidiary, see Boys (b), Frogs

Chremes, an old man, E p21, p28, p30, p32, E 74n, 311n, 322n, 327-356n, 369n, **372-477,** 564n, 746n, 931n, 1113n, We p19, We 22n, 332n

Chremon, (nickname of) a frequent prosecutor, W 401

Chremylus, name of two Euboeans (v-iv), We 22n

Chremylus, hero of *Wealth,* A p11, T p6, E p13, p27, p28, p31, E 277-9n, 311n, 369n, 571-709n, 608n, 651n, 730n, **We** pp4-5, p7, pp13-19, p20, p22, p23, pp24-25, p26, **1-252,** 253, 260,

262-5, 319, 321n, **322-626**, 626/7n, 633, 654-663, 740, 767, 770, **782-801**, 801/2nn, 819-820, 824n, 844n, 857n, 859n, 864-5n, 870-1n, 958/9n, **965-1096**, 1103, 1153-63n, 1162n, 170n, 1171, **1172-1209**
children of, We 383, 1104, 1194-1209n
son of, We 35, 47, 250-1
Chromon (2), politician, W 401n
Chronos, see Time
Chrysis, mistress of Demeas in Menander's *Samia,* W 1353n
Chrysus, a slave of Bdelycleon, W 1251*, 1263ff*, 1264n*
Cillicon, a semi-legendary traitor, P 363
Cimon (8429, 11), son of Miltiades of Laciadae, politician and general (v), A p5, p6, K 407n, 1312n, C 1005n, P 804n, B 619n, L 1137-44n, 1138n, 1143-4, T 446n, We 627n
Cinesias (8438, 2), son of Meles, dithyrambic poet, K 1363n, C 333n, B 1332-3n, 1360-1n, **1372-1409***, F 153, 366n*, 1435-66n, 1437-41, E 329n, 330
Cinesias, husband of Myrrhine, L p3, p5, L 441-2n, 686n, 830n, 831-844, **845-1013**, E p25
Circe, sorceress who befriended Odysseus, B 1561n, We 290-321n, 302-315
Cironides or Scironides (12730, 1), general, L p3
Citizens attending the Assembly, **A 40-173**
Cleaenetus (8460, 11) of Cydathenaeum, father of Cleon, K 574
Cleidemides (3), politician(?), F 791
Cleigenes (8488, 1) of Halae, politician, F p7, p14, F 708-717, 729n, 1442-50n, 1531-3nn, E 77n
Cleinarete, a member of the chorus, E 41
Cleinias (8510, 22) of Scambonidae, father of Alcibiades, A 716
Cleisthenes (8526, 1), son of Megacles, of Alopece, founder of Athenian democracy (vi), B 33n, L 273n
Cleisthenes (8525, 2), a beardless man, A 118, K 1374, C 355, W 1187, B 831, L 622, 1091, T p7, p8, T 235, **574-654**, 763, 929, F 48-51, 57, 423-7, 431-3n, E 65n, 167n

Cleitagora of Lesbos(?), a courtesan(?), C 684n, W 1246, L 1237
Cleitagora, typical woman's name, C 684
Cleito (8552, 2), mother of Euripides, A 457, 478, K 19n, T 387, 456n, 910n, F 840, 947n
Cleitophon (8546, 5), son of Aristonymus, politician, K 1281n, C 156n, F 967, 1442-50n
Cleocritus (8569, 4 or 8570, 3?), a fat man, B 876, F p19, F 1435-66n, 1437-41
Cleomachus (10), tragic actor, E 22-23n
Cleombrotus (1), "son of Partridge", B 766n
Cleomenes I, king of Sparta (vi/v), B 1282n, L 273-282, 1150-6n, 1254n
Cleomenes of Rhegium, lyric poet (vi/v?), F 1302n
Cleon (8674, 43), son of Cleaenetus of Cydathenaeum, politician and general, A pp2-3, p6, p10, p16, pp32-33, A 6*, 88n, 134n, 299-300, 377-382, 502-3, 630n, 659-664, K pp2-4*, 44n, 48-49n, 51n, 54-57n, 61n, 63-70n, 75n, 103n, 137n, 224n, 231-3n*, 247n, 255-260nn, 281n*, 313n, 314n, 336n, 358n, 361n, 394n, 438n, 449n, 465n, 478n, 511n, 574n, 575n, 658n, 668-9n, 715-8n, 732n*, 765n, 774n*, 775n, 786n*, 805-8n, 809n, 812n, 818n, 835n*, 852-7n*, 862n*, 946n, 956n, 973-996, 1017n, 1030n, 1044n, 1054n, 1071n, 1099n*, 1102-3n, 1128n, 1256n, 1319n, 1341n, 1408n, C 400n, 549-550, 581-594, W pp.xv-xviii, W 34-45*, 62-63*, 133n, 134n, 197, 240n*, 242-4, 342n, 345n, 409-410, 417n, 596-7, 671n, 759, 895n, 896n, 903-4n, 909n, 930n, 970n, 1031-7, 1183-4n, 1220, 1221n, 1224-37, 1238-9n, 1284-91*, 1467n, P p.xv, p.xvii, P 47-48, 217n, 219n, 271-2, 313-320*, 395n, 507n, 637n, 639n, 640n, 642n, 647-656, 667n, 669n, 687n, 752-760, 928n, 1084n, B 440-1n, L p5, L 536n, 683n, T 451n, 605n, 805n, 834n, 640n, F 368n, 419n, 549-578n, 569, 570n, 577, 680-1n, 710-3n, 764n, 765n, 1431n, E p18, E 78n, 252n, 292n, We p19,

We 31n, 48-50n, 175n, 288-9n, 417n, 1061n; *see also* Cerberus, Hound, Paphlagon

Cleonyme, derogatory feminine name for Cleonymus, C 680

Cleonymus (8680, 2), politician, A 88*, 844, K 958, 1293-9, 1372, C 353-4, 400, 673-6, W 16n, 19-27, 592, 666-7n, 822-3, P 446, 673-8, 756n, B 289-290, 1473-81, 1556n, T 605, F 534-541, E 51n
    son of, *see* Boy (d)

Cleophon (8638, 5), son of Cleippides of Acharnae, politician, A p6, K 765n, C 109n, L 1270n, T 803n, 805, 840n, F pl, pp6-7, pp10-11, p14, p18, p22, F 141n, 678-685, 708n, 710-3n, 715-6n, 729n, 730n, 1442-50n, 1504, 1506n, 1528-33nn, 1532-3, E 252n

Cleophon (8639, 2), tragic(?) poet (iv), F p9

Clouds, see Chorus (c)

Clytaem(n)estra, wife and murderer of Agamemnon, C 621n, T 560n, F 470-8n*, 951n, 1044n, 1126-68nn, We 134n, 647n, 935n

Cnemon, title-character of Menander's *Dyskolos,* P 743-2n, E p28, We 58n

Coalemus, see Blockhead

Cocytus, infernal river-god(?), F 472n

Coesyra (F1545) of Eretria, grandmother of Megacles (vi/v), A 614, C 48, 800, E 943n

Colaconymus ("Flatteronymus"), nickname for Cleonymus, W 592

Colotes of Heraclea, sculptor, B 515n

Comarchides, name of the chorus-leader in *Peace,* W 230n, P 1142

Comias, name of a member of the chorus, W 230, P 1142n

Comic Production (Comoedodidascalia), goddess/personification, K 517n*

Conisalus, an ithyphallic god, L 982

Connas, *see* Connus

Connus (8697, 1), son of Metrobius, musician, K 534*, W 675*, F 134n

Conon (8707, 21), son of Timotheus of Anaphlystus, admiral, F pp3-4, F 1512n, E pp2-3, p6, p7, E 102n, 195-6n, 197n, 201-3nn, 644-5n, 825n,

1107n, We pl, p2, p3, We 173n, 176n, 179n, 196n, 550n

Conon (8715, 41) of Paeonidae, member of a young men's hellfire club (iv), F 366n*, E 663-4n, We 597n
    sons of, E 640n

Corinthian Woman, L 77-253

Corinthus, eponymous hero of Corinth, F 439, E 828

Coronis, mother of Asclepius, We p8, p9, pll

Corpse, F 170-7

Corybantes, gods worshipped with ecstatic dancing, W 8*, 119, L 558, E 1069, We p10

Cranaus, an early king of Athens, A 75, B 123n, L 481

Crates of Athmonum, candidate for ostracism, T 861n

Crates (8739, 3), comic dramatist (v), A p8, K 537-540, B p2, T pll, E p8

Crates of Mallos, scholar (ii), A p4, P p.xix, We p29

Cratinus (8755, 2), son of Callimedes, comic dramatist, A p6, p7, p8*, p9, p24, p28, p32, A 530n, 848-853, 1173, K p2, K 400, 526-536*, 537n, 1225n, C p2, C 524n, P 700-3, F pll*, F 13-15n, 94-95n, 357, 765n, 1259n, We pp5-6, p27

Creditors:
    (a) **C 1215-58**
    (b) **C 1259-1301**

Creon, brother-in-law of Oedipus, L 450n, F 619n

Creusa, mother of Ion, L 721n, T p5

Critias (8792, 7), son of Callaeschrus, leader of the Thirty, C 876n, 1421-2n, B 1282n, F p10, F 541n, 1244n, E 385n

Critius (8796, 1), artist in bronze (v), L 633n, E 682n

Crito (8823, 18) of Alopece, friend of Socrates, W 386n

Critylla, one of the women in the Acropolis, L 323

Critylla, priestess of the Thesmophorian goddesses, **T p7, p8, 292-654, 759-946,** 1024-5, 1129n (named 898)

Crius ("Ram") of Aegina, aristocrat and wrestler (vi/v), C 1356*

Crobylus, see Hairbun

Croesus, king of Lydia (vi), L 254-387n*, We 287n, 1002n

Cronus, father of Zeus, K 561, C 381n, 398*, 905, 929, 1028-9*, 1070, W 652, 1480, B p2*, B 469, 586, 701-2n, E p8, We p6, p16, We 581

Ctesias (6), "informer", A 839

Ctesiphon, a fat man, A 1002

Curetes, Cretan gods associated with Zeus' infancy, L 558n

Cybele or Cybebe, "mother of the gods", W 8n, B 746, 874-5, L 2n, 3n, 558n, E 1068-9n

Cyclops (Polyphemus), one-eyed giant tricked by Odysseus, W 181-6nn, 193n, 1208n*, T 1218ff.n, F 299n, We 290-301

Cycnus, son of Poseidon, ally· of the Trojans, F 963

Cydias of Hermione, lyric poet (vi/v), C 967n

Cylon (8943, 1), would-be tyrant of Athens (vii), K 445-6n

Cynegeirus (8944, 1), son of Euphorion of Eleusis, killed at Marathon (vi/v), F 1296-7n

Cynna (1), a courtesan, K 765, W 1032, P 755, T 805n

Cypris, see Aphrodite

Cypselus, tyrant of Corinth (vii), K 1037n, F 1431n

Cyrene (1), a courtesan, T 98, F 1328

Cyrus, founder of the Persian empire (vi), We 1002n

Cyrus, younger son of Darius II of Persia, F p4, pp5-6*, p7, p13, F 365n, E pp1-2, We p3

Damastes, alternative name for Procrustes, E 1021n

Danaë, mother of Perseus, P 296-8n, T 1101n

Danaus, king of Egypt, F 1206-8nn
   daughters of, F 951n

Dancing-girls, A 1196-1234

Daos, slave in Menander's Aspis, P 742n, We p23

Dardanis, music-girl, W p.xviii, 1326-85

Darius I, king of Persia (vi/v), B 484, F p6, p10, F 1027n, 1028

Darius II, king of Persia, B 484n, L 1133n, F p4, pp5-6, p22, F 791n, E p1

Datis, Median general (v), P 289-291

Daughter(s):
   (a) of Dicaeopolis, A 241-283
   (b) of the Megarian, A 729-835, B p5
   (c) of Trygaeus, P 111-2, 113-149

Dawn, see Eos

Day, goddess/personification, E 105n

Death, god/personification, F 1392, E 905, 995-6(?), We 11n, 549n

Decanter (Stamnias), imaginary father for Dionysus, F 22

Decree-seller, B 1035-45, 1049-51, 1054-5, 128n

Deianeira, wife of Heracles, L 283n, T p5

Deidameia, princess of Scyros, mother by Achilles of Neoptolemus, T 406n

Deiphobus, son of Priam, who lived with Helen after Paris' death, L 155-6n

Delight (Tryphe), goddess/personification, E 974

Demaenetus (3265, 5), politician and general, K 648n*, L 397n, E 202-3n, 208n, We 550n

Demagogocleon, see Demologocleon

Demeter, goddess, A 47, 709(?), B 580, L 254-387n*, 643n, 1129-32n, T p11, T 299n, F 337, 338n, 383-393, 441, 444n, 446, 459n, 886-7, 892n, 1526-7n, E 18n, We p5, p8, We 515, 872
   and Kore ("the Two Goddesses", "the Thesmophorian Goddesses"), W 378, 1396, P 420n, L 113, 148, 452, 682, 731, T p10, T 83, 89, 101, 282, 285-8, 294n, 297, 299n, 301n, 312-330n*, 383, 566, 594, 655n, 658n, 718, 719n, 748n, 948, 1148-59, 1229, F p18, F 378n, 686n, E 18n, 155, 156, 158, 223[a]n, 443, 532, We p5, We 820n, 845n, 1006; see also Persephone
   Chloe, L 835
   sworn by, A 708, K 435, 461, 698, 812, 833, 942*, 1021, C 121, 455, W 629, 1442, B 517, L 271, 500, T 225, F

42, 668, 1067, 1222, E 662, We 64, 364, 555

Demetria, typical woman's name, C 684

Demetrius Poliorcetes, Macedonian dynast (iv/iii), We 1193n

Democracy, goddess/personification, E 685n

Democritus of Abdera, philosopher, C 377n, 380n*, 404-7n

Democritus of Chios, lyric poet, B 1385n

Demologocleon ("Demagogocleon"), nickname invented for Bdelycleon, W 342

Demophon (3701, 12), son of Hippocrates of Cholargus, reputed a half-wit, C 1001

Demos, the personified People of Athens, A p6, p11, K pp2-3*, K 40-62, 396, 710-727, **728-1263**, 1321-30*, **1331-1408**, P p.xvii, L 696-7n, F 345-9n, 1453n, 1510-4n, E pp11-12, E 685n, We 770/1n

Demos (3573, 1), son of Pyrilampes, in youth a noted beauty, A 63n, W 98, B 102-3n*, E 428n

Demosthenes (3585, 16), son of Alcisthenes of Aphidna, general, represented by a slave in *Knights,* A p11, **K** p3, **1-497, 742, 1254-6,** P 219n, L 104n, 394n, 800n

Demosthenes (3597, 37), son of Demosthenes of Paeania, orator (iv), A 704n*, K 1017n, C 353-4n, B 194n, 946n, 1403n, F 289-296n, 680-1n, 833-4n, E 22-23n, 252n, 356n, 808n, We 328n, 377-385n

Demostratus (3611, 4), politician, L 390-7, 398n

Demostratus (3612, 32) of Cerameis, archon 393/2, E p5

Demostratus (3620, 9), archon 390/89, E p5

Deo, see Demeter

Dercetes (3) of Phyle, farmer, **A 1018-36**

Dercippus, an old man in Menander's *Encheiridion,* We 332n

Dercylidas, Spartan general, E p2

Dercylus (3247, 1), W 78

Desire (Pothos), god/personification, P 456, B 1320

Destitution (Ptocheia), goddess/ personification, We 549

Dexinicus (1), politician(?), We 800

Dexitheus, citharode, A 14

Diagoras of Melos, atheist, C 229n*, 830n, W 377-8n, B 1073*, F 320

Diallage, see Reconciliation

Dicaearchus of Messene, scholar (iv/iii), F p21

Dicaeogenes (3771, 8), tragic poet (iv), F p9, E 1-18n

Dicaeopolis, hero of *Acharnians,* A p10, pp32-33*, **1-202,** 237, **241-327, 331-357, 366-625, 719-728,** 748, 749-815, 823, **824-835,** 836-859, **864-970,** 971-7, 988, **1003-1142,** 1143-9, 1196, **1198-1234,** K 1388-9n, C 1070n, P p.xvi, P 1000n, L p4, T p6, p9, T 776-784n, F 345-9n, 565n, 1039n, E p25, pp26-27, p32, E 49n, 277-9n, 400-2n, We p21, We 223n, 332n, 544n

Dictynna, goddess of hunting, W 368, F 1331-63n, 1358

Didymon, an adulterer (iv), We 312n

Didymus of Alexandria, scholar (i), A p16, P 1254n, F 55n

Dieitrephes (3755, 8), son of Nicostratus or Hermolycus of Scambonidae, general, B 798, 1442, L 103n

Dike, see Justice

Dindorf, Wilhelm, scholar (xix[P]), A p20

Dinos, see Vortex

Diocles, Megarian hero, A 774*

Diocles (3984, 7), archon 409/8, We p26, p28

Diocles (4061, 160) of Phlya, nicknamed Orestes, A 1167-8n

Diodotus (3889, 3), son of Eucrates, politician, K 834-5nn*

Diogenes of Apollonia, philosopher, C 229n*, 264n, 272n, 380n*, 627n

Diogenes of Sinope, Cynic philosopher (iv), We 312n, 885n

Diomedes, son of Ares, owner of man-eating mares (or daughters), E 1029n

Diomedes, son of Tydeus, hero of the Theban and Trojan wars, A 418-9n, W 351n, F 634n, E 1029

Diomedon (4065, 1), general, L p3, F pp3-4

Diomus, eponymous hero of the deme Diomeia, F 651n

Dionysius I, tyrant of Syracuse, A p8(?), B 1372-1409n, F 153n, E p4, E 246n, 330n, 825n, We p3, p17, p29, p30, We 290-321n, 550

Dionysius II, tyrant of Syracuse (iv), A p8(?)

Dionysius (4092, 17), general, We 550n

Dionysodorus of Chios, sophist, F 25-32n

Dionysus, god, A p13, A 247, 1224n, K 408, 536, C 311, 603-6, 1484-5n, W 9n, P 185-7n, 267, 348n, 442, 829n, B 95n, 276n, 558-9n, 873n, 918n, L 1n, 3n, 388n, 723-5n, 1282-4, T 134-5n, 136n, 140n*, 255-6n, 680n, 748n, 975n, 987-1000, F p6, p8, pp9-14*, p15*, pp16-17, p18, p19, p20, p23, 1-673, 694n, 738-743, 759n, 765n, 810-1, 830-1481, 1500-33, E p27, p28, E 14, 39n, 332n, 346n, 772n, We p27, We 46n, 287n, 327n, 929n, 935n, 1129n

  priest of, A 1087, F 297, E p27

  sworn by, C 91, 108, 519, 1000, W 1046, 1474, P 109, 1277, B 171, 501, 1370, E 344, 357, 422

Diopeithes (4309, 3), politician, K 1085*, W 380, B 988

Diopeithes of Sparta(?), expert on oracles, W 380n, B 988n

Dioscuri, see Castor and Pollux

Diotima of Mantinea, wise woman quoted by Socrates in Plato's *Symposium,* A pp7-8, E 3n

Dirce, water-nymph, T 855n

Dissident, E pp20-21, p25, p28, p30, p32, E 221-8n, 471-2n, 730-745n, 746-876, We p20

Ditylas, a Scythian archer, F 608, 609-622

Divus, Andreas, Italian scholar (xvi[P]), T p14

Doco(?) (1), mother of Hyperbolus, C 552, T 785-845n*, 839-845

Dog of Cydathenaeum, see Hound

Donkey:

  (a) W 169-178, 179-197*

  (b) F 1-37

Doorkeeper, L 1216

Dorilaus (Δόριλλος 1), tragic dramatist, T p4

Dorkion, name for a prostitute/courtesan, T 1172n

Doro, comic goddess of bribery, K 529

Draces, stock name for a member of a chorus, A 612n, E 293, L 254

Dracis, name of a satyr in Sophocles' *Ichneutae,* L 254n

Dracon (4553, 1), codifier of the Athenian homicide laws (vii), C 1425-6n, F 1167-8n

Dracontides (4549, 9) of Bate, father of Lysimache, W 157n

Dracontides (4551, 14), son of Leogoras of Thorae, politician and general, W 157n

Dracontides (4546, 4) of Aphidna, politician, W 157n`

Dracontides, a prospective defendant, W 157, 438

Dracyllus, name of a member of the chorus, A 612, L 254n, E 293n

Dread Goddesses (Semnae), worshipped near the Areopagus, K 1312, T 224, F 1525n

Earth (Ge, Gaea), progenitress of all the gods, C 364, 366, P 188, 1117, B 194, 469n, 470-7, 586, 693n, 702, 971n, 1230n, T 11-18n, We p16, We 771n

  children of, *see* Giants, Titans

Echidna, a monster, F 473*

Echo, goddess/personification, T p8, 1007-81n, 1015n, 1018-21, 1056-97*

Ecphantides (4654, 2), comic dramatist, W 151n

Eileithyia, see Hileithya

Elaphion, see Fawn

Electra, daughter of Agamemnon, C 534, L 283n, T p5, F 304n

Empedocles of Acragas, philosopher and poet (v), C 377n, B 586n, 700n

Empusa, a monster, F p12, F 285-307, E 1056

Enipeus, river-god, L 139n

Enyalius, god of war, P 457

Eos, goddess of dawn, F 963n, 1365n

Epaenetus of Andros, lover of Neaera and of her daughter, We 168n

Ephialtes (6157, 1), son of Sophonides, politician (v), A p8*, L 1137-44n

Ephorus of Cyme, historian (iv), P 603-4n, F 1032n, 1266n*

Ephudion of Maenalus, pancratiast (v), W 1191-4, 1383-5

Epialus (or Epiales or Epioles), nightmare-demon, W 1038-9nn*, E 639-640n

Epicharmus of Syracuse, comic dramatist (v), A p8*, C p2*, We p7

Epicrates (4859, 70) of Cephisia, politician, E p7, E 71, 97n, 102n, 195-6n, 248n

Epicrates of Ambracia, comic dramatist (iv), E p10

Epicurus (4853, 3), (?)son of Paches (q.v.), E 644-5

Epigenes, a young man in love, E p21, p29, p30, p31, p32, E 877-1111n, 912, 931-6, **938-1111**, 1112-26n, 1150n, We p20, We 904n, 1092n, 1201n

Epigonus (107), a man who could be taken for a woman, E 167-8

Epimenides Buzyges, ancestor of the Buzygae, L 397n

Erasinides (5021, 1), politician and general, F p2, F 417n, 1196

Eratosthenes ([5035], 3) of Oë, allegedly a serial adulterer, L 723-5n, We p15

Eratosthenes of Cyrene, scholar (iii/ii), P p.xix, T 395*, We p28

Erebus, the primeval Darkness, B 691, 693, 694, 1193

Erechtheus, an early king of Athens, K 1015, 1022, 1030, We p21

Ergasion, a wine-grower, W 1201

Ergocles (5052, 2), general, We p2, We 381n, 385n, 483n, 550n, 567-570n

Erichthonius, early Athenian hero, L 759n, T 17n

Erinyes, see Furies

Eris, see Strife

Eros, god of sexual desire, A 991-2, B 574, 693n, 695n, 696-700, 703, 704n, 1737, L 551, E 3n, 958, 966, 1032n

Eryxis (5090, 2 = 5191, 3), son of Philoxenus of Cephisia, military officer(?), F 934

Eteocles, son of Oedipus, P 1270n, F 1021n

Eteonicus, Spartan admiral, F p7, We p3

Euaeon (5253, 1), a poor man, E pp18-19, E 18n, 408-421

Euagoras, king of Salamis (Cyprus), E p4, We p3, We 178n

Euathlus (5238, 1), son of Cephisodemus, a frequent prosecutor, A 704-712, W 592, 666-7n, 947n

Eubule, typical woman's name, T 808

Eubulus (5359, 37), son of Euphranor of Cettus, comic dramatist (iv), A p3

Eubulus (5369, 61), son of Spintharus of Probalinthus, politician (iv), A p28, B 762n

Eucharides (14), greengrocer, W 680

Eucleides (5674, 9), archon in 403/2, B 1662n, We 1193n

Eucles (5732, F7636), son of Philocles, herald of the Council and People, E 825n

Eucrates (5759, 41) of Melite, politician, K 129*, 254, L 103n

Eucrates (5757, 36), son of Niceratus of Cydantidae, general, L 103

Eucrates of Corinth, lover of Neaera (iv), We 1003n

Eudamus or Eudemus, dealer in drugs, amulets, etc., We 884

Euelpides, companion of Peisetaerus, B p3, p4, p5, **1-675***, **801-847**, 1122-63n*, E 133n

Euenus, Aetolian hero, F 194n

Euenus of Paros, sophist, C 876n

Euergides, a deceased ex-juryman, W 234

Euetion (5460, 1), general, B 1369n

Eumolpus, founder of the Eleusinian Mysteries, F 145-153n, 1033n

Eunuchs, A **94-125**

Euphemius (1), a man widely regarded as worthless, W 599

Euphiletus (6049, 4), speaker of Lysias 1, E 1056-7n, We p15, We 168n

Euphorides, name of a member of the chorus, A 612

Euphorion (6079, 2), son of Aeschylus of Eleusis, tragic dramatist, We p5

Euphranor of Corinth, painter and sculptor (iv), E 685n

Euphronius, Alexandrian scholar (iii), A p16, We 385n

Eupolis (5936, 1), son of Sosipolis, comic dramatist, A p4*, p7, p24, p28, p29, p32, K p4*, K 1225n, 1288-9n, C p2*, C 553-6*, P p.xv, F p9, p11

Euripides (5953, 13), son of Mnesarchides of Phlya, tragic dramatist, A pp4-5, p6, p10, p12, p13, 394-409, **410-479**, 484,. K 18, 522n, C 265n, 627n, 1358n*, 1369-72, 1377-8, W 61, 1414, P 126n, 147, 532-4, B 1444-5n, L 283, 368, 369n, 706-717n, 1222n, T p1, pp4-6, pp7-10, p11, **1-279**, 331-351n, 337, 377-9, 386-431, 434n, 437n, 450-6, 465-519, 530n, 542, 584-591, 649, 660n, 693-5n, 766-9, 776-784n, 778n, 781n, **871-927**, 1008-14, 1015n, 1039-46, 1056-97n*, 1061, 1092n, **1098-1132**, **1160-1209**, 1218ff.n*, F p1, pp7-9, p10, p12, p13, pp14-17*, p19, p20, p23, F 25-32n, 52-53n, 57n, 64n, 66-71, 71-88n, 73n, 76, 80-81, 91, 96-106, 177n, 209-268n, 311n, 686-7n, 758, 771-8, 791n, 794, 797-801n, 801-2, 814-829, **830-1478***, 1491-9, 1520-1, E p25, p27, p28, E 18n, 1182n, We p5, p30, We 385n, 544n, 647n, 929n, 935n
imitates Ar.?, B 213-4n, T 255-6n
marriages of, F 944n*
mother of, *see* Cleito

Euripides (5952, 14), son of the above, We 647n

Euripides (politician), *see* Heurippides

Euripides' Relative, see Inlaw

Euryalus, bastard son of Odysseus, T 547-8n

Eurycles, ventriloquist, W 1019

Eurydice, wife of Orpheus, F p9

Eurymedon, name of a character on an early fifth-century oinochoe, F 57n

Eurymedon (5973, 2), son of Thucles, general, K 355n, 742n, W 965n

Eurystheus, king of Tiryns and enemy of Heracles, We 385n

Eurytion, centaur slain by Heracles, F 38n

Euthydemus of Chios, sophist, F 25-32n

Euthymenes (5640, 3), archon in 437/6, A 67

Execestides (20), allegedly a false pretender to citizenship, B 11, 764, 1527

Execestides, lyre-player, B 11n

Fates (Moirai), B 1734, T 700, F 453

Fawn (Elaphion), a dancing-girl, T **1160-1201**, **1210-4**, 1218ff.n*

Flamingo, B 267n, **268-?***

"Flatteronymus", *see* Colaconymus

Follies (Bereskhethoi), gods of stupidity(?) invoked by the Sausage-seller, K 635

Fraud (Apaeole), divinity invoked by Strepsiades, C 1150

Frogs, subsidiary chorus in *Frogs*, A p28, F p12, F 205-7, **209-268**

Fullfruit (Opora), attendant of Peace, afterwards bride to Trygaeus, P p.xvii*, **520-728***, **819-855**, **1329-59**

Furies (Erinyes), hideous goddesses of vengeance, L 810, T 224n, F 294n, 472n, 1126n, E p23, We 423-5

Gabinius, A., Roman politician (i), F 420n

Gaea, see Earth

Galanthis or *Galinthias, see* Acalanthis

Galatea, sea-nymph loved by Polyphemus, We 290-301nn

Ganymede, cupbearer and catamite of Zeus, P 724

Garland-seller, T **292-458**, E 877-1111n

Ge, see Earth

Gellius Poplicola, L., friend then enemy of Catullus (i), E 470n, We 295n

Georgia, see Agriculture

Geras, see Old Age

Geres (1), ambassador, A 605, E 932(?)

Genetyllis, Genetyllides, goddess(es) of procreation, C 52, L 2, T 130

Geron (1), a poor, elderly man, E 848-9; *see also* Hieron

Geryon(es), monster slain by Heracles, A 1082, K 416n

Getas, slave in Menander's *Dyskolos*, E p31, We p23, We 958/9n

Geusistrate, a member of the chorus, E 49

Giants, defeated by the Olympian gods at Phlegra, B 824, 1250n, F 825n

Girl(s)
(a) E pp21-22*, pp25-26, p29, p31, p32, E 327-356n, 877-1111n, **884-936,**

938, 942, 947-8, **949-968***, 970-5,
998n, **1037-51**, 1051-70n, 1054-5,
1080, 1111-2n, We 1201n
(b/c) E p13, p25, **1129-79**
see also Dancing-girl(s), Dardanis,
    Daughter(s), Peace-terms
Giunta, Bernardo di, Italian editor (xvi[P]), T
    p14
Glanis, alleged source of the Sausage-
    seller's oracles, K 1004, 1035, 1097
Glauce, Corinthian princess, wife of Jason,
    murdered by Medea, P 1014n*
Glaucetes (2944, 1), a gourmand, P 1008, T
    1033
Glaucippus (2979, 4), archon 410/09, We
    p28
Glaucothea (2989, 1), daughter of Glaucus
    of Acharnae, mother of the orator
    Aeschines, W 9n, F 289-296n
Glaucus of Potniae, who was eaten by his
    own horses, F 1403n
Glaucus, son of Minos, raised from the
    dead by Polyidus, F 1082n
Glyce, poultry-thief, F 1331-63n, 1337n,
    1342-3, 1344n, 1352n, 1363, E 43n
Glyce, a member of the chorus, E 43
Glycera, a young woman in Menander's
    Perikeiromene, E 994-7
Gnathaena, courtesan (iv/iii), L 962n
Gobbler-bird, B 287-?*
Godschild (Amphitheus), son of Demeter
    and Triptolemus, A 47
Godschild (Amphitheus), an immortal,
    great-grandson of the above, **A 45-
    55***, 57-58, **129-133**, **175-203***,
    216n*, We p21
Goliath, Philistine giant, T 822n
Good Spirit (Agathos Daimon), K 85, 106-
    8, W 525, 1217n, P 300, E 1123n
Gorgasus, mocking patronymic for
    Lamachus, A 1131
Gorgias of Leontini, rhetorician, A p6, W
    421*, B 636-7n, 1701, T 5-21n*,
    29n, 1102-3n, F 83n, 1021n, E 571n
Gorgias, Cnemon's stepson in Menander's
    Dyskolos, E p28, p31, We 958/9n
Gorgon(s), hideous female monster(s), A
    567n, 574, 964, 1095, 1181, P 474n,
    561, 810, L 560, T p8, T 1011-2n,

1101, 1103, F 289-296n, 477, 929n,
    963n, 1039n
Gorgopas, Spartan commander, We p2
Gorgus, secretary to an unknown state
    board, T 1102-4
Graces (Charites), goddesses of beauty, A
    989, C 773, P 41, 456, 797, B 782,
    1100-1, 1320, L 1279, T 101-129n,
    122, 301, F 334, 1299-1300n*, E 974
Great King, the, *see* Artaxerxes I,
    Artaxerxes II, Cambyses, Cyrus,
    Darius I, Darius II, Xerxes I
Grypus (Γρύππος 1), disfranchised for
    having been a male prostitute, K 877,
    E 365n
Groomsman, **A 1048-1066***
Gylippus, Spartan general, L 57n

Hades, lord of the underworld, W 763; *see
    also* Pluto
Hagnon (171, 22), son of Nicias of Steiria,
    politician and general, L 421n, F
    970n
Hairbun (Crobylus), supposed ancestor of
    Amynias, W 1267
Hard Man, The, see Orthagoras
Harmodius (2232, 1), tyrannicide (vi), A
    980, 1093, K 449n, 786*, W 1225, L
    619n, 632n, 634n, 664n, E 682, 834n,
    938-945n, 943n
Harmodius (2) of Aphidna, A 1093n, K
    786n*
Harpies, hideous female monsters, P 811
Harpocration, lexicographer (ii[P]), L 152n
Hauainos, comic distortion of the name of a
    hero(?), F 194n
Health, see Hygieia
Heath, Sir Edward, English politician
    (xx/xxi[P]), K 44n
Heaven, see Uranus
Hecate, goddess, W 804, L 64*, 443, 700,
    738, T 858, F 293n, 366*, 1144-5n,
    1331-63n, 1361-2, E 70, 330n, 1097,
    We p18, We 594-7, 764, 1070
Hector, son of Priam, L 520n, 1255-8n, F
    828n
Hecuba, queen of Troy, L 283n, T p5, T
    838n, F 956n, 1331-7n, We 424n,
    541n
Hegelochus (10), actor, F 303-4, E 22-23n

Hegesander (6307, 11), son of Hegesias of Sunium, lover of Timarchus (iv), E 103n

Helen, wife of Menelaus, whose elopement with Paris caused the Trojan War, A 524-5n*, B 1104n, 1639n, L 155, 191-2n, 723-5n, 1162-3n, 1314, T p6, p7, p8, T 480n, 547-8n, 838n, 850-919, 975n, F p10, p11, F 956n, 1331-63n, 1425n, E 225n, 1098-1111n

Helenus, a Trojan seer, We p11

Heliodorus, metrician (i[p]), P 1359*

Helios, see Sun

Hellanicus of Lesbos, historian and mythographer, B 1021n

Helle, daughter of Athamas, drowned in the Hellespont, C 257n, W 308, F 1225-6n

Hellen, eponymous ancestor of the Hellenic people, F 1244n

Helmet-maker, P 1208-64

Hemera (goddess), see Day

Hephaestion, close friend of Alexander the Great (iv), C 621n*, W 392n

Hephaestus, god of fire and metalwork, C 1063n, We 661
temple of, B 1556n

Hera, goddess, P 1078n, 1126n, B 1104n, 1536n, 1633, 1654n, 1731, 1741, L 1286, T 974-6, F p11, E 80n

Heracleides (6489, F2901), politician, a naturalized Clazomenian, E 301n

Heracles, hero/god, A p4*, p7*, A 284, 807, 1018, 1082n, C 184-202, 257n, 1048-52, 1372n, W 60, 420, P 180, 422n, 699n, 741*, 1078n, B p3, B 93, 277, 553n, 558-9n, 567, 814, 859, 1129, 1242n, 1470-81n*, 1565-1693, L 254-387n*, 283n, 296, 577-8n, 678n, 928, T p5, T 26, F p9, p10, p11*, p12, p13, p20, 1-20n, 35-37n, 38-165, 187n, 273-4n, 278-282, 289-296n, 298, 311n, 323-459n, 430n, 431-3n, 460ff.n, 463, 464n, 465-6n, 468n*, 470-8n*, 495n, 499, 501n, 503, 504-511nn*, 518n, 523, 531, 560n, 565n*, 581, 582, 588n, 592n, 593, 594n, 634n, 635n, 651, 1033n, 1206-8n, 1468n, 1469n, E p27, p28,

E 76n, 328n, 639-640n, 1068, We p8, We 69-70n, 374, 417, 586n, 1127n
Aristophanes compared to, W 1029-43, P 752-760, We 417n
children of, We 385
daughter of, in Euripides, We 385n
sworn by, A 860, K 481, W 757, B 1391, We 337

Heraclitus of Ephesus, philosopher (vi/v), C p2*, C 627

Herald:
(a) A 40-173, 1000-2, 1004
(b) B 844-5, 1269-70, 1271-1307
(c) B 1706-19
(d) L 723-5n, 980-1013

Heraldess, E p30, p31, p32, E 713, 832n, 834-852
see also Critylla

Hermaphroditus, androgynous god, We 1126n

Hermes, god, A 816, K 639*, C 1234*, 1478-85, P p.xvi, p.xvii*, 180-233, 362-728*, 924, B 572-3, 1176n, 1203-4n, 1552n, 1673n, T 301, 977, 1202, F p9, F 39n, 234n, 465-6n, 911-2n, 1126, 1138, 1141-9, 1169, 1266, E p27, E 80n, We p10, p13, p16, p21, p26, p30, We 288-9n, 660n, 820n, 1097-1170, 1173n, 1189-90n, 1194-1209n
images of, mutilated, P 395n, B 1556n, L 103n, 489n, 490n, 1093-4*, 1099n
pours libation to himself, P 433-457n*, 456
sworn by, A 742, 779, K 297, C 1277, P 963, E 445

Hermione, daughter of Menelaus and Helen, L 276n, T p5, F 121-134n, 750n, E 1098-1111n

Hermippus (5112, 1), son of Lysis, comic dramatist, A p8, C 557

Hermocrates of Syracuse, politician, K 1303n

Hermolycus (5164, 7), son of Euthoenus of Scambonidae, athlete and war hero (v), B 798n

Herodotus of Halicarnassus, historian, C 1420n, B 1125-31n, 1130n, 1145n, L 759n, E p16

Hesiod of Ascra, didactic poet (viii/vii?), B 685-702n, 1193n, F p14*, F 1033*, We 50n

Hestia, goddess of the hearth, W 844, 846, B 95n, 864, 865n, We 395, 768-9n

Hesychia, see Tranquillity

Heurippides (5949=5955=5956, =Euripides 11), son of Adeimantus of Myrrhinûs, politician, E p5, p6, p7, E 823-9

Hierocles (7473, 2), expert on oracles, **P** p.xvii, 1024n, 1031n*, **1043-1125***, B 959n, 975n

Hieron I, tyrant of Syracuse (v), B 926-7, 945n

Hieron (7522, 8), auctioneer, E 757, 848n

Hieronymus (2), son of Xenophantus, tragic poet, A 389*, C 349*

Hieronymus (7552, 3), politician and general, E p7, E 201

Hileithya, goddess of childbirth, L 742, E 369

Hipparchides (1), ambassador, A 603

Hipparchus (7598, 1), son of Peisistratus (vi), A 980n, K 786n, W 1225n, 1410n, L 619n, 632n, 665n, 1150-6n, E 682n, 943n

Hippias (7605, 1), son of Peisistratus, tyrant of Athens (vi/v), A 980n, K 449, 786n, W 502, 1225n, B 1074-5n, L 619, 632, 664n, 665n, 1150-6n, 1153, T 331-351n, E 682n, 943n

Hippias of Elis, sophist, C p3, B 1005n

Hippo, mother of Melanippe, L 1126-7*

Hippocinus, obscenely distorted form of Hipponicus, F 429

Hippocrates (7640, 18), son of Ariphron of Cholargus, general, K 479n, T 273(?) sons of, C 1001; see also Demophon, Pericles, Telesippus

Hippocrates of Chios, mathematician and astronomer, B 1005n

Hippodameia, daughter of Oenomaus, F 1232-3n

Hippodamus of Miletus, town planner (v), K 327*, B 1001-9n

Hippolyte or Astydameia, wife of Acastus, C 1063n

Hippolytus, bastard son of Theseus, A p4*, B 1372-1409n, L 785n, T 153n, F 101-2n, 1043n

Hippomenes, in some accounts the successful suitor of Atalanta, L 785n

Hippon of Samos(?), natural philosopher (v), C 95-96n, B 1001n

Hipponax of Ephesus, iambic poet (vi), B 904-953n*, L 361, F 661, We p6

Hipponicus (7658, 13), son of Callias sr. of Alopece, general, B 283, F 429

Hippopenis, see Hippocinus

Hippostratus, a man prosecuted by Cleon(?), K 247n

Hippothoon, son of Poseidon and Alope, B 558-9n

Hippyllus (7672, 1), W 1301*

Historis, see Acalanthis

Homer of Chios(?), epic poet (viii/vii?), C 1056, P 1089, 1096, B 575, 910, 914, F p14*, F 814-829nn, 868n, 924n, 1004n, 1016-7n, 1033n, 1034*, 1035-6n, 1038n, 1039n, 1040n, 1144-5n, We 937n

Homichle, see Mist

Honest Man, W 248n, E p28, **We p15, p20,** p25, p26, We 782-3n, **823-958,** 1194-1209n

Honour or Shame (Aidos), goddess/ personification, C 995

Hoopoe: (a) see Tereus (b) B 279-?*

Horae, see Seasons

Hound of Cydathenaeum, A p3, K 775n, W 841-3, 894-7, **899-1008**, F 569n, E p31; see also Cleon

Hounds, the, recipients of preliminary offerings at Asclepiea, We p10, We 660n

Hunt, Sir David, English diplomat and Hellenist (xx[P]), L 1234n

Hunters, the, recipients of preliminary offerings at Asclepiea, We p10, We 660n

Hurlyburly (Kydoimos), servant to War, **P 255-262, 268-275, 279, 280-8**

Hyades, daughters of Atlas who became stars, P 832-3n*, L 254-387n*

Hybrias, reputed composer of a popular song, B 1697-9n

Hydra, monster slain by Heracles, F 473n

Hygieia (Health), goddess/personification, B 603; daughter of Asclepius, We 639n

Hylas, beautiful youth loved by Heracles, We 1127n

Hylas, a slave of Demos, K 67

Hyllus, son of Heracles, We 385n

Hymen(aeus), god of weddings, P 1332-56, B 1736, 1742

Hyperbolus (13910, 5), son of Antiphanes of Perithoidae, politician, A p6, A 846, K 173-4n, 739n, 864-7n, 1300-15, 1363, 1377n, C p2, C 551-8, 615-6n, 623-5, 876, 1065-6, W 1007, P p.xvi, p.xvii, P 680-692, 921, 1319, B 440-1n, L p4, L 1270n, T 804n, 840, F 570, 678n, 710-3n, 1039n, E 252n, We 175n

mother of, *see* Doco

Hypereides (13912, 3), son of Glaucippus of Collytus, politician (iv), We p12

Hypermestra, the only daughter of Danaus not to murder her bridegroom, F 1206-8n

Hypnos, see Sleep

Hypsipyle, princess of Lemnos, F 1211-3, 1305-28nn, E p10

Iacchus, Eleusinian god identified with Dionysus, T 975n, F p13, F 313-4n, 316-7, 320, 323-336, 338n, 340-353, 357n, 394-413, 414-5n, 886n, 1517-8n

Iadmon of Samos, master of Aesop (vi), W 566n, P 129n, B 471n

Iapetus, brother of Cronus, C 998

Iasius or *Iasion*, mortal lover of Demeter, T 299n, We p5

Iaso, daughter of Asclepius or Amphiaraus, We p20, We 639n, 660n, 701

Ibycus of Rhegium, lyric poet (vi), T 161-3

Idas, son of Aphareus, L 118n, We 210n

Imbecility, see Blockhead

Imps (Kobaloi), gods of mischief invoked by the Sausage-seller, K 635, We 508n

Inachus, king of Argos, B 1203-4n, We 802-818n, 1189-90n

Incapacity, goddess/personification, We 549n

Informer:
  (a) **A 818-828**
  (b) **B** 1332-3n, **1410-68**, We 31n, 921-5n
  (c) B 1423n, E 1027n, **We** p4, p13, p15, p17, p20, p25, p26, We 824n, **850-954**, 955-7, 958-9n
  see also Nicarchus

Initiates, see Chorus (j)

Inlaw of Euripides, chief character of *Thesmophoriazusae*, A p26, T pp6-9, p11, p12, **1-946, 1001-1209**, 1212, 1218ff.n*, 1219-20, E p28, E 332n, We 476n

wife of, T 1021, 1206

Innkeeper, **F 549-578**; *see also* Plathane

Ino, daughter of Cadmus and wife of Athamas, A 434, C 257n, W 1414, F 1225-6n

Inspector, **B** p6, **1021-32, 1046-8, 1052-3**

Intellect, see Sagacity

Invernizi, Filippo, scholar (xviii[p]), A p20

Io, daughter of Inachus, loved by Zeus, B 1203-4n, F 1208n, E 80n

Iolaus, nephew of Heracles, A 867, We 385n

Ion, son of Apollo and ancestor of the Ionians, B 525n, L 721n

Ion of Chios, poet and prose-writer, P 835-7*, F p7, F 82n

Ion of Ephesus, rhapsode, F 1035-6n

Iophon (7584, 7), son of Sophocles of Colonus, tragic dramatist, C 1484-5n*, F 73, 78-79

Iphicrates (7737, 4), son of Timotheus of Rhamnûs, general, K 281n*, E 810n, We p1, We 173n

Iphigeneia, daughter of Agamemnon, L 217n, 447n, T p6, T 1218ff.n, F 1232-3n, E 1056-7n, We 647n

as daughter of Theseus and Helen, T 480n

Iphitus, son of Eurytus, murdered by Heracles, We 69-70n

Iris, goddess of the rainbow, **B** p6, B 575, 576n, 1172-85, 1197-8, **1199-1261**,

1494-1552n*, 1596-7n, F 470-8n, We 1099n

Isagoras (7680, 1), son of Teisander, politician (vi), L 273n

Ischomachus (?=7725/6/7, 1), character in Xenophon's *Oeconomicus*, L 894-5n

Ischys, lover of Coronis, We p8, p9

Ismene, daughter of Oedipus, L 676n

Ismenia, a Theban woman, L 77-**253**, 697

Ismenias or *Ismenichus*, servant of the Theban, **A 860-958**

Isocrates (7716, 13), son of Theodorus of Erchia, rhetorician and educator, B p5, E 571n, We 180n

Isyllus of Epidaurus, poet (iv/iii), We p9

Itys, son of Tereus and Procne, B 15-16n, 100-1n, 212, L 563n, F 683-4n

Jason, leader of the Argonauts, K 1321n, P 629n*, 1014n*, E p10

Jocasta, mother and wife of Oedipus, F 1193n

Junket, see Showtime (P 523n*)

Jurymen, see Chorus (d)

Just Argument, see Better Argument

Just Man, see Honest Man

Justice (Dike), goddess, C 902-6, B 1240, 1536n, 1753n

Kapnias ("Old Smoky"), a nickname, W 151, 324n, F 22n

Kesey, Ken, American novelist (xx[P]), F 430n

Kitchen Utensils, **W 936-9, 940-1008**

Knights, see Chorus (b)

Kobaloi, see Imps

Kore, see Demeter and Kore, Persephone sworn by, W 1438

Kourotrophos, see Nurser of the Young

Küster, Ludolph, scholar (xviii[P]), A p20

Kydoimos, see Hurlyburly

Labes, dog accused of stealing cheese, W 835-843, 893-8, **899-1008**, 1151n, E p31; *see also* Laches

Lacedaemonius (8965, 3), son of Cimon of Laciadae, politician and general, K 407n, L 1138n

Lachares, reputedly a former male prostitute, E 97n

Laches (9019=9010, 25), son of Melanopus of Aexone, politician and general, A p6, W p.xv, p.xvi, p.xviii*, W 62n, 240-4*, 288n, 836n, 895n, 924-5n, 926n, 952-965nn; *see also* Labes

Laches, a member of the chorus, L 304

Lacrateides, an eponymous archon (vi/v), A 220n

Lacrateides, name of a member of the chorus, A 220

Laertes, father of Odysseus, We 312

Laespodias (8963, 5) of Coele(?), politician, B p1, B 1569, F 153n

Laïs of Corinth, courtesan, We p28, p29, We 179n

Laius, father of Oedipus, F 1185n

Lamachus (8981, 7), son of Xenophanes of Oe(?), general, A 270, 566-8*, **572- 622***, 625, 722, 960-8, 1071, **1072- 1141**, 1143-6, **1190-1226**, P 241n, 304, 473-4, B p5, B 363n, L 560n, 1270n, F 1039, 1478n, E 400-2n

mother of, T 841

son of, *see* Boy (c), Tydeus

Lamia, a child-eating ogress, W 1035, 1177, P 758, E 76-80nn

Lamius, nickname of Mnesitheus (q.v.), E 77

Lampas (1), courtesan (iv/iii), E 1150n

Lampito, mother of Agis II of Sparta, L 77n

Lampito, a Spartan woman, L p3, **77-244**, 696, 830n, 998, 1148n

Lampon (8996, 3), diviner and expounder of religious law, C 332, P 1084n*, B 521, 988, We 396n

Lamprocles (1), lyric poet (v), C 967n

Lamynthius of Miletus, lyric poet, F 1302n

Lartius, see Laertes

Lasus of Hermione, lyric poet (vi), W 1410-1*

Leaena (4), mistress of Harmodius or Aristogeiton (vi), A 1093n*

Leda, mother of Castor, Pollux, Helen and Clytaemestra, L 1314, T 860n

Leocrates (9083, 3), alleged traitor (iv), F 953

Leogoras (9075, 7), son of Andocides of Cydathenaeum, a very rich man, C 109, W 1269, T 805n, F 678n

Leon (9100, 5), general, L p3, F 1431n

Leonidas, king of Sparta (v), L 1254

Leotrophides (9159=9160, 1=2), afterwards a general, B 1406

Leto, goddess, mother of Apollo and Artemis, K 1081, B 870, T 101-129n, 118, 120, 123, 129, 321, 332-3n, F 1361-2n

Leucippus, brother of Tyndareos, We p8

Leucippus of Miletus(?), philosopher, C 377n, 380n*

Leucolophides (9061, 2) of Scambonidae, father of Adeimantus, B 1311n, F 1512

Leucolophus (2) son of Adeimantus of Scambonidae, F 1512n, E 644-5 see also Leucolophides

Leucon (9065, 2), comic dramatist, W p.xv, P p.xv

Libanius of Antioch, rhetorician (ivᵖ), A p17*

Lichas, Heracles' herald, We 69-70n

Licymnius, half-brother of Alcmene, killed by Tle(m)polemus, B 1242

Light Infantrymen (Odomanti from Thrace). A 155-173

Love, see Eros in Empedocles' cosmogony, B 700n

Loxias, see Apollo

Lucian of Samosata, prose humorist (iiᵖ), B p2, F 464n, E 891n

Lyca, courtesan (iv), We p6

Lyceas (9191, 1), alleged to be a bastard(?), B 11n

Lycinus, father of Godschild, A 50

Lycis (5), comic poet, F 14

Lycon ([9271], [19]), father of Autolycus, W 1301*, L 270

Lycon (9271, 19) of Thoricus, accuser of Socrates, W 1301n, L 270n

Lycophron (9255, 2), a client of Hypereides, We 948-9n

Lycurgus, king of the Edonians and enemy of Dionysus, T 135-6, F 605-673n*

Lycurgus (9249, 3), son of Lycomedes of Butadae, an aristocrat with interests in Egypt, B 1296*

Lycurgus (9251, 4), son of Lycophron and grandson of the above, politician, B 1296n, 1463n, T 395*, We 1013-4n

Lycus, Athenian hero, W 389-394*, 819-823, 875n

Lycus, son of Pandion, uncle and enemy of Theseus, W 389n

Lynceus, the only son of Aegyptus not murdered by his bride, F 1206-8nn

Lynceus, son of Aphareus, L 118n, We 210

Lysander, Spartan general, B 1427n, F p4, p6, p7, p22, F 365n, 1299-1300n*, 1422n, 1431n, E p1, p2, E 243n

Lysanias (9324, 53) of Sphettus, friend of Socrates, C 1162n*

Lysanias (9312, 54) of Thoricus, father of Dexileos, C 1162n*

Lysias (F6988), son of Cephalus, metic speechwriter, B 1372-1409n, F p22, F 157, E 593n, 602n, We 550n

Lysicles (9417, 4), politician and general, K 132, 173-4n, 765

Lysicrates (9443, 2), politician or official, B 513

Lysicrates (44), short man who dyed his hair black, E 630, 736

Lysilla, typical woman's name, C 684, T 374

Lysimache (9470, 1=7), daughter of Dracontides of Bate, priestess of Athena Polias, P 992, L p5, L 554; see also Lysistrata

Lysistrata, heroine of Lysistrata, A p12, B 491n, L pp3-5, 1-253*, 430-613, 706-780, 829-864, 1012n, 1086, 1103-4, 1106-88, 1273-1321*, F 942n, E pp8-9, p26, p27, p28, E 261n, W 770/1n

Lysistratus (9630, 39) of Cholargus, a poor man noted for verbal and practical jokes, A 855-9*, 1267, W 787-795, 1302*, 1308-13, E 408n

Lysistratus (9611, 9=37), son of Macareus of Amphitrope(?), reputedly a passive homosexual, W 787n, L 1105

Macareus, son of Aeolus, who raped his sister, C 1371n, F 850n, 1081n, 1475n, 1491-2n

Macaria, see Heracles, daughter of

Machaon, son of Asclepius, We p8, p9, p11, We 639n

Magistrate (Proboulos), L p4, L 1-3n, **387-610**, T p7, F 1478n

Magnes (9651, 1) of Icaria, comic dramatist (v), A p8, K 520-5*, F p11, F 15

Maid(servant(s)):
  (a) of Persephone, **F 503-520**
  (b) of the innkeepers, **F 549-571**
  (c) of Praxagora, E p12, pp21-22*, p25, p27, p30, p31, p32, E 1111-2n, **1112-79**
  (d) of the Old Woman, **We 959-1094**

Maleatas or *Maleates,* healing god, We 660n; *see also* Apollo (sub-entry "... and Asclepius")

Manes, a slave, **L 845-908**
  see also Manodorus *and* P 1146*, B 523n, L 1212, F 965n, 1344n

Mania, nurse to Mica, **T 292-764**

Mania, the upstairs neighbour(?), F 1344n, 1345

Manodorus or Manes, slave to Peisetaerus, **B 1-450***, **451-464, 465-675, 851-1057, 1187-1312, 1317, 1324, 1326-9, 1335-6, 1468-9, 1579-1693**

Manto, daughter of Teiresias, We 41-43n

Marilades, name of a member of the chorus, A 609

Marpsias (1), nickname (?) of a frequent prosecutor, A 702

Masyntias, a slave, W 433, **435-522**

Medea, Colchian sorceress and mistress of Jason, K 1321n, P 1012, 1014n*, L 283n, T p5, E 1-18n

Mede-bird, **B 274-?***

Medusa, see Gorgon

Megabazus, Persian general (vi/v), B 484

Megacles (9695, 16), son of Hippocrates of Alopece, of the Alcmeonid family (v), A 614-5n*, C 46, 64n, 69n

Megacles (9697, 17), son of the above, A 614, C 46, 64n, 70, 124, 815

Megaenetus (1), military officer(?), F 964n, 965

Megarian, A **729-835**, P 1000n, We 147n, 1155n

Meidias (9714, 2), politician and gambler, B 1297-9

Meidias (9719, 10), son of Cephisodorus of Anagyrûs, enemy of Demosthenes (iv), B 1403n, E 808n

Melanion, the successful suitor of Atalanta, C 997n*, B 1549n, L 784-796, 807, 808n, 818n

Melanippe, daughter of Aeolus, L 1126-7n*, T 547*, F 1244n

Melanthius ([9767], [3]), elegiac poet (v), P 804n

Melanthius (9767, 3), son of Philocles(?), tragic dramatist, P 804-818*, 1009-15*, B p2, B 151, T p4

Meleager, slayer of the Calydonian boar, F 864, 1238-41n, 1402n

Meles (9802, 2), son of Peisias, lyre-player, B 766n

Melesias (9812, 2=7) of Alopece, father of Thucydides, a wrestling trainer, A 710n

Melesias (9813, 8), son of Thucydides of Alopece, A 710n, C 686n

Melesias (3), a man of doubtful masculinity, C 686

Melesippus, Spartan envoy to Athens in 432/1, P 435-6n

Meletus, composer of love-songs (vi?), F 1302

Meletus (9829, 13) of Pithus(?), tragic poet, F 1302n

Meletus (9830, 4=14), son of Meletus of Pithus, accuser of Socrates, F 1302n

Melissus of Samos, philosopher (v), F 634n

Melistiche (1), wife of Smicythion of Halae(?), a member of the chorus, E 46-48

Melitides, proverbial fool, F 991

Memnon, son of Eos, killed at Troy, C 622, F 963, 1365n

Memory (Mnemosyne, Mnamona), goddess/personification, L 1249

Men assaulted by Philocleon, W 1326-40

Menander (9875,75), son of Diopeithes of Cephisia, comic dramatist (iv/iii), A p4, p8, p26, p27, T p11, F 1480n, E p31, E 729-730n, 867-8n, 1146n, 1182n, We p23, We 321/2n, 322n, 1194n

Menecles (9905, 4), politician, We 725n

Menelaus, brother of Agamemnon and husband of Helen, B 509, L 155, 276n, T p6, p7, p8, T 850n, 858n,

867, 871-919, F 841-2n, 942n, 1284n, E p16, p25

Menippus (10033, 1), politician and general (v), B 1293n

Menippus (10034, 2=4), politician, B 1293

Mercury, Roman god identified with Hermes, We 1170n

Meriones, a Cretan warrior in the Trojan War, E 1165-6n

Messenger:
(a) A 1073-7
(b) A 1085-94
(c) A 1174-89*
(d) B 1118-63*
(e) B 1168-85

Metaneira of Corinth, mistress of Lysias, F\ 157n

Metellus Numidicus, Q. Caecilius, Roman politician and general (ii/i), L 1039n

Metis, child of Erebus and Night, B 693n

Metis, swallowed by Zeus when pregnant with Athena, We p16

Meton (10093, 1), son of Pausanias of Leuconoeum, astronomer and geometer, C 95-96n, B 992-1020, T 273n

Miarotatos, see Archvillain

Mica, a woman at the Thesmophoria, T p12, 292-764, E 51n

Micon (10200, 1), son of Phanomachus, painter and sculptor (v), L 679

Midas, king of Phrygia (viii/vii), W 433n, We 287

Midas, a slave, W 433*, 435-522

Miltiades (10209, 3), son of Cypselus, grandfather of the next-mentioned (vi), C 1407n

Miltiades (10212=10206, 13), son of Cimon of Laciadae, the victor of Marathon (vi/v), K 1325, F p9, F 1086n, E 105n, 1089n

Minos, king of Crete, later judge of the dead, F 464n

Minotaur, monster destroyed by Theseus, W 303-316n

Mist (Homichle), divinity worshipped by Socrates' pupils, C 814

Mnemosyne, Mnamona, see Memory

Mnesilochus (10329, 8), father-in-law of Euripides, T 1n; see also Inlaw

Mnesitheus (Γνησίθεος 1), politician(?), nicknamed "Lamius", E 77

Moirai, see Fates

Molon (1), actor, F 55

Moon (Selene), goddess, C 607-626, 1507, P 406-415

More, Sir Thomas, English politician and author of Utopia (xviᴾ), E 673-4n

Mormo, a nursery bogy, A 582n, K 693, P 474, F 925n

Morsimus (10416, 1), son of Philocles, tragic dramatist, K 401, P 803-818, B 151n, T p4, F 151, 1488-9n, E 364n

Morychus (10421, 4), a gourmand, A 887*, W 506, 1142, P 1008

Moschopoulos, Manuel, scholar (xiii/xivᴾ), A p18

Moschion, a young man in Menander's Perikeiromene, E 994-7n

Moschion, a young man in Menander's Samia, We 46n

Moschus, citharode, A 13

Mothon, see Cheek

Mountain Mother, see Cybele

Musaeus, legendary poet, B 693n, F 145-153n, 1033*

Muse(s), goddess(es) of the arts, A 665-675, K 505, C 972, 1030, W 1022, 1028, P 736, 775-780, 817, B 659, 724, 737-9, 782, 906, 909, 913, 924, 937, 950n, 1719, L 1248n, 1250, 1295n, 1297, T 41, 975n, F 227n, 229, 356, 674, 762n, 871n, 874-881, 1299-1300n*, E 882, 974

Muse of Euripides, F 1305-7, 1308-28

Music, goddess/personification, B 1372-1409n

Musurus, Marcus, first editor of a printed text of Ar. (xv/xviᴾ), A p18, p19*, P p.xxii*, T p14, E p38

Myrmex (2), a person allegedly deserving death, F 1506

Myronides (10509, 1), son of Callias, general (v), L 281n, 801, E 304

Myrrhine (10485, 1), wife of Hippias the tyrant (vi), K 449*, E 943n

Myrrhine, mistress of Leogoras, C 109n

Myrrhine (7), daughter of Callimachus, priestess of Athena Nike, L p5*

Myrrhine, wife of Cinesias, L p3, p5, **69-253***, 441-2n, 686, **830-844**, 850-861, 864-6, **870-884,885-8, 889-918**, 919, **920-4, 925-7, 929-935**, 936, **937-9, 941-5, 947-951**, 952-979, E p23, p25, We 1055n

Myrtia, a bread-seller, W 1372, **1388-1412***, B 14n, L 365n

Myrtilus, charioteer to Oenomaus, F 1232-3n

Naïs of Corinth, courtesan, We p28, p29, We 149n, 179, 303n, 305n, 306n, 312n

Nannion (6), courtesan (iv), We p6

Nauphante, personified warship, K 1309

Nauplius, father of Palamedes, T 769-770n

Nausicydes (10567 = 10571, 5) of Cholargus, a rich miller, E 426, 608n

Nausimache, typical woman's name, T 803n, 804

Nausimenes (10578, 1), son of Nausicydes(?) of Cholargus, a rich man, E 426n

Nauson, "father" of Nauphante, K 1309

Neaera (1), courtesan, We 149n, 1003n

Neighbour of Blepyrus, E pp20-21, p24, p29, p30, p31, p32, E 221-8n, 322n, **327-353, 356-7, 564-729, 730-871**, 1113n, We p20

Neith, Egyptian goddess identified with Athena, E 999n

Neleus, son of Tyro and Poseidon, father of Nestor, L 139n

Neocleides (10631, 4), politician, E p5, E 254-5, 398-407, 408n, We p9, p10, p13, p20, We 665-6, 716-726, 747

Neoptolemus, son of Achilles, P 109n, We p11, We 69-70n

Nephele ("Cloud"), wife of Athamas, C 257n

Nereus, sea-god, father of Thetis, C 1068n daughters of, T 326

Nesiotes (10668, 2), artist in bronze (v), L 633n, E 682n

Nessus, centaur slain by Heracles, F 38n

Nestor, sage king of Pylos in the Trojan War saga, C 1057, E 392-3n

Nicarchus (10718, 2), "informer", **A 908-958**, We 935n

Nicias (10808, 95), son of Niceratus of Cydantidae, politician and general, represented by a slave in *Knights,* A p6, A 846n*, K p2, p3, **1-98, 101-112, 115-154**, 234, 358, 604n, 1377n, W p.xv, p.xvi, W 52n, 81n, 210n, 240n, 959n, P 681n, 1031n, B p5, B 363, 593n, 639, L 57n, 390-7n, T 840n, We p28

Nicias (10809, 96), son of Niceratus of Cydantidae, grandson of the above, E 428

Nicobulus, name possibly invented for sake of pun, K 615

Nicochares (11083, 4), son of Philonides of Cydathenaeum, comic dramatist, F p1, E p10, We p1, We 290-321n

Nicodice, a woman of the chorus, L 321

Nicolochus, Spartan admirai, We p3

Nicomachus (10934, 4), member of law review commission, F 1084n, 1506

Nicophemus (11066, 2) of Rhamnus, general, E 201n

Nicophon (11077, 1), son of Theron, comic dramatist, We p1

Nicostratus (11011=11051, 146), son of Dieitrephes of Scambonidae, general, W p.xvi, W 81-84, 210n, 240n, B 798n

Nicostratus (11038, 86), possibly son of Ar., comic dramatist (iv), A p25, We p8

Night, primeval goddess, B 693, 695, T 1054n, 1065, F 1331, 1334, E 105n, We 425n

Nike, *see* Victory, *also* Athena

Nilus (Nile), river-god, T 855n

Niobe, mother of fourteen children slain by Apollo and Artemis, W 580, 741n, F 912, 920, 922n

Nobody, name assumed by Odysseus and Philocleon, W 184-6

Nostrils, divinities worshipped by Euripides, T 451n, F 893

Nurser of the Young (Kourotrophos), goddess, T 300

Nymphs, goddesses of various aspects of nature, C 271, P 1070-1, B 1098, L 254-387n*, T 326, 978, 993, F 1344, E p28

Ocean, father of many water-deities, C 271, 278, B 691n, 701

Oceanides, nymphs, C 271n

Ocnus, underworld ropemaker, F 186

Odomanti, *see* Light Infantrymen

Odysseus, hero of the Trojan War and of the *Odyssey,* K 1056n, W 181-6, 188n*, 351, B 720n, 1553-64n, 1561, T 547-8n, 769-770n, 877n, 1218ff.n, F p11, F 121n, 299n, 518n, 1266n, 1425n, E 1029n, We 290-315nn, 312

Oeagrus (1), tragic actor, W 579

Oeax, brother of Palamedes, T 770n, 776-784n

Oedipus, king of Thebes, B 998n, F 750n, 841-2n, 850n, 1021n, 1023-4n, 1182-95, E p14, E 1042

Oeneus, king of Calydon, father of Meleager and Tydeus, A 418-420, F 1238, 1240

Oenomaus, king of Pisa, F 1232-3n

Oeonichus, musician(?), K 1287*

Old Age (Geras), god/personification, We p7, We 80n

Old Smoky, *see* Kapnias

Old Woman/Women:
  (a) **L 439-613,** E p23, E 261n
  (b) **L 443-613,** E p23, E 261n
  (c) **L 447-613*,** E p23, E 261n
  (d) **L** 177-9, 240-2, 453-8, **459-461,** E p23, E 261n
  (e) E **pp21-22*,** pp25-26, p29, p31, p32, 877-937, 938n, **942-6,** 949-950, **976-1044,** 1046, We p20, We 1092n
  (f) E **pp21-22*,** pp25-26, p29, p31, p32, 877-1111n, **1049-1111*,** We p20, We 1092n
  (g) E **pp21-22*,** pp25-26, p29, p31, p32, 877-1111n, 1051-70n, **1065-1111*,** We p20, We 422n, 1092n
  (h) E 877-1111n, **We** pp15-16, p20, p25, p26, We 958/9n, **959-1094,** 1095, 1172n, 1194-1209n, **1197-1209**
  see also Chorus (g)

Olympiodorus, commentator on Plato and Aristotle (vi[P]), We 327n

Olympus, musician, K 9

Omphale, queen of Lydia to whom Heracles was enslaved, F 531n

Onomacritus (11481, 1), editor of early poetry (vi), F 1033n

Opheltes, child whose death occasioned the foundation of the Nemean Games, F 1319n*

Opora, *see* Fullfruit

Opuntius (1=2) of Oa, a one-eyed man, B 153-4*, 1294

Oracle-monger, B 959-991

Orestes, son of Agamemnon, who killed his mother, A 1167-8n, C 534n, W 523n, B 712n, L 447n, T p12, T 689-758n, 717n, 1218ff.n, F 364n, 750n, 942n, 1124-68nn, 1139, 1167-8, 1331-63n, E 1098-1111n, We 9n, 39n, 935n

"Orestes", son of Timocrates, reputedly a footpad, A 1167, B 712, 1490-3

Orion, hero and constellation, P 832-3n

Orpheus, seer and singer, F p9, F 1032*, 1033n

Orsilochus (1), a serial adulterer, L 725

Orthagoras ("the Hard Man"), nickname for a dildo, E 916

Orthannes, erotic divinity, E 916n

Orwell, George, English novelist etc. (xx[P]), B p3

Paches (11746, 1), son of Epicurus, general, W 523n, E 644-5n

Paean, see Apollo

Palamedes, Trojan War hero treacherously murdered, T 770, 848, F 1451

Pallas, see Athena

Pamphilus (11545, 52) of Ceiriadae, politician and general, We p2, We 174, 175, 176n, 385

Pamphilus of Amphipolis, painter, We 385n

Pan, god of the mountains and wilds, B 745, L 2, 721, 911, 998, T 978, 1092n, F 227n, 230, E p28, E 1069 (plural), We 287n

Panacea, daughter of Asclepius or Amphiaraus, We p20, We 639n, 660n, 702, 730-2

Panaetius (11566, 4), a cavalry officer, K 243*

Panaetius (11567, 7), son of Polychares of Aphidna, denounced for impiety in 415, K 243n*

Panaetius ([11567], [7]), denounced for impiety in 415, K 243n*

Panaetius (3), called "monkey" and "son of a cook", B 440-1n

Pandeletus (1), politician, C 924

Pandion, an early king of Athens, P 1183, B 15-16n, 368n, L 563n

Pandora, chthonic goddess, P p.xvii*, B 971

Pandora, the first woman, B 971n, E 14-15n, We 87n

Pandrosus, daughter of Cecrops, L 439

Panhellenes, see Chorus (e)

Pantacles (5), an imbecile, F 1036-8

Paphlagon, villain of Knights, A p11, p24, K p3, 1-7, 44-79, 102-4, 109-111, 115-7, 125-7, 134-7, 199, 203-5, 222-4, 230-4, 235-481, 487, 491, 625-673, 684, 691-972, 997-1110, 1151-61, 1164-1263, 1392-1408, 1408, C 559n, 581, P 314n, B 1423n, L p5, L 466, T 805n, F p16, F 569n, 754n, 830n, 861n, 1453n, 1478n, 1510-4n, E pp11-12, p27, We 508n, 872-3n, 935n; see also Cleon

Pardocas, a Scythian archer, F 608, 609-622

Paris (Alexandros), son of Priam and abductor of Helen, B 1104, L 723-5n, T p6, T 850n, F p11, F 499n

Parmenides of Elea, philosopher and poet (v), C 377n

Parmenon, slave to the Neighbour, E p30, 730-745n, 738-871

Parmenon, slave in Menander's Samia, We 46n

Parricide, see Young Man

"Partridge", nickname of a "lame tavern-keeper", B 1292; see also Peisias

Pasias, a creditor of Strepsiades, C 20-21, 30, 1224n

Pasion (11672, 5) of Acharnae, freedman banker later given citizenship, E 102n, 366n, We 176n

Pasiphaë, wife of Minos, F 849n, 850n, 1082n

Patrocleides (11685, 3), politician, A p24, B 790, L 581n, F pp21-22, F 686-705n

Patrocles, a miserly rich man, We 84-85

Patrocles of Thurii, tragic dramatist, We 84n

Patroclus, friend of Achilles, C 621n*, B 807n, 1420n, F 911-2n, 924-7n, 928n, 933n, 1041, E 392-3n, We 583n, 937n. 951n

Paul of Tarsus, apostle (iᴾ), W 1019-20n

Pausanias, regent of Sparta (v), W 236-7n

Pausanias (11717, 20) of Cerameis, lover of Agathon, T 29n, F 83n

Pausanias, king of Sparta, E p2

Pauson (4), painter, A 853, T 949, E 408n, 932n, We p29, We 602

Paxamus, sexologist etc. (i), F 1327-8n

Peace, goddess/personification, A p7, P p.xvi, p.xvii*, p.xix, P 221-6, 294, 300n, 307-8, 315-7, 319n*, 338, 372, 391, 417, 429n, 445, 469, 500-7, 508-511n, 520-1359, E p27, p28, We p7, p21, We 288-9n, 1191n
Athenian cult of, P 1020n

Peace-terms, girls/personifications, K 732n, 1388-9, 1390-1408*

Peasants, see Chorus (e), (l)

Pegasus, winged horse, P 76, 135, 140n*, 154, 722n

Peirithous, friend of Theseus, F p10, F 142n, 464n

Peisander (11770, 3), son of Glaucetes of Acharnae, politician, A 88n, P 395*, 1008n, B 11n, 1470-81n*, 1556-64, L pp1-3*, L 489n, 490, 577-8n, T pp2-4, T 1143-4n, F 689n

Peisetaerus, hero of Birds, B p1, p3*, 1-675*, 801-850, 859-1057, 1118-1469, 1495-1552, 1579-1693, 1706-19, 1720-65, L 1065-7n, T p6, p9, F 345-9n, 505-511n, E p12, p24, pp26-27, E 122n, 133n, 179n, E 277-9n, We p21, We 223n, 332n, 770/1n, 859n, 1099n, 1133n, 1189-90n

Peisias (11777, 1), nicknamed "Partridge", B 766-7, 1292(?)
son of, allegedly a traitor, B 766

Peisistratus (11793, 3), son of Hippocrates, tyrant of Athens (vi), A 614n*

descendants of, Xerxes' attempt to restore, W 490n

Peitho, see Persuasion

Pelasgus, Arcadian hero, C 398n

Peleus, virtuous father of Achilles, C 1063-70, B 569n, F 464n, 863, We 937n

Pelias, son of Tyro and Poseidon, L 139n, F 1403n

Pelops, father of Atreus, F 1232

Peltasts, see Light Infantrymen

Penelope, wife of Odysseus, L 696-7n, T p6, T 547, 550, F 1193n
suitors of, We 1159n

Penia, see Poverty

Pentheus, grandson of Cadmus, king of Thebes, T 134-5n, 255-6n, 680n, 996n, F 605-673n*

Pericleidas, Spartan envoy to Athens in the 460s, L 1138-41, We 382-3n

Pericles (11811, 3), son of Xanthippus of Cholargus, politician and general, A p8, p15, A 530-4, 538n, 548n, 710n, K 262n, 283, 732n, 1085n, C 64n, 213, 332n, 859, 969-971n*, 1001n, W 98n, 947n, P 270n, 500-2n, 606-611, 612-3n, 619-620n, 621n, B 521n, 540-3n, 1584n, 1652n, L 390-7n, F p9, F 569n, 680-1n, 1431n, 1463-5n, E p11, p20, E 171-2n, 304-5n

Pericles (11812, 5), son of the above by Aspasia, general, F p2

Pericles (11810, 4), son of Hippocrates of Cholargus, reputed a half-wit, C 1001

Persephone, daughter of Demeter and queen of the underworld, P p.xvii*, F p9, p17, p18, F 142n, 337, 338n, 503n, 504-511*, 518n, 519n, 671, 1480n, 1500-33
forms of name, in tragedy, L 742n
Soteira, F 378n
see also Demeter and Kore

Perses, son of the Titan Creius, F 1361-2n

Perseus, hero who slew the Gorgon, C 556n, P 296-8n, 832-3n*, T p7, p8, T 1009-14n, 1011, 1015-1135n, 1015n, 1056-97n, 1092n, 1098-1134, F 52-53n

Persuasion (Peitho), L 203, F 1391, 1392n, 1395-6

Pestle, see Kitchen Utensils

Peter, Simon, apostle (iᴾ), F 464n

Phaeax (13921, 1), son of Erasistratus of Acharnae, politician, A 846n*, K 1377-80, C 1172-3n

Phaedra, daughter of Minos and wife of Theseus, A p4*, L 283n, T p5, T 153, 497, 547, 550, F 57n, 101-2n, 849n, 1043, 1044n, 1052, E 225n, 915n

Phaedrias, a member of the chorus, L 356

Phaeinus, commentator on Ar. (iii/ivᴾ?), A p29

Phaenarete, grandmother of Godschild, A 49

Phaenippus (13979?, 6=?7), ambassador, A 603

Phaleas of Chalcedon, political philosopher (iv), W 959n, We p18

Phales, personification of the phallus, A 263-279

Phanias (14010, 2), politician, B 1372-1409n, F 153n, E 330n

Phanus (14078, 4), associate of Cleon, K 1256, W 1220

Phaon, man of irresistible sex-appeal, E pp7-8

Pharnabazus, satrap of Dascylium, W 1183-4n, B 1028n, L p1, L 1133n, We p3

Pharnaces, satrap of Dascylium, father of the above, B 1028, 1030

Phayllus of Croton, athlete (v), A 214, W 1206

Pheidias (14149, 1), son of Charmides, sculptor (v), K 1169n, P 605, 616-8*, B 515n, L 390-7n, 751n, T 1142n, We 185n

Pheidippides (14156, 1), long-distance runner and herald (v), C 67n

Pheidippides, son of the hero of Clouds, A 615n, C 1-125, 795-802, 814-1113, 1143, 1148-66, 1167-1213, 1229, 1268-70, 1313-20, 1322-1475, 1489n, B 1443n, 1555n, F 1087-8n, We 487-618n
how name decided upon, C 60-67*

Pheidon, father of Strepsiades, C 134

Pheidonides, proposed name for Strepsiades' son, C 65

Phenakes, see Bamboozlers

Pherecrates (14195, 1), comic dramatist, A p8, L 158, E p9

Pheredeipnus, (nickname of) a frequent prosecutor, W 401

Pheres, father of Admetus, C 1415n, T 194n

Pherrephatta, see Demeter and Kore, Persephone

Phertatus (1), dealer in amulets etc. (iv), We 884n

Philaenete, a member of the chorus, E 42

Philagrus (14205a, 33), son of Asclepiodorus, We p12

Philemon (94), nicknamed Phrygilus, B 763

Philemon (14277, F6998), son of Damon, of Diomeia, comic dramatist (iv/iii), A p4*

Philepsius (14256, 1) of Lamptrae, politician, We 177

Philetaerus (14253, 7), possibly son of Ar., comic dramatist (iv), A p25, We p12, We 1082n

Philinna, typical woman's name, C 684

Philip II, king of Macedon (iv), K 656n, L 1231-5n, We 385n

Philippides, *see* Pheidippides

Philippus (14399, 87) of Cydathenaeum, father of Ar., A p2

Philippus (14368, 6), a frequent prosecutor, W 421*, B 1470-81n*, 1701, 1703

Philippus (14400, 88=89) of Cydathenaeum, son of Ar., comic dramatist, A p3, T p12

Philiste, a woman at the Thesmophoria, T 292-654 (mentioned 568)

Philochorus (14782, 4), son of Cycnus of Anaphlystus, historian (iv/iii), E pp3-4, p5, We p28

Philocleon, father of the hero of *Wasps,* A p26, C 1387-8n, W pp.xvii-xviii*, W 4, 69-133*, 138-144*, **144-7**, 148-155, **156-173**, 174-8, **179-197***, 198, **205-9**, 209-221, 264-5n, 266-289, **316-407**, **415-833**, 834, 839, **844-1008**, **1122-1264**, 1290n*, 1292-1325, **1326-1449**, 1450-73, 1476-81, **1482-1537**, B 815-6, T p6, F 298n, 345-9n, 1466n, 1478n, E p31, E 47n,

179n, 327-356n, 1165-6n, We p10, We 321n, 917n, 935n

Philocles (14529, 3), son of Philopeithes, tragic dramatist, K 401n, W 461, B 151n, 281, 1295, L 563n, T 168, F 1453n*, 1488-9n

Philocles (14518, 44) of Anaphlystus, archon 392/1, We p28

Philocrates (14571, 5), a dealer in birds and bird-meat, B 14-18, 1077-83

Philocrates (14574, '15), a trierarch on Thrasybulus' last expedition, We 381n

Philoctemon, a rich man (fictitious, or grandfather of the next-mentioned?), W 1250

Philoctemon (14641, 10), son of Euctemon of Cephisia, a rich man, W 1250n

Philoctetes, famous archer abandoned on Lemnos by Greeks en route to Troy, A 424, F 841-2n, 1383n, We p11

Philodoretus, husband of a member of the chorus, E 51

Philomela, sister of Procne, B 15-16n, L 770-1n, F 683-4n

Philon, a chariot-racing acquaintance of Pheidippides, C 25

Philonides (14904, 47) of Cydathenaeum, comic dramatist and producer for Ar., A p2*, p28, W p.xv*, B p1, T p2, F p1, We p1

Philonides (14907, 52), son of Onetor(?) of Melite, an uncouth rich man, We p28, p29, We 179, 303, 305n, 310n

Philostratus (2), a pimp, nicknamed "Fox-dog", K 1069, L 957

Philoxenus (14707, 32) of Diomeia, reputedly a passive homosexual, A 605n, C 686-7*, W 84, F 934n

Philoxenus ([14707], [32]) of Cephisia, father of Eryxis, F 934

Philoxenus, son of Eryxis of Cephisia, grandson(?) of the preceding, F 934n

Philoxenus of Cythera, dithyrambic poet, W 84n, E 1169-75n, We p29, We 290-301nn

Philoxenus of Leucas, gastronomic poet, E 1169-75n

Philurgus, name of a member of the chorus, L 266

Phineus, blind Thracian prophet-king persecuted by Harpies, P 811n, We p11, We 634-6n

Phocus (2), man allegedly cuckolded by Callias jr., B 285n, We 168n

Phoebus, see Apollo

Phoenix, son of Amyntor, later tutor to Achilles, A 421-3

Pholus, centaur who entertained Heracles, A p4*

Phormio (14958, 21), son of Asopius of Paeania(?), admiral, K 562*, P 348, L 804*, F p11, E 999n

Phormisius (14945, 1 = 6), politician, F 964n, 965, 967n, E 71n, 97

Photius, patriarch of Constantinople (ix^P), A p17, E p9

Phrixus, son of Athamas, C 257n, F 1082n, 1225-6n

Phryne (3), courtesan (iv), E 1101n

Phrynichus (15008, 1), son of Polyphrasmon, tragic dramatist (vi/v), W 220, 273-289n, 462n, 1490, 1518-37n*, 1524, B 750, T 164, F p9, F 910, 1005n, 1254-5n, 1299

Phrynichus, tragic actor(?), C 1091n

Phrynichus (15011, 16), son of Stratonides of Deiradiotae, politician, W 1302*, L p3, T 1143-4n, F p10, F 686-705n, 689, 1196n

Phrynichus (15006, 3), son of Eunomides, comic dramatist, C 556*, B p1, B 1297n*, F p1*, p12, p20, F 13, 14n

Phrynichus (15007, 7), prizewinning dancer, denounced in 415 for mutilation of Hermae, W 1301-2n*

Phrynion (15021, 12), son of Demon of Paeania, lover of Neaera (iv), We 1003n

Phrynis of Mytilene, citharode, C 969-971n*, T 68n

Phrynondas, a proverbial villain, T 861

Phryx, a slave, **W 433, 435-522**

Phthia, concubine of Amyntor, A 421n

Phucus of Dickeleia, see Sebinus

Phyromachus (15054, 1 or Κλεόμαχος 10), actor(?), E 22

Pindar of Thebes, lyric poet (v), B 904-953n, 919n, 930n, 939, 941-4n, 945n, 1321-2n*, F 1299-1300n*, 1483n

Piper(s), **A 860-6**, E 255n

Pissuthnes, satrap of Sardis, A 100n*, B 1028n

Pittacus, tyrant of Mytilene (vii/vi), K 1044n, W 1232-5n

Pittalus (4), doctor, A 1032, 1222, W 1432, We 408n

Plangon, unmarried mother in Menander's *Samia*, We 46n

Planudes, Maximus, scholar (xiii/xiv^P), A p18*

Plathane, an innkeeper, **F 549-578**

Plato (11845, 1), comic dramatist, C 558n, F p1, E pp7-8

Plato (11855, 24), son of Ariston of Collytus, philosopher, A pp7-8, p25, C p3, C 103n*, 331n, 902n, W 98n, T 156n, F p15, F 126n, 141n, 868n, 1053-6nn, E p8, pp13-18*, p21, p27, E 571n, 606n, 635-643nn, 673-4n, 678-9n, We p12, We 461-3n, 833n, 925n

Plautus, T. Maccius, Roman comic dramatist (iii/ii), We p23

Pleiades, daughters of Atlas who became stars, P 832-3n, B 710n, 711n

Pleistoanax, king of Sparta, C 859n

Ploutoi, see Titans

Pluto, lord of the underworld, T p10, F p13, p14, p16, p17, p20, F 142n, 163, 432, 436n, 460n, 464n, 468n, 503n, 508n*, 670, 755n, 765, 784, **830-1481***, **1500-33**
see also Hades *and* Wealth

Plutus, son of Demeter and Iasion, T 299

Plutus, blind god, *see* Wealth

Podaleirius, son of Asclepius, We p8, p9, p11, We 639n

Poet, **B 904-955, 956-7**
see also Aeschylus, Agathon, Carcinus, Cinesias, Euripides, Xenocles

Poetry (Poiesis), goddess/personification, A p4

Polemarchus (F6993), brother of Lysias, F 967n

Polemon, a soldier in Menander's *Perikeiromene*, E 994-7n

Polemos, see War

Pollux, see Castor and Pollux

Polybius of Megalopolis, historian (ii), E 6n

Polybus, king of Corinth, adoptive father of Oedipus, F 1192

Polycrates, tyrant of Samos (vi), We 1002n

Polydectes, king of Seriphos and enemy of Perseus, T 1101n

Polydeuces, see Castor and Pollux

Polydorus, youngest son of Priam, murdered by Polymestor, F 1331-7n

Polygnotus of Thasos, painter (v), F 186n

Polyidus, a seer and wonder-worker, F 1082n

Polymestor, wicked Thracian king, F 956n

Polymnestus of Colophon, musician (vii), K 1287*

Polyneices, son of Oedipus, P 1270n, F 619n, 750n, 1021n, 1167-8n

Polypemon, alternative name for Procrustes, E 1021n

Polyphemus, see Cyclops

Pontus, see Sea

Poros, see Resourcefulness

Porphyrion, one of the Giants, B 553, 1249n, 1252

Porphyrion, Attic hero, B 881n

Poseidon, god, A 510, 682, K 551-564, 609, 839-840n, C 84-85*, 401n, 566-8, 587n, 1067n, 1234*, W 143, P 433-457n, B 294, 558-9n, 566, 586*, 868n, 1131, 1470-81n*, **1565-1693,** 1751-3n, L 139, 1142n, T 86, 109-110n, 318-9n, 322-5, 547n*, 1011-2n, 1047n, F 491, 664, 963n, 1341, 1430, E p28*, E 474-5n, We 1050

swears by himself, B 1614

sworn by, A 560, 798, K 338, 366, 409, 845, 899, 1035, 1201, C 83, 665, 724, W 163, L 403, 1165, F 183, 276, 295, E 339, 451, 568, 748, 832, We 396-7

Posthaliscus, see Willykins

Pot, see Kitchen Utensils

Pothos, see Desire

Potter, P 1197-1208

Poverty (Penia), goddess/personification, A p11, p26, F 1478n, E 571-709n, 651n, **We** p4, p13, p14, pp17-19, p20, p22, p25, p26, p27, p30, We 131n, 224n, 288-9n, 410-1n, **415-612,** 618, 907-919n

Praxagora, heroine of *Ecclesiazusae,* A p12, L 536n, E p7, pp11-13*, p14, p15, p17, pp18-22, pp23-24, pp26-27, p28, p29, p30, p31, p32, **1-29, 32-284,** 311-2, 318-9, 323n, 331-2, 335-7, 348-350, 374, 396-7n, 412-426n, 427-454, 491-2, 500-1, **504-513, 514-729,** 835, 870, 1013n, 1015n, 1042n, 1113, 1114n, 1126, 1137, 1138n, We p23, We 332n, 461-3n

Praxilla of Sicyon, poetess (v), W 1238-9n

Praxiteles (12172, 38), son of Cephisodotus(?) of Sybridae, sculptor (iv), F 313-4n

Prepis (12184?, 2=?3), reputedly a passive homosexual, A 843*

Priam, king of Troy, B 512, 1104n, We 1159n

Priapus, ithyphallic god, L 553n

Priest:

   (a) B 849, **859-894*,** T 295-311n

   (b) We p16, p20, p24, p26, **1171-1209**

   see also under Dionysus

Princess (Basileia), a heavenly maiden, Peisetaerus' bride, B p3, B 549n, 1536-43, 1634-9, 1674-82, 1687, **1720-65,** We p21

Prinides, name of a member of the chorus, A 612

Proboulos, see Magistrate

Procne, Tereus' wife, transformed into a nightingale, **B** p3, B 15-16n, 100-1n, 203-224, 268-292n*, 368, 659-666, **667-(?)800*,** 858n*, L 563n, 770-1n, F 683-4n

Procoptes, alternative name for Procrustes, E 1021n

Procrustes, brigand slain by Theseus, E 1021

Prodicus of Ceos, sophist, A p6, C p3, C 361*, 659n, B 692, F 970n, 1181n, We 548n

Proetus, king of Tiryns and enemy of Bellerophon, A 427n, T 401-4n, F 1043n, 1217-9n

Prometheus, the god who gave fire to mortals, K 759n*, **B** 686, 1182-3n, 1470-81n*, **1494-1552*,** 1751-3n, F

p19, F 131n, E p28, We pp5-6, p13, p16, p21, We 87n, 942-3n, 1133n

Pronapes (12250=12251=12253, 3), father of Amynias, W 74

Pronomus (1), politician(?), E 102

Protagoras of Abdera, sophist, A p6, A 710n, C p2*, C 112-5n, 419n, 659n, 1229n, 1421-2n, W 592n, T p7, F 1112n, 1475n

Proteas (12298, 6), son of Epicles of Aexone, general, T 876, 883

Proteus, king of Egypt, T 850n, 874, 881, 888n, 891, 897

Protomachus (12318, 2), general, F p2

Proxenides (12257, 1), a boaster, W 325, B 1126

Pruninghook-maker, see Sickle-maker

Prytanis/Prytaneis:
  (a) **A 40-173**
  (b) (in audience) **P 887-908**
  (c) T p7, T 763-4n, 854, 855-923n, 923, 929-946

Psammetichus, name of three kings of Egypt (vii-vi), We 178n

Pseudartabas, a high Persian official, A p15, 91-92, **94-125***, B 1615n

Ptocheia, see Destitution

Ptolemy I, king of Egypt (iv/iii), We 385n

Puppies, **W 976, 977-1008**

Pussy (Choirion), imaginary daughter of disguised Inlaw, T 289

Pylades, friend of Orestes, T 1218ff.n, F 830n, 1331-63n

Pyrilampes (12493, 1), son of Antiphon, once ambassador to Persia, A 63n*, W 98

Pyronides, hero of Eupolis' *Demes,* F p9, p10

Pyrrhander (1) of Anaphlystus(?), K 901*

Pyrrhander (12496. 5) of Anaphlystus, grandson of the above(?), politician, K 901n*

Pyrrhias, stock comic name for a slave, P 743-2n, F 730n

Pythagoras of Samos, philosopher (vi), C 219n

Pythangelus (5), tragic dramatist, F 87

Pythias, wife of Aristotle, W 386n

Ram, *see* Crius

Raven, **B 851-(?)1057***

Reconciliation (Diallage), goddess/personification, A 989-999, L 1114, **1115-88,** 1247n

Relative of Euripides, see Inlaw

Resourcefulness (Poros), god/personification, father of Eros, We 549n

Respiration (Anapnoe), divinity worshipped by Socrates, C 627

Rhadamanthys, virtuous brother of Minos, B 521n, F 464n

Rhea, mother of Zeus etc., B 971n, L 558n
  see also Cybele

Rhesus, Thracian king and ally of the Trojans, F 963n

Rhodia, wife or mistress of Lycon, W 1301n, L 270

Rhodippe, a woman of the chorus, L 370

Sabazius, Phrygian god, W 9-10*, B 873, L 3n, 388

"Sacas", *see* Acestor

Sadocus (12546, –), son of Sitalces, A 145-7

Sagacity or *Intellect (Synesis),* goddess/personification worshipped by Euripides, T 451n, F 893

Salabaccho (1), a courtesan, K 765, T 803n, 805, F 678n

Salmoneus, father of Tyro, L 139n

Samothracian Gods, P 277-8n*

Sannyrion (1), comic dramatist, A p25

Sappho of Mytilene, poetess (vii/vi), T 162n, F 1302n

Sarapion, Q. Statius (18) of Cholleidae, a distinguished Athenian (iii[P]), We p11

Sardanapallus, Greek name of a king of Assyria (vii), B 1021, We 287n
  see also Ashurbanipal, Ashur-uballit II

Sarpedon, son of Zeus and king of the Lycians, killed at Troy, C 622

Satyrus, ruler of Bosporus, E 102n, We 176n

Saucies (Skitaloi), gods of friskiness invoked by the Sausage-seller, K 634

Sausage-seller (Agoracritus), hero of *Knights,* **K pp2-3, 141-6*, 146-497*,** 498-502, **611-972, 998-1110, 1151-61, 1165-1263, 1316-1408,** B 1150n,

T p6, F p16, F 179n, 754n, 861n, E pp11-12, p27, E 171-2n, We 48-50n, 508n, 770/1n, 872-3n

Saviouress (Soteira), title of Athena, F 378, We 1175n

Scamander, river-god, We 1005n

Scamandrius, archon when the Peisistratid tyranny fell (vi), A 220n

Sceblyas, a Scythian archer, F 608, **609-622**

Scellias (12727, 1), father of Aristocrates, B 126

Scironides, see Cironides

Scott, Sir Walter, Scottish poet and novelist (xviii/xix[P]), T 1180n

Scythian, see Archer, Ditylas, Sceblyas, Pardocas

Scythian Girl, servant to Lysistrata, **L 184-199, 200**

Sea (Pontus), father of various water-deities, B 1230n

Seasons (Horae), goddesses of the annual cycle of nature, P 456, 1168

Sebinus of Anaphlystus, derogatory name for woman's or pathic's lover, F 427, E 980

Selene, see Moon

Sellus or *Sellartius* ("Brag"), patronymic applied to boasters, W 325, 459, 1243, 1267

Semele, mother of Dionysus, B 559, T 991, F p9, p11, F 58-60n, 323-353n

Semiramis (Sammu-ramat), queen of Assyria (ix/viii), We 287n

Semnae, see Dread Goddesses

Servant(s), see Slave(s)

Seuthes, nephew and successor of Sitalces, A 134-n, We p3

Shagathon, see Sebinus

Shakespeare, William, English dramatist (xvi/xvii[P]), B 1203n*

Shame, see Honour

Showtime (Theoria), attendant of Peace, P p.xvii*, **520-728*, 819-908***, B 794

Sibylla, an ecstatic prophetess, K 61*, P 1095, 1116

Sibyrtius (2), proprietor of a wrestling-school, A 118

Sickle-maker, P p3*, **1197-1208**

Sicon, slave to the Neighbour, E p30, E 730-745n, **735-871**

Sicon, typical name for a cook in comedy, F 499n, We p24

Sidero, stepmother of Tyro, L 139n

Silas, companion of Paul (i[P]), W 1019-20n

Silenus, father of the satyrs, We 287n

Simaetha (1), courtesan, A 524

Simon (12686, 9), politician, C 351, 399

Simon (12687=12689, 6=10), a cavalry officer, K 242*

Simonides of Ceos, lyric poet (vi/v), C 1356*, 1362, W 1410, P 697-9, B 919, 930n, We 327n

Sinis, "pine-bender" killed by Theseus, F 966n

Sinope, courtesan (iv), We p6

Sisyphus, hero famous for his craftiness, A 391, F 177n

Sitalces, king of the Odrysians, A 134-154, B 1529n

Skitaloi, see Saucies

Sky (Aether), god worshipped by Socrates and Euripides, C 265, 271n, 569-570, B 693n, 1193n, T 14, 272, 273n, 451n, F 100, 311, 889-891n, 892

Slave(s):

(a) of Dicaeopolis, **A 241-283, 805-6, 887-958, 1003-1142**; *see also* Xanthias (a)

(b) of Euripides, **A 395-479,** L 1222n

(c) of Lamachus, **A 959-968, 1097-1141, 1174-89***

(d) of the bridegroom, *see* Groomsman

(e) of Demos, **K 1331-1408**; *see also* Demosthenes, Nicias, Paphlagon

(f) of Strepsiades, **C 1-59*, 847-851**; *see also* Xanthias (b)

(g) of Bdelycleon, **W 525, 531-7, 805-1008, 1122-70**; *see also* Chrysus, Masyntias, Midas, Phryx, Sosias, Thratta, Xanthias (c)

(h) of Trygaeus (1), **P 1-2, 4-8, 11, 15-18, 38-49**

(j) of Trygaeus (2), **P 1-149, 824-855, 868-938, 948-9, 956-1022, 1039-41, 1042-1126, 1191-6,** B 1469n

(k) of Trygaeus (3), **P 1191-6*, 1329-59**

(l) of Tereus (1), **B** p3, B 60, **61-84**

(m) of Tereus (2+3), **B 270-450***

(n) as auxiliary troops defending Cloudcuckooville, **B 1187-(?)1261**

(o) of the Magistrate, **L 387-610**

(p) of the Spartan delegates, **L 1072-1224, 1239-40**

(q) of Agathon, **L 1222n, T 37-38, 39-70**

(r) of the women, **T 292-654**

(s) of Pluto (1/2), **F 605-673**

(t) of Pluto (3), **F 738-813**

(u) of Chremylus, **We 26, 816, 1105, 1194-1209n, 1197-1209**

see also Archer(s), Boy, Carion, Dancing-girls, Dardanis, Ditylas, Fawn, Hurlyburly, Hylas, Ismenias, Maid(s), Manes, Mania, Manodorus, Pardocas, Parmenon, Sceblyas, Scythian Girl, Sicon, Thratta, Woodworm, Xanthias

Sleep (Hypnos), god/personification, B 1181n, We 549n

Smicrines, old man in Menander's *Aspis* and *Epitrepontes*, P 742n, E 293n

Smicythe, *see* Smicythus

Smicythion (4), a frequent prosecutor, W 401

Smicythion (12769, 12) of Halae, a minor official in 407/6, W 401n, E 46(?), 293n

Smicythus (9), reputedly a passive homosexual, K 969*, E 293n

Smicythus, assumed male name of a member of the chorus, E 293

Smoeus (1), allegedly a cunnilinctor, E 846-7

Socrates (13101, 30), son of Sophroniscus of Alopece, philosopher, A p6, pp7-8, K 534n, **C** p2*, p3, C 94n, 102-4*, 137n*, 140n, 144-183, 188, **218-509***, 563-574n, **626-699, 723-6***, **731-813**, 830, 837n, 853n, 866-7, **867-888**, 957n, 1024-5n, 1105n, **1145-64, 1167-70**, 1358n*, 1432, 1450, 1465-6, 1477, **1502-9**, W 83n, 240n, 386n, 1408n, B 1282, 1296n, 1553n, 1555, 1561n, L 593n, T p7, T 451n, 795n, 1225n, F 126n, 876-8n, 889-891n, 1035-6n, 1114n, 1302n, 1478n, 1491, 1496-8n, E p1, p9, p12, p15, p16, p27, E 3n, 617n, 1064-5n,

We p12, p16, We 155n, 487-618n, 942-3n

Soldiers, A 572-622, 1190-1226

see also Light Infantrymen

Solon (12806, 1), son of Execestides, creator of the Athenian legal code, C 448n, 1187-95, B 1287n, 1354n, 1660, F p9, We 147n, 908n

Sopaeus, chief minister to Satyrus of Bosporus, E 102n, We 176n

son of (speaker of Isocrates 17), E 102n, We 176n

Sophia, see Wisdom

Sophocles (12834, 17), son of Sophilus of Colonus, tragic dramatist, K 522n, P 531, 695-9*, B 100, 998n, 1444-5n, L 283n, 421n, 450n, 563n, T p1, pp4-5, F p1, pp7-9, p12, pp20-21, F 71-88n, 73n, 76-82, 96-97n, 148n, 177n, 359n, 786-794*, 824n, 844n, 849n, 868n, 876-8n, 939n, 946-7n, 1122n, 1198-1247n, 1254-5n, 1314n, 1516-9, We p5, p11, p30, We 953n

Sophocles (12827, 2), son of Sostratides, general, K 355n, 742n, W 965n

Sophron of Syracuse, mimographer (v), F 1331-63n

Sophrone, Pamphile's nurse in Menander's *Epitrepontes*, E p31

Sosias (13177/8, 9/10/13), son of Pythis or Parmenon, reputedly a drunkard, C 65n, W 78-79

Sosias, slave to Bdelycleon, C 65n, **W 1-141**, We 170-9n

Sostrate, stock name for a citizen woman, C 678, W 1397, T 374, 380n

Sostrate, a member of the chorus, E 41

Sostratus, young man in love in Menander's *Dyskolos,* E p31, E 110n, We p23

Soteira, see Saviouress

Spartan Delegates, L 1072-1188, 1222n, 1223-6, 1236-8, 1241-1321

Spartan Women, L 77-253, 1273-1321

see also Lampito

Spartocus, king of Bosporus (v), F 608n

Spear-maker, P 1208-64

Spercheius, river-god, B 569n, We 937n

Sphinx, a man-snatching monster, F 473n, 929n, 1182n, 1193n, 1286, 1337n

Spintharus (?12855, 3=?12) of Probalinthus(?), allegedly a false pretender to citizenship, B 762

Spondai, see Peace-terms

Sporgilus (1), barber, B 300

Stalin, Josif V., Georgian/Russian tyrant (xx[P]), E 665n

Stamnias, see Decanter

Stephanus (12884, 23), son of Thucydides of Alopece, A 710n

Stephanus (12887, 33), son of Antidorides of Eroeadae, politician, We 168n

Stesichorus of Himera, lyric poet (vi), C 967n, T p6

Stheneboea, wife of Proetus, who fell in love with Bellerophon, W 111-2n, P 126n*, 140n*, T p5, T 401-4n*, F 1043, 1044n, 1049, 1217-9n, E 225n

Sthenelus (8), tragic dramatist, W 1313, F p9

Stilbides (1), diviner, P 1031*

Stilbonides, name apparently applied to Peisetaerus, B 139n

Strato (12964, 7), a beardless man, A 122, K 1374

Stratonice, typical woman's name, T 807

Strattis (1), comic dramatist, E 330n

Stratyllis, leader of the women's chorus, L 365

Strepsiades, hero of *Clouds*, A p6, p12, p13, C p3, p4*, **1-509**, 510-7, 627-633, **634-807**, 808-9, **814-843**, 844-6, 847-1114, 1131-1213, 1219-21, 1221-45, **1247-1302**, 1303-20, **1321-1509**, P 451n, B 111n, T p6, p7, T 1225n, F 420n, 1114n, E p12, p28, We p16, We 223n, 332n, 487-618n, 1082n

Strife (Eris), in Empedocles' cosmogony, B 700n

Strongylion (1), artist in bronze, B 1128n*

Struthas, satrap of Sardis, E p3, We p3

Strymodorus, stock name for an old man, A 273

Strymodorus, name of a member of the chorus, W 233, L 259

Strymodorus of Aegina, banker, W 233n, L 259n

Students, C **133-221**, 1493, **1495-1509**

Sun (Helios), god, C 571-4, P 406-415, T 17n, E 1-18n, We 771

Swindlers (divinities), *see* Bamboozlers

Sykophant, see Informer, Nicarchus

Symmachus, commentator on Ar. (ii[P]?), A p29

Synesis, see Sagacity

Synesius of Cyrene, intellectual and bishop (iv[P]), We 290-321n, 298n

Syra, stock name for a female slave, P 1146*

Syracosius (13041, 1), politician, B 1297*

Syrus, slave in Menander's *Dis Exapaton*, P 742n

Tantalus, father of Pelops, F 1232

Taraxippus, an evil spirit haunting racecourses, K 247n

Tartarus, the nethermost darkness, B 693

Teisamenus (3), ambassador, A 603

Teisamenus (13443, 4=6), son of Mechanion, politician, A 603n

Teisiades (1), a frequent prosecutor, W 401

Telamon, father of Ajax, L 1237, F 1041n

Teleas (13500, 2), son of Telenicus of Pergase, politician, P 1008, B 11n, 167-170, 1025

Telemachus, son of Odysseus, L 696-7n, E 1161n

Telemachus of Epidaurus(?), founder of Athenian Asclepius cult, We pp10-11

Telephus, king of Mysia, wounded and healed by Achilles, A 318n, 326n*, 429-472, 497-8n, 555, C 922, T p6, p12, T 93n, 466-519n, 689-758n, 776-784n, F 855, 864, 1080n

Telesippus (13541, 7), son of Hippocrates of Cholargus, reputed a half-wit, C 1001

Telesis, courtesan (iv), We 1082n

Teleutias, Spartan admiral, We p3

Temenus, first Heraclid king of Argos, F 1206-8n

Teredon, see Woodworm

Terence (P. Terentius Afer), Roman comic dramatist (ii), E 41-42n, 369n, 867-8n

Tereus, Thracian king transformed into a hoopoe, B p3, p5, p6, B 15-16, 46-48, 57-60, 71-84, 92, **93-208**, 209-

226*, **227-262***, 265-7, **270-675**, L 563, 770-1n, F 683-4n

Terpander, lyric poet and musician (vii), A 16n, F 1298n, 1308n, E 741n

Terpsichore, one of the Muses, F 674n

Tethys, mother of the rivers, B 691n

Teucer, half-brother of Ajax, T 850n, F p16, F 1041

Thales of Miletus, natural philosopher (vi), C 171-3n, 180, B 1009

Tharreleides (6583, 2), father of a man nicknamed "Jackdaw", B 17-18

Thatcher, Margaret, Baroness, English politician (xxᴾ), We 175n

Thaumas, father of Iris, B 1230n

Theaetetus (6632, 14), son of Euphronius of Sunium, mathematician, We 833n

Theano, priestess of Athena at Troy, T 101-129n

Theban, **A 860-958***, P 1000n, 1004n, E 255n

Themis, see Justice

Themisto, second wife of Athamas, A 434n, W 1414n

Themistocles (6669, 39), son of Neocles of Phrearrhii, politician and general (v), A p8*, K 84*, 812-9*, 884, 1325n, 1350-3n, W 220n, 499n, B 493n, E 1107n, We 327n

Theoclymenus, son of Proteus, T 850n, 891

Theodectes of Phaselis, tragic poet and rhetorician (iv), F p9

Theodorus (9), ambassador, A 605

Theogenes (6703, 15) of Acharnae, politician, W 1183, P 928, B 821n, 822, 1127, 1295, L 63, 64n

Theognis (6736, 4), tragic dramatist, A 11*, 140, T 170

Theonoe, daughter of Proteus, T 850n, 897, 921-2n

Theophrastus of Eresus, philosopher (iv/iii), W 386n

Theopompus of Miletus, pirate, B 1427n

Theopompus (7010, 6), son of Theodectes(?), comic dramatist, E pp9-10, We p12

Theoria, see Showtime

Theorus (7223, 1=2), politician, **A 134-173**, K 608*, C 400, W 42-51, 418, 599-600, 1220, 1236, P 756n

Theramenes (7234, 7), son of Hagnon of Steiria, politician and general, K 1281n, T 1143-4n, F p1, p3, p6, p13, p15, p22, F 367n, 541, 967-970, 1442-50n, E 97n

Theseus, greatest of Athenian heroes, K 1312, L 678n, 1162-3n, T 153n, 480n, F p9, pp10-11, F 142, 464n, 966n, 1043n, E 685n, 1021n, We 627n

Thesmophorian Goddesses, see Demeter and Kore

Thespis (7206, 1), first Athenian tragic dramatist (vi), W 1479

Thetis, sea-goddess, mother of Achilles, A 883n, C 1067-70, B 929n, F 840n, 1365n, We p16

Thoas, king of Lemnos and father of Hypsipyle, T 605n, F 1211-3

Thoas, king of the Taurians, T 1218ff.n*

Thomas Magister, scholar (xivᴾ), A p18, C p5, We p14

Thorycion (7419, 2), tax-collector accused of disloyalty, F p13, F 362-4, 382

Thracians, *see* Light Infantrymen

Thrasybulus, tyrant of Miletus (vi), We 1002n

Thrasybulus (7310, 22), son of Lycus of Steiria, restorer of Athenian democracy, F p3, F 541n, E p4, p5, p6, p7, E 102n, 195-6n, 202-3, 208n, 356, 428n, We p2, p3, p17, p28, p30, We 172n, 176n, 550, 567-570n, 1146n

daughter of, E 428n

Thrasybulus of Calydon, assassin of Phrynichus, B 1274-5n

Thrasybulus (7305, 14), son of Thrason of Collytus, general, We 550n

Thrasyllus (7333, 3), general, F p2

Thrasymachus of Chalcedon, sophist, C 902n, 903n, 1038-40n, 1060n, F 967n

Thrasymachus, character('s husband) in Theopompus' *Stratiotides,* E p10

Thratta, stock name for a female slave, A 273, W 828, P 1138, T 279-280, 284-5, 293

Thucydides (7268, 7), son of Melesias of Alopece, politician, A 703-712, W 592n, 947

Thucydides (7267, 11), son of Olorus of Halimus, historian, P 609n, B 481-521n, L 653n, F 569n

Thumantis (1), a poor man, K 1268-73

Thuphanes (7074, 1), politician or official, K 1103

Thuphrastus (7162, 1), W 1302*, 1314-8

Thyestes, son of Pelops and brother of Atreus, A 433

Timachidas of Lindus, scholar (ii/i), F 1269-70n, 1294n

Timaea, wife of Agis II of Sparta, F 1422n

Timanoridas of Corinth, lover of Neaera (iv), We 1003n

Timarchus (13636, 36), son of Arizelus of Sphettus, politician (iv), E 103n, 365n, We 155n

Time, god/personification, F 311

Timocleia, chairwoman of the Women's Council, T 368

Timocrates of Argos, musical assistant to Euripides, F 944n*

Timocreon of Rhodes, lyric poet (v), A 532n, We p6

Timon, a misanthrope, B 1549, L 808-820, T 861n, F 129n

Timotheus of Miletus, lyric poet, T 100n, F 1336n

Timotheus (13679, 32), son of Conon of Anaphlystus, general, We 180

Tiribazus, satrap of Sardis, E p3, p4, We p1, p3

Tissaphernes, satrap of Sardis, L p1, p2, L 1133n, T pp2-4, T 1143-4n, F 1422n, E pp1-2

Titans, brothers of Cronus, C 904-6n, B 469, 701-2n, We pp5-6, We 327n

Tithonus, husband of Eos, who was given immortality but not agelessness, A 688, F 963n

Tle(m)polemus, son of Heracles, who killed his great-uncle Licymnius, C 1266, B 1242n

Tongue, divinity worshipped by Socrates and Euripides, C 424, T 451n, F 889-891n, 892, We 1082n

Tragedy, goddess/personification, F 95

Tranquillity (Hesychia), goddess/personification, B 1321, L 1289

Triballian God, A p28, **B** p5, B 1470-81n*, 1533, **1565-1693***; cf. B 1520-30

Tricksters (divinities), *see* Imps

Triclinius, Demetrius, scholar (xiv[P]), A p19, p34, K p6, C p5, W p.xx, P p.xxii*, B pp8-9*, L p8, F p30, We 968/9n, 1170-1n

Triptolemus, Eleusinian hero, A 48, 55

Triton, sea-god, L 347

Trophonius, Boeotian hero with an oracular shrine, C 508, We 658n

Trygaeus, hero of *Peace*, A p14, P p.xvi, p.xvii, P 56-78, **79-728, 819-1126, 1191-1311, 1316-59**, B 1673n, L 723-5n, T p6, p9, T 1009-14n, F 345-9n, 465-6n, E p27, p28, p32, E 277-9n, We p21, We 223n, 288-9n, 859n, 1099n, 1191n

Tryphe, see Delight

Twelve Gods, W 1372n*, B 95, F 121-134n

Twin Gods, see Amphion and Zethus, Castor and Pollux

Two Goddesses, see Demeter and Kore

Tydeus, son of Oeneus and father of Diomedes, A 418-9n, P 1290n

Tydeus of Chios (son of Ion), politician, P 835n

Tydeus (13884, 1), son of Lamachus of Oë(?), A 965n, P 1290n

Tyndareos, father of Castor and Clytaemestra, foster-father of Helen, P 285n, L 191-2n, 1300, T 860, 919, F 499n

sons of, *see* Castor and Pollux

Typho(eu)s, a hundred-headed monster, K 511, C 336, W 1032-5n, P 755-8n, F 473n, T 847n

Tyro, daughter of Salmoneus, seduced by Poseidon, L 139n

Tzetzes, Johannes, scholar (xii[P]), A p18, C p5, We 1127n

Ulius (11496, 1), son of Cimon of Laciadae, minor official, K 407

Unjust Argument, see Worse Argument

Uranus, first ruler of the universe, C 381n, B 469n, 701, 824-5n, T 11-18n, We p16

Velsen, Adolf von, scholar (xix[P]), A p20

Victorius, Petrus (Pier Vettori), scholar (xvi[P]), P p.xxii

Victory (Nike), goddess/personification, K 586-590*, B 574, L 317, F 720n, 725n, E 815n, We 185n; *see also* Athena

Void (Chaos), primeval being in various theogonies, C 424, 627, B 470n, 691, 693, 694n, 698, We 1082n

Vortex (Dinos), "god" whom Strepsiades supposes to have supplanted Zeus, C 379-381, 833, 1471-4

War (Polemos), god/personification, A 979-987, P p.xvi, P 204-6, 223-235, **236-288***, 310, 319n*, 624, We 80n, 288-9n, 1040n, 1108n

"Wasps", see Chorus (d)

Wealth (Plutus), god/personification, A p12, T 299n, E p20, p24, p28, E 608n, We pp4-8, p11, pp12-17, pp20-21, p24, p25, p26, **1-252,** 265-270, 277-8n, 284-5, 321n, 327, 331, 391-405, 406n, 410-1nn, 418n, 446, 452, 459, 468-470n, 494-7, 505-6, 510, 558-560, 564, 569n, 580, 587-9, 621, 625, **626,** 634-6, 647n, 654-662, 727-746, 749-750, 752-3, 767, 770, **771-801,** 801/2n, 804-5n, 806-818n, 823, 824n, 827-8, 840, 844, 849, 858-9, 864-8, 875n, 878-9, 925, 937, 938n, 940, 946-950, 956n, 958, 960, 968-9, 1008-37n, 1025-30, 1081n, 1088-90, 1114, 1159, 1162, 1173, 1189-90n, 1191-3, 1194-1209n, 1195, 1196, **1197-1209**
multiple identities of, We pp4-7

Wells, Herbert George, English novelist etc. (xix/xx[P]), We 566n

Wife:
  (a) of Dicaeopolis, A **241-283,** We p20
  (b) of Strepsiades, C 41-5, 60-70, 83n*, 438, 800, 1443-5, We p20
  (c) of Chremylus, W e p20, p26, We 384, **641-769, 788-801,** 1104, 1194-1209n

Willykins (Posthaliscus), imaginary son of disguised Inlaw, T 291

Winstanley, Gerrard, English revolutionary (xvii[P]), E 665n

Wisdom (Sophia), goddess/personification, B 1320

Witness:
  (a) C 1214-58
  (b) W 1415-41
  (c) We 850-929, 933

Woman/Women:
  (a) L 727-780
  (b) L 735-780
  (c) L 742-780
  (d) L 760-780
  (e) E p23, p29, p32, E 30-284n, 33-35, **35-284,** 327-356n, 503n, 509-510n, 746n
  (f) E p23, p30, p32, E 30-284n, **54-284,** 503n
  see also Athenian Women, Brideswoman, Chorus (g),(h),(j),(k), Corinthian Woman, Dancing-girl(s), Garland-seller, Girl, Maid, Old Woman/Women, Slave, Spartan Women, Wife, *and under names of individual women*

Woodworm (Teredon), a boy piper, T p7, **1160-1203**

Worse Argument, C p3, p4, C 112-8, 244-5, 361n*, 657, 882-6, **891-1112,** 1148-9, 1229, 1336-7, 1400n, 1427n, 1437-9n, 1444-51, B p6*

Xanthias, stock name for a slave:
  (a) A 241-283
  (b) C 1485-7, **1487-1509**
  (c) W 1-436, 456-522, **835-843, 899-1008, 1264*, 1292-1325*, 1474-1515*,** P 743-2n, L 186n, E p31, We 170-9n
  (d) B 1-450*, 451-464, 465-675, 851-1057, 1187-1312, 1468-9, 1579-1693
  (e) B 721n, F pp12-13, **1-196,** 209-268n, 271, **272-673,** 694n, **738-813, 1500-33,** E 772n, 1056n, We p23, We 46n

Xanthippus (11169, 7), son of Ariphron of Cholargus, politician and general (v), C 64n

Xanthippus (11170, 8), son of Pericles of Cholargus and grandson of the above, C 64n

Xanthippus, proposed name for Strepsiades' son, C 64

Xenarchus (11183, 2), son of Carcinus of Thoricus, tragic dancer, **W 1500-37**

Xenocles (11222, 86), son of Carcinus of Thoricus, tragic dramatist, C 1261n, 1264-5n, **W** 1501n, **1507-37**, P 289n, 788n, 791n, T p4, p5, T 169, 441, 848n, F 86

Xenophanes of Colophon, philosopher and poet, C 1280-1n, F 634n

Xenophantus (4), father of Hieronymus, C 349

Xenophon (11307, 22), son of Gryllus of Erchia, historian etc., F 1457n

Xenotimus (11269, 15), son of Carcinus of Thoricus, tragic dancer, **W** 1501n, **1505-37**, P 784n

Xenylla, woman at the Thesmophoria, T 633

Xerxes I, king of Persia (v), W 490n, B 1074-5n, L 653n, 675n, T 1200n, F p5, p6, F 1028n

Xuthus, son of Hellen, We 41-43n

Young Man:
   (a) B 1332-3n, **1337-71**
   (b) E 877-1111n, We pp15-16, p20, p25, p26, We 816n, 975-1024, 1029-33, 1038-41, **1042-94**, 1096, 1096/7n, 1194-1209n, 1197n, 1201-3
   see also Epigenes

Zan, see Zeus
Zeno of Elea, philosopher (v), 876n
Zethus, see Amphion
Zeus, king of the gods, A 171, 223, 435, 1153, K 410*, 500, 1188, 1253, 1390, C p3, C 2, 265n, 302-310n, 314, 366-411, 563-4, 602n, 817-829, 904-6, 984n, 1048, 1067n, 1080-2, 1150, 1234*, 1241, 1279-80, 1468-71, W 261, 323-333, 1448n, P p.xvi, P 41, 57-59, 61-62, 68, 77, 104-8, 133n, 161, 178-9, 195, 320n, 371-2, 376-381, 420n, 722, 736, 1126n, 1158, B p2, p3, B 130, 216, 223, 468,

480, 510n, 514, 519, 553n, 554-6, 558-9n, 568-570, 576, 586*, 610, 619n, 667, 689n, 716n, 728, 865n, 929n, 1172, 1230, 1237, 1240, 1242n, 1246-52, 1259, 1263, 1372-1409n, 1494, 1500n, 1501-2, 1506, 1514-5, 1522-3, 1527n, 1532, 1534-43, 1550-1, 1595n*, 1601, 1605, 1611, 1633, 1642-70, 1671n, 1714, 1731-2, 1740, 1745-54, 1757, L 254-387n*, 397n, 476, 558n, 694-5n, 716, 717, 773, 940, 967, 972, 1285, 1287n, 1300, T 1, 14n, 71, 272, 273n, 315, 369, 850n, 860n, 870, 990, 1009, F p11, F 100, 216, 246, 298n, 378n, 439, 464n, 465-6n, 631, 750n, 756, 875, 889-891n, 892n, 1144-6n, 1146, 1148-9, 1244, 1278, 1356n, 1361-2n, 1365n, E p27, p28, E 80n, 378, 685n, 776, 828, 1118, We p8, p13, p16, p18, p20, p21, p24, We 1, 82, 87-94, 119-133, 141-3, 185n, 210n, 215n, 233n, 269n, 327n, 351n, 382-3n, 385n, 406n, 408n, 578n, 579-592, 770/1nn, 802-818n, 845n, 859n, 898, 1095, 1099n, 1107-9, 1111, 1175, 1186, 1189-90, 1194-1209n

Pericles compared to, A 530
Philocleon compared to, W 556-7n, 619-627, 652
"Sons of", *see* Castor and Pollux
statue of, at Olympia, P 605n
sworn by, A 368, 730n, 911, K 280, 282, 319, 338, 417, 719, 725, 801, 901, 941*, 972, 1000, 1092, 1163, 1347, 1350, 1382, C 217, 328, 330, 408, 652, 694, 733, 1066, 1227, 1228, 1234, 1239, 1331, 1379, W 97, 134, 173, 181, 193, 205, 209, 217, 231, 254, 297, 298, 299, 310, 396, 416, 426, 461, 477, 508, 512, 665, 680, 832, 841, 912, 934, 954, 966, 997, 1126, 1141, 1152, 1231, 1371, 1387, 1400, 1404, 1409, 1496, 1506, P 218, 489, 566, 630, 979, 987, 1046, 1096, 1233, 1236, 1290, B 11, 24, 81, 89, 135, 176, 269, 275, 297, 462, 465, 470, 572, 574, 581, 607, 638, 661, 673, 801, 860, 954, 956, 1017, 1148,

Index III: General[1]

abaton or *adyton* (place of incubation at an Asclepieum), We p13, We 733-4n
abstinence, sexual, in ritual regulations, P 151n*
Abydos, We p3 n10
    battle of (411), T p2
Acanthus (Chalcidice), A 709n
Acarnania, A 604n
accents misplaced, F 304n, E 22-23n
Achaea, B 1421n
Achaeans, Homeric term for Greeks, F 1270, 1285
Achelous, River (N.W. Greece):
    used as metonym for "water", L 381
Acheron, River (in underworld), L 606n, F 137-8n, 471, We p7
Acherusian lake, B 721n, L 606n, F p12, F 137-140, 180n, 181-270, We 278n
Achillean cake, K 819
acoustics, W 1410n
act-breaks, in Menander, E 729/730n, We 321/2n
acting, paradox of, T p8*
actors, A p15*, K 537n, 1280n, C 64n, W 78n, 579n, 1279, 1480, 1498, 1505
    boys as, A p15, W 1501n
    number of, L 133-6*, 447*, E p31, We p27
    occupational hazards of being an, F 778n
    rest periods arranged for?, E p31 n121, We p27 n111
    silent, P 1192n, 1210n, We p27 n110
    songs for, We p23
    speaking in name of author, A 299-302n, 377-382*, 499, 500n
    speaking *qua* performers, A 299-302n, 416, 442-3n, B 1169n, 1273n, L

1218-20nn, T 531n, 1056-97n, 1060-1, 1077, F 1-20n, 297n, 783n
    tragic, thought effeminate, C 1091-2
    verbal blunders by, F 303-4, E 22-23n
address, forms of, A 397n, K 725n, C 1192n, 1432n, 1464n, W 163n, 609, 1297-8, 1307n, P 90n, 298n, B 57n, 139n, 977n, 1216n*, 1257n*, 1581-2n, L 7n, 762n, 891n, 1098n, 1171n, T 64n, 882n, 890n, F 44n, 58-60n, 116n, 239-241n, 565n, 1175-6n, E 37n, 526n, 531n, 609-610n, 631n, 915n, 934n, We 823n, 963n
    none available for a mixed audience, F 598n
    see also gods (addressed as "man"); slaves (addressed deferentially; address masters disrespectfully)
Adonia (festival), P 420, L 389-396, 409n
adultery, A 265, 849*, W 42n, 1353n, P 979-985*, B 558n, 793-6, 1652n, L p2 n9*, L 107, 212, 270n, 723-5n, T p7, T 339-340n, 340-1, 343-5, 396-404, 417, 466-519n*, 477-501, 558n, F 983-8n*, 1043-51, 1217-9n, 1422n, E 8n, 225, 323n, 348-350n, 522-6, 675n
    betrayed by creaking door, F 604n
    compensation privately paid for, F 428n, 810n, We 168n
    facilitated by foolish husbands, L 407-419
    how to get away with, C 1075-82, L 798n, T 494-501, We 168
    in Euripidean tragedy, T p5 n28, F 849n, 1043-52
    in Euripides' home life, F 944n*, 1045-6nn, 1408n

---

1   In alphabetical sequencing, *comma, space* and *hyphen*, in that order, precede all the letters of the alphabet; hence *hair, tearing of* precedes *hair colour*; *hair styles* precedes *hair-nets*; and *fire-walking* precedes *fireships*. Cross references ("see ..." or "see also ...") are to main entries unless marked with §, in which case they refer to an indented subheading within the same main entry.

prosecuted as "subversion of democracy", We 948-9n

summary execution of man taken in, C 1077n, E 1056-7n, We p16 n74

unofficial punishments for, C 1083*, 1084n, T 537n, We 168n, 312n

with slaves, T 491-2, E 225n

adyton of Asclepieum, see *abaton*

Aeaea, home of Circe, We 303n

Aegae (Achaea), F 666n

Aegae, Cape (Euboea?), F 666

Aegean Sea:

as theatre of naval war, F pp1-3, p10 n47, F 1463-5n

origin of name, F 666n

Aegina, A 538n, 653*, 654n*, K 1253n, C 1356n, W 122-3, 233n, P 763n, L 259n, F p5, p13 n58, F 363, We pp2-3, p4, p10, We 174n, 385n, 411n

coins of, E 413n

aegis, garment/implement of Athena, K 1177n, C 602, L 1273*, E p27 n101

Aegospotami, battle of (405), B 1427n, L 103n, F p2 n12, pp3-4 n17, p5, p21, F 686-705n, 694n, 1422n, 1435-66n, 1512n, E 243n, 644-5n

aerial warfare, F 1437-41

Aetna (Sicily), P 73n, B 926

Aetolia, K 1n, 79

Africa, see Libya

a fable from, B 471n*

home of the Shadefeet?, B 1553n

Agathyrsi (tribe of present-day Romania), E 987n

age, of characters or chorus, L 7n, 69-253n, T 345n, E 471-2n, We 277-8n

agōn (formal debate), A pp9-10*, p11, p26 n49, K 303-460n*, 761-835n, C p4 n9, C 476-7n, B 451-635n, L 476-607n, F p16, F 830-1478n, 895-1098n, 1214n, E p10, pp12-15, p24, E 514-9n, 571-709n, 729/730n, We pp17-20, p24, pp28-29, p32, We 487-618n, 569n, 611n

anapaests and iambics in, K 761-835n, C 959-1023n, F 905-991n

chorus as judges in, W 521n

determining who speaks first in, K 335-341, C 940-8

first speaker in, normally the loser, A pp9-10, F p16 n73, E 1158-9n, We p17 n78

in Euripidean tragedy, T p4 n27, F 775n, 956n

introduced by prayer, F 871n

mischievous interjections by third party during, F 1023-4n

with only one main speaker, B 451-635n

agriculture:

as metaphor for sex, A 995-8n, L 1173n

Hesiod as authority on, F 1033-4

air, in physical theory of Diogenes of Apollonia, C 229-233nn, 264n

aithēr (upper air), C 265n, 285n, 570n, P 832-3n, T 14n, F 892n

Alcmeonidae, Athenian aristocratic family, A 614n, C 46n, L 665n, F 1512n

Aldine edition of Ar. (Venice, 1498), A pp18-19*, P p.xxii*, E p38

Aletrides, see Grinders

Alexandria, library of, P p.xix, B 870n, F 1269-70n

Aristophanic texts missing from, We p30

all-night celebrations, see *pannychides*

allegory, mixture of tenor and vehicle in, K 50n, L 574-586n

alliance, four-power, in Corinthian War, E p5, E 193-6; see also Argos, Corinth, Thebes

"allied" (subject) states, A 6n, 192*, 506, 633-645n*, 642, K 839, 1034n, 1408n, C 609, W 657, 669-671, 707, 1098-9n, P 45-46n*, 619-622, 760n, 936, B 1021n, 1035-50nn, L p1, L 582n, 653n, 1177-80n, F p2, p4

and the Athenian courts, B 1046-7n, 1422-60

Athenian citizenship suggested for, L 582n

autonomous (Chios and Methymna), B 879n

fined if Athenians are killed in their territory, P 170-2n

rich citizens of, persecuted, K 326, P 639-646

allies of Sparta, see Peloponnesians

Alpheus, River (Elis), B 1121n

altar, A 308, P 938, 942, 957, 1020-31, 1040n, T 279d, 888, F 875d, We 382-3n, 660, 679
direction of circling, P 957n
in orchestra, see *thymele*
of Apollo Agyieus, T 489, 689-758n, 748, We 1114n
pollution of, threatened, T 695
ambassadors:
age of, L 1247n
chosen for their connections in receiving state, L 1138n
ambition, as merit and/or fault, T 383-4n`
Ambracia, K 1n
Ammon (oracular sanctuary), B 619*, 716, 724-5n
amnesty:
of 405, F p21
of 403, C 1425-6n, F 1512n, E p1, We p32, We 1146n
proposed in *Frogs*, F p14, F 691n
Amorgos, We 1015n
Amphictyonic Council, C 624n, L 1129-32n, T 841n
amphidromia (carrying of baby round hearth), L 757
Amphipolis (Thrace), C 549n, W p.xv, W 35n, 475n, P p.xv, P 47n, 282n, B 1369n, L 421n, F p2 n12, F 569n
amphoras, Panathenaic, E 744n
amulets, T 504n, We 883-5
Amyclae (Laconia), L 1298
anabolai (preludes; astrophic dithyrambs), P 830, B 226n, 1385, F 366n
"anapaests", name for main speech in *parabasis*, A 627, K 504, P 735, B 684
Anarrhysis (second day of Apaturia), P 890n
andrōn (dining-room), E 675n
anecdotes of famous men, C 156n
angling, W 174n, 381n
animal diseases, K 376n, T 222n
animal noises, W 903, F 209-268, We 293n; *see also* bird calls
animals[2]:
antelope, F 937n
ape, see §monkey

ass, K 254n, 1246n, 1399*, C 1273, W 616-8nn, 1306, 1310, 1367n, P 4, 82n, B 721, 1328, L 290, F 1-20n, 159, 186n, 196n, We 179n, 287; *see also* Donkey *in Index II*
baboon, see §monkey
bat, C 104n, W 1408n, B 1296, 1564
reckoned a bird?, B 1296n*
bear, L 645, F 1273-4n
boar, wild, W 1202, L 1255-6, F 822n, 863-4n
camel, W 1035, P 758, B 278, 1559-63
cat, A 879
cattle, K 655-6, 1344n, C 347, 386n, W 279n, P 925-6, B 582, 585, 856n, 1500n, L 81, 188n, 1063n, T 325n, F 290, 467n, 506, 804, 850n, E 80n, We 819n, 820n
choruses of, B p2
deer, C 354, T 1172n, 1218ff.n*
dog, K 289, 415-6, 819n, 1017-34*, 1074, 1246n, 1399, C 491, W p.xvi, W 701-2n, 835-843, 894-994, 1031n, 1402-5, P 24, 313n, 482, 641, 754n, 1065n, 1078n, 1178n, 1204, 1297n, L 158n, 298, 363, 791, 957n, 1215, T 416, F p6 n36, F 292, 293n, 467n, 472, 605, 893n, 1287, 1292, 1359, E 255, We 157, 1105; *see also* Cerberus, Hound of Cydathenaeum, Labes, Puppies *in Index II*
meat of, offered to Hecate, We 594n
dolphin, K 560, F 1317-8, 1319n
donkey, *see* §ass
ferret, *see* §polecat
fox, A 878, K 1067-78, W 1241, P 1067-8, 1100n, 1189, B 429, 652, 1295n, L 957n, 1270, T 1133, E 255n
frog, *see* Frogs *in Index II*
gazelle, T 1172n
gecko, *see* §lizard
goat, A 853n, K 660-1, 1344n, C 45n, 71, P 813, 1159n, B 620n, 651-3n, 856n, 859d, 901-2, 959, L 1063n, 1262n, F 230n, We 294, 295, 313, 820
hare, A 878, 1006, 1110, 1112, K 1192-9, W 289n, 709, 1202, 1448n, P

2   This entry covers mammals, reptiles and amphibians; for other animals *see* birds, crustaceans and molluscs, fish, insects and arachnids, sea-urchin.

133n, 1142-58n, 1150, 1178n, 1196, 1312, L 789, F 1289n, 1291-2n, E 843, 1174

hedgehog, A 879, P 789, 1086, 1114, L 1168-9n

horse, K p4, K 551-8, 595-610, C 13-16, 21n*, 23, 32, 83-84, 109n, 122, 125, 243, 438, 1224n, 1225-6, 1298, W 135n, P 74-75, 81, 83-86n*, 126, 155-6, 1282, B 1128, 1293n, 1470-81n*, 1702-3n*, L 191-2, 561, 676-9, 1307, T 153, 325n, 1174n, 1211n, F 429n, 467n, 818n, 904n, 929n, 932n, 963, 1073n, 1403n, E 1029n, We 157; see also cavalry, sport (chariot-racing, horse-racing)

leopard, C 347, B 1250, L 1015

lion, K 1037-43, P 1065n, 1189, L 231, T 514, F p17 n79, F 815n, 823n, 1041, 1427-32n, 1431

lizard, C 169-176, W p.xviii n3, W 206n

marten, A 880

mole, A 879, W 1509n

monkey, A 907n*, K 416, 887, P 1008n, 1065-6, 1100n, B 11n, 440, T 1133, F 708, E 907n, 1072

mouse, A 255n, C 173n, W p.xviii n3, W 140, 204-5*, 206n, 1182, 1185, T 559n, E 924n, We 693n

mule, T 491, F 32n, 290

otter, A 880

pet-names for, W 179n

pig. A 739-835, K 416n, W 36, 573n, 844, P 24, 374, 387, 927-8, L 203, 683, 1062-4, 1073, T 237, F 338, E 128n, 606n, We 304, 305n, 308, 315, 820, 1024n, 1106, 1170n; see also §boar

polecat, A 255n, W p.xviii n3, W 364, 1182, 1185, 1078n, 1151, B 721n, F 196n, 304n, E 128, 792, 924

as scapegoat for vanishing food etc., P 795-6, T 559

rebellion by, against humans, B p2

sacrificial, rules governing, A 785n, 793n

seal, W 1035, P 758

sheep, K 264, 1017n, C 45, 1203, W p.xviii, W 32-34, 181n, 295-6n, 572, 672n, 955, 1467n, P 530-8n, 535,

929-937, 1076, 1112, B 566, 568, 571n, 583, 620n, 713, 856, 959n, 971, 1559-60, L 1063n, F p11, F 404-6n, 467n, 847, We 293, 296, 299, 820, 922

snake, K 198, 206-210, C 506-8n, W p.xviii n3, W 17-18, 206n, 438n, 1032-5n, P 336n, 756, L 364n, 670-1n, 809-811n, F 473n, E 909, We 689-690, 884n

Aesculapian, We 690n

in Asclepian miracle healings, We 733-6, 741

toad, L 1242n, E 1101

tortoise, W 429, 1292-5

shell of, as component of lyre, F 234n

whale, W 35, 38, P 1008n, F 549-578n

wolf, K 1017n, C 347, 352, W 952, P 1076, 1112, B 369, 967, L 629

see also meat

annual plants, K 518n

anodos (rescue of goddess from underworld), P p.xvii*; see also Pandora, Persephone, Semele in Index II

Anthela (Trachis), L 1129-32n

Anthesteria (festival), A 961n*, 1224n, T 746-7nn, F 180n, 216-9nn; see also Choes, Chytroi

Anthesterion (Athenian month, ~ February), A 961n, C 408n, T 746n, We 845n

Antlētriai, P 151n

aparkhē (first share of sacrificial meat), P 1056n

Apaturia (festival), A 146, C 1198n, P 890n, T 558, F 418n, 798

aphrodisiacs, L 723-5n, T 561n, E 1092n

Aphytis (Chalcidice), B 790n, 1025n

aposiopesis, C 1378, T 536

aposterein (failure to repay/restore a loan/deposit), We 373n

apotheosis, see deification

apotympanismos, method of execution, T 930-1n, We 476n

apprentices, K 1236, B 1150n

aprāgmosynē (avoidance of involvement in troublesome affairs), B 44n, 471n

Arabia, B 278n

Aradus (Phoenicia), W 220n
Arcadia, K 797n, 798, 801, C 398n, P 507n,
  B 745n, L 785n, F 1266n, 1402n, E
  80n
  dialect of, F 1144-5n
archers, mounted, in Athenian army, K
  225n
archery, A 707n, F 1357; *see also* Archer(s)
  in Index II
Arginusae, battle of (406), B 126n, F pp2-3,
  p6, p7 n32, F 33n, 49-50n, 191n,
  365n, 417n, 541n, 693n, 694n, 696n,
  1072n, 1196n, 1422n, 1431n, 1512n,
  E 202-3n, 366n, 550n
  condemnation of commanders after, F
  pp2-3, F 1196n, E 202-3n, 1089n,
  We 550n, 725n
Argo, Jason's ship, K 67n, F 1382
Argonauts, We p11 n54
Argos, A 430n, 793n, K 1n, 465-7, 479n,
  813, W 240n, P p.xv, P 414n, 475-7,
  493, 508n, B 399n, 1569n, L 394n,
  513n, T 1101, F 1072n, 1126-8n,
  1208, 1276n, E p2, p4, E 193n, 197-
  8n, 201, 237n, We p1, p2 n7, p4, We
  601
  union with Corinth, E p3, E 200n, We
  p2 n7
aristocracy, B 125
arithmetic, invention of, F 1451n
arkhōn (governor), title of Peisetaerus, B
  1123*; *see also* Athens, political and
  legal institutions (archon, archons,
  arkhontes)
Arkteia, L 643-5
arms and armour, A 279n, 574n, 581-9,
  964n, 1103-40, 1181-2, K 849n, P
  356, 395, 438, 553, 561, 662, 678,
  1128, 1173, 1177-8, 1186, 1193n,
  1274-5, 1298-9, 1303, 1328, B 94n,
  270*, 290, 292n, 359-360n, 434*,
  1185-7, 1360-9*, 1697-9n, L 49-53,
  106, 184n, 188-190, 555-564, 627,
  632-3, 985, T 140, 218n, 822-3n,
  825-9, 929d, 1127, 1197n, F 564,
  928-9, 966, 1016-8, 1036-8, 1039n
  makers and sellers of, P 447, 545-9,
  1210-64

Arrephoroi (girl cult-servants of Athena), L
  642, 643-4n
arson, C 1465-6n, 1484-1505, B 997n
Artemisium, battle of (480), L 1251
aryballos, T 139n, F 1200n, E 1101n
asafoetida, K 895n.
Asia, *kithara* associated with, T 120n
Asia Minor:
  Athenian naval expedition to (390-388),
  E 102n; *see also* Agyrrhius,
  Ergocles, Thrasybulus (7310) *in
  Index II*
  Greeks of, *see* Ionia(ns)
  Spartan campaigns in (390s), E p2, p3,
  We p3
asides, A 45d, 809-810d, K 752d, 1193d,
  1237d, C 1112d, W 137d, 826-7d*,
  906d, 992d, P 244-254, 262d, B
  1494, L 1088, 1149n, T 1-2, 72-73,
  603-9, F 33, 87-88, 107, 115, 159,
  254-5, E 946, We 99, 106, 111, 147-
  8, 343, 1008-37n
askōliasmos, *see* wineskin-hopping
Aspendus (Pamphylia), E 202-3n, We 550n
assassinations, political, *see* Androcles,
  Hipparchus, Hyperbolus, Phrynichus
  (15011) *in Index II*
Assyria, B 1021n
astronomy, C 171-3*, 194, 201, 361n, P
  1031n, B 692n; *see also* stars and
  constellations; Venus
  criminalized, K 1085n, W 380n, B 988n
atheism, C pp2-3, C 247-8, 365-7, 423-6,
  830n, 853n, 1240, 1469-77, 1506-9,
  B 1073n, T p11, T 451, F 320n,
  871n, 889-891n, 1114n
  criminalized, K 1085n, W 380n, B 988n
Athenian League, Second (formed 378/7),
  K 901n*, E 208n
Athenians "do everything too late", L 56-57
Athens, annihilation of, feared (405), F
  pp4-5, p14, F 358n, 736-7, 1392n,
  1419n, 1448n
Athens, avoidance of ill-omened words
  about, P 252n, L 37-38
Athens, places and buildings (ancient):
  Academy (park), C 1005, F 129n, 131n
  Acropolis[3], A p13, A 75n, K 267, 581n,

---

3   This entry includes subheadings only for buildings, etc., *on top of* the Acropolis, not for those on its sides or slopes.

1015n, 1092, 1312n*, 1325n, C 69, W 31n, 895n, P 699n, B p1 n3, B 123n, 515n, 826-836nn, 1128n*, L p4, L 1n, 174n, 176-9, 184n, 263n, 341-9n, 678n, 751n, 754, 758, 759n, 912, 1012n, 1150-6, 1183, T 224n, 533n, 658n, 811-2, 1223n, F 216-7n, 651n, E p30, E 745n, We p26, We 772

Athena Nike, temple of, L p5 n31, L 317n

Athena Polias, old temple of, L 174n, 439n, 759n, We 1193n

Athena Promachos statue, L 751n

Erechtheum, L 262n, 722n, We p22 n91, We 1193n

guardian serpent of, L 759

Hecate sanctuary, L 443n

occupation of, in *Lysistrata*, L p4, L 176-9, 240-251, 262-488, 698n, 706-780, 900n, E p8

opisthodomos, L 174n, E p28 n104, We p19, p22, We 1193

Pandrosus precinct, L 439n

Parthenon, K 580n*, 586-9n*, 1169n, F p3, F 720n, E 815, We 185n, 1193n; frieze of, E 730-745nn

residence on, forbidden, L 482n

siege of (508/7), L 281-2

treasuries on, L p3, p4, L 174n, 492n

Zeus Soter and Athena Soteira, sanctuary of, F 378n

Aglaurus, sanctuary of, T 533n

Agora, A p32*, A 21, 125n, 164n, 533, K 165, 181, 218, 293, 297, 333n, 410n, 500n, 677, 744n, 751n, 852-7n*, 1258, 1312n, 1373-6, C p3, C 991, 1003, 1055, W 16, 492-9, 1108n, 1372, P 119-121n, 609n, 999, 1010, B 395n, L 328n, 458, 555-564, 633n, T 457, 578, 654n, F 129n, 320n, 501n, 1071n, 1351, E p13*, p24 n91, p27, p29 n110, p30, E 62, 378n, 382n, 504n, 681, 711, 712-3nn, 728, 757n, 759, 802n, 818n, 819, 876/7n, 877-1111n, 1113n, 1128n, 1138n, 1152n, 1176n, 1181n, We p5 n19, p12 n26, We 162n, 787, 874

altar of Twelve Gods, W 1372n*, B 95n

areas of, devoted to specific trades, K 852-7n*, 1375, W 789, B 13, 1288n, L 557, T 448, E 302

decrees displayed in, B 1288n

dramatic performances in(?), T 395*

Eponymous Heroes monument, K 979n*, P 1183n, B 450n

itinerant vendors in, W 496-9n, B 14

perischoinisma, K 852-7n*

private, created by Dicaeopolis, A 719-730, 838-841, 847, 854, 896

statue of Zeus Soter/Eleutherios, We 1175n

Stoa Alphitopolis (Cornmarket Colonnade), K 852-7n*, E 14n, 686; *see also* Peiraeus

Stoa Basileios (Royal Colonnade), K 852-7n*, E 685

Stoa of Zeus Eleutherios, E 685n

Stoa Poikile (Painted Portico), K 846n, 852-7n*, B 997n, We p2 n7

see also *kyrbeis*

Areopagus, K 1312n, W 31n, L 678n, T 224n, 658n; *see also* Athens, political and legal institutions (Areopagus)

Asclepieum, W 123n*, We p11, We 411n, 660n

Barathron (place of execution/exposure of criminals), K 1362, C 1449, F 574, E 1089n, We 69-70n, 431, 487-618n, 1109

Cerameicus, K 772, 1246n*, B 1296n*, F 129, 131n, 1093

cemetery in, K 772n, B 395

city walls, A 72, B 497, 1484n, T 495, F 129n, E 197-8n

Clepsydra (spring), B 1695n, L 913

Council Chamber (*bouleutērion*), A 379, K 395, 485, 641n, L 696-7n

Court at Lycus (?), W 389n

Cynosarges gymnasium, F 651n

Demeter Chloe, sanctuary of, L 835

Dionysus in the Marshes, temple of, C 303-4n, F 180n, 216-7, 218-9nn

Dread Goddesses (Semnai Theai), shrine of, K 1312, T 224

Eleusinium, K 242-3n, T 658n

Enneakrounos fountain-house, L 328n, 378n, 381n

Eridanus (stream), K 852-7n*
gates, K 1246
 Dipylon, K 1246n*, F 129n, 131n,
  324n, 1093-4n, We p29 n118
 Phalerum, F 216-7n
 Sacred, K 1246n*, F 324n
Hephaesteum, K 1312n, P 395n, B
 1556n, L 490n
Heracleum in Diomeia, F 651n
Heracleum in Melite, F 501n
Iaccheion, F 324n
Ilissus (stream), F 216-7n
Long Walls, K 656n, 1362n, C 1449n, L
 1170n, F p1, p5, F 574n, E p2
Lyceum, W 386n, P 356
New Court, W 120
Odeum, W 1109
Olympieum, A 887n*, W 506n*
Pan's Grotto, L 721, 911, 913n
Parabyston court, W 1108n
Peisianacteum, see §Stoa Poikile
Pelargikon (= Acropolis), B 832
Pnyx, A 1*, 20, 21n, 22n, K 42, 165,
 313n, 395, 749, 751, 956n, 1109,
 1126, W 31, P 680, B 998n, L 392n,
 696-7n, T p10 n60, T 658*, E p11,
 p23 n84, p30, E 89n, 95n, 173-
 240n, 243, 279-284nn, 312n, 369n,
 378n, 381n, 384, 390-1n
 altar of Zeus Agoraios, We 382-5nn
 bēma (speaker's platform) on, E 87n,
  We 377-385n, 382
 benches on, in fourth century?, E 21n
Potters' Town, see §Cerameicus
Propylaea, A 1093n*, K 1326, L 1n,
 265, 317n, 835n, 913n
Prytaneum, A 125, K p2, K 167, 281*,
 535, 709, 766, 786n*, 1312n*, 1404,
 W 711n, P 1084*, F 764, 765n,
 1480n, E 834n
Theatre of Dionysus, A pp13-16*, K
 173-4n, C 275-328*, 323n, 521-3n,
 W 1109n, T 964n, 1060n, E p30, E
 128n, 330n, We p26
 honorific inscriptions in, B 1372-
  1409n
 seating in, T 395*
Theseum, K 1312*, L 679n
Thesmophorium, T p10, T 83, 88, 276n,
 278, 281n, 624n, 658n*, 763-4n, 878,

 930n, 964n, 1012n, 1046, 1060n,
 1149, E p28, We p5
Tholos, P 906n, T 654n
Tower of Timon, F 129n
Tower of Timotheus, We 180
Athens, places and buildings (modern):
 Adrianou St., K 852-7n*
 Aghiou Philippou St., K 852-7n*
 Cerameicus Museum, K 1246n*
 National Archaeological Museum, F
  651n
Athens, political and legal institutions:
 adeia (immunity from prosecution), B
  1293n
 adoption, W 478n, 583-6n, F 970n
 affidavits, see §antōmosiai
 agoranomoi (market commissioners), A
  723, 824, 968, W 1407
 allotment machines (klērōtēria), A p25
  n24, E 681-8, 1158-9n
 ambassadors, A 61-110, 134-173, 192,
  601-614, 615n*, K 327n, 465n,
  1377n, C 686n, W 42n, 74n, 98n,
  506n, 1139n, 1183-4n, 1247n, 1268-
  9n, 1271, P 714n*, 928n, 1008n, B
  147n, 284n, 822-3n, 1532-3, 1565-
  1693, 1569n, L 63n, 570, 801n,
  1009-12, 1231-5, T 342n, F p9, F
  428n, 965n, 1071n, 1072n, E 71n,
  97n, 208n, 248n, 303n, 932n, We
  377-385n, 550n
  drunkenness recommended for,
   L 1229-35
  plenipotentiary (autokratores),
   B 1595*, L 1010, T p2
  see also Ambassador, Athenian
   Delegates, Spartan Delegates,
   Theorus in Index II
 anagraphēs (law consolidation board,
  410-399), F 1506n
 anakrisis (preliminary hearing of court
  case), A p3, W 1284-91nn, 1407n, B
  1455n
 ancestral gods (patroioi), B 1527
 ankhisteiā (close kinship), B 1661n
 antidosis (exchange of property), F
  1065n
 antigraphai (written statements of a
  case), C 472n

antōmosiai (sworn statements of facts), W 544-5, 1041, E 603n

apagōgē (summary arrest), C 1175n, F 772n

aphaireisthai eis eleutheriān (rescue of person claimed as slave), E 1023-4n

arbitrators, private, W 524, F 1412n

arbitrators, public, C 64n, W 1287n

archers, Scythian, A 40n, 707n, K 665, L 184n, 433-462*, F 608n, E 143, 258-9, 688n; *see also* Archer(s) *in Index II*

archon, chief ("eponymous"), A p14, A 220n, C 528-9n, 615-6n, W 1108, 1109n, B 876n, T 372-9n, F 1437n, E p5 nn26,28

archons, the nine, W 304, B 1527n, T 834n, F 694n, E 282-4n, 290n, 655, We 278n

Areopagus, Council of the, W 663n

arkhē (magistracy), scope of term, W 587n, We 917n

arkhontes (resident officials in allied states), B 1049n

Assembly (*ekklēsiā*), A 19-173, 45n, 685n, 846n, K 76, 165n, 305, 410n*, 746, 751n, 763n, 794-5n, 936, 937-8n, 1054n, 1227n, 1304n, 1340, 1358n, C 432, 551n, 1019n, W p.xvi, W 31-45, 590, 594, 663n, 1007n, 1501n, P 420n, 605n, 680n, 681n, 906n, 931, B p5, B 720n, 1027, 1030, L p2, p3, L 390-7, 421n, 513-4, 696-7n, 1010n, T p2, p3 n21, T 294n, 295-371n, 342n, 359n, 372-9nn, 808-9n, 840n, 936-7n, 1143-4n, E p11, p30, E 17n, 20-23, 74n, 84-310, 352, 369n, 372n, 376-457, 490, 550-7, 740, We 171, 381-3nn, 875n, 949-950

agenda of, E 396-7n

assessing/declaring results of voting in, We 725n

concluding formulae for speeches in, T 432n, E 239n

debate on "saving the City", E 396-7n

disqualifications for speaking in, T 819-820n, E 400-2n

dress-rehearsal for, E 30-284n, 82n, 116-267

factions sitting together in, K 852-3n*, E 296-7

formula for opening debate, A 45, T 379, E 130, 396-7n

never errs but may be deceived, K 1356-7

opening gambits for speeches in, E 132-168n, 151-2n, 171-2n, 173-4n

pay for attending, E p11, p18, E 96n, 102n, 183-8, 280-1, 284n, 290n, 292, 300-310, 380-393, 396-7n, 547-8, We 171n, 176n, 329-330; tickets for, E 284n, 292n, 296, 378n, 381n

prayers and curses recited at, B 1074-5n, L 619n, T 295-371nn, E 128-130n

presidency of, E 87n

procedural obstructionism in, E 254n, We 725n

quorum for, E 183-4n, 296n, We 171n

"regular" meetings of (*kyriai ekklēsiai*), A 19n

sacrifices preceding, K 410n*, E 128n

sign displayed at start of session, W 690n, T 277-8

time of commencement, A 19-20, T 375, E 20-21, 84-85, 312n, 377n

trials before, W 987-8n, F p2, E 1089n; *see also* Arginusae

were late-comers admitted to?, E 284n, 378n

auditors, see §*logistai*

basileus, see king-archon

bastardy, B 1649-70

board of control for Eleusis, W 401n, E 46n

Boule, *see* Council

boulomenos, ho ("anyone who wishes"), as prosecutor, We 31n, 907-918; *see also* informers

chairman of Prytaneis, *see* §*epistatēs*

challenges, in litigation, F 615-641, 1065n; *see also* torture (of slaves)

citizenship law, B 1652n; *see also*
§naturalization, §prosecutions for
(*xeniā*) *and* foreigners (citizens
accused of being)
"collectors of the people" (*syllogēs tou
dēmou*), E 290n
Council of Five Hundred, A p2, p3, p25
n24, pp32-33, A 23n, 88n, 379, 603n,
685n, 705n, K 166, 300n*, 363, 475,
615, 626-682, 710n, 722, 774, 969n*,
1358n, W 590, 1187n, P 52n, 714*,
846, 872, 878, 882n, 886n, 887,
893*, 906n, 907n, B 794, 800n,
1372-1409n, 1527n, L 421n, 489n,
980n, 1010n, T p1 n4, p3 n21, T 372-
3, 432n, 808-9, 936-7n, E 87n, 102n,
128n, 143n, 171-2n, 290n, 304-5n,
444, We p30, We 176n, 382-3n,
875n, 949-950; *see also* §Prytaneis
    did not normally meet on festival
    days, T 79, 943n
    factions sitting together in, K 852-
    3n*
    power to impose death penalty?,
    T 78-79n, 943-4
    secret information leaked from,
    E 444-5
    secret sessions of, K 648n*, E 444n
Council of the Areopagus, *see*
§Areopagus
cross-examination, in trials, A 687n, C
1174n
debts, lawsuits for, C 34-37, 241, 1131-
42, 1151-3, 1214-56, 1277-8, E 567,
657-661
debts to state:
    collection of, C 37n
    imprisonment for, E 102n, We 176n
    incur disfranchisement, L 581n
decrees (*psēphismata*) of the Assembly,
C 1019, 1429, W 157n, 377-8n,
917n, B 790n, 798n, 988n, 1021n,
1024-5n, 1035-51, 1052n, 1288n,
1289, 1293n, 1296n, 1297n, 1372-
1409n, L 391n, 654n, 698-704, F
153n, 967n, 1196n, 1512n, E 248n,
825n, 1013-20, 1089n
    called "laws", B 1037-8
    detailed drafting of, T 432

honorific, F pp21-22, E 330n,
We 550n
language of, parodied, L 1012n,
T 372-9, E 1013-20
penal, against individuals, B 1052n
prescript formula, T 372-9n
proposed *after* a speech, T 432n
tend to be ephemeral, E 812-829
demarch, C 37
demes, A 319, 328, 675, K 320, C 210,
1209, 1219, 1322, B 33n, L 685n, T
300n, 834n, F 694n, E 1023, 1115,
We 254, 1167n; *for individual demes
see* Attica, demes and localities
(ancient)
democracy:
    abolition of (404), W 157n; *see also*
    Thirty
    and wealth redistribution, C 205n
    Ar.'s attitude to, A pp5-6, W p.xviii*
    attempted limitation of (403), E 97n
    ascribed to Solon, C 1187n
    conspiracies against (real or
    imaginary), W 342-3n, 413-4n,
    466n, B 766-7n, 1584n, L pp1-3*, L
    313n, 489n, 577-8n, T pp2-4, T
    804n, 805n, 840n, 1143-4n, We
    550n, 875n; *see also* "conspiracy",
    hetaireiai, tyranny
    elects ill-qualified officials, B 1570-1
    establishment of (508/7), L 273n
    extreme interpretations of, F 952n,
    E 626n, 631n
    Euripidean tragedy and, F p14,
    F 952-3
    fears for (411), T 361-2n, 1143-4n;
    see also tyranny
    overthrow of (411), T pp2-4; *see also*
    Four Hundred
    restoration of (410), E 456-7n,
    We 948-9n
    restoration of (403), F 367n, 965n,
    1506n, E p1, E 97n, 102n, 202-3n,
    456-7n, We 550n, 1146n
    some more equal than others in,
    E 633n
    Spartan disdain for, L 170-1
    subversion of, as a crime, E 452-3,
    767n, We 948-9n

deposits (*prytaneia*), lodged by plaintiffs in lawsuits, C 1136, 1179-95n, 1181-2, 1185n, 1191, 1255, W 659

dikastēria, see lawcourts

diōbeliā (two-obol dole to the poor), T 805n, F 141n, 678n

disfranchised persons, restoration of rights to, L 581n, F pp21-22, F 687-702; *see also* §punishments (*atīmiā*)

distraint, C 35, 37n, 242, B 1460, E 567

divorce, B 284n

dockyard commissioners, K 912-3n

dokimasiā (scrutiny):
   of boys reaching majority, W 578
   of officials, councillors, public speakers, etc., K 877n, T 808-9n, F p3 n14

dowries, T 446n

draftsmen, commissions of (*syngraphês*), A 1150, F 967n

eisangeliā (form of prosecution), A pp32-33, K 774n*, W 590-1n, F 362n, 367n, We 385n

eisphorai (property taxes), A 6n, K 774n, 924-6*, W 660n, L 654, F p4, E 197-8n, 825n, We p2

ekklēsiā, see §Assembly

elections:
   by lot, A 724, K 41n, W 557n, B 1111n, E 290n
   by voting, A 598, 607, C 581-7, W p.xv, T 432n, F p3, E 246-7, 517, 714-5

Eleven (prison controllers), W 1108

endeixis (type of prosecution), K 278n, 281n

epiklēroi, see §heiresses

epilakhontes (shadow councillors available to fill vacancies), T 808-9n

episkopoi (imperial inspectors), P 1008n, B 1021-53

epistatai (boards supervising specific projects), P 605n

epistatēs (chairman of Prytaneis), A 23n, P 906n, T 372-9n, 373, 654n

euthynai (audit of outgoing officials), A 938, K 259, 825, W 102, 523n, 554n, 961n
   jurors not subject to, W 587

executioner, E 81

exēgētai (expounders of religious law), A 171n

exile, voluntary, T 805n, F p3, p10 n47, F 417n, 678n, 1512n, E p4, E 71n, 180n, 196; *see also* §punishments

exōmosiā (oath of excusal), E 1026

extradition, We 377-385n, 390n

genē (clans), A 322n, B 33, L 1094n; *see also* Alcmeonidae, Buzygae, Eteobutadae, Kerykes, Mesogeioi

generals, A 566n, 569, 593*, 601n, 685n, 1073-8, K p2, K 166, 288, 355, 438n, 574n, 742, 912-3n, C 580n, 582, 586, 1001n, 1261n, W p.xv, W 81n, 157n, 240n, 961n, 964n, 970n, 1501n, P 53n, 296-8n, 304n, 444n, 450, 782n, B 126n, 284n, 397, 448-450n, 798n, 800n, 1293n, 1406n, 1569n, L 103n, 390-7nn, 801n, T 804n, 805n, 833, 837n, 841n, 876n, F pp2-3, p7 n35, F 367n, 428n, 541n, 689n, 1039n, 1072n, 1196n, 1422n, 1431n, 1512n, E p7 n33, p11 n47, E 102n*, 201n, 202-3nn, 246-7, 303, 366n, 491, 500, 504n, 517, 558n, 678-9n, 727, 810n, 834n, 835, 870, 1113n, We 174n, 176n, 179n, 192, 381n, 550n, 800n; *see also*, 385n
general (sole)

graphai (indictments), A 714, K 306, W 848, 894-7, 907, P 107n

graphē xeniās, see §prosecutions for (*xenia*)

guardians of fatherless minors, T 446n

heiresses (*epiklēroi*), W 135n, 583-6, 589, B 1652-4, 1657-8n

Hellenotamiae (treasurers of the Athenian Alliance), A 1093n, W 459n, B 822-3n

herald of the Council and People, E 825n; *see also* heralds, *and* Herald *in Index II*

hieromnemon (head of delegation to Amphictyonic meeting), C 624, T 841n

hipparchs (cavalry commanders), K 242-3n, B 799

homicide law, C 1425-6n, W 654n, F 1167-8n

hypogrammatēs, see §under-secretaries

hypōmosiā (sworn challenge to Assembly vote declaration etc.), We 725

imprisonment pending trial, P 605n, F 417n, E 1064-5n, 1089n

indictments, *see* §*graphai*

inheritance, C 39-40, B 1352n, 1643-70*, T 819-820n, 822-3n

insanity, court adjudication of, C 845, 1413-4n

inspectors, imperial, see §*episkopoi*

juries, *see* §lawcourts

jury-pay, K 48-49n, 51, 255, 555n, 715-8n, 798, 800, 804, 807, 1019n, 1099n*, 1126n, 1359, C 863n, W pp.xvi-xvii, W 241n, 300, 525, 606-9, 661-4, 674n, 684, 701-2, 785-795, 813, 1113n, 1118, 1121, P 621n, 639n, B 1541, L 624, F 1466, E 197-8n, 296n, 303-5nn, 563n, 982-4n, We 277n

kakourgiai (summarily arrestable offences), C 1175, W 1108n, F 772n

king-archon (*basileus*), A p14, A 1224, T 730n, E 22-23n, 685n

kings, prehistoric, A 1224n; *see also* Aegeus, Cecrops, Cranaus, Erechtheus, Erichthonius, Pandion, Theseus *in Index II*

klērōtēria, see §allotment machines

klepsydrā, see §water-clock

kōlakretēs, see §paymaster

lawcourts (and juries), A p6, A 375, 656n, 679-718, K 50n, 255, 897-8, 968n, 977n, 1317, 1332n, 1358-60, C 208, 447, 620, 755-782, 1141-2, 1211, W pp.xvi-xviii, W 88-1008 *passim*, 1340n, 1367n, P 349, 505, 607n, B 38n, 40-41, 109, 1283-4n, 1539-41n, L 270n, 380, T 1031n, E 292n, 460, We 277n, 916-8
  admission to, W 104n, 689-690, 775, 892
  bēma (speaker's platform) in, E 677-8
  benches in, W 1110n
  cases settled out of, C 1179-95n, 1193-4, W 1284-91(?)*, 1419-26
  character, arguments from, W 952-8n

children brought into, W 568-573, 976-8, We 382-3n
closed on festivals, T 78-79
converted into dining-halls, E 676-8
did not always sit daily, W 304-5n
dryphaktoi (railings), W 124n, 386, 830
duration of trials, W 243n
emotive pleas by defendants, W 279, 390, 392, 553-574, 882, 967-978, F 1066n
entertainment as defence strategy, W 566-7, 579-580, We 177n
factions sitting together in, K 852-3n*
fraudulent multiple registration by jurors, We 1167n
judgements given by default, B 1455n
juries identified with Athenian people, W 917n
juror's oath, We p19 n83
kinklis (bar at court entrance), W 124, 775
moratoria on certain types of lawsuit, F 1463-6nn, E 982-4n
notice-boards in or near, W 105n, 349, 848
number of jurors in, W 662
number of sitting days per annum, W 663n
one-man jury, W 891-1008, F p1
paid half-holidays for, K 50, W 595
rate at which cases disposed of, W 595n
sign displayed at start of session, W 690
speeches in, interrupted by jurors, W 621n, 980-1n
symbola (tokens issued to jurors), We 278n
tied vote, effect of, F 684-5n
vote-counting in, W 332-3, 993-4
voting-tokens in, K 1332, W 94, 109, 987; *see also* §mussel-shells
voting-urns in, K 1150n, W 321-2, 349n, 674, 754, 853-5, 987-994, 1339, B 1032, 1053, T 1031, F p1 n3
laws:

alleged duty to enforce, We 911-8
curse against subverters of, T 361-2
duty to obey, E 762-8, 942-5, 950n,
　1022, 1049, 1055-6, 1077n
indiscriminately ascribed to Solon,
　C 1187n, B 1660
recodification of (410-403), A 603n,
　F 1084n, 1506n, We 948-9n
liturgies (compulsory public services),
　A 392n, F 1065n, E 426n, We 195n;
　see also chorēgoi, §trierarchs
logistai (auditors), W 102n
lottery between letter-classes:
　for dining, in Praxagora's society,
　　E 683-8, 836-7
　for jury selection, E 290n, E 683n,
　　688n, We 277, 972n, 1166-7
　for seating in Council, We p30
lottery within letter-classes, for jury
　selection, We 972n
merchants, legal privileges of, E 1027,
　We 904
mussel-shells, as voting-tokens, K 1332,
　W 333n, 349
naturalization, A 145, K 327n, 449n*, W
　283n, F 694n, E p4, We p3
　of fighters for democracy, after 403,
　　E 202-3n, We 550n
nautodikai, E 1027n, We 904n
nomothesia (4th-century law-making
　procedure), W 1187n
nomothetai (4th-century legislative
　commission), We p17 n75, p19 n83
notheia (permitted bequests to bastards),
　B 1656n
oath of allegiance, P 457n, B 540-3n*, E
　767n
office, refusal to accept, E 1026n
oikos (patrilineal family), T 825-6n
ostracism (temporary banishment by
　popular ballot), A 703n, 846n*, K
　852-7n*, 855n*, 1304n, 1377n, C
　551n*, W 947n, 1007n*, P 681*, L
　1137-44nn, T 804n, 805n, 840n*,
　842n, F 570n, 678n, E 1089n
outlawry, W 417n, B 1072-84*, F 320n
pay for office-holding, A 66, 597, 602,
　608, 619, W 683, 691, B 1025, F
　1466n, E 197-8n, 206, 304-5n; see

also §Assembly (pay for attending),
　§jury-pay
paymaster (kōlakretēs), W 695, 724,
　1541
penalty, assessment of, W 106-8, 167,
　847, 850n, 897, We 480-4, 859n
peristiarkhos (purifier of meeting-
　places), E 128n
phasis (type of prosecution), A 726n,
　819-823*, 911-4, K 300*
phratries, K 255n, B 765, 1669, T 558n,
　F 418
phylarchs (tribal cavalry commanders),
　B 799, L 561
pinakia (jurors' personal tickets), E
　683n, We 277n
polemarch (third archon, responsible for
　metics), W 1042*, 1187n
police, see §archers
poristai (Revenue Board), F 1505,
　1506n*
probouleumata (draft decrees proposed
　by Council), W 590-1n, T 372-9n,
　658n*
probouloi (special advisory board, 413-
　411), L 387n, 421, 450n, 467, 609,
　980n, T 808-9n; see also
　Magistrate in Index II
proedria (privileged seating as honour),
　K p2, K 536, 575, 702, T 834n, F
　765n
proedroi (presidium of Assembly in 4th
　century), E 87n
prosecutions for:
　abusive language, W 1207
　adultery, F 428n, E 810n, We 168n
　assault, C 494-6, W 1255, L 435-6n,
　　F 1133n, E 662-4
　being a sykophantēs, W 1042n
　bribery, A 6n, 685n, K 442(?), 834-5,
　　C 591, F 367n, E 71n, We 550n
　cowardice, A 1129n, K 368
　damage (blabē), W 1255n, 1407
　"deceiving the people", F p22 n101,
　　F 417n, 1086n
　desertion, A 1129n, K 368n, T 805n,
　　F p22, F 678n, E 982-4n
　diverting public watercourses,
　　K 814n

embezzlement, K 442n, 444n, 828-9, W 554n, 759, 896n, P 605n, F 417n, 1196n, E 71n, 102n, We p2, We 174n, 176n, 177n, 385n, 550n
evading military service, A 1129n, K368n, 443
exercising citizen rights when disqualified, K 278n, 281n, 877n
failure to tithe war booty, K 301-2n*
false testimony, W 783n, E 560-1n
forcing up prices, E 424n
homicide, C 1413-4n, W 654n, We p16 n74
household offences, in mock court, W 765-1002
hybris, W 1418*, 1434n, B 1046, E 663-4n
impiety, A 703n, 710n, K 242-3n*, 1085n, C 109n, 1481-2(?), W 592n, B p4, B 145-7n, 1297n*, L p1, T 451n, F p19, F 320n, 886n*, E 248n, We p12
"injuring the Athenian people", E 1089n
misconduct as ambassador (parapresbeiā), E p4, E 71n, 102n
misconduct in office, E 644-5n
moving illegal decrees (graphē paranomōn), B 1372-1409n, L 421n, F 153n, E 248n, 330n, We pp19-20 n83
"not proposing what is best for the people", F 367n
proposing an inappropriate law, We pp.19-20 n83
slandering an individual, E 639-640n
"slandering the City", A p2, p32, A 502-3, 630-1, C 549n
subversion of democracy, K 248n*, We 948-9
throwing away one's shield, A 1129n, K 368n
theft, K 444, C 591, B 1625n, F 605-617; see also §embezzlement
trading with the enemy, K 278n
treason, A 685n, K 248n*, 327n, 819n, W 288n, 1270n, P 108, 639n, B 145-7n, F p10 n47, F 362n, 953n, We 381n, 385n

xeniā (falsely claiming citizenship), A pp2-3, W 718, 1284-91n
prosecutions withdrawn, W 1284-91n; see also informers (silence of, bought)
prosecutors:
acting on behalf of leading politicians, K 1256
penalties for unsuccessful, We 482n
rewards for successful, A 819n, K 300n*, B 1460n, We 31n
see also §boulomenos; informers
prostatēs (patron of a metic), P 684n, F 549-578n, 569n
prostatēs tou dēmou (leading radical politician), P 684n
Prytaneis (business committee of Council), A 1*, 23, 40, 56, 167, 173, K 665, 674, P 887, 905-6, L 981, T 372-9n, 654, 764, 854, 1084, E 87, 183-4n, 377n, 396; see also Prytanis in Index II
prytanies (divisions of Council year), A 19n, 23n, 843n, C 584-5n, B 800n, T 432n
public enemies, We 948-9n
punishments:
atīmiā (loss of citizen rights), A 1129n, K 327n, 368n, 877n, C 351n, W 917n, B 766-7n, 790n, T 808-9n, F p14, pp21-22, F 686-705nn, 692-705
burial denied, K 327n, 819n, B 1585-6n, We 30n
confiscation of property, A 522n, K 103, 256n, 327n, 774n*, 1019n, 1359n, C 109, W 241n, 659, 1113n, P 395n, 639n, B 1460n, 1556n, L 103n, 490n, T 805n, F 678n, 1512n, E 563n, We 31n, 174n
death, K 327n, 1359n, 1362n, 1377n, W 241n, 421n, 898, P 364n, 365*, 395n, B 766-7n, 1297n*, 1460n, 1585-6n, L 490n, T p9, T 78-79n, 816-8, 930n, 931-946, 1001-8, 1026-8, 1109, F p22, F 417n, 541n, 574n, 613, 617, 678n, 772n, 886n*, 1012n, 1086n, 1196n, 1504n, E p28, E 71n, 81n, 424n, 563n, 1089n, We p2, p12, p16 n74,

We 30n, 381n, 385n, 390n, 476, 483-4, 524n, 550n, 910n, 948-9n; see also *apotympanismos*; Athens, places and buildings (ancient) (Barathron); hemlock

demolition of house, K 327n

disfranchisement, see *atīmiā*

enslavement, A p3, W 718n

exile, K 819n, W 241n, B 1297n*, F 1167-8n, We 910n

fines, K 442n, 814n, 1019n, W 241n, 769n, 1113n, 1255, 1263, 1407n, B 38, 1052n, 1460n, 1625n, L 490n, E 563n, 662-4, 1064-5n, We 31n, 176n, 910n

for dangerous dogs, W 897n

imposed without a hearing, T 943-4n

imprisonment, K 248n*, F 367n, E 102n, We 176n, 177n

of offender's descendants, K 327n

pillory, confinement in, We 476, 606

stocks, confinement in, K 248*, 367, 394n*, 705, 1049, C 592, P 479, L 680-1

summary killing, F 688n, We 948-9n; *see also* adultery (summary execution of man taken in)

purifier, see *peristiarkhos*

retrospectivity in legislation, C 1425-6n, F 688n

Revenue Board, see *poristai*

rewards, official:

for capture of Artemisia, L 675n

for information, L 489n

for killing/capturing public enemies, B 1072-84, L 619n, F 320n

see also §prosecutors (rewards for successful)

rope, dyed, used for crowd control, A 22n, E 378-9, 380n

sanctuary, places of, K 445-6n, 1311-2*

sanis (execution board), T 930-1, 940, 1001-8, 1124, 1165; see also *apotympanismos*

searching for stolen goods, C 499, F 1363

secretaries (to Council, magistrates, etc.), A 603n, 614n, 843n*, 969n*, C 46n, W 157n, 401n, P 1008n, B 168n, T 372-9n, 374, 432, 1103, F

367n, 708-9n, 1084, E 46n, 102n, We 176n

sītēsis (state maintenance as honour), K p2, K 281n*, 282n, 283n, 574-5, 709, 786n*, W 711n, P 1084*, F 764, E 834n; *see also* Athens, places and buildings (Prytaneum)

sītophylakes (corn-controllers), K 407*

skēpsis (plea of exemption), A 392n; *see also* §merchants

summons, C 875, 1189, 1221-2, 1277, W 1041, 1334-5, 1406, 1417, 1445, B 849n, 1455, F 578, E 863

server of, abroad (*klētēr*), B 147, 1422-6

witness to (also *klētēr*), C 1218, W 189, 1408, 1412-4, 1416, 1445, We 945n

sureties, E 1023-4, 1059-60n, 1064-5

suspension of magistrates pending trial, W 240n

synēgoroi (state-appointed prosecution speakers), A 679-688, 704-716, 1358-61, C 1089-90, W 102n, 482n, 687-694

syngraphês, see §draftsmen

taxes, W 658-9, E p5, p6, p7, E 823-9

harbour dues, W 658n, 659

on confiscated goods, W 658n

on foreigners trading in Agora, A 896, W 659

on imports and exports, W 659n, F p4 n19, F 363

on property, see §eisphorai

on real estate, hard to evade, E 197-8n

on sales, E 1006-7n

taxiarchs (tribal infantry commanders), A 569, P 395n, 444, 1172-81, B 126n, 353, 1556n, L 490n, T 833, F 363n

theōriai (state delegations to festivals etc.), W 1187, 1382, P 523n, 714n*, B 188-9n; *see also* Showtime *in Index II*

theoric fund, A pp15-16*

thesmothetae, W 304n, 775, 935n, E 282-4n, 290, 296n

thiasoi (religious associations), W 728n, E 167n, We 508n

treasurers of Athena, A 614n, K 969n*,
   C 46n, W 157n, P 1008n, B 168n,
   We 1193n
treasurers of the Other Gods, We 1193n
tribes, A 23n, 568, P 887n, B pl n3, B
   33, 368, 1404, 1407n, F 694n, E 87n,
   683n, We 550n
   Acamantis, C 134n
   Antiochis, B 368n
   Cecropis, B 1407n
   Erechtheis, K 321n
   Hippothontis, B 558-9n
   Leontis, A 406n*, W 81n, 1223n
   Oeneis, A 406n, 568n
   Pandionis, P 1183n, B 368n
trierarchs (naval ship-captains), A 546,
   887n*, K 912-8, P 1234n, B 997n, T
   837, F p3, F 48n, 1065-8, E 197-8n,
   202-3n, 366n, 624n, We 195n, 550n
trittyes (regional subdivisions of tribes),
   A 406n*, W 1223n
under-secretaries (*hypogrammatēs*), F
   1084
voluntary contributions, in emergencies,
   E p3
voting:
   by ballot, W 656n*; *see also*
      §lawcourts (voting-tokens in),
      §ostracism
   by show of hands, W 656n*, E 263-
      7, 297; *see also* §elections (by vote)
   under Thirty, W 987-8n
water-clock (*klepsydrā*) for timing court
   speeches, A 693, W 93, 857-8, B
   1695
water-supply controller, K 814n
wills, W 386n, 583-6n, 589n
witnesses, C 777, 1052-3, W 936-9, 962-
   6, E 560-1n, We 932n, 933
   appeal for, A 926n, C 495, 1297,
      W 1436, 1437, 1439, P 1119,
      B 1031, F 528, We 932
   depositions by, W 1041, E 1026n*
   oath of inability to testify, E 1026n*
   see also Witness in *Index II*
Athens, population of, W 708n, E 1132-3n
Athens, sack of (480/79), W 1079n, L 254-
   387n*, 318n, We 1193n
Athens, siege of (405/4), F p21, p22

athletes and athletics, A 214n, 483n*, K
   1159-61, C 1005-6*, W 1005n,
   1023n, 1203-4, 1206-7, 1301n, P
   1084n, L 270n, F 91n, 764n, 1319;
   see also Olympic Games, sport
   diaulos (footrace of 2 stadia), B 292, F
      91n
   dolichos (footrace of 12 stadia), F 91n
   hoplite *diaulos*, B 292n
   starting gate (*hysplēx*), L 1000n
   starting signals, B 507n
Attica, demes and localities (ancient):
   Acharnae, A p33, A 180, 200, 203, 222,
      286, 322, 324, 329, 348n, 406n,
      568n, 667, K 321n, 1377n, W 1183-
      4n, P 395n, 928n, 1008n, B 737n,
      822-3n, 1556n, L 62, 63n, 490n, T
      562-3, 805n, F 678n
   Acherdûs, E 362n
   "Achradûs" (imaginary deme of
      "Pearswick"), E 362
   Aegaleos, Mt, A 855n
   Aexone, W 240n, 895, T 876n
   Agrae, We 845n
   Alopece, A 614n, 703n, W 947n, B
      284n, F 428n, E 810n
   Amphitrope, A 855n*, W 787n, L 1105n
   Anagyrûs, A p4*, A 322n, L 67
   Anaphlystus, K 901n*, F 427n, E 979n,
      We 180n
   Aphidna, A 1093n, K 1n, 79n, 786n, W
      157n
   Athmonum, P 190, 918, B 881n, T 861n
   "Ballene" (imaginary village of
      "Peltingham"), A 234
   "Bangwell", *see* §Paeonidae
   Bate, W 157n, P 992n
   Brauron, P 874
   Butadae, B 1296n
   Ceiriadae, We 174n
   Cephale, B 476n
   Cephisia, K 321n, W 1250n, F 934n, E
      71n
   Cephisus (river), A 855n, K 321n
   Cholargus, A 855, K 1267n, C 1001n, W
      787n, T 273n, E 426n
   Cholleidae, A 406*
   Cicynna, C 134, 138n, 210, 1322n
   "Clopidae" (imaginary village of
      thieves), K 79

Coele, F 367n

Colias, Cape, C 52, L 2, T 130n

Collytus, A 202n, F 367n, E 102n, 248n, We 176n, 550n

Colonus Agoraios, B 998

Colonus Hippios, W 1187n

"Compasus" (imaginary deme of "Boaston"), B 1126

Conthyle, W 233

Cothocidae, T 620

Coprus, K 899, E 317

Corydallus, F 378n

Crioa, B 368n, 496n, 645

Cycloborus (stream), A 381, K 137

Cydantidae, K 6n, L 103n, E 428n

Cydathenaeum, A p2, p25 n13, K 336n, 775n, 852-7n*, C 549n, W 35n, 895, 1268-9n, P 47n, B 590n, T 898n, F 569n

Cytherrus, E 366n

Deceleia, A 322n, P p.xix, P 395n, B 1556n, L p1, L 62-63n, 490n, 555-6n, 1163n, T 495n, 806-7n, 977n, 1147n, F p1, p6, F 651n, 720n, 1023-4n, 1422n, 1463-5n, E 243n

Deiradiotae, W 1302n, F 689n

Diacris, W 1223

"Dickeleia" (imaginary deme), see Anaphlystus

Diomeia, A 605, C 686n, W 84n, F 651

Eleusis, A p3, p27 n61, A47-52n, 774n, K 899n, W 401n, B 645n, L 643n, F p12 n55, p19, F 886n, 887n, 1500-27n, E 317n, We p31 n126, We 820n; see also Mysteries

Hall of Initiation (Telestērion) at, C 303-4n*

Erchia, T 300n, We 1138n

Eroeadae, F 1506n

Gargettus, T 898

Halae (Aexonides or Araphenides?), W 401n, F 708-9n, E 46n

Halae Araphenides, L 447n

Halimûs, B 494-8n, 496, T 80n

Hymettus, Mt, C 156n, W 233n, P 252n, B 227-262n*, L 67-68n, T 1192n

Ilissus (stream), We 845n

Lamptrae, E 1089n, We 177n

"Larcenadae", see §Clopidae

Laurium, K 362n*, 1350-3n, W 659n, B 593n, 1106, L p1, F 720n

Leipsydrium, L 281n, 664n, 665, 852n, 1150-6n

Leuconoeum, B 997n

Lousia, L 67-68n

Marathon, B 227-262n*, 245, L 285n, T 300n, F 1296, We 385n

battle of, A 181, 697-8, K 660-1n, 781, 1334, C 67n, 986, W 711, 1078n, 1085n, P 289n, L 254-387n*, 285, 619n, 721n, 1262n, T 696-7n, 806, F 694n, 887n, E 105n, We p2 n7

Marathon Bay, marsh adjoining, L 1032n

Marathonian Tetrapolis, L 285

Melite, K 129n, B 998n, F 501

Munichia, B 876n, F 1437n

Myrrhinûs, B 872n, E 825n

Oa, B 153-4n*

Oë, A 566n, P 304n, T 841n, F 1039n

Oenoe (near Marathon), L 285n

Paeania, K 562n*, L 804n

Paeonidae, L 852

Paralia (S.E. coastal districts), L 58

Parnes, Mt, A 348, 1023n, 1075n, C 275-328*, 323*, 325n, W 1223n, L 665n, F 1056-7n

"Pearswick", see "Achradûs"

Peiraeus, see separate entry

Pelekes, F 417n

Pergase (Upper and Lower), K 321, P 1008n, B 168n

Perithoidae, A 846n, K 1304n, C 551n, W 1007n, P 681n, T 840n, F 570n

Phalerum, A 901, C 52n, W 895n, B 76, 496n, L 2n, 1150-6n, T 130n

Phlya, A 1167-8n, W 234, We 327n

Phrearrhii, K 812n

Phyle, A p24 n10, A 855n, 1023, 1028

occupation of, by democrats (404/3), F p3 n14, F 1167-8n, E 202-3n, We p30, We 550n, 1146

Prasiae, W 74n, P 244n

Probalinthus, B 762n, L 285n

Rhamnûs, W 1270n

Salamis, K 449n*, L 59, 411, F 139-140n, 204, 1041n

battle of, A 214n, K 785, W 1085n, 1086n, 1206-7n, L 675n, T 1200n, F 1027-8nn

ferry to, E 1087n

sexual stamina of male inhabitants, L 59-60, E 38-39

Scambonidae, A 716n, W 44n, 81, 895n, B 798n, T 100n, F 1422n, 1512n, E 644-5n

"Shittington", see Coprus

Sphettus, C 134n, 156, We 720

Steiria, F 541n, E 202-3n, We 550n

Sunium, K 560, B 476n, 868, F 427n, 666n, E 979n

Teithras, F 477

Thoricus, C 1261n, W 1501n, P 782n, T 169n, F 86n

Thria, B 645n

Thymaetadae, W 1138

Tricorythus, L 285n, 1032

"Wanksbury", see Anaphlystus

Zea, W 123n, We p11 n51, We 411n, 733-4n

Attica, localities (modern):

Aspropyrgos, T 620n

Glyphada, W 895n

Ieraka, T 898n

Kato Souli, L 1032n

Khalandri, W 234n

Pikermi, F 477n

Vari, L 67-68n

Atticism, in Roman period, A p16

auctions, E 757

audience, A p8*, pp15-16, A 705n, 911n, C 1102n*

addressed, A 497, K 36, 300n, C 1262n, 1437-9, W 54-135, P 20-37, 50-77, 263-7, 276-9, 296-8n, 819-823, 1115, B 479-480, T 531n, F 354-371, E 173-240n, 363, 1002-4, 1154-62, We 802n; see also parabasis

admission charge for, F 141n

age-groups in, P 50-53, 766n, E 1146

appeal to opinion of, F 1475n

applause solicited, K 546-550, P 761n, E 1146n

brought into play, A 40*, W 73-84, P 905-8, 962*, 1115-6

children in, C 539

cries from, W 1526-7

presupposed by script, L 1219d, 1220n, E 888n

fickleness of, K 518-540

flattered, C 521, 526, 527, 535, W 65n, 1014n, F 676-7n, 700, 1109-18

food thrown to, W 58-59, P 962n, We 796-801

foreigners in, A p16, A 502-8, T p11, F p15 n65

generous promises to, made and snatched away, L 1043-71, 1189-1215, E 1141-8

"girl" presented to a member of, P 905-8

individuals in, picked out, W 74-84, 325n, P 543-9, 883, 906-8, T 809, E 167-8, We 800

influence on judges' decision, B 445, F 141n

insulted, C 1096-1104*, 1201-3, P 9n, 55n, 821-3, 968n, F 276, 734, 783, 808, 1109-18n, 1503, E 439-440, We 47n, 1082n(?)

intentionally kept in dark, E 17n, 107n

misled, F 1109-18n, E 107n, We 802-818n

old men in, C 1437

presence of, ignored to good comic effect, E 322n

referred to, K 146*, 163, 228, 233, P 658-9, 1192n*, F 954, 1475, E 578-587, 888-9, We 409, 1061d

size of, A pp15-16, W 1010, F 676-7

status groups in, P 52-53, 296-8n

supposed reactions of, P 43-48

surveyed, C 1096-1100, P 545-9, We 409

unintentionally kept in dark?, We 53-54n, 1030n

varying tastes among, E p22

women in, A p16*, P 966n, L 1050, T 386n

augury, see omens

autochthony, Athenian pride in, W 1076, L 1082

autocracy, in comic fantasies, B p3, B 163n, 1584n, 1708n, E p11 n47

"autonomy" of Greek states, as Spartan policy, E p3

Avernus, Lake (Italy), F 1266n

Babylon(ia), W 1137n, B 552, 590n*,
   1021n, 1125-31n
babies, L 878-884, 889-890, 907-9, T p12,
   T 608, 688-732; see also birth, child
   substitution
"baby" proves to be a wineskin, T 733-
   761
boys preferred to girls, T 503n, 564-5, E
   549
in New Comedy, T pp11-12
represented by dummies?, L 879n
baby-talk, C 1380-5*, F 990n
bacchants, see maenads
Bacchic societies, L 1
backgammon, see pettoi
bad news, precautions when breaking, E
   554n
baldness, A 849n*, K 550, C 540, P 767-
   774
bankers, E 102n, 366n, We 176n
barbarians, A 168, K 1253n, W 439, B
   199n, 500n, 1470-81n*, 1700
as threat to Greek world, P 406-413, L
   1133; see also Persia
"copulate in public", T 489n
crude sexual tastes of?, T 1210n
implicitly excluded from human race,
   We 461-3n
inversion of Greek norms among, B
   1529n
"like daytime sex", W 500n*, P 290
lives of, deemed expendable?, T p6 n34
religion of, P 406-413
shown behaving outlandishly, in
   tragedy, F 1028-9
struggling with Greek dress, B 1567-73
struggling with Greek language, A 104,
   P 289n, 291, B p5, B 1293n, 1628-
   9*, 1678-82, T 1001-7, 1082-1135,
   1176-1201, 1210-25
"subtle schemes wasted on", T 1128-32
unintelligible words uttered by, A 100, B
   1615*
wars against, not deprecated, L 566n
see also under names of particular non-
   Greek countries and peoples
barbers, B 299-300, L 382n
barbers' shops, as centres of gossip, B
   1440-1, We p26, We 338
bargaining, P 1215n

basket, ritual, at a sacrifice, P 948, B 43n,
   850, 863, E 732n
basket-bearer (kanēphoros), at a sacrifice,
   A 242, 260, B 670n, 1551, L 646,
   1194, E 732, 733n, We 1198n
bathing:
early, associated with party invitations,
   B 131-2, L 1065-6, We 85n, 615n
ritual, W 118, P 843n, L 378, We p10,
   We 656-8
Spartan disapproval of, B 1282n, L 279-
   280n
baths, hot, condemned and defended, C
   1044-52
baths, public, K 1060, 1091, 1401, 1403, C
   837, 991, 1044n, 1054, P 1103n, B
   139n, L 338, F 1070n, 1200n, 1279,
   We 616
as warm refuges for the poor, E 419n,
   We pp4-5, We 535, 952-7
battle-cries, C 1508n, B 364n
bean-trefoil, stinking, L 67-68n
beard, theatrical, cut off during
   performance, T 232n*
beards and beardlessness, A 120, K 1373,
   1374n, C 355n, W 476, 1187n, B
   831n, L 279-280n, 621n, 809-811n,
   1072, T p7, T 33, 190-1, 235n, 574d,
   575, 583, F 48n, 58-60n, 965n, 966,
   E p7 n35, p32, E 17n, 24-25, 30-
   284n, 68-72, 97n, 99-102, 104n, 118,
   121-7, 167n, 173-240n, 273-4, 277-
   9n, 494, 502-3
beatings, ritual, F 621-2n, 733n
bedding, as part of traveller's luggage, F
   439n, 567n, We 624
beds, C 254, 633-745, W 815-6n, L 916-
   937
Bee-wards (Melissonomoi), priestesses of
   Artemis, F 1273
beggars, A 412-594, K 1083n, C 921-5nn,
   P 193n, 955n, F 842, 855n, E 400-2n,
   We p5, We 298n, 544n
bells (attached to armour, horses, etc.), F
   963n
bestiality, F 67n, 850n
betrothals, T 795n
bile, C 833, B 14n, E 251n, We 12n, 903n
biology, C 144-168, F 1114n

bird calls, B 227-8, 237, 242, 260-2, 267, 310, 314, 505, 738, 741, 743, 747, 752, 770, 773, 775, 779, 784, 857n, 1122-3n(?), 1170n, L 761n, F 1285n, 1380n

birdlime, B 527n

birds, K 522n, 1344n, P 116, B p3, B *passim*

as destroyers of pests, B 1063-71

as pets, B 1084-5, W 129n

blackbird, A 970, B 306n*, 806, 1081, E 1172

bunting, B 297-304n*, 304

black-headed, B 304n

buzzard, W 1534n, B 1181, 1206

chaffinch, P 1149, B 1079n

chough, B 303*

classed as "quadrupeds", C 661

coal-tit, B 887*

cock, *see* §fowl (domestic); *also* sport (cock-fighting)

crowing in evening, W 100, B 495

control of, in sanctuaries, B 525n*

coot, A 875, B 565, E 1173

corncrake, B 870n, 1138, 1407

crane, B 710, 1136-7, 1428-9

crow, K 1051, B 1d*, 1-161n, 5, 23, 49, 61d, 89, 609, 967*, We 369n

cruelty to, by dealers, B 1077-83

cuckoo, A 598, B 303, 504-7, 819n, F 1380n

dabchick, A 876, B 304

dove, P 1067n, B 575, E 1174; *see also* §palm dove, §pigeon, §ringdove, §stockdove, §turtledove

duck, A 875, P 1004, B 566, 1148*, 1302, We 1011

mallard, B 1148n*

eagle, K 197, 203-5, 1013, 1020n, 1051n, 1087, 1093n, W 15-16, 1446-8nn, P 133-4, B 515, 571n, 653, 807n, 978, 979n, 987, 1110, 1181, 1248, 1306n, 1332-3n, 1337, 1341, L 694-5, F 1289n, 1291-2n

lesser spotted, B 883n

falcon, red-footed, B 303*

"Fearfowl", B 65

finch (not further specifiable), B 763n

firecrest, B 303*

flamingo, B 273

fowl (domestic), C 4, 661-7, 847-853, 1427, 1430-1, W 100, 794, 815-7, 934, 1490, B p6*, B 277n, 483-495, 507n*, 515n, 707, 757-9nn, 833-6, 1332-3n, L 896-7, F p16, F 566n, 932n, 935, 1331-63n, 1337n, 1342-55, 1380n, E 30-31, 390-1, 739n, 741n, 1165-6n, 1173, We p12

francolin, A 875, W 257, B 248, 297, 761

gallinule, purple, *see* §porphyrion

goldfinch, P 1078n, B 871

goose, A 878, P 1004, B 707, 805, 1145, 1295n, 1302

great tit, B 888

grouse, B 884

halcyon, B 251, 298, 299-300n*, 1594, F 1309

hawk, K 1052, B 303, 516*, 564-5n, 868n, 1112, 1179, 1306n, 1332-3n, 1454, L 770-1n

her(o)n, B 886, 1142

hoopoe, B p6 n21, B 471n, L 563n, 771n, F 683-4n; *see also* Hoopoe, Tereus *in Index II*

ibis, B 1296

jackdaw, A 875, K 1020, 1022, W p.xviii n3, W 129, B 1d*, 1-161n, 7, 17, 50, 61d, 86, 88, 571, 1174, 1212

jay, B 302, 1297

kērylos, B 299-300n*

kestrel, B 304, 589, 1181, 1332-3n, 1335, 1454

kingfisher, B 251n, F 1309-12n; *see also* §halcyon

pied, B 299-300n*

kite, P 1099, B 499-503, 713, 865, 891, 1624-5

lammergeyer, B 304, 1294

laws and customs of, B 755-768, 1342-59

lapwing, B 303*

lark, B 281-2n, 302, 472-6, E 1173n

live, problems of using as stage-properties, B 86-87n*

marsh harrier, B 883

nightingale, B 280-4n, 682-3n, 739n, 744n, 769-784n, 1332-3n, 1381, L 770-1n, F 682n, 684; *see also* Procne *in Index II*

osprey, B 891
ostrich, K 1105, B 874-6, 887*, F 1437n
owl, K 1092, W 1086, 1509n, B 261n,
    301, 358, 515n, 516, 589, 1083n, L
    760-1*
    as coin emblem, B 1106
    eagle-, B 1181
oystercatcher, B 303*
palm dove, B 303*
partridge, B 297, 767-8, 1083n, 1292
    black, see §francolin
peacock, A 63n, W 98n, B p6, B 102*,
    269, 277n, 884
pelican, grey, B 883
pelican, white, B 882, 1155n
Persian fowl, see §fowl (domestic)
petrel, stormy, P 1067n, We 912n
pheasant, A 726n, C 109, W 1268-9n, B
    68n
pigeon, A 1104, 1106, P 1004, B 302,
    1082, 1302, L 755, E 1172; see also
    §dove
pipit, B 297-304n*
plover, B 79n
    Egyptian, W 1513n
poet compared to, P 830n
porphyrion, B 304, 553n, 707, 882, 1249
quail, P 789, B 707, 870n, 1083n, 1298-
    9
raven, A 93, K 1053n, P 1125, B 521n,
    582, 609n, 851d, 858n*, 861, 1293,
    1611-3, T 868, 942, 1028, F 187n,
    189n, 607n, We 394n, 604n, 782n
redshank, B 303*
reed-warbler, B 302, 885
ringdove, B 303, E 1172, We 1011n
robin, W 927-8n
rook, B 579
    said to have "hands", B 1135
seagull, K 956, B 567
shelduck/drake, B 1295
"Shitterling", B 68
siskin, B 1079
skua, B 886(?)
sparrow, W p.xviii n3, W 207, 208n, B
    300n, 578, 874-5n, 1077n, L 723
starling, C 1225n
stilt, black-winged, B 303*
stockdove, B 303*
stone-curlew, see §thickknee

stork, B 501n, 757-9n, 832, 868n, 1139,
    1213, 1353-7
swallow, K 419, 422, P 800-1, B 15-16n,
    501n, 714, 769-784n, 1151*, 1293,
    1301, 1407n, 1412, 1416n, 1417,
    1681-2, L 770, 774-6, T 1n, F 93,
    681, 683-4n
swan, K 1093n, W 1064-5, B 769-784*,
    869, T 860n, F 207
    mute, B 771-2n*
    whooper, B 771-2n*
teal, B 885
tern, B 887
thickknee, B 266, 1141
thrush, A 970, 1007, 1104, 1108, 1116,
    K 1192n, C 339, P 531, 1149, 1195,
    1197, B 591, 1079, E 1172
    blue rock-, B 979
    trapping of, B 194, 525-8
turtledove, B 302, 979, 1181
vulture, B 891, F 1291-2n
    Egyptian, B 303n
wagtail, E 1173
wheatear, B 302*
widgeon, B 298, 1302n
woodchat, B 303*
woodpecker, B 304, 480, 882-3n, 979,
    1155-7n
wren, A 876, W 1513n, P 788n, 1004, B
    79n
    as "King bird", B 568
    see also Chorus (f), Flamingo, Gobbler-
    bird, Hoopoe, Mede, Procne, Raven,
    Slave(s) (l, m, n), Tereus in Index II
"birds' milk", W 508, B 734, 1673
birth, P 1014n*, 1078, L 700-1n, 742-757,
    E 369n
    charms to ease, T 504
    forbidden in sanctuaries, L 742-3, 754-
    5n, F 1080
    men forbidden to be present at, T 409n,
    508-9
    offstage, in New Comedy, T p12 n71
    women friends assisting with, E 528-
    534, 549-550
birthdays of gods, We 1126n
blackmail, W 1025-8nn; see also informers
    (silence of, bought)
Black Sea, W 700, L 45n
    corn trade to, E 818n

Milesian campaigns in, We 1002n

blinding, as (barbaric) punishment, We 859n

blockade, B 186-193, 556-560, 1520-4, 1576, 1591-5n

blood, substituted for by wine, L 195-7n

boats, A 920n, P 143; see also navy, ships and seafaring
  as stage-property, F p11 n49, F 180-270

Boedromia (festival), W 682-718n

Boedromion (Athenian month, September), P 420n, We 845n

Boeotia(ns), A p32, A 160, 624, 721, 860*, 872, 873, 900, 920*, 953, 1023, 1077, 1082n, 1187n, K 479-480, 857n, 1271-3n, W p.xv, W 234n, 345n, 1191n, P 466, 481n, 507n, 1000n, 1003, B 189, L 35-36, 75, 86-89, 699n, 702, 703n, F 1023-4n, E p3, p4, E 200n, We p4 n13, We 550n; see also Thebes
  conquered by Athens (457), L 801n, E 303n
  dialect of, A 860*-954, 905*, L 6n
  low intellect of, A 878-880n*, 902n
  music of, A 14, 862-3
  Spartan invasion of (395), E p2

bogies, A 582, 693, W 1035n, P 474n, 758n, T 417n, F 925n

books, B 967-989, 1288-9, F 52-53n, 943*, 1109-18nn, 1114, 1409

bookstalls/booksellers, B 1288-9, F p10 n46

Bosporus (kingdom in Crimea), F 608n, 680-1n, E 102n, We 176n

Bosporus (strait of Byzantium), F p2, We 178n

Bottiaea (Macedonia), C 1425-6n

bovicide, ritual, see Buphonia

brain, W 683n; see also diseases and ailments (concussion of the brain), meat (brains)

brand-marks, on horses, K 603n, C 23, 122, 438, 1298, B 1293n

Brauronia (festival), P 874n, L 643-5

breasts, A 1199, W 1339n, 1374n, P 536n, 863, L 83, 155, T 143, 640, 1185, F 412, E 903, We 1067-8

breath, bad, F 1150n

breathlessness, phonetic imitation of, B 1122-3n

breeding, in Plato's Republic, E p14 n62, p17, E 614n, 635-643n

bribery, A 6n, K 361n, 402-3, 438n, 707n, 802, 834-5*, 853n, 996n, 1034n, 1083n, 1197n, W 101-2, 669-671, 675-7, 693, 1036, P 192-5, 378-9, 416-425, 622, 907-8, B 513, 521n, 1403n, L 103, 861-3nn, T 331-351n, 346n, 936-7, F 361, 965n, E 71n, 77n, 97n, 248n, 782n, We p19 n83, p22 n92, We 177n, 178n, 379, 381n, 800n; see also Athens, political and legal institutions (prosecutions) and informers

brickmaking, C 1126, B 1139-46, F 799-800

bride, clothing and adornment of, E 1034n, We 529n

brigandage, P 449

bronteion (thunder-making device), C 292n, B 1751n

Bronze House, temple of Athena at Sparta, L 1321

Bronze Race, mythical, F 730n

brothels, K 1246n*, 1285, W 1283, F 113

buggery, heterosexual, L 231n, 417n, 1158n, 1162-3n, 1171n, 1174n

building, B 837-840, 1124-67, L 722n, E 197-8n, 310

bull's blood, believed poisonous, K 83*

Buphonia ("ritual bovicide") at Dipolieia, C 985

buttocks:
  erogenousness of, E 907n, 963-4n
  wear and tear on, F 1070-1n

Buzygae, Athenian genos, L 391n, 397n

byes, in knockout sporting tournaments, F 791-2

Byzantine Empire, scholarship in, A pp17-19*

Byzantine triad (Wealth, Clouds, Frogs), A pp17-19

Byzantium, C 249, W 236, We 550n

"Cachinnatia", see "Catagela"

Caesarean section, We p10 n44

calendar, C 17, 615-626, 754-6, 1131-4, P 414-5

Metonic cycle, B 997n
stopped to delay a festival, P 414n
see also New Moon, Old-and-New Day,
Hecatombaeon, Boedromion,
Pyanopsion, Poseideon, Gamelion,
Anthesterion, Elaphebolion,
Munichion, Thargelion, Scirophorion
Callichoron (sacred well at Eleusis), F 451n
Calligeneia, last day of Thesmophoria, T
pp11-12, T 299n
Calydon (Aetolia) and the Calydonian
Boar, A 418-9, B 1274-5n, F 863-4n,
1238-41n, 1402n
Camarina (Sicily), A 606
camping, at festivals, P 879-880n, T p10, T
624
cannibalism, W 1035n, P 758n, B 15-16n,
100-1n, L 563n, F 683-4n, E 77n, We
p17 n76, We 297n
Caphereus, Cape (Euboea), F 666n
caprification, B 590n*
captives, war, F 1235n, We 179n, 521n
caravans, homes of Scythian nomads, B
941-4n
Cardia (Chersonese), B 1475
Caria, K 132n, 173, W 1259n*, P 126n*, B
p5 n18, B 11n, 292, 764, 1028n, F
1302, We 1n, 1002n
Carpathos (Dodecanese), A 1030n
carriages, A 69-70, We 1013-4
Carthage, K 174, 1303, C 1372n
cartoons, animated, comic fantasy
compared to, W 127n
Carystus (Euboea), L 1059, 1181
castrated animals, forbidden in certain
sacrifices, B 569n
castration, of humans, T 172n, We 859n;
see also eunuchs
casualties, Athenian:
in Corinthian War, We p4 n15
in Peloponnesian War, F p2
"Catagela" (fictitious Sicilian [?] city), A
606
"catamite", origin of word, P 724n
Catana (Sicily), B p4, B 639n
catoptromancy, A 1128-9n*, We 382n
Caucasus, F 187n
Caunus (Caria), L p2 n13
cavalry, A p6, A 6n, 7, 301-2, K pp3-4*, K
225*, 242-7, 272*, 290-1n, 577n,

597n, 604n, 1370n*, C 21n*, 120, P
356n, B 1442-3nn, L 676-9, F 653,
1023-4n, E 846, We 174n; see also
Athens, political and legal
institutions (hipparchs, phylarchs)
cavern, theatrical representation of, P p.xvii
Cayster, river of Asia Minor, A 68
ceilings, decorated, W 1215n
cemeteries, as haunt of prostitutes, F 423n*
Cenchreae (Corinthia), T 647-8n
centaurs, C 346, 350, F 38, 429n, 902n,
929n; see also Cheiron in Index II
Ceos (Cyclades), B 692n, F 970, E 652n
Cerberians, tribe living near entrance to
Hades, F 187
cereals:
barley, W 718, P 449, 1322, B 506, 565,
622, L 1212n, E 424n
daily requirements of, We 986n
wheat, W 718n, 1405, P 1145, B 506,
566, 580, 622, 626, L 1203-12, T
813, E 424n, We 986
see also corn, food
Chaeroneia (Boeotia), battle of (338), C
353-4n, E 396-7n
chair, as symbol of honour, F 764, 768,
777, 787, 790, 830, 1515-23
Chalcidice, K 438n, W 210n, P 283-4n, B
172n*, 824n
Chalcis (Euboea), K 237-8, 1043n, W
1232-5n
Chalkeia (festival), L 642n
chamber-pots, W 806, 858, 935-940, P
1228n, 1266-7n, T 633, F 544, E 371,
We 1096d, 1133d
Chaonia (Epirus), A 604, 613, K 78
characters:
assumed to know what audience know,
E 558n, We 401n, 1088-9n
depart with plans/threats that are then
forgotten, E 875n
disappearing, to release actors for other
parts, B 837-847n, 1122-63n*
fictitious, kin to real people, C 46n, T
p6, T 1n
forgotten once dramatic purpose is
served, E 509-510n, We 35n, 321n,
782n
identifiable or anonymous?, A 395n, K
p3, T 1n, F 464n, 738n

identification of, within and across scenes, E pp25-26, E 327-356n, 372n, 564n, 730n, 746n, 1113n, 1138n, We 824n, 964n, 1172n

poet recommended to adopt personalities of, T 148-156

real-life, usually named at once, T 574n

thinking of themselves *as* characters of a play, T 910n, 930n, 1060-1

uncertainty in audience's identification of, F 1-20nn

chariot of Night, T 1066-7

chariot of the Sun, C 571n, T 17n

chariots, *see* sport (chariot-racing)

  in processions, C 69n, L 1189n, 1190n, T 811-2

  in war, F 1403, 1405

Charybdis, mythical whirlpool, K 248

"Chasmos", *see* Chaonia

chemical warfare, F 1440-1

Chersonese, Thracian, K 262, B 1474-5n

chewing, as means of easing nerves, E 554n

chewing gum, beans as Athenian equivalent of, K 41n, L 537n

child performers, A p15, A 241-279, 729-835, W 230-414, P 111-149, 1265-1304, We 823-958

child substitution, P 678n, T p7, T 339-340, 407-9, 502-516, 564-5

children, pledged as security for loans?, We 147n

Chios, C 273n, P 171, 835n, B p1 n3, B 879-880, L p1 nn4,6, L 361n, T 647-8n, F p3, p7 n32, p7 n35, F 82n, 970, E 208n, 248n, 1139

Choes (Pitcher Feast), A 179n, 961, 1068, 1076, 1211, T 746, F p8 n37, F 218-9n

choregoi, A p14*, A 886n, 1154-5n*, 1173n, K 574n, 967n, C 338n, W p.xv, W 220n, P 531n, 1022, B p6, B 105-6n*, 126n, 1372-1409n, F p4, F 153n, 404-6n, 407n, E 330n, 366n, 825n, We 195n, 1162n

  joint, in 406/5, F p4, F 404-6n

choreography, A 284-302n*, W 1517n, B 327-335n, 750n, 1755-65n, T 164n, 667-686n, 953-968n, F 910n, 1331-63n; *see also* dancing

chorodidaskalos, P 508n, E 809

chorus, A pp9-13, p14, p15*, F 729

  departure and return of, E p23, E 285-310n

  divided, A 557-571n, P p.xviii, L pp4-5, F 323-459n, 398-413; reunites, L 1042

  entrance of, fast or slow, L 254-318n

  exaggerated caution of, in tragedy, We 632n

  exit of, misleadingly foreshadowed, P 551-2n*, L 1291-4n

  exits dancing, W 1537n, L 1321d, E 1163-83

  feast for, after performance, A 1154-5

  fluid identity of, in *Peace*, P pp.xviii-xix

  formations of, We 953n

  formed up in couples, L 1279d

  how coordinated, T 121-2n

  identifies itself with another chorus, A 1154-5n

  ignored, L p5 n26, L 441-2n, 907n, E pp24-25

  in New Comedy, E p25, E 729/730n

  inactive in a crisis, T 654n, E 261n

  interludes for, often devoted to satire on individuals, L 1043-57n, T p11, T 962-5n

  interludes for, thematically linked with each other, L 1043-57n

  interludes for, thematically linked with preceding scenes, B 1470-81n*

  irrelevant interludes for, in comedy?, E p24 n90, We p23

  irrelevant interludes for, in tragedy, T 29n, F 83n

  leader of, see *koryphaios*

  long songs by, in Aeschylean tragedy, F 914-5

  members of, individualized by mask/costume?, B p6

  moving to/from edge of orchestra, L 539n, 829d, 907n, 954d

  normally enters from left (west), E p30-31 n116, We p26

  of boys, F 729n

  of maidens, L 1307-15*, T 1029, 1031n; see also *partheneia*

  persuaded to disarm, A 341-6, W 727n, B 400-2

  pretended reduction in size of, P pp.xviii-xix*, P 508n

prolonged absence of?, E p24 n91
regrouping of, P 508d
representing men and women, F 323-459n
silent entrance of, E p23
singing offstage, C 275-328*
singing technique, T 127n
songs by, omitted from book-texts, A 1234n, K 1408n, L 1320-1n, E p21, p24, E 729/730, 875n, 876/7, 1111/2n, We pp23-24, p34, We 321/2, 626/7, 770/1, 801/2, 958/9, 1096/7, 1170/1n, 1209n
speaking in name of author, A 659-664, C 518-562, W 1284-91, P 754-774, 775-818n*
speaking in name of comedy, P 749n
speaking *qua* performers, A 299-302n, 1154-5n, K 589, C 601n, 1352n, P p.xviii, B 445n, L 1055n, T 947-1000n, 1231n*, F 324n, 352-3n, 375n, 376n, 385-393n, 404-6n, 416-439n, 444n, 459n, 1005n, E 1155-62n, 1181n
still significant in Ar.'s late plays, E p25
sub-plot involving, L pp4-5
subsidiary, A p15, P p.xviii, F p12
temporarily lose their fictive identity, F 459n
temporary exit by part of, P 428-430dd
use of first person plural by, B 789n*
use of first person singular by, W 727n, 1093n
used to mean "dramatic performance", B 787n
words of, must be clearly heard by all, T 986n
see also dancing, dithyramb, *parabasis, parodos*
chronological
     implausibilities/impossibilities:
     Cratinus' death antedated, P 700-1
     extreme old age, A 181n, L 281n, 665n
     rapid travel, A 133-175, P 261n
chryselephantine statues, K 1169n, P 605n
Chytroi (Pot Feast), A 1076, F 218
Cimmerians, people to north of Black Sea, L 45n, F 187n
Cimmerians, tribe living near entrance to underworld, F 187n

Cimolos (Cyclades), F 713n
circumcision, A 158n, 592n, K 964*, C 538-9n, B 507, L 143n, We 267n
cisterns, E 154n
Cithaeron, Mt (Attic-Boeotian border), T 996, F 1190n, We 162n
Citium (Cyprus), L 1144n
citron, used as aromatic, W 1056*
City Dionysia, *see* Dionysia
Cius (N.W. Asia Minor), K 67n
civil war, Athenian (404-403), B 876n, F 1437n, E 71n, 208n, 825n; *see also* Athens, political and legal institutions (democracy: restoration of); Attica, demes and localities (Munichia, Phyle); Ten; Thirty
Claros (Ionia), F 659n
class hatred, allegedly fomented by demagogues, W 40-41n
Clazomenae (Ionia), L p1 n6, We p4
"Cleitagora" (symposiac song), L 1237
cleruchs, C 203, P 1047n, L 582n
clitoris, L 1004n
clothes-stealers, see *lōpodytai*
clothing:
     batrachis (frog-green robe), K 1406*
     "Cimberic" and other diaphanous, unbelted *khitones*, L 45, 48n, 52, 150
     described by weight of wool, E 413n
     diphtherā (leather smock), C 72, W 444n, 933n, E 80
     diploïs (outer garment, worn folded), E 318n
     enkyklon (woman's outer garment), T 250n, 261, 499, E 536
     everyday, how much would one own?, E 315-6n, 415n, 730n
     everyday, often replaced twice yearly, B 715, E 315-6n
     exōmis (off-one-shoulder tunic), B 1492*, L 662, 1021, F 180n
     fawnskin (worn by Dionysiac worshippers), F 1211
     gold-spangled garments, K 967n, C 912n
     halourgis (purple robe), K 967n
     hēmidiploidion (type of woman's *khiton*), E 318
     high-class, cost of, We 982-3
     hitched up to dance, T 656

hitched up to leave hands free, L 536n
kalasīris (Egyptian robe), B 1296n
katōnakē (slave's coarse garment), L
  1151, 1155, E 724
kaunakēs (tufted cloak), W 1138
khitōn(ion) (tunic), K 881-6, B 933, 944,
  F 641n, 1066n, 1067, E 268, 318n,
  332n, 374, We 984
khitōniskos (short tunic), B 946
khlaina (thick warm cloak), W 738,
  1122d, 1132, B 493, 712, 715,
  1421n, L 586, 1156, T 142, F 1459,
  E 416, 606
khlamys (soldier's cloak), P 1193n
khlanis (fine cloak), W 677, P 1002, B
  1116, B 1693, L 1190, T 840-1n, E
  848
Krētikon (Cretan robe), T 730
krokōtos (woman's saffron-dyed dress),
  C 51n, 1102n*, L 44, 47, 51, 219-
  220, 645, T 138, 253, 637d, 642d,
  941, 945, 1044, 1220, F 46, 308n,
  627n, E 318n, 329-332, 879
lēdarion (thin summer cloak), B 715,
  915n
lion-skin, F 46, 430, 501n, 627n
making of, L 574-586; *see also* women
  (and clothes-making)
Megarian woollen cloaks, A 519-521n,
  P 1002
mitrā (hair-band), T 163, 257, 941
mourning, A 1024n
of slaves, W 443-7; see also §*katōnakē*
outer, how draped, B 1567-8n
outer, used as blanket, C 54n, E 334n,
  536n; see also §*sisyra*
Persis (tufted cloak), W 1137
phoinīkis (officer's or Spartan's red
  cloak), A 320n, P 303*, 1173-5, L
  1140
ragged garments, A 412-438, B 1416n,
  T p6 n36, T 838n, 871d, 910, 935n, F
  404-6, 412-3, 459n, 842, 855n, 863-
  4n, 1063, 1066, We 267n, 540, 845n
sheepskins, P 1122-4
sisyrā (hairy skin cloak/blanket), C 10n,
  W 738, 1139, B 122n, L 933n, F
  1459, E 347, 420n, 421
spolas (leather jerkin), B 933, 944
storage of, W 1056-9

strophion (breastband), L 931, T 139,
  251, 255, 637d, 638
tasselled, seen as un-Athenian, W 475-6
tribōn(ion) (coarse homespun cloak), W
  33, 116, 738n, 1122d, 1131, L 278, E
  850, We 714, 842-6, 882, 897, 935
trousers, worn by barbarians, W 1087*,
  T p7 n42, T 1187-8dd
used to conceal ugly legs, B 1569n
veils, L 530-3, T p7 n41, T 1160d
washing of, We 1061n
white, (in)appropriate occasions for, A
  1024, B 1116, T 840-1
white, of Asclepian pilgrims, We p12
  n60, p27, We 626d
women's, not purchased by men, We
  983-4n
xystis (rich smooth robe), C 70, L 1190
zōnion (waistband), L 72
see *also* costumes and properties, cross-
  dressing, footwear, undressing
"Cloudcuckooland", as naturalized English
  expression, B p1 n2
Cloudcuckooville, A p12, K 1013n, C
  333n, P 1008n, 1085n, B p1, p3, B
  175n, 819ff, 821n, E 330n
a second Athens?, B p1, B 826-836n,
  879n, 1283-4n
judicial system(?) of, B 1584n
plural form of name, B 819n, 917, 963,
  1023
whether a democracy, B 1584n
clubs, political, see *hetaireiai*
Cnidians, *leschē* of, at Delphi, F 186n
Cnidus, L p1 nn4,6, L 57n
battle of (394), K 656n, E p2, p4, p6, We
  p3
Cocytus, River (in underworld), F 470n,
  472
coins/coinage, A 517-8n, C 249, 1041n, P
  1200n, B 1106-8, E 601-613
Athenian, quality of, F 721-3
Athenian decree on, B 1040-2
bronze, emergency issue of (406/5), F
  p3, F 725-6, E 815-822, We 862n;
  withdrawn, F 725n, E 815n, 821-2
carried in mouth, W 609, 791-2, P 645n,
  B 502-3, E 818, We 379n
darics, E 602, We 816-7n

electrum (gold/silver alloy), P 1176n,
We 816-7n
gold, emergency issue of (407/6), F p3,
F 720, 725n, E 602n, 815n
miraculous abundance of, We 808-9
non-Athenian, circulating in Athens, C
1041n, P 1176n, E 602
placed in mouth of corpse, F 140n
silver, scarce by 406/5, F p3, F 725n
smaller, sometimes in short supply, W
786-9
staters, E 413n, We 816-7n
value of, in weight of metal, C 21n
Colchis, C 257n, F 1382n
collaboration:
in comic scriptwriting, K p4*, K
1225n*, 1288-9n, W 1018-20
in tragic scriptwriting etc., F 78-79,
944n*, 1452-3*
colonies, Athenian, L 582-5
colonnades (stoai), E 676, 677n, 682n, We
385n; see also Athens, places and
buildings (Agora: Stoa Alphitopolis,
Stoa Basileios, Stoa of Zeus
Eleutherios, Stoa Poikile)
Colophon (Ionia), K 763n
colour terms, P 1178n, B 800n, T 318n, F
308n, 483n, We 690n
columns, in façades of great houses, C 815
Comedy, New, T pp11-12, T 339-340n
Comedy, Old:
"acquainted with justice", A 500
and the Athenian ideal, C p2*
basic aims of, A p13*
below the dignity of young aristocrats?,
K 509n
claims to benefit society, F 1008-9n,
1500-27n
difficulty of producing, K 516
disregards its own fictiveness, T p9 n55
favourable references in, rare, K 6n,
327n
formal structure of, A pp9-11*
functional structure of, A pp11-13*, E
pp22-23, We p23
innovations in, C 547-8, W 1044, 1053,
1535-7
legal restrictions on?, B 1297n*
lyrics from, sung at symposia, K 529-
530, 976n

makes mythical enemies into friends, B
15-16n
nothing impossible in, We p20
offers fantasy remedies for real evils, E
p18*, We p20
painful subjects taboo in, E 183-4n
performed in southern Italy, T p12
political exploitation of, A p8*
serious elements in, F 390, 686-7
should be immune from political
interference, F 368n
spoken of in mystery-cult language, F
320n, 354-371nn
time intervals in, A 961n, C 1131n, B
1515n, L 723-5n, We 626/7n
triumphs over tragedy, T pp9-10*, T
1160-1225n
used to further personal quarrels, W
1025-6n
vulgar features of, disowned and
employed by Ar., C 537-546nn*, W
60n, 63n*, P 739-748, L 928n, 1218-
20, F 1-20, 30n
communal meals, in Eccl. and Republic, E
p14, E 606n, 675-690, 715-7, 835-
876, 1112-53, 1163-83
premises for, E 675n
communism, E pp12-22, E 579n, 590-1111
community, interests of, seen as paramount,
E 471-2, 853-862
comparison game, W 1308-13, F 906
concubinage, facilitated by decree (ca.412),
L 593n
conscience, W 999-1000
conspicuous consumption, A 988n, We
820n
"conspiracy", as political smear, K 236,
257, 452, 476, 628, 862*, W p.xvii,
W 345, 483, 488, 507, 930n, 953, P
642n
consumerism, E 606n
cookery, poetry on, E 1169-75n
cooking own food, mark of the good
citizen, A 1017n*
cooks, A 1017n, P 1017n, 1060n, B 440-1n,
1637, F 517, We p12 n58, p25 n104
Copais, Lake (Boeotia), famous for eels, A
880, 883, 962, P 1005, L 36
coprophilia, E 647n, We 314-5n
Corcyra, W 81n, P 990n, B 1463, T 876n

Coresia (Ceos), E 652n
Corinth, A 391n, 793n, K 1037n, C 710n, P
   p.xv, p.xvi, P 622n, 990n, B 968-9, T
   404, 647-8, 876n, F p5 n25, F 439n,
   1043n, 1192n, 1431n, E p1, E 199-
   200, 237n, 810n, 828n, We p29, We
   149, 173, 179n, 303; see also
   Isthmus, Lechaeum, Oenoe
   (Corinthia)
Athenian expedition against (425), K p2,
   K 6n, 268n, 599-610
Athens' ally in Corinthian War, E pp2-4,
   p6, E 193n, 197-8n, We pp1-2, p4
battle at (369/8), E p15 n63
union with Argos, E p3, E 200n, 201n,
   We p2 n7
Corinthian Gulf, T 647-8n
Corinthian War (395-387), F 367n, E pp1-
   7, E 208n, 248n, We pp1-4; see also
   Argos, Corinth, Persia, Sparta,
   Thebes, and under names of battles
   and (in Index II) of leaders
corn:
   Egyptian gift of, to Athens, We 178n
   free distributions of, K 1100-6, W 716-
      8, B 581n, E 424-5
   hulling of, W 201n
   price of, E 547n, We 982-3n
   stolen from household stores, T 419-
      420, 556-7
   supply route to Athens, F p2
   trade in, and Agyrrhius, E 102n*, We
      176n
   see also cereals, food (barley-groats,
      flour and meal, whole grains)
corn-dealers, unpopularity of, C 640, E 424
cornucopia, We p5, p8
corona tortilis, We 686n
Coronea, battles of:
   (446), F 1023-4n
   (394), E p2, p6, E 195n, We p4 n15
corporal punishment:
   by parents, C 1409-26, 1433-6
   female slaves generally spared, L 503n
   of master by slave, in fantasy, F 545-8
   of schoolboys, C 493, 497n
   of slaves, K 5, 29n, 68-70, C 7, 58,
      450n, 870n, W 3n, 438n, 450-1, P
      746, L 1240n, F 501n, 546-7n, 741-2,

747-8, 756, 812-3, We p16 n73, We
   1144-5
   see also parents (violence against),
      slaves (beaten without cause),
      women (physical abuse of)
Cos, F 970n
cosmetics, L 44, 49n, 149, 219-220, F 289-
   296n, 1308d, E p32, E 877d; see
   also perfumes
   rouge (alkanet), L 48, E 929, 1049d,
      1056n
   white-lead (lead carbonate), E 732n,
      878, 929, 991n, 1065d, 1072, 1073n,
      We 959d, 1064
cosmogony and cosmology, C 95-97, 361n,
   380n*, B 470n, 685-702, 1000-1, T
   11-18nn*, F 889-891n, F 1114n
costume changes, time required for, E p31
   n118, We 958/9n
costumes and properties, A p15, A 63d,
   187d, 241d, 244d, 326n*, 331d,
   366d, 412*-479, 572d, 594n, 719d,
   806d, 918d, 1003d, K 101d, 115d,
   146d, 235d*, 487d, 490d, 493d,
   771n, 873d, 922n, 948, 959d, 997d,
   998d, 1151d, 1161d, 1195d, 1214d,
   1218d, 1250d, 1316d, 1331d, 1384d,
   1408d, C 21d, 56d, 91n, 254, 261d,
   500d, 509d, 543, 633-4, 694-745,
   848d, 889n, 1247d, 1473, 1478d,
   1489d, 1492d, W 1d, 131-2n, 148d,
   179d*, 230d, 314-5n*, 399-415n,
   400d, 408d, 423n, 456d, 456-460n,
   525d, 538d, 727n, 805d, 806n, 811d,
   817d, 844d, 851d, 855d, 863d,
   1008d, 1122d, 1313, 1326d, 1363d,
   1374n, 1388d*, 1500d, P 1-18dd,
   82d, 192, 236d, 242-252dd, 301d,
   424d, 428d, 431d, 550-5*, 563d,
   729-730, 886*, 948d, 956d, 1024n,
   1039-43dd, 1052d, 1102d*, 1191-6*,
   1193d*, 1197d, 1204n, 1214d,
   1224d, 1240-2dd, 1250d*, 1315n,
   1329d, B p6, B 1d, 43n, 79n, 105-6n,
   306n*, 357-363dd*, 386-7*, 434*,
   450d, 465d, 511-3, 672n*, 801d,
   851d, 904d, 915, 933, 959d, 992d,
   1021d, 1035d, 1170n, 1188d, 1199d,
   1271d, 1313-36dd, 1364-6dd*,
   1398d, 1410d, 1463d, 1494d, 1495d,

1504n, 1552n, 1579d, 1693d, 1720*, L p4, L 78d, 184d, 199d, 254d, 288n, 319d, 357n, 387d, 424-432, 532-5dd, 539n, 567d, 602-4dd, 613d, 751d, 768d, 828d, 863d, 920-947dd, 953d, 1027-32, 1077d, 1087d, 1092-6, 1217d, T p7, p8, p12, T 42d, 95d, 101d, 137d, 142n, 219d, 234d, 239d, 254-6dd, 258-263dd, 292d, 295n, 372d, 380d, 443d, 466d, 574d, 636-642dd, 654d, 655-6, 688d, 730-4, 739d, 749-750dd, 755-7dd, 758-9dd, 764d, 776-784, 871d, 929d, 1001d, 1009-14nn, 1056-97n, 1083d, 1085-6dd, 1098d, 1160-75n, 1160d, 1202d, 1203n, F p12 n55, F 1d, 37d, 46-47, 160d, 165d, 169d, 179-180dd, 180n, 308, 315d, 323d, 404-8, 437-9dd, 459n, 464d, 483dd, 495n, 525, 528, 533d, 607d, 608n, 622d, 627n, 628d, 673d, 797-801n, 813d, 830d, 875d, 1061n, 1308d, 1384-5n, 1478d, 1481d, 1504-7dd, E p30, p32, E 1d, 2n, 6d, 28n, 30d*, 35d, 87d, 122n, 311d, 369n, 504d, 513-4d, 520d, 729-745dd, 785d, 833d, 877d, 1049d, 1055d, 1077d, 1081d, We p27, We 1d, 227d, 267n, 626d, 770/1n, 782d, 788n, 802d, 822d, 850d, 935-945dd, 958d, 959d, 1097d, 1099n, 1133d, 1197d, 1199, 1203d; see also clothing, cross-dressing, garlands, mirrors, padding, phallus, role-swapping, stage business, torches, undressing, vehicles
cottabus (symposiac game), A 525*, K 277, C 1073, P 343, 1244, B 523n, T 94n
country vs. town, A 32-36, K 805-8, 1394-5, C 47, P 508, 551-600, 1318, B 111n, 590n, T 977n, E 197-8, 277-9n, 300-310, 432n, We 162n, 223n
courage, rewards for, in *Eccl.* and *Republic*, E 678-9n
courtesans, *see* sex-sellers
cowardice, punishment of, in *Eccl.* and *Republic*, E p14, E 679-680
craftsmen, despised by peasants, We 162n, 617-8n
Cranaa, name for Athens or the Acropolis, A 75, B 123, L 481

cress, soaks up moisture, C 235, T 616-7
Crete, W 303-316n, B 521n, 570n, 798n, 1697-9n, L 558n, F 849, 1331-63n, 1356, E p17, E 1165, We p5
crime, and poverty/inequality, E p19, E 667-671, We 565
Crimea, W 1501n, P 784n; *see also* Bosporus (kingdom)
Crisa (port of Delphi), F 1319n
Cronia (festival), C 398*
cross-dressing, L 531-8, T pp7-9, T 92, 95d, 161-2n, 249-1209, E p11, p32, E 17n, 26-27, 40, 47, 48n, 74-75, 82n, 173-240n, 189n, 268-276, 311-9, 327-356n, 329-353, 374-5, 478-546
Croton (S. Italy), A 214n, C 1484-5n, W 1206-7n, 1259n, P 344n
crowns, W 677, 710
   funerary, E 538n
   gold, L 1190n, We 586
   honorific, A p3, B 1274-5, F pp21-22
   see also garlands
crustaceans and molluscs:
   crab, K 606-610*, W 1500-37, P 784n, 1083
   pea-, W 1510-1
   crayfish, W 1509, E 102n, We 176n
   cuttlefish, *see* §squid
   limpet, W 105, We 1096
   murex, P 1174n
   octopus, L 757n
   shrimp, W 1522
   squid, A 1158n, K 929-940, L 757n, E 126-7, 554
cult-titles, We 1153-65
Cumae (Italy), K 61n, P 1094n, F 1266n
Cunaxa (Babylonia), battle of (401), E p1
cunnilingus, K 1281n, 1284-6, W 1283, P 716, 883n, 885, T 647-8n, E 129n, 470n, 846n, We 1005n
curses, T 331-371, 1081n, F 746, E 128-130n, 906-910
   hereditary, K 445-6n, P 1250n
   inscribed, F 295n, 1144-5n
cutpurses, F 772
Cyclades, F 363n
cyclic choruses, *see* dithyramb
Cyclopes, B 1695-6n; *see also* Cyclops (Polyphemus) *in Index II*

Cyllene (Elis), A 263n, K 1081n
Cyllene, Mt (Arcadia), F 1266n
Cyme (Aeolis), F 1266n*
Cyme (Italy), see Cumae
Cynossema, battle of (411), C 553n, T p1
Cynthus, Mt (Delos), C 596
Cyprus, A 793n, 989n, C 28n, W 98n,
    1259n*, L 833, 1144n, 1290n, F
    1512n, E p3 n12, p4, We p3, p4, We
    178n, 1002n
  Athenian campaign in (ca.450), T 446n
  Athenian expedition to (390), E 201n
  dialect of, F 1144-5n
Cyrenaica, K 895n, B 534n
Cyrene, B 619n*, We 925n
Cythera, P 625n, L 833
Cyzicus, P 1176, E 413n
  battle of (410), T p2

dáidoukhos (second priest, Eleusinian
    Mysteries), B 284n, F 428n, E 810n
daimōn, denoting an impersonal power, B
    544n
dancing, K 20n, 697*, C 271n, 540, 555, W
    1478-1537, P 322-336, 337-345*,
    784, 788, 976, 1319, P 784n, 791n,
    864n, B 1169, 1372-1409, 1720*,
    1759-62, L 2n, 82n, 392, 409n, 541-
    2, 558n, 615n, 982n, 1243, 1246,
    1248d, 1292d, T 94n, 102, 120-1,
    663d, 666n, 667d, 953-968n, 961n,
    1031n, 1174, 1175n, 1178-80, 1186-
    8, F 674, 1303, E p25, p27, E 1163-
    83, We 190n, 277-8n, 288-9, 321/2,
    761
  and "benign madness", T 961n
  gods taking part in, L 1273*, 1279-90,
    1314-5, T 975, 987-8, 1136-59
  in couples, L 1275-6n, 1279-1321
  mimetic, F 849n, We 290-315
  mismatched to rhythm of music?, T 120-
    1n
  ritual, W 8n, T 953-962, 969-970, 977-
    1000, 1136-59, F 157n, 330-6, 352,
    354, 356, 370, 396, 403, 407-413,
    450-3, 1213
  see also choreography, emmeleia,
    pyrrhic dance
dancing-girls, see sex-sellers
Dardania (= Troad), W 1371n

darkness, imaginary, easily forgotten, We
    1041n
Dascylium (Phrygia), B 1028n
dead:
  abused in comedy, P 47n, 651-6n
  dropped food dedicated to, T 401-4n*
  praised in comedy, having been abused
    while alive, P 304n, 700-1nn, T
    841n, F 357n, 1039n
Dead Sea Scrolls, E 665n
death:
  forbidden in sanctuaries, L 743n, T 930n
  imagery of, in Eccl., E p21, E 537-8,
    905, 926, 994-7, 1030-6, 1073, 1105-
    11, 1112-26n
  mock, L 599-613
  possible in comedy, for informers only,
    We 942-3n
  symbolic, on stage, F 1478n
  threat of, used to force captive to talk,
    We 67-71
death and life, inversions between, F 177n,
    420, 1082, 1333, 1477
debt, enslavement for, We 147-8, 217n,
    521n
debts, cancellation of, We p19 n83
decapitation, T 1126-7, We 859n
"deceiving the people", offence of, F 1086,
    1453n, 1466n; see also Athens,
    political and legal institutions
    (prosecutions)
dedications, E p28 n104, We p12, p22, We
    842-9, 937-9, 943, 1088-9
defaecation:
  as demonstration of contempt, E 640
  as political protest, B 1054n
  caused by blows, K 70, C 1389-90, L
    440-1, T 570
  caused by terror, K 1058, C 293-4, W
    626, 941, P 174-6, 185-7n, 241n,
    1176n, B 66n, 68n, T 248n, F p13, F
    308, 479-491, E 1059-63
  in street or alley, C 1385n, P 99n, 157-
    8n
  simulated, on stage, E 369n
  see also diseases and ailments
    (constipation, diarrhoea), gods,
    scatology
defeat, consequences of, F pp4-5

deformities, K 1085n, C 1001n, W 462n, P
    789-790*, B 281-2n, 988n, 1569n, T
    168n, F 1192, We 177n
dei ex machina, F 1322n
deification, W 392n, B p3, B 1765
dekatē (baby's naming feast), B 494, 922,
    L 757n, T 795n
Delium (Boeotia), battle of (424), A 920n,
    C 353-4n, 362n, W p.xv, W 19n,
    98n, 240n, P p.xv, P 446n, 507n, B
    289n, F p2, F 1023-4n
Delos, C 596, B 869, 870n, T 101-129n,
    316, F 659
    gods of, addressed collectively, B 868n,
    T 333-4
Delphi (= Pytho), K 220, 534n, 1015n,
    1016, 1229, 1273, C 104n, 605,
    624n, W 159, 869, 1408n, 1446, B
    189, 525n, 556n, 618, 620n, 716,
    724-5n, 769-784n, 869, 968n, 1296n,
    1522-3n, L 1129-32n, 1131, T 101-
    129n, 110n, F 186n, 659, 1056-7n,
    1211-3nn, 1319n, E p14 n62, We p2
    n7, p21, We 9n, 39n, 213, 227n,
    287n, 357n, 377-385n, 390n, 1002n
dēmagōgos, early meaning of, K 191n*, F
    419n
demigods, *see* heroes
demons of the night, W 1038-42
demons of the underworld, We 422n
denunciation, of demagogues by their own
    supporters, W 342n, 418n, 758-9n;
    see also self-condemnation
depilation, *see* hair (pubic)
Derveni papyrus, C 229n*
diagrams, C 177-8, B 1001-9
dialects, Ar.'s use of, A 729n*, We p28
    n117
    see also Arcadia, Boeotia, Cyprus,
    Doric, Ionic, Italy, Laconia, Megara,
    Mycenaean
Diarrhoea, River of (in underworld), F 146n
Diasia (festival), C 408, 864
dice, W 75, 295-6n, P 1081*, F 970, 1400,
    E 672, 825n, We p6, We 243
    special table for playing with, We 1037n
didaskalos (producer of a performance), A
    pp14-15, A 628n*, K 507n, C 530n,
    W p.xv*, W 1018-29n, B p1, L p1, T
    p2 n4, F p1, F 14n, We p1, p25

Ar. as his own, K 512-7, 541-550, W
    1018-29n, We p1 n4
    how assigned to tribes for dithyrambic
    contests, B 1403n*
    term used interchangeably with *poietes*,
    A 628n, P 737n, B 912n, We 797n
Diisoteria (festival), We 1175n
dikē "justice", in sense "the law of nature",
    C 1292n, 1419n
dildoes, L 109-110, 158n, E 45n, 890n,
    916-7nn
diminutives, A 404n, 450-1n, 872n, 954n,
    1206n, K 726n, 823n, 906-9n, 1215n,
    C 80n, 92n, 132n, 223n, W 655*, P
    202n, 263n, 1002n, L 906n, 1052n, F
    58-60n, 405n, 582n, 1200n, 1203n, E
    332n, 953n, We 1011
dining before sunset, as symbol of luxury,
    E 652n
dinners for two, in courtship, F 518n
Diocleia (Megarian festival), A 774n
Dionysia, City (festival), A p2*, p3, pp4-5,
    pp13-16*, p32, A 504n*, 505n, K
    520n, 537n, 574n, 967n, C p2, C
    311-3, 333n, 521-3n, 557n, 595-
    606n, W p.xv, W 220n, 225n, 1023n,
    1044n, 1479n, 1501n, P p.xv, p.xvi
    n1, P 1n, 45-46n, 414n, 700-1n,
    760n, 782n, 803n, 804n, 829n, B p1,
    B 510n, 800n, 918n, 1046-7n, 1072n,
    1403n, 1444-5n, L p2, T pp1-3, T
    p11, p12 n74, T 67-68, 164n, 747,
    1060n, 1061n, F p6 n36, p15 n65,
    p22 n99, F 14n, 73n, 76n, 151n,
    404-6n, 910n, 1419n, E p7, E 203n,
    825n, We p1 n4
    Ar. refused chorus for?, W p.xv
    curtailed in wartime?, A p13, T 1147n
    "old" tragedy at, F p8, We p32
    parade of war-orphans at, B 1361n
    proclamations at, B 1072-87*
    schedule of, B 786-9n*, F 376n
    unsuccessful dramatists relegated from?,
    W p.xv n1*
Dionysia, City or Country?, A 195, P 530
Dionysia, Country (festival), A p27 n61, A
    202, 237-279, 961n, L 646n, We p31
diphrophoros, *see* stool-bearer
diplomacy:

language and protocol of, B 1581-2n, T 1163n

technique of, B 1591-5nn, 1596-7n, 1605-25n, 1633n, L 1113n, 1117n, 1234n

Dipolieia (festival), C 398n*, 984, 985n*, P 420

discord, civil, deprecated, L 567-586, F 359-360, 686-705

discrimination, positive, E p13, p17 n75, E 617-634, 694-709

disease, theories of, C 332n

diseases and ailments, C 243n
  ague, W 1038
  arthritis, W 235n
  back trouble, E 10n
  black eyes, A 551, W 1386, P 541, L 444n, 472
  blindness, A 421, T 24-27nn, 299n, E p5 n25, We p5, pp6-8, p11, p13, p21, p22 n93, p27, We 13-15, 48, 86-92, 115n, 120-1, 249n, 327n, 403-4, 494, 634, 665, 747, 858-9
    healed, We 634-746
    in one eye, B 153-4n, 1294
  blisters, W 1119, 1167, F 236, E 1057, We 535
  boils, W 1172, E 1101
  burns, T 247n, We 535n
  calculus, P 1211n
  chilblains, see blisters
  concussion of the brain, C 1275-6
  constipation, E 355-371, 808n
  consumption, B 1372-1409n*, F 153n, E 330n, 935n, We p12
  cramp, L 845, 967, 1089
  deafness, K 43, T 24n
  delirium, temporary, W 8n; due to hunger, We 873n
  diarrhoea, W 1128n, B 1372-1409n, T 485-7, F 153n, 366n, E 329-330nn, 355n; see also Diarrhoea, River of
  dropsy, L 1085n*, F 940-4n*
  earache, W 701-2n
  eye troubles, C 327, L 299-300n, F 192, 417n, 1247, E p5 n25, E 254-5, 311n, 398-407, We p21, p29, We 115n, 332n, 665n; see also §blindness
  fainting, W 995-8, P 702, F 479, 482n, 1478n

  fevers, W 284, 813, 1038, P 755n
  fistulas, W 1172n
  flatulence, T 486n
  foreskin, adhesion of, K 964n*, We 267; see also circumcision
  gout, P 1211n, We 559
  head injuries, P 71
  heart palpitations, F 482n
  hangover, W 1255, F 218, We 297n
  hemiplegia, B 1490-3n
  indigestion, P 529, 712n
  jaundice, C 74n
  lameness, A 410-1, 427, 429, P 147, B 766n, 1292-3, 1378, T 24
  lovesickness, We 1034n
  lung disease (pleurisy), B 1372-1409n*, E 417
  mental disorders, C 833n, W 8n, 71-132, 651n, 1486-96, P 54-55, 64-66, 90, 95, B 14n, 712n, 798n, L 336n, 397n, 558n, T 680, E 250-2, 1068-9n, We 1-17, 364, 366, 903n, 1066n, 1132n
  oedema, F 940-4n
  palpitations, T 3n
  paralysis, W 948, B 1490-3n
  pneumonia, P 1069n
  prolapse of uterus or bladder, E 906n
  seasickness, T 882
  senile dementia, W 1370n, We 1066n
  skin diseases, P 804n, B 151n
  spleen, abnormalities of, P 1211n, T 3n
  swellings in groin, W 277, L 987-8, F 1280n
  swollen feet, F 1192n
  tuberculosis, see §consumption
  urine, difficulty in passing, W 810, T 616
  war wounds, A 1178-1226, P 443
  see also plague

dissidents, isolation of, used as evidence against them, A 290, 493, T 544-5n, We 948

distance, telescoping of, in drama, C 138n

dithyramb, K 574n, C 333-9*, 595n, 985n, W 84n, 1410n, P 829-831*, B p1 n3, B 672n*, 918, 1372-1409*, T 119n, F 153n*, 366, 729n, 1336n, E 1-18n, 330n, We p31 n128, We 293n, 515n, 529n
  choruses of, called "tribes", B 1407n

quasi-dramatic, We 290-321n
divination, *see* omens
diviners, C 332, P 1026, 1031n*, 1044n, 1046, 1056n, B 521n, 593-7, 602
doctors, A 1030-2, 1222, K 401n, C 332*, W 1432n, B 584n, E 363, We p9, p10, We 406-9
equipment of, We 710-1
eye specialists, P 803n, F 151n, E 364n, We p7
must not be squeamish, We p13 n63
publicly employed, We 408n
Dodona, C 402n, B 716, T 416-7n
"Dog's Arse", alleged name of a Boeotian melody, A 863
Dolopes (people of N. Greece), A 421n
doorkeepers, P 182-3n, L 1216d, F p13, F 37n
doors:
creaking of, T 487n, F 604
shrines at, W 804n, 875n; *see also* · Apollo (Agyieus), Hecate *in Index II*
see also knocks on doors, *skēnē*
Dorians, ethnic/linguistic division of the Greek people, L 1129-32n
Doric dialect, 555n
Aeginetan, K 1253n(?)
Cretan, B 570n
Laconian, K 1225n(?), P 214, L 81-240*, 980-1013, 1076-1188, 1242-1321
stereotypical expressions in, L 81n, 198n
Megarian, A 729n
poetic, C 339n, W 1438n
doss-houses, free public, E 418-421n
"doughnutting", E 296-7n
drama:
failure to understand nature of, T pp8-9*, T 1129n
theories of, T p9
dramatists:
actions of characters attributed to, F 15n
competing, singled out for derogatory comment, A 847-853, 1173, K 400, 526-536, F 13-15n
early, acting in own plays, K 522-3n, W 1479n, F 15n
fees paid to, F 367, 1463-5n

identity known even when not own *didaskaloi*, C 533n*, W 1018-29n
increasing use of assistants by, F 944n*; *see also* collaboration
dreams, C 16, 25-32, W 13-53, 1218, F 51n, 1331-40
comic fantasy compared to, W 127n
evil, exorcism of, F 1338-40
healing, We p13, We 695n
interpreters of, W 52n
prophetic, K 809, 1090-5, W 51n
dressing and undressing, sequence of, L 931n, T 255n, 636-642n
Dromos, exercise-ground at Sparta, L 1301n
drugs, dangerous, T 561; *see also* aphrodisiacs, poisoning
drunkenness, A 981, K 104, 1054, W 9n, 1253-5, 1292-1449, 1474-1515, P 537, L 1226-38, F 715, E 143n, 948, 1112-26, 1166-7n, We 297n, 1042n, 1048; *see also* diseases and ailments (hangovers)
dryness, association with death, F 194n
dung, *see* defaecation, insects (beetles), scatology, scatophagy
sinners wallow in, in underworld, P 48n, F 145-153
used to clear goats' air passages, We 313n
washed out of fleeces, L 574-5
dung-collectors, W 1184, P 9
"Dustyfeet", epithet for the (rural) poor, L 664*
Dyme (Achaea), T 1142n
dystopias, B p2 n4*

earthquakes, A 511, C 567-8, 584-5n, L 1137-44n, 1142, E 791
eating on stage?, P 1315n
Ecbatana, capital of Media, A 64, 613, K 1089, W 1143-4
Echinus (Thessaly), L 1168-70nn
eclipses, C 584-6, P 1031n
editions of Ar., printed, A pp19-21
Edonians (Thracian tribe), T 134-5n
education, traditional, C 961-976, F 729, We 190n
educational disadvantage:
an excuse for crime, W 958-9

an excuse for judicial perversity? W 989n

a qualification for politics, K 188-193

effeminacy, W 1169n, 1301n, T 163, 191-2, F 424n, 966n, 983-8n*, E 428n; *see also* homosexuality

of Dionysus, F 46-47nn

egg, cosmic, B 695-7

Egypt, K 416n, C 109n, 398n, 1130, P 1253, B 272n, 504-7, 1130n, 1133, 1296n, T 850n, 856-7, 878, 922, 935n, F 442n, 1208n, 1406, E p4, E 222n, 364n, 999n, We p3, We 178, 267n, 1198n

Assyrian conquest of, B 1021n

Athenian expedition to (459-454), E 293n

eiresiōnē (harvest-wresth), K 729, W 398-9, We 1054

eisodoi (entrance-passages in theatre), A p27 n65, C 275-328*, 326n, B 296n, T 658n, E p30

ejaculation, F 753n

ekkyklēma, A p14, A 395n, 408-9, 479d, 1003d, 1096n, K 1249n, 1252d, 1263d, 1327-8n*, 1329d, 1334d, C 91n*, 184n, 508n, W 1475n, P p.xvii, P 430d, 516-520dd, 726n, B 1579d, 1693d, T 95d, 96, 265, 1001n, F 830d, 1478d, We p25

Elaphebolion (Athenian month, ~ March), A p13, P p.xv

elegy, B 218 (in sense "lament"); *see also* metre (elegiac)

Eleon (Boeotia), K 123n, P 1070n, B 962n

Elis, P 605n, B 149*, 515n, 1121n

Elymnium (island off Euboea), P 1126

embatērion (Spartan marching-song), F 372-382n

embezzlement of public funds, K 258, 438n, 715-8n, 824-6n, 826-7, 1032n, C 351, 591n, 1199, W 554, 556-7, 666-7, 836n, 924-5n, 1101n, B 168n, 1111-2, 1297n, L 103n, 490, T 811, F 1453n, 1505n, E 77n, 254n, 438n, 630n, 667n, We p18 n80, We 569, 665; *see also* Athens, political and legal institutions (prosecutions)

emmeleia (tragic dance), F 897n

encomium (song of praise), C 1205-8

encore, planned, L 1295n

enemies, learning from, B 375-382·

enemies, perversity of deliberately making, We 910n

Englottogastores, *see* Tongue-to-Belly Men

enslavement:
   after capture by pirates/bandits, B 1427n
   as legal penalty, *see* Athens, political and legal institutions (punishments)
   for debt, We 147-8
   mass, on capture of a city, F p5

entertainers, itinerant, P 763n

entertainment, mass, moral and social effects of, F pp15-16

enthronement, in initiation-rites, C 254-262n

entrances and exits:
   choral farewell to departing actor, A 1143, K 498, C 510, W 1009n
   directions of, P 262*, 725-6dd*, B 849n, 1185n, E p30, We pp25-27
   dragged feet first, T 1001n
   entrance from *skēnē*, drawn by noise outside, A 864, C 1221, P 824, B 1469n, T 1083, E 564n, We 641
   entrance from *skēnē*, "driven out by smoke", We 821-2
   entrance in mid-conversation, C 1214n*
   entrance in mid-soliloquy, E 746, We 335
   entrance unnoticed by other characters, E 564n
   exits with poor or no motivation, C 887n, L 654n, 763-4n; *see also* characters (disappearing)
   of the four exotic birds, B 268-292n*
   running, T 1225n; *see also* slaves (*servus currens*).
   through audience area, C 275-328*, 1102n*, P 301n*, T 1223n
   unsummoned entrance, L 431n, T p8
   via chimney, W 144d
   via gap under eaves, W 205d, 209d
   see also chorus, windows

Ephesus (Ionia), A 68-69n, C 598, W 1139n, B 971n, F 733n

Epidaurus, K 1n, P 414n, L 513n, F p13 n58, F 364, We pp9-11, We 411n, 690n, 733-4n

epideixeis (display-performances by sophists), F 771n

epiparodos (song for chorus's second entrance), E p23, E 478-509

epirrhematic syzygy, A p9, p10, W 395n*, B 336-8n, L 614-705n

Epirus, A 604n, B 1522-3n, T 416-7n

epitaphs, F 84n, 1296-7n

eranoi (funds of a club of friends), A 615n*, L 651n, 653n

Eretria (Euboea), A 614n*, C 48n*, P 289n, E 943n

erotic art, subjects avoided by, E 470n, We 295n

Erythrae (Ionia), K 61n, C 273n, P 1095n, B 1021n, L p1 n4, We 678n

esparto grass, B 816, F 186n

Eteobutadae, Athenian *genos,* W 157n, B 1296n

Ethiopia(ns), C 622n, T p8, T 856-7n, 1011-2n, 1015n, 1060n

ethnic anecdotes, W 1259n*

Etna, Mt, P 73, B 926-7n

Etna (city), *see* Aetna

Étoile, Place de l' (now Place Charles de Gaulle), Paris, B 1007n*

etymology, C 394n. B 1530n

Euboea, K 238n, C 211-3, W 715, P 1046n, 1047n, 1084n, L 1168-9n, T p3, F 666n, We 22n

Eumolpidae, chief priestly family at Eleusis, F 1033n

eunomiā (law and order), B 1540

eunuchs, A 117-122, F 1331-63n

euphemism, K 1151n, C 1075n*, F 1280n, E 104n, 338n, 613n, 920n, We 57n, 977-8n, 1055n

Eurotas, River (Laconia), L 1298n, 1307

Eurymedon, River (Pamphylia), battle of the, L 1144n

evil, problem of, P 105n

evil spirits:
    amulets etc. protecting against, We 884n
    formula for banishing, F 301n

exclusus amator, E 952-975n, 962n, We 297n

exile, unauthorized return from, F 1163-8

exit-songs:
    omitted from script, A (end)n, K (end)n, L 1320-1n, We 321/2n

replaced by short anapaestic chant, C 1510-1n, T 1227-31

exodos:
    = "finale of a play", A p11
    = "music accompanying choral exit", W 582n

exposure of infants, C 530-1, L 139n, F 691n, 1189-91, We 521n

"Extortia", *see* Aetolia

fables, K 1038n*, W 566, 1181-2*, 1446-8nn, P 129, B 440-1n, 651, We 177n; *see also* Aesop *in Index II*

falsetto, T 101d, 267-8

family, abolished by Praxagora, E p13

family cults, B 1527n

farting, W 1183-4n, F 10n, 236-9, 1097, E 78, 327d, We p13 n63, We 698-706
    and anal sex, K 639n
    and other uninhibited behaviour, W 1305
    as defensive weapon, W 1177n, P 1077, E 77n
    as omen, K 639*
    compared to thunder, C 293-4, 386-394
    foods liable to cause, K 894-900, We 925n
    in fright, K 224, C 293-4, L 354n, We 693
    in sleep, K 115, C 9, E 464n
    symbolic of carefree joy, P 335, E 464, We 176n
    symbolic of contempt, P 547, F 1074, E 890n, We 618

fasting:
    at Thesmophoria, B 1519, T p10, T 570n, 693-5n, 733-4n, 949, 984
    in mourning, C 621*

father:
    addressed as if he were a public meeting, C 1408n
    helping look after children, C 1380n

feasting, at end of a comedy, C 1212-3n, F 1480n, E p22, p25, p32, E 834-852

fellatio, A 79, K 167, W 1345n, 1346, 1350, P 855n, T 57, F 1308n, E 920n, self-, K 1010, E p32, E 469-470, 471-2n, We 295d

ferries, F 139-140n, 180n, 185-7n, E 1086-7; *see also* Charon *in Index II*

festivals:
  curtailed in wartime, T 1147n
  international, P 342; see also under
    festival names underlined below
  mistimed through calendar adjustments,
    C 617-620
  new, in honour of Wealth, We 1162n
  profusion of, at Athens, C 307-310
  see also Adonia, Anthesteria, Apaturia,
    Boedromia, Brauronia, Chalkeia,
    Choes, Chytroi, Cronia, Diasia,
    Diisoteria, Diocleia, Dionysia,
    Dipolieia, Geraestia, Hephaestia,
    Heracleia, Isthmian Games, Lenaea,
    Mysteries, Nemean Games, Olympic
    Games, Panathenaea, Prometheia,
    Pyanopsia, Pythian Games, Scira,
    Stenia, Tauropolia, Thargelia,
    Thesea, Thesmophoria
fiction and deception, problem of
    differentiating, T pp8-9
figs, necklaces of, K 755*, L 647
figwood:
  acrid smoke from, W 146n
  punningly linked with sykophantai, W
    145n, 897n, We 946n
  used for toys, C 880n
  useless as timber, L 110n, We 946n
finance, Athenian public, W 656-660, L p1,
    L 174, 488-496, 653-4, We p2, We
    1192n
fire:
  and water, in myth, L 254-387n*
  covered at night, B 841n
  how contrived on stage, C 1484-5n*,
    1494*
  how to call for help, T 240-2
  lit around person who has taken
    sanctuary, T 721-2n, 726-730
  property destroyed by, B 997n, T 273n
  ritual involving, at Lemnos, L 299-300n
  temples destroyed or damaged by, C
    401, We 1193n
fire-walking, L 133-4, 136
fireships, A 920n*
fish:
  and gluttony, K 608n, B 151n
  and luxury, arrogance, etc., C 983n*, P
    804n, F 1068, E 606n
  and women, A 893-4n*

barracuda, European (spet), C 339
bass, K 361, E 1170n
boiled, W 679
catfish, K 1004n
cheap, offered to Hecate, We 594n
croaker, K 1053n, L 560n
dogfish, E 1169
eel, A 880n, 893-4n*, K 864-7, C 528-
    9n, 559, W 510, P 1005, L 36, 702
flat, thought of as "cut in half", L 115n
flounder, L 116, 131
grouper, W 493*
mackerel, K 1008
mullet, W 790, E 1173n
murry-eel, F 470-8n*, 475
picarel, blotched, F 984-5n, E 554n
pike, C 339n
pilchards, K 662*
ravenfish, K 1053n, L 560
salted, A 967n, K 1247, W 491, P 563, F
    558, E 385n
sardines/anchovies, A 640n, K 645-650,
    666, 672, 678, 895n, W 496, E 56
shark, E 1169
skate, W 510, P 810
sliced, K 1177, F 517, 1040n, E 606,
    842, 1169, We 894
sole, L 115n
sprats/whitebait, A 671n, 901n, W 328-
    331n, 493-4, 1127, 1329-31, B 76-
    77, 1546, F 984-5, E 252n
tunny, K 313, 354, W 195n, 1087n*
turbot, P 1008n, L 115n
fishbones, E 56n
Five Thousand (semi-democratic regime,
    411/0), T p1 n4, F 1466n, E 456-7n
flowers, A 637, 992, K 1323, 1329, C 910,
    911, 1005-8*, 1027n, 1174n, 1330, P
    520n, 577-8, B 1067-8n, T 746n,
    902n, 910n, F 351, 372, 441, 448-9,
    1150n, We 807n
fly-whisks, K 59n
folktales, W 1177-9, B 280-4n, 471n*, 479-
    480n; see also fables
food:
  acorns, P 1137
  ambrosia, K 1095n*, P 724, 854
  barley-groats, K 1009, 1104, C 106n,
    648, 669, W 300, P 368, 477, 636, B
    503n, E 819, We 219n, 628, 763, 806

beans, P 772n, L 690, We 816n; *see also* chewing gum

black-eyed, *see* §cowpeas

bread, A 872n, 1123, 1168, K 414n, C 95-96n, W 238, 1391, P 120, 123, 741n*, 853, 1196, B 567, L 1208-9, F 505, 507, 551, E 307, 606, We p6, We 190, 320, 543, 627, 765, 1136, 1142

brine, W 328-331n, 1515

bulbs, edible, C 188-190

cakes, A 246n, 1125-30, K 103n, 819, 1105, 1181-2, 1190-1, 1219, C 507, P 869, 1159n, 1195, 1314, 1359, B 161n, L 601, 759n, T 94, 570, F 507, E 223, 742n, 843, We 191, 677, 995, 999

cheese, K 479-480, W 676, 838, 896-7, 911, 913, 925, 956, P 250d, 368, 1129, B 533, 1579-80, F 559, 1369, E 404n, We 298n, 719n

chickpeas, P 772n, 1136, E 45, 606

cowpeas, P 1144

cucumber, A 519-521n, P 1001

daily requirements of, E 424n

deprivation of, as punishment, E p19, E 469, 665-6; *see also* slaves (punished by deprivation of food), women (punished by deprivation of food)

eggs, P 242-252n, B 673-4, L 856

fig-juice, P 1185n

fig-leaf, stuffed (*thrion*), A 1102n, K 954-5, L 663, F 134n

figs, A 802n, K 259-260, 755n, W 296, 302, P 574-5, 634, 772n, 1145, 1165-6, 1169n, 1217-23, 1249, 1324, 1348, 1699, L 564, T 1114n, We 191, 677, 768-9n, 798, 801, 811

flour and meal, preparation of, A 507-8n

fruit, A 519-521n, 967n, K 755n, 1077, C 978, W 449, 1268, 1289n, P 63n, 634, 711n, 1001, 1154n, B 82, 160, 1100, L 856, 1169-70n, T 1185n, F 1320-1n, E 355, 362, 817, We 768-9n, 1142n

as love-token, C 997*, L 785n

garlic, A 519-521n, 526n, 813-4n, K 492-3, 600, W 679, 680, P 246d, 258, 502, 1000, L 689, F 555, 861n, 987, E 291

used as toilet-paper, in Wealth's new world, We 817-8

herbs and seasonings, A 254n, 861, 874, K 629-630n, 631n, 676, 682, 894-900, C 421, W 455, 676, 1357, B 534, 1579, 1582, 1585, T 456, 910n, F 603n, 942n, E 292n, 648n, 1171, We 253, 283, 925

honey, A 1130, K 755n, W 676, 878, P 252, 830n, L 475n, T 1192, E 742-3, 1171

kandaulos, P 123n

leaves of root vegetables, eaten by the destitute, We 544

mallow, wild, We 544

māza (uncooked barley cake), A 732n, 835n, K 819n, 1166, W 301n, 610, P 565, 853, F 1073n, E 606, 665, 851, We 192, 219n, 544

milk, W 710, P 1150, 1159n, 1185n, We 298n, 1206n

nettles, K 422

nuts, W 58-59, We 768-9n, 816n, 1142n

olive oil, A 35, P 242-252n, B 533, 1589, We 810

olives, F 988, E 308

pickle, A 671n

porridge, W 737, L 562, E 1178

salt, A 760n, 813-4n, 835n, C 1236, P 1074, F p9 n40, E 814, 1171

sauces, K 343n, B 534-7, 1637, E 292, 1170

savoury (*opson*) versus staple, K 707n, C 983n*, C 1073n, W 301, P 123

savoury mash (*myttōtos*), A 174n, K 771, W 63n, P p.xvi, P 242-252n

soup/broth, K 1007, 1171-6, C 386, W 264-5n, 811, 814, 855n, 882n, 906, 918, 982-4, P 716, B 78, L 1061, F p19, F 62-65, 505-6, E 252n, 845, We 192, 627, 672-695, 1004

sweetmeats, We 768, 789, 798, 996

vegetables, A 469n, 894n, K 19, 41, 600, 677, 827n, 895n, C 982, 1001n*, W 239, 480, 496-9, P 242d, 529d, 1014, 1129, L 798, T 1185, F 303n, 654, 942n, E 307, 1092, We 167, 820n

vinegar, W 1367, P 242-252n, B 534, F p9 n40, We 812

whole grains, K 806n, P 595

see also animals, birds, crustaceans and molluscs, fish, meat
"foot", metrical sense of, F 1323n
football referees, mockery of, E 255n
footfall, contrast of male and female, E 483n, 544-6
footpads, see *lōpodytai*
footwear, K 315-321, 869-875, W 275, 1154n, 1157-73, B 973-4, L 416-8, T 1183, F 405, E 47, We 847, 983, 1012
  blacking of, W 600
  koṇipodes (light sandals), E 848
  kothornoi, B 994, L 657, T 263n, F 47, 541n, 557, E 346
  lack of, We 942-3n
  "Laconians", W 1158-65, T 142, E 47n, 74, 269, 345, 508, 542-5
  peribārides ("riverboat slippers"), L 45, 47, 53
  Persian boots/slippers, C 150, L 229-230, T 734n, E 319, 346n
  Socrates' reluctance to wear, C 103n, B 1553n
  winged sandals, T 1011-2n, 1098d, 1099
  worn by a wineskin, T p12, T 734
foreigners:
  Athenian citizenhip suggested for some, L 580n, F 696n
  citizens accused of being, A 517-8n, 704n*, 705n, K p3, W 1042n, 1221n, 1301n, B 11n, 31-32, 764, 798n, 876n, 1527n, 1700n, L 103n, T 805n, 840n, F p1, F 417n, 678-682, 694n, 730-2, 970n, 1532-3, E 254n, 932n, We 665n; *see also* Athens, political and legal institutions (prosecutions for *xeniā*)
  visiting, in Attica, A 505n, K 975n
foreskin, retraction of, in sexual arousal, P 903, B 507n, 560n, L 143n, 158n, 739-740n, 953, 978-9n, 1136, 1187-8n, We 267n, 295
forgiveness, considered praiseworthy, We 910n
Four Hundred (oligarchic regime, 411), K 327n, W 1270n, 1302n, P 395n, B 126n, 798n, 1556n, 1569n, L p3, L 421n, 490n, 1059n, T p1 n4, p3 n21, T 1143-4n, F p14, F 541n, 686-705n,

689n, 729n, 967n, 1072n, 1422n, 1466n, E 456-7n
freed(wo)men, T 515n, F 1345n, We 1n
  as under-secretaries, F 1084n
  rich, W 1309, E 102n, 366n
freedom, academic, F p14 n64
freedom of speech, T 540-1
friends:
  fair-weather, We 782-3, 829-838
  should treat their property as common property, We 345n
frogmarching of arrested offender, E 258n
fullers, C 870n, W 1128, F 713, E 415, We 166
funerals, C 838n, B 474n, L 600-613, F 167-170, 170-7n, 1302-3n, E 537-8, 1030-6nn, We 1008
  games at, in heroic legend, F 1319n, 1403n
  prothesis, E 537-8nn, 1030-4nn
  public, B 396
  triple farewell to deceased, F 184n, 271n, 1176n
  see also death, *lekythos*
fungi, W 262

gait, peculiarities of, W 688, 1168-73, E 482n
gambling, A 855n, 1115n, C 686n, W 75, B 1297n, E p20, E 672, We 243; *see also* dice, *pettoi*, sport (quail-fighting, quail-tapping)
games, children's, K 855n*, C 763, W 295-6n, B 1151*, 1460-2, 1465, We 307-8n, 816-7, 1055-9
Gamelion (Athenian month, ~ January), A p13, E 1027n, We 904n
"Gargantuans", *see* Tragasae
garlands:
  as badge of office, K 1227-8, 1250-2, C 625, L 602n
  as love-gift(?), T 400-1, We 297-8nn
  at sacrifices etc., C 256n, 257n, 309, W 861, B 43n, T 37, 448n, F 329-330, We p6, We 820
  at symposia, A 1091, 1145, P 1154n, B 463n, L 632n, T 457-8n, F 218-9n, 1500d, E 133, 606, 691, 844, 938d, 1129d, We 1041
  dedicated, We 108°-9

for athletic victors, We 269n, 585-592

for bringer of good news, K 647n, We 21n, 757

for two-year-olds at Choes, T 746n

funerary, L 602, E 538

of ivy, worn by Dionysiac worshippers, T 988n

of loaves (!), We 765

of sacred olive, as honour, F p21

sacred, make wearer sacred, We 21n

worn by athletes, C 1005-8*

worn by diviners, P 1044

worn by those consulting the Delphic oracle, We 1d, 21-22, 357n

worn by priests, B 893n*

worn by public speakers, K 1227n, B 463, T 380, E 122, 131, 145d, 148, 163, 165d, 171-3dd

see also Garland-seller in Index II

garlic, used for poultices etc., W 1172n; see also food, sport (cock-fighting)

gastronomic poetry, E 1169-75n

Gates, The, see Thermopylae

Gela (Sicily), A 606

gender, confusions and inversions of, C 518-562n*, 687n, W 35-36n*, 1035n, P 758, B 673-4n*, 830-1, 1172-1201, 1296n*, 1494-1552n*, L 145, 454n, 527-538, 917n*, T pp7-10, T 35, 92, 97-98, 101-175, 184-192, 204-7, 211-268, 571-6, 584-596, 850-922, 855n, 1012-1135, 1160-1225, E 519, 952-975n, 1024-5n, 1037-97n; see also cross-dressing, gynaecocracy, women (use or threaten violence)

gender, grammatical, C 658-693, 847-853, 1247-51, 1258, L 217n, T pp7-8, p9, T 134-5n, 903n, 1001n, 1015n, 1056-97n, 1077, 1109n, 1114n, 1133n*, 1160-75n, F 1443-4n, E p9, E 31n, 172n, 285-8n, 298-9, 549-550n, 572n, 589n, 738n, 739n, 890n

gender-doubling, in prayers to all the gods, B 866-7n, T 331-4

genders:

most distinctions maintained, in Eccl., E p17

near-indistinguishability of, in Republic, E p8, p17

strict dichotomy of, in Lysistrata, L 908n

general, sole, Praxagora elected as, E 246n

generations, inversion of, W p.xviii, W 1333, 1336n, 1351-9, 1364-5n

generosity, laudable whatever its motive, We 831n

genocide, B 186n, F p5

geometry, C 177-8, 202-5, B 995-1009, F 799-801nn, 813d, 956n

gephyrismos (raillery during Athens-Eleusis procession), F 416-439n

Geraestia (festival at Geraestus), K 561n

Geraestus (Euboea), K 561, F 666n

gerousia (Spartan senate), L 980n*

gestures, A 54d, 111d, 113d, 114d, 204d, 444n, 1123d, K 922d, 1025d, 1220n, 1254d, 1381n, C 81d, 83d, 187d, 200d, 211d, 217d, 324d, 654, 806n, 1131d, 1237d, W 209d, 279n, 437d, 654d, 820dd, 821d, 850n, 858d, 1001d, 1062d, 1122d, 1150d, 1161d, 1214-7dd, 1328d, 1373d, 1389d, 1500d, P 15d, 36d, 52n, 53n, 57d, 114d, 142d, 376d, 538d, 545d, 549, 883d, 942d, B 380d, 424-5n, 438d, 1258dd, 1395d, 1688d, L 85d, 92d, 123-5dd, 126-7, 167d, 311d, 317n, 362d, 634-5d, 657d, 856d, 862d, 956d, 988-9dd, 992d, 1172d, T 25d, 219d, 245d, 252d, 285d, 536d, 748d, 809d, 927d, 929d, 936d, 1009-14n, 1092d, 1170d, 1216d, F 26d, 87d, 139d, 141d, 173d, 175d, 308d, 437d, 508d, 622d, 653d, 830d, 843d, 913d, 954d, 1012n, 1024d, 1029n, 1136d, 1198-1247n, 1345n, 1413n, 1475d, E 28n, 105d, 129d, 167d, 171d, 246-7dd, 255d, 260d, 369d, 555n, 614d, 622d, 720d, 785d, 805-6n, 890d, 1029n, 1043d, 1098-1101n, 1106n, 1108d, 1140d, We 1d, 53-54n, 57d, 74n, 86d, 226n, 271d, 287d, 425d, 452d, 575n, 926-934n, 1037d, 1061d, 1067-79n, 1087n

conveniently impossible, E 1080n

"girl" (pais), implying affection rather than age, L 697n, 700-1n

glass, A 75, C 766-772

gleaning, F 92n

goatherds, autoerotic tendencies of, P 290n

"Goatland", *see* Tragasae

gods:

a human invention, according to Prodicus, B 692n

absence of, in *Wasps* and *Eccl.*, E pp27-28*, We p21

addressed as "man", B 1638, F 1160n, 1472n, We 78-79n, 118n, 208-9n

averse to manifestations of grief, W 392n

barbarian, 1520-33; *see also* Triballian God *in Index II*

behaviour of, used to justify human delinquencies, C 902-7, 1080-2, E 778-783

cease to be worshipped, We pp16-17, We 1114-6, 1172-85

cooking own food, F 505-511n

cult-images of, B 515, L 262n, T 773n, F 16n, We p22 n91

death of, envisaged, B 1223-4, 1514n, 1642-68

do not defaecate, P 723n

do not feel pain (?), F 633-673

"foreign", We n12

forgiving of Athenian errors, C 587-9, E 474-5n

identify themselves with Athenian cause, F 1448n

invented by Ar., B 1536n

join a rebellion they can't beat, We 1189-90n

make offerings to themselves, P 433-457n*

mortal equates himself with, C 223n, W 556-7n, 619-627, 671, 946-7

mortals equated with, A 405n, 530n, 567n*, K 1338, W 418n, 556-7n, 652, 1532-3n, B 1765, L 1252, 1273*, T 43-50n, 1106, F 851n, 1259n, E p27 n101

nature stilled in presence of, B 777-8n

novel, F 889-894; *see also* Air, Chorus (c), Mist, Nostrils, Respiration, Sagacity, Sky, Tongue *in Index II*

origins of, B 685-702

praying to a human, F 297n

praying to lesser divinities, F 871n

punishment of impiety by, T 667-685

quarrels among, E p27 n103

rebellion against, P 102-8, 361-519, B pp2-3, B 186-193, 554-587, 629-635, 843, 1168-1268, 1494-1765, E p27 n103, We p13 n65, p17, We 112-221, 1096-1190

revered for their power not their goodness, We p17

spiritual maturation of, in Aeschylus and Ar., F p19 n88

startling utterances ascribed to, C 1260-1n

statues of, B 514-9

swear by themselves, B 1614

"take and don't give", E 778-783

tempting sinners to their doom, C 1452-61

treat Aeschylus as their equal, F 1479n*, 1517-8n

ubiquitous in *Wealth*, We pp21-22

worship a mortal?, T 41n

see also apotheosis, atheism, deification

gold, associated with gods, F 483n

gold, mined in Thrace, B 670n

Golden Age, C 1028-9*, B p2, B 586n*, We p6

Golden Fleece, C 257n

Golden Hills, fabulous mountains (or privies?) of Persia, A 82

Gortyn (Crete), law code of, C 1425-6n, We 147n

graffiti, amatory, A 144, W 97-99

grammar, study of, C 658-691, F 1114n

grandmothers, not necessarily elderly, L 549n

Great Idea, A pp11-13, We p5, p23, We 95n

Great King, *see* Persia

Greece (Hellas):

Athens as destined ruler of, K 797, 964-5, 1330, 1333

common welfare of, A 8, P 93, 105-8, 292-8, 406-413, 435-6, 866, 995-8, 1097-8n, 1320-8, L 29-41, 49-50n, 343, 525, 1110, 1128-34, We 430n

greeting, formulae of, C 1145n, We 322-4, 1042n

Grinders (Aletrides), girl cult-servants of Demeter(?), L 643

Guardians, in Plato's *Republic*, E pp13-17,
    E 589n, 614n, 635-643n, 656n, 663-
    4n, 673-4n
Gulag, E 665n
gymnasia, C 178n, 179, 417, 1002, 1054,
    W 527, 1025, P 356n, 762, B 139n,
    140, F 1087-8n, 1198-1247n, 1200n,
    E p17, We 168n; *see also* sport
    (wrestling)
gymnastic training, of Spartan women, L 82
gynaecocracy, E pp8-22, E 173-240n, 210-
    1, 229-240, 427-477, 504n, 555-
    1183; *see also* Amazons *in Index II*

Hades (underworld), A p4, p12, p13, W
    1031n, P 48, 313, 650n, F p18, F 69-
    1533 *passim*
    descent to, as comic theme, F pp9-13
    eating in, dangerous?, F 508n*
Haerae (Ionia), L p1 n4
hail, C 1124-7, F 852
hair, facial, plucking of, E 904n
hair, long, on men, A 390n, K 580, 1121, C
    14, 332, 348, 1100, W 74n, 1267n,
    1317n, B 911, 1282, L 279-280n,
    561, 1222(?), E 955n
    and conceitedness, C 545
    modern prejudices about, W 476-7n
    seen as anti-democratic, W 466
hair, pubic and/or perineal:
    female, W 1374n, P 892-3n, E 97n
    female, plucked or singed, L 89, 151,
        825-8, T 537-543, F 516*, E 12-13,
        724
    male, C 978n, L 800-4
    male, plucked or burnt off, as
        punishment for adultery, C 1083n*,
        T 537n, We 168n
    male, singed, for purpose of disguise, T
        216, 236-248, 590-3
    male, torn in grief, F 424
    of slaves, not to be plucked, E 724
hair, shaken in dance, L 1311
hair, tearing of, F 424, We 168n
hair colour, A 243n, C 1485n, W 1n, 1064-
    5, 1192, L 595, 685n, T 190, F 730,
    We 1043
    artificial, L 43n, E 630n, 735-6
hair styles, A 849n*, C 528-9n, W 1069,
    1267, B 806n, T 258n, 838, 841

on theatrical masks, E 1150n
hair-nets, T 138, 161-2n, 257
halcyon days, B 1594; *see also* birds
    (halcyon)
Haliae (Argolid), W 240n
Haliartus (Boeotia), battle of (395), E p2,
    p5, E 193n, 202-3nn, We 550n
Halicarnassus, L 675n, T 1200n
handclasp, as pledge of faith/friendship, A
    309n, C 81, F 754-5, 789*, We 753n,
    1202-3
handwashing, before and after meals, K
    357n, W 1216-7nn, B 463-4, 603n, E
    133n, 419n
"Harmodius" (symposiac song), A 980
harness, P 155-6n
head, covering of, in shame or grief, F 911-
    2
headgear, K 580n*, 968n, C 268, B 487n,
    1203-4n, L 604, F 180n; *see also*
    garlands, ribbons
headpiece, *see* (1) masks, (2) wigs
healing, *see* Asclepius *in Index II*
"Heartford", *see* Cardia
hearth, B 864n, 865n, We 768-9n
Hebrus, River (Thrace), B 769-784n, 771-
    2n*, 774
hecatomb, K 656n
Hecatombaeon (Athenian month, ~ July), C
    386n, 398n*, P 418n, F 1090n
hegemony, joint, of Athens and Sparta, P
    935n, 1082
Hellas, *see* Greece
Hellas (ancient region of Thessaly), A 421n
Hellespont (Dardanelles), C 553n, W 308,
    F p2, p3, p20, F 1422n, E p4, We p4,
    We 178n, 550n
Hellespontine satrapy, We p3
helots (Spartan serfs), K p2, K 849n,
    1225n, 1330n, P 219n, 625n, B 149n,
    L 106n, 1137-44n, 1166n, E 651n
helping friends / harming enemies, K 94, C
    1161, B 419-420, We 910n
hemlock, F 123-6, 1051
Hephaestia (festival), W 1203-4n, F 131n
Heraclea-in-Trachis, K 238n, L 1168-9n
Heraclean baths, C 1051
Heracleia (festival) at Diomeia, F 651
Heraeum, Cape (near Epidaurus), K 1n

heralds, A 1000n, K 668n, 751n, W 753, P 551n, 968n, 1060n, B 448-450n, 561n, 843-4, 845n, 1269, 1705n, 1706-19n, 1726-30n, T 1163n, E 684, 713, We 1110n; see also Herald, Heraldess in Index II

see also Athens, political and legal institutions (herald of the Council and People); Mysteries (herald of)

herbal remedies, see medicine (plant extracts used in)

Hermae, C 1478n, P 924n, We 1153n

mutilations of (415), K 242-3n*, C 109n, W 795n, 1268-9n, P 395n, B 766-7n, 1293n, 1297n*, 1556n, L 103n, 489-490nn, 1094*

Hermione (Argolid), W 1410n, F 194n

hero, comic, A pp11-13, P p.xvii, B pp3-4, T p6, p9 n55, E p26

agenda hidden until power secured, E pp11-12, p26

atypicality of Strepsiades as, C p3*

divine assistance for, E pp27-28, We p22

enemy of gods if anti-social, E p28

failure of enemies of, sometimes taken for granted, E p21

female, problems of handling, in finale, E p27

prolonged absence of, E pp26-27, We p24

spouse of, E p22, We p21

heroes, A 575, 578, 709n, W 823, B 881, F 1060; see also under names of individual heroes in Index II

as patrons of households, W 389n*

becoming gods, We pp8-10, p11 n53, p12 n55

dangers of encountering, C 315n, B 1485-93

libation to, W 1217n

shrines of, W 389n*, 819-820

heroines, C 315

Hestiaea or Histiaea (Euboea), A 6n, P 1047n, F p5

hetairai, see sex-sellers

hetaireiai (political clubs, often anti-democratic), L p3 n17, L 490n, 577-8, T p3, E 22-23n

"Hidings, The", see Lepri

hidrysis (installation of a cult-statue), P p.xvii, P 918ff, 1091, We 1191-3

hierarchy of the universe (god>man>[woman]>beast), B pp3-4*, E p8

hierophant (chief priest of the Mysteries), F p19 n91

hired labourers, W 681n, 686n, 712, B 1152, E 310n

Histiaea, see Hestiaea

history, edited for a political purpose, L 1137-44, 1150-6

holy war, B 556; see also Sacred War

homicide, justifiable, C 1077n, B 558n, We 168n

homoeopathy, A 717-8n

homonymous plays confused, We pp29-31

homosexuality[4], A p7, A 79, 119n, 265, 388n, 592, 605n, 664, 716, 843, 855n, 1093n, K 371n, 428, 523n, 639n, 721n, 732-740*, 877-880, 969, 1277n*, 1321n*, 1382n*, 1385-6, C 178n, 349n, 350n, 529, 686n, 909, 973-980, 1023, 1073, 1084-1104, 1330n, W 84, 98n, 687-8, 787n, 1025-8, 1070, 1187n, 1278n*, 1493n*, P 12n, 724n, 804n, B 137-142, 151n, 168n, 521n, 703-7, 831n, 876n, 1296n, 1569n, L 621n, 723-5n, 1092, 1105n, 1113n, 1222n, 1270n, T p7, p9, T 29n, 35, 50, 59-62, 132-3, 163n, 200-1, 204-7, 235n, 1119-20, 1123-4, F p1, F 48n, 56-57, 83n, 148, 339n, 417n, 422-7, 934n, E 103, 112-3, 167n, 364n, 365n, 626n, 932n, 1037-97nn, We 153-9; see also sex-sellers (male)

and blackmail, W 1025-8nn

and heterosexual promiscuity, L 723-5n

and the successful dramatist, W 1025, P 762-3

rare between two free adults, F 57n

---

4 This term is used here merely as a label to denote sexual desire by one male for another, and actions resulting therefrom; it is not meant to imply any view on the question whether anything corresponding to the present-day distinction between heterosexual and homosexual "orientations" existed in classical Athens.

stable relationships, T 29n
honeycomb, used to soothe infants, T 505-6
honours, public, to Ar., F pp21-22, F 686-705n
horse-riding, unwomanliness of, L 676n
horsecock (fabulous beast), P 1177, B 800
horses, wooden or "pantomime", K p4
hospitality:
emphasized in Eleusinian doctrine, F 145-153n
outrages against, punished in Hades, F 147
unknown among Triballi, B 1529n
hostages, A 325-351, K p2, L 244, T p8, p12, T 689-759
household, new inmates of, how welcomed, We 768-9n, 789-790, 794-5
houses:
all merged into one, E 673-5
heinousness of entering uninvited, E 675n
layout of, W 129-130n, 139n*
walls of, We 204n
husband:
basking in wife's reflected glory, E 725-7
in tragedy, never survives bringing mistress home, E 1138n
known by wife's name, under gynaecocracy, E 727n
reluctant to believe ill of wife, E 348-350n
hybris, A 479, K 727n, C 1068n, 1083n*, 1299n*, 1506n, W 1303, 1441, P 1229, 1264, L 399-400, 425n, T 63, 465, 670, 719, F 21n, E 663-4n, 1138n, We 564n, 886n, 1003n, 1099n; *see also* Athens, legal and political institutions (prosecutions)
against shrines of Hecate, F 366n*
and age, T 63n
and wealth, We 564
hydriāphoroi (jar-bearers), in Panathenaic procession, E 738
Hymettus, Mt (Attica), We 720n
hymns, K 551-564, 581-594, C 563-574, 595-606, T p11, T 43-50n, 947-1000, 990-4n, 1136-59, F 318-352, 372-413, 448-459, E 3n
Hyperboreans, B 769-784n

hypnosis, W 8n

iambic poetry, A p8*
Iapygia (toe of Italy), We 550n
Ida, Mt (Crete), B 570n, F 1356
Ida, Mt (Troad), L 723-5n, F p10 n45, p11, F 1356n
idiōtai (private individuals), comedy's attitude to, F 459n
ill-luck, treated as contagious, A 1019n, C 1263
ill-omened words, attempts to neutralize, C 1372n, W 536
Illyria, B 1521
Imbros, E p3, p4, E 644-5n, We p4
immortality:
birds claim to possess, B 688, 700n
granted to favoured individuals, P 832-3n
how attainable, K 1095n*
of gods, ignored, B 1224
shared by Dioscuri, P 285n
impalement, as (barbaric) punishment, We 859n
impiety, E p28 n105, E 330n, We 859n, 946n; *see also* Athens, political and legal institutions (prosecutions)
excused on plea of revenge, T 721-2
impossible orders, followed by interruption/distraction, W 201n, L 186n
incendiary devices, in war, A 920n, B 1248
incense, offerings of, W 96, 860-874, T 37-57, F 871, 885-8, We 1114, 1126n
incentives, material:
argued to be essential, We 507-534
not considered immoral, We p15 n71
incest, C 1371-2, W 1178n(?), P 114-123n, F 850, 1081, 1193-4, 1475n, 1491-2n, We p25 n104
Oedipal, E p14 n62, E 1038-42
incubation, We pp12-13, We 411-2, 653-747
India, B 471n, 485n, 1553n
inequality, abolished by Praxagora, E p19, E 592-4
infertility, T 407-8, 641
informers (*sykophantai*), A 515-522*, 559, 725n, 840, 904-958, K 259, C 104n, 923-4n, W 74n, 146n, 421n*, 502n,

1038-9nn, 1042n*, 1096, 1187n, 1408n, P 191, 653, B 153-4n, 285*, 289n, 1296n, 1297n, 1470-81n*, 1475n, 1479, 1699-1705nn, L 490n, F p9 n43, F 1453n, E 254n, 439, 452, 562-3, 603n, We p15, p20, We 31, 665n, 970; see also figwood, and Informer, Nicarchus in Index II
inhuman and degrading treatment of, in comedy, We 942-3n
needed for democracy to work?, We 907-920
silence of, bought, K 63-70n, 439, 529n, 775, 824-6n, P 639n, 645-6, We 31n, 370n
initiation rites, C 254-426, F p18; see also Mysteries, mystery-cults, Samothrace
innovation for innovation's sake, F 1446-50, E 218-220, 455-7, 586-7
inscription, Aristophanic text on an, F p30
insects and arachnids, K 518n, T 1009-14n
ants, B 590, T 100, 1175n
bedbugs, C 12n, 37n, 634, 699, 701-4n, 707-715, 742, F 115, 439n, We 541
beetles, A 920n, C 150n, W 179n, 1448-9, P 1-181, 720-4, 865, 1077, L 694-5
cockchafer, C 763, W 1341
bumblebees, A 866n, W 107
cicadas, A 871n, C 1360, W 1159-60, B 39-40, 769-784n, 1095-6
golden, as ornaments, K 1331*, C 984*
fleas, C 144-152, 831, T 1180, We 537-9
flies, W 597
gadfly, A 427n, T 325n
gall-wasps, K 523n, B 590*
gnats, K 1038, C 156-168, W 352, B 82, 245, 247n, 569, 570, L 1025-34, We 537-9
honeybees, K 755n, 794n, C 45, W p.xviii n3, W 107, 366, 1082n, 1116*, B 498n, L 475n, F 1273-4n, E 973
poets compared to, P 830n, B 749-751, F 1299-1300n
lice, P 740, We 537-9
locusts, A 871n, 1116n, W 1311-2, P 627n, B 185, 588

mosquitoes, L 1032n
moths, A 1111, W 1056-7n, L 730
scorpions, T 528n
spider, poisonous, W 1509
spiders, F 1313-5
spoken of as two-footed, C 150n, P 7n, 35n
wasps, W p.xvii, W 146n, 223-9, 376-7n, 404-460, 1062n, 1071-90, 1102-21, P 1216n, L 475, We 561-2; see also Chorus (d) in Index II
woodworm (furniture beetle), K 1308, T 427n, 1175n
interest, C 18-20, 34, 241, 739, 755, 1166, 1285-95, L 1056n, 1057n, T 843-5
argued to be unnatural, C 1294-5n
Internet, F 1114n
interpolations, A 436n, K 1062, C 653, 1176, W 1282, 1293, P 273, 365*, 744, 896b(?), 1218, B 192, 336-8n(?), 386-7n, 1343, T 12, 276, 298, 306(?), 360, 1187, We 281, 805a, 897(?), 967-9n(?)
interruptions, marked by metrical imbalance, C 700-6n, W 395n*
Ionia(ns):
as Persian term for Greece/Greeks, A 104, 106, We p3 n11
ethnic/linguistic division of the Greek people, A 104n, L 582n, 584n, 721n, 1129-32n, F 696n
in Asia Minor, K 327n, P 46*, B 172n*, L p1, L 1133n, F 187n, E pp1-2, p3, We pp3-4, We 1002n
music of, E 883
thought of as effeminate/lustful, T 163, E 883n, 918
Ionic dialect, K 659n, P 47-48, 929-933
Iron Age, wickedness of, We 50n
"islands", term for allied states, K 170n, 1034n, 1319n, P 298n, 760, B 1422n
Isles of the Blest, W 638n, 639-640
Ismenus (river at Thebes), A 861n, L 697n
Isthmian Games, W 1191n, P 879, T 647-8n
Isthmus of Corinth, P 879-880n, F 966n, E p2, E 202n, We p1, p2 n7, p4, We 173n
causeway across, T 647-8
Italy:

Athenian allies in, W 700n
embassy to (422), K 1377n
far south of, conquered by Dionysius I,
We 550n
Greek dialects of, K 963n
performances of Athenian drama in, C
521-3n*, T p12, T 390-1n, F p7 n35
Ithaca, W 185
Ithome, Mt (Messenia), L 1137-44n
ithyphalloi, alleged sacrilege-club, F 366n*
ivory, B 219, 1463n, We 815
ivy, attribute of Dionysus, T 988, 999-1000

jailers, E 77n
jealousy, pretended show of, We 1067-79n
Jerusalem, temple of, We 678n
jewellery, W 677, B 670, L 408-413, 1190,
T 822-3n, E 447
theft of, at festivals, A 258, T 893-4
Judaism, C 252n
judges, at dramatic festivals, A p14*, A
1224, B 445, 447, E p7, p25, E 1154-
62
biased or corrupt, E 1142n
promises/threats to, by chorus, C 1115-
30, B 1102-17, E 1142
varying tastes of, E 1155-7
Juntine editions of Ar.:
first (Florence, 1515), A p19
second (Florence, 1525), P p.xxii

kakodaimonistai, club allegedly founded by
Cinesias, B 1372-1409n, F 366n*
kalos kāgathos (term of commendation), K
185n, 227n, 735n, C 101n, 797n, W
1256n, 1301n, L 1059-60, *F 719n*
kanēphoros, see basket-bearer
Karneios, sacred month among Dorians, P
414n
katakeleusmos, B 336-8n, 638-640n, L
484n, E p24, E 571-709n, We p24,
We 487-618n
katēlips (high storage shelf bisecting room),
F 566n
Kerykes (family), B 284n
keys, T 421-3
khorou, marking choral song omitted from
script, E p24, E 729/730, 876/7,
1111/2n, We p23, p24 n99, We
321/2n, 770/1n

kidnapping, K 1030n, C 749n, T 818, We
461-3n, 521, 524n
King's Eye, title of Persian official, A 92,
94, 124
King's Peace, *see* Peace of Antalcidas
kinship system, abolished by Praxagora, E
p13
kinship terms, T 1n
kisses:
as metrical units, A 1190-7n
as pledge of faith/friendship, C 81, F
754-5, 788*, 790n
onion-eaters unlikely to get, L 798n
specialized, A 1201n, K 352n, C 51,
52n, W 609, T 131-2, 1190-2
symbolizing peace, L 1036
kissing the soil, We 771n
kistē (handbox), A 1086n, W 529, L 1184,
T 284
Knights, *see* cavalry
knocks on doors, A 395d, K 725d, C 136n,
P 179d, B 56-60, F 36d, 460-4, E 33-
36, 975-6, 989, We 1097-1101
kommation khorou, marking short choral
song omitted from script, We 770/1n
kommōtria (maid-in-waiting), in
Panathenaic procession, E 737
kōmoi (bands of drunken revellers), A
982n, W 1254n, 1301-2n*
consisting of one person, W 1322-41,
We 1040
koryphaios (chorus-leader), A p15, W 863-
7*, F 323-459n, E p23 n85, E 30-
284n, We 953n
speaking in name of author, A 377n,
659-664, C 518-562
kyrbeis, pillars bearing Solon's laws, C
448n, P p.xx n13, B p1 n3, B 1354n

labia, T 912n
Lacedaemon, *see* Sparta
Laconia, *see* Sparta
Athenian raids on, P 625n, 627n, B p5,
B 1569n, We p10 n48
dialect of, A 905*
Laconian keys, T 421-3
Laconian shoes, *see* footwear
Laconian spurge, E 405n
lacunae (gaps in text), A 1094, C 661, W
1283/4, 1410/1, P 440/1*, 1345*, B

868(?), 1343, L 507-8n, 814, 884, T 994, E 382n(?), 560, 1166-7, We 967-9n

lamps, A 920n*, E 1-18*

land battles, Athens' poor record in, T 806-7n

lāsismata (witty sayings ascribed to Lasus), W 1410-1nn

laundries, F 710-3

laurel, P 1044, T 489, We 21, 213, 1114

lawyers, C 467-475n

lead, symbolism of, C 913, F 295n

leave-taking formulae, A 1143, K 498, C 510

Lebadeia (Boeotia), C 506-8n

Lebedus (Ionia), L p1 n4

Lechaeum (Corinthia), E 810n
    Long Walls of, E p3, p6

lēkythos (oil-jar or -flask):
    as gymnasium accessory, F 1198-1247, E 1101n
    at funerals and tombs, E 538, 996, 1032, 1101n, 1111
    white-ground, E 996n

Lemnos, A 424n, P 277-8n, 1162, L 299-300n, F 1305-6n, 1383n, E p3, p4, E 102n, We p4, We 176n
    women of, E p10

Lenaea (festival), A p3, pp4-5, pp13-16, p32*, A 504*, 505n, 1154*, 1224n, K p2, K 537n, 547, C 521-3n, W p.xv, W 1023n, 1038n, P 760n, L p1, p2*, T pp1-3, p11, p12 n74, T 29n, F p1, p3 n14, p15 n65, p22, F 13n, 14n, 83n, 323-353n, 376n, 404-6n, 444n, 1419n, E p7, We 550n

Leontini (Sicily), A 606n, W 421n, P 250n, B 1701n

Lepreus/Lepreum (Elis), B 149*, 151

Lepri ("The Hidings"), an unknown (perhaps imaginary) place, A 724

lesbianism, when first so termed, E 920n

Lesbos, K 107n, 203n, W 660n, 1245-7n, T 163n, F 1298n, 1308, E 920; *see also* fellatio, Mytilene

Lethe, plain (later river) in the underworld, F 186n

letters of the alphabet, obsolete or regional, C 23n, 122n

libations, P 424-456, 1059, 1060n, 1089-1111, 1319, B 975, F 479n, E 140
    after meals, W 1217n, We 1175n

Libya, W 1259n*, B 65, 710, 1136, We 925n; *see also* Cyrenaica

light-armed troops, T 232n; *see also* peltasts

lightning, potentially ominous, W 625n*, E 792

literacy, K 189-190, W 960

literary criticism:
    Frogs and, F pp14-17*; *see also* poetry
    technical terms of, T 52-57nn

literature, and the public good, C 361n; *see also* poet (social responsibilities of)

litigation to disappear as private property does, E p14, E 560-1(?), 655-662

livestock-rustling, F 467n

loans, C 1214-1302, W 98n, L 1055-7, We 239-241; *see also* interest, moneylenders
    informal, E 446-9n
    misleadingly presented as gifts, L 1050-4
    of utensils etc., P 261n, F 1159, E 991n
    social duty to make, C 1216n, E 446-9n, We 240n

location of action, imaginary:
    ambiguous, B p4, T p8, T 1015-1135
    forgotten/ignored, P 301*, 314n, 543n, 611n, B 175n, 301n, 755n, T 930n
    tacitly changed, A 174n, W 1372n, L 1n, T 276n

Locris, B 152, 153-4n, E p2 n6

lōpodytai (clothes-stealers, footpads), A 1167-8n, C 178n, 179, 497-509, 856, 1498, B 497, 712, 1490-3, T 817, F 55n, 715-7, 772, 1075, E p19, E 544n, 565, 668, We 165, 932n

love, romantic, in tragedy, T 1011-2n, 1105-22, F 52-53n, 863-4n

love (*erōs*) as one of life's blessings, We 190n

love-gifts, We 1011n
    as coded request for assignation, We 995n
    by men to boys, B 705-7, We 153-9
    by men to women, E 1034n
    by women to men, T 345n, We 979-1002

love-songs, E 952-975, We 297n
lucerne, as fodder, K 606n
Lycabettus, Mt, F 1056
Lycia, A 427n, K 1240, C 622n, P 126n*
Lydia, K p3, C 599-600, W 1139n, P 123n,
    290n, P 1174n, B 1244, T 1217n, F
    531n, We 1002n
lyrics, much reduced in Ar.'s late plays, We
    p23

Macedon(ia), A 134n, K 129n, C 109n, W
    1268-9n, P 283-4, L 431-2n, 1231-
    5n, T p11 n65, T 29n, F p8, F 83n,
    84n, 85n, 953n, 1206-8n, 1299-
    1300n*, E p1, We 287n, 377-385n
performances of Athenian drama in, T
    390-1n
maenads, C 605, L 3n, 1283, 1312, T
    140n*, F 1211-3nn, We 162n
Maenalus (Arcadia), W 1191n
Maeotis, Lake (Sea of Azov), C 273
magic, sinister, C 718-9n, We 302, 309-310
magical objects and acts, A 390n, 447n,
    1029n, 1066n*, K p2, C 766n, B
    654-5, 1033n, We 883-5
Magnesia-on-Maeander (Ionia), K 84n, W
    499n
maidservant, preferred to bride?, B 1253-
    4n*
male supremacy, myth of establishment of,
    E p28*
Malian Gulf, L 1168-9n, 1169-70, F 1383n
Malis, F 1383n
man, creation of, B 686n
mannerisms, linguistic, We 833n
Mantinea (Arcadia), A p7, L 394n
    battle of (418), C 553n*, 580n, W 81n,
        240n, L 513n
    battle of (362), E 685n
    broken up by Spartans (385/4), E p15
        n63
manual stimulation, W 739-740, 1344, L
    673n, We 305n
manuscripts, medieval, A pp17-19, pp34-
    35, K pp5-6, C pp5-6*, W p.xx*, P
    p.xxii*, B pp8-9*, L pp8-9, T p14, F
    pp30-31*, E p38, We p34
maps, C 206-217
marriage:

abolished by Praxagora, E pp12-13, E
    727n
abolished for Plato's Guardians, E p14
abolition of, forgotten, E pp21-22*, E
    727n, 1125-6n
against parental opposition, T 1011-2n
age differences in, T 479n,. F 1193n, E
    323-4
and the Fates, B 1734n
and the priestess of Athena Polias, L
    1273*
early, E 428n
Hera as goddess of, T 973-6
importance of securing favourable
    auguries for, B 718n
impossible between citizen and non-
    citizen, B 1652n
of half-siblings, C 1372n, 1444n
of old men, allegedly discouraged by
    Euripides, T 410-3
rejected and restored, L p4, L 1186-7,
    1273-6
rites of passage preparatory to, L 644-
    5nn
to a goddess, dramatist's problems with,
    B 1536n
to an older woman, a dire fate, F 1193
woman promises herself in, T 1115n
women denied, because of war, L 592-7
masks/headpieces, A p15, p24 n6, A 94d*,
    388n, 418-9n, 1069-70n, K p3, K
    230-3*, 1331d, C 103n*, W 901, P
    1315n, B 61d, 79n, 92d, 99, 307,
    667d, 672n*, 673-4n*, 801d, 806n,
    1170n, 1271n, L 7-8, T 1160-75n, E
    p26 n96, p32, E 996n, 1101n, 1150n,
    We p27, We 415d, 422, 424n, 771d,
    1051
objects nailed to forehead of, We 942-3n
stock,   for   frequently-satirized
    individuals?, T 574n
Massagetae (tribe near Caspian Sea), E
    987n
masturbation, K 24n, C 676, 734, 966n, P
    290, L 1099n, F 545-6nn, E 470n,
    707-9, 979n, We 295n, 305n
    female, L 720n, E 890n; see also dildoes
Matapan, Cape, see Taenarum
matchmakers, C 41
matrilineality, E p13 n59

mean, ethically superior to extremes, We 245n

measures, weights, etc., A 108n, 814n, 1000n, 1053n, K 95n, C 21n, 430n, 640, 643-5, 1238n, W 440n, 481n, 716n, 718n, 1147n, P 254n, 630n, 1144n, B 6n, 154n, 292n, 1125-31nn, L 337-8n, 1207n, T 347-8n, 743n, 746n, F 91n, 799n, E 44-45nn, 413n, 547n, 1024-5n, We 436n, 546n, 986n regulations on, B 1040-2

meat, P 192, 378, 717, 955n, F 553-4, 560n, We 227, 298n, 320, 693n, 894, 1137
beef, A 85-87, K 361, P 1159n, 1280, 1282, F 506
black pudding, C 409n; see also §sausages
boiled, K 1178
brains, F 134n
eating of, prohibited in animal utopia, B p2
for men only, at Apaturia, T 558n
gravy, K 357, 360
mince, K 372, 770
offal, K 410n*, P 1040, 1059n, 1068-9n, 1092, 1100n, 1101-5, 1110n, 1111, 1115-8, B 519, 651-3n, 975-6, 984, 1524, We 1130-1, 1169
overcooked, W 1156n
portions sent to absent friends, A 1049n
poultry, B 1583-6, 1590, F 509-510
sausages, A 146, 1119, K 143*, 161, 197-208, 214-6, 315, 364, 432, 454-5, 1242, 1246, 1398-9, W 1144, P 717, F 339, 576, We p6, We 1169n
sheep's feet, W 672n
tripe, K 160, 200, 300-1*, 356, 454, 488, 1179, 1184, B 1552n, W 820n, 1169
see also animals

Medes, Media, W 1087n, B 277-8, 1021n; see also Ecbatana, Persia

Median grass (= lucerne), K 606n

medical treatment:
bathing, F 1280n
birth-inducing drugs, T 504n
dietetic therapy, F 939-944
exercise in, F 942
laxatives, F 942n

mock, designed to worsen patient's condition, E 404-6n, We p21, We 716-726
plant extracts used in, K 895n, 898n, W 1172, 1489, P 712n, 1254n, T 486, F 942-3nn, 1033n, E 355n, 404-6
plasters, We 716-721, 724
theories of, C 332n*
see also diseases and ailments

mediums, W 1018-29n

Megara, Megarians, A 519-538*, 624, 721, 729-835, K 1n, W 475n, P p.xvii, p.xviii, P 246, 249, 282n, 481-3, 500-2, 508n, 1000, B 1406n, L 699n, 801n, F 439n, E 828n
comedy at, A 738n, W 57
councillors (probouloi) at, A 755
decree against, A 530-8, P 605n, 609, L 390-7n
dialect of, A 729*-835
Long Walls of, L 1170
reputation for cheating, A 738n

Megarid, Athenian campaign in (460 or 459), E 303n

mēkhanē, A p14, C 217-238, 869n, P p.xvii, P 82-181, 791n, B 1199-1261, T p8, T 1009-14n, 1056-97n, 1098-1104, We p25
operator of, P 174, E 891n

Melissonomoi, see Bee-wards

melody, sung without words, in comic scripts, K 10, B 953n, L 99-100

Melos, C 830, W 377-8n, B p5, B 186, 191-3n, 1073, F p5

Mende (Chalcidice)., W p.xvi

mercenaries, A 153-166, B 798n, 1369n, We pp1-2, p29, We 173

mermaids, impermanence of marriages with, C 1068n

Mesē, penultimate day of Thesmophoria, B 1519-20n, T p10, T 79, 375-6, 658n*, 693-5n, 949n

Mesogeioi (Athenian clan), F 651n

Messene (Peloponnese), submerged state of, L 1141n

Messene (Sicily), L 1141n

messenger-speeches, in tragedy, We 647n

Messenia(ns), K p2, K 1330n, P 219n, B 149n, L 104n, 513n, 1137-44n, 1141, 1166n

metamorphosis, W 49, B 15-16n, 72-73, 100-1n, E 909n

metaphor, A 231n, 320n, 376n, 445n, 484n, K 314n, 343n, 345n, 355n, 479n, 481n, 496n, 528n, 538n, 546n, 571n, 920-1n, 921-2n, 1034n, C 602n, 1007n, 1108n, W 29n, 30n, 174n, 671n, 727n, 1050n, 1503n, P 199n, 310n, 610n, 747n, 753n, 996-8n, 1339n, 1348n, B 35n, 224n, 433n, 462n, 498n, 1013-4n, 1438-9n, L 324n, T 52-57nn, 75n, 557n, 986n, 1041n, 1133n*, F p13 n58, F 462n, 472n, 578n, 691n, 791n, 797-801n, 896n, 970n, 1113n, 1365n, E 39n, 208n, 253n, 356n, 640n, 707-8n, 826n, 829n, 1091n, 1104n, We 379n, 1154n

metatheatre, T pp7-9*

metempsychosis, P 832-3n*

meteorology, C 332n, 368-407, 1279-84, F 1114n

meteors, P 838-840, B 1710n

Methone (Macedonia), K 1085n, W 380n, B 988n

Methone (Thessaly), A 424n

Methymna (Lesbos), B 879n

metics (foreigners resident in Attica), A p28 n78, p28 n94*, A 508, K 347n, W 1221, P 297, 684n, L 580, F 549-578n, 696n, E 424n, 738n, 742n

metre:

aeolic, K 551-564n, W 317-333n, 1232-5n, B 676-684, 1393-1400n, L 1247-72n, T p2 n12, T 985-1000n, F 1309-28n, 1323n, 1331-7n, 1341-51n, E 289-310n, 911-923n, 952-975n; see also §aristophanean, §asclepiad, §dodrans, §glyconic, §hagesichorean, §hipponactean, §phalaecian, §pherecratean, §reizianum, §telesillean, §wilamowitzianus

aeolo-choriambic dimeters, W 1450-61n

anapaestic tetrameters, A 626-718n, K 498-610n, 761-835n, C p4 n8, C 263-274n, 476-7n, 518-562n, 959-1023n, W 346-364n, 379-402n, 546-630n, 648-724n, 725-8n, 1015-59n, P 729-733n, 734-774n, 1316-28n, B 460-538n, 548-626n, 627-8n, 658-660n,

685-736n, L 484-538n, 549-607n, 1072-3n, 1108-11n, T p11 n68, T 655-8n, 785-845n, 947-952n, F 354-371n, 383-4n, 1004-98n, E p24, E 514-9n, 571-709n, We p24, p32(?), We 487-618n, 1208-9n

anapaests (lyric), A 284-302n*, C 510-7n, 708-722n, 1154-70n, W 1009-14n, P 939-955n, B 209-222n, 310-326n, 327-335n, 451-9n, 1313-22n*, 1393-1400n, L 476-483n, T 667-686n, 707-725n, 776-784n, 1065-97n, F 372-382n, 1331-7n, 1352-5n, E 478-509n, 952-975n, 1163-7n

anapaests ("recitative"), A 1143-9n, K 498-610n, C 889-948n, 1510-1n, W 317-333n, 736-742n, 863-7n, 868-890n, 1482-95n, P 82-101n, 154-172n, 459-472n, B 400-5n, 1726-30n, 1743-7n, L 954-979n, T 39-62n, 947-952n, 1065-97n, 1227-31n, F 1206-8n, 1500-27n, We p24 n98

archilochean, W 1518-37n*

aristophanean, K 551-564n, P 775-796n, T 955-6*, 985-1000n, E 893-910n

asclepiad, W 1238-9n, B 1410-2n

bacchiac, C 708-722n, W 317-333n, L 706-717n, T p2 n12, T 1018-9n, 1136-59n, F 316-7n

chironean, B 1313-22n*

choriambic, B 1372-4n, 1376-7n, 1720-5n, T 352-371n

"choriambic dimeter", see §wilamowitzianus

cretic(-paeonic), A 208-233n, 280-3n, 284-302n, 665-675n, 971-999n, 1214-25n, K 303-313n, 322-332n, 616-623n, W 403-429n, P 1127-39n, B 243-9n, 327-335n, 1058-71n, L 476-483n, 658-671n, 1043-57n, T p11 n69, F 1356-60nn

cyrenaic, B 1410-2n

dactylic hexameters, K 197-201n, 1015-95n, P 114-123n, 1063-1114n, 1298-1301n, B 967-988n, L 770-6n, F 1264-77n, 1528-33n

dactylo-anapaestic, T 312-330n

dactylo-epitrite, K 1264-73n, C 457-475n, W 273-280n*, P 775-796n, B

451-9n*, 1337-9n, F 209-268n, E 571-580n

dactyls (lyric), K 322-332n, C 275-290n, 457-475n, 563-574n, 1154-70n, P 114-123n, 775-796n, B 230-7n, 250-4n, 737-752n, 1748-54n, L 1247-72n, T 101-129n, 1015-55n, F 674-685n, 814-829n, 875-884n, 1264-77n, 1282n, 1284-95n, 1338-40n, E 1168-78n

dochmiac, A 358-363n, 490-6n, 1214-25n, C 1154-70n, W 729-735n, 868-890n, B 230-7n, 406-433n, 1188-95n, T 667-686n, 700-1n, 707-725n, 913-4n, 1015-55n, 1284-95n, 1341-51n, We p23, We 637-640n

dodrans, W 1245-7n, E 938-945n

elegiacs, P 1298-1301n

"enoplian" (ancient term), C 651

enoplian (modern term), W 1518-37n; see also §prosodiac-enoplian

eupolidean, C 518-562n*

euripidean, K 756-760n

glyconic, K 551-564n, 973-984n, C 563-574n, W 317-333n, B 676-684, T 352-371n, 1136-59n, F 1251-60n, 1309-28n, E 911-923n, 1179-83n; irregularity in, F 1324n

hagesichorean, W 1241n, T 1158-9n

hipponactean, T 1158-9n, E 952-975n

iambic dimeters, among spoken trimeters, B 1196n, 1380-1n

iambic monometer, among spoken trimeters, L 706-717n

iambic tetrameters, A 1226-34n, K 333-381n, 756-760n, 761-835n, 841-940n, C 959-1023n, 1351-90n, W 230-247n, 526-545n, P 508-511n, 856-867n, 939-955n, 1305-10n, B 1313-22n, L 254-318n, 350-386n, 467-475n, 539-540n, T 381-2n, 531-573n, F 905-991n, E 285-8n; syncopated, W 248-272n, E 289-310n, We p23 n96, p28, p32, We 253-321n

iambics (lyric), A 490-6n, 836-841n, 929-951n, 1008-17n, 1190-7n, 1204-13n, 1214-25n, C 708-722n, 1113-4n, 1154-70n, 1206-13n, 1303-10n, 1345-50n, W 729-735n, 868-890n,

1009-14n, 1326-31n, P 512-9n, 856-867n, 939-955n, 1127-39n, 1305-10n, B 227-9n, 230-7n, 406-433n, 451-9n, 629-635n, 851-8n, 1313-22n, 1393-1400n, 1755-65n, L 254-318n, 476-483n, 1296-1315n, T 101-129n, 312-330n, 352-371n, 667-686n, 707-725n, 955-6*, 969-984n, 985-1000n, 1015-55n, F 209-268n, 215-6n, 385-393n, 394-7n, 398-413n, 416-439n, 448-453n, 875-884n, 1284-95n, 1352-5n, E 478-509n, 911-923n, 952-975n, 1168-78n, 1179-83n, We p23 n96, We 290-321n

iambics (spoken), A 404n, 440-1n, K 1015-95n, C 222n, 235n, 642, 1351-90n, W 868-890n, L 879n, F 204n, 1133, 1203n, 1206-8n, E 911-923n, We p24, p33

iambo-choriambic, A 1150-61n, C 510-7n, 563-574n, 700-6n, 804-813n, 949-959n, W 526-545n, L 319-349n, E 952-975

iambo-trochaic, K 322-332n

ibycean, T 1136-59n

ionic, C 1206-13n, W 273-280n, 290n, B 238-242n, T 101-129n, F 323-353n

ithyphallic, A 1150-61n, K 1264-73n, C 457-475n, 1113-4n, W 1518-37n, P 775-796n, B 629-635n, L 781-804n, F 674-685n, E 1168-78n

lecythia, B 1755-65n, F 814-829n, 1208n, 1284-95n, E 255n

molossi, B 1720-5n

paeonic tetrameters, A 971-999n, W 1275-83n

pentamakron, E 1163-7n

phalaecian hendecasyllable, W 1227n, 1248n, B 1416n, E 938-945n

pherecratean, K 551-564n, 973-984n, C 563-574n, B 1380-1n, 1731-6n, T 985-1000n, F 1251-60n*, 1309-28n, E 1179-83n

pnīgos (long unbroken run of recitative), A p9, p11, A 626-718n, 1226-34n, K 242-302n, 333-381n, 498-610n, 761-835n, 841-940n, C 263-274n, 959-1023n, 1351-90n, W 346-364n, 546-630n, 648-724n, 1009-1121n, P 299-345n, 553-581n, 729-818n, 734-

774n, 1140-58n, 1316-28n, B 352-399n, 460-538n, 548-626n, 685-736n, L 350-386n, 484-538n, 549-607n, T 785-845n, F 905-991n, 1004-98n, E p24, E 571-709n, We p24, p28, We 487-618n

Porson's Law, C 1452-64n

prose, A 43, K 941-2, W 868-890n, P 433-4n, B 414n, 864-888, 910, 1035-50, 1661-6, T 295-311

prosodiac-enoplian, F 1361-3n

reizianum, A 836-841n, K 1111-20n, C 1345-50n, P 856-867n, 939-955n, 1329-59n, T 969-984n, F 448-453n, E 289-310n

spondaic, C 1154-70n, B 1058-71n, F 372-382n

strophic correspondence, irregular, A 231n*, C 700-6n, 953n, 1303-10n, W 308*, 403-429n, 542-5*, 636*, 646-7*, P 491n, B 327-335n, 1553-64n, L 331n, 664*, 809*, 814n, F 592n, 895-904n, E 486-8n, 952-975n

study of, C 636-655

syllable quantities, irregular or inconsistent, K 416n, W 1526-7n, P 1154n, 1178n, T 120-1n

telesillean, K 1111-20n, W 317-333n, P 856-867n, 939-955n, 1329-59n, 1731-6n, F 448-453n, E 289-310n, 952-975n

trisyllabic (tribrach/dactyl), L 1279-90n, E 1168-78n

trochaic tetrameters, A 204-7n, 284-302n, 676-691n, 971-999n, K 242-302n, 303-460n*, 322-332n, 565-580n, C 575-594n, 642, 1115-30n, W 334-345n, 403-429n, 430-460n, 488-525n, 1071-90n, 1275-83n, P 299-345n, 383-4n, 426-430n, 553-581n, 601-656n, 729-733n, 1140-58n, B 268-309n, 310-326n, 336-342n, 352-399n, 753-768n, 1072-87n, L 614-705n, 1014-42n, T 659-666n, 687-8n, 702-6n, 707-725n, 726-7n, 785-845n, 1015-55n, F 686-705n, 718-737n, E p9 n41, p25 n93, E 1155-62n, 1163-7n

trochaics (lyric), A 280-3n, K 616-623n, C 1303-10n, W 273-280n, 334-345n,

403-429n, 1009-14n, 1060-70n, 1265-74n, 1326-31n, P 1127-39n, B 230-7n, 255-262n, 737-752n, 1393-1400n, 1470-81n, 1720-5n, L 108, 658-671n, 781-804n, 1043-57n, 1247-72n, T 101-129n, 433-442n, 459-465n, 659-666n, 667-686n, 953-968n, F 209-268n, 534-541n, 895-904n, 1099-1108n, 1370-8n, 1482-99n, E 893-910n, 899/900n, 952-975n

wilamowitzianus, F 1309-28n

midwives, L 694, 746, T 505n, E 528-9n

presents for, if baby was male, E 549n

Miletus, A 6n, 527n, K 327n, 361, 932, P 363n, 667n, B 1427n, L p1 nn4,6, L 57n, 108, 729, F 543, 659n, We 1002, 1075

philosophy at, C 180n, B 1009n

women of, L 109n

military life:

bell patrols, B 842, 1160

bivouacs, K 605*, P 348*

call-up lists, A 1065n, K 1369-71*, P 1179-84

duties of youngest soldiers, K 604-5*, E 845n

evasion of service, C 692, W 74n, 1117-9, F 1084n, E 366n; see also Athens, legal and political institutions (prosecution)

fire-signals, E 6n

good for young males, B 1360-9

Homer as authority on, F 1035-6n

marines (epibatai) on board ship, F 48

mounted archers, B 1179

non-combatants mobilized in emergency, B 1186-7

orders parodied, K 242-6, W 422-4, P 551-5, B 343-6, 353, 364, 383, 387-392, 400-2, 448-450, L 451-2, 456-461

over-age soldiers, L 177n

parades, P 564-7n

peripoloi (border patrols), B 1177

physical fitness and, F 1087-8n

pilfering on campaign, K 1077n, W 238, 354-8, F 1075n

sentries, W 359-364, B 391-2n, 841, 842n, 1161, 1174, L 847-9

sieges, B 1212-6n*, 1576n
signal-fires, B 841n, 1161
soldiers' food, P 527-9, 1129
soldiers' jokes, B 507n*
soldiers' view of generals, L 103n
"three days' rations", A 197, W 243, P
    312, 367-8n, 1182n
training, P 355-6
treasurer to a general, W 964, 965n
volunteering for service abroad, B 1369n
walls of circumvallation, B 1576n
watchtowers, B 841n
see also arms and armour; Athens,
    political and legal institutions
    (generals, hipparchs, phylarchs,
    taxiarchs); cavalry; mercenaries
mills, hand, E 739n
Mimas, Mt (Ionia), C 274
mime (minor dramatic genre), F 1331-63n,
    E 952-975n*
mīmēsis, see role-playing
mind, materialistic analysis of, C 229-233
mines, silver, leased by state, K 362*, W
    659*, B 593, 718n, E 428n
Minoa (island off Nisaea), A 760n, P 246n
Minoan art, B 515n
mirrors, C 752, T 140, 234-5, E 124-7dd
misanthropy, B 1549n, L 805-820, We 58n,
    107-111
miscarriage, T 339-340n
misdirection of a pursuer, to facilitate an
    escape, T 1218ff.n
mishearing?, We 269n
Molossian dogs, T 416
money, see coins
    effective abolition of, E 412-426n, 605n
    useless if there are no goods to buy, We
        p18 n79
moneylending, C 552n, 1155*, 1216n, T
    842-5, E 660-1; see also interest,
    loans
monodies (solo songs), C 1154-70n, W
    317-333, 1326-41, P 1012, B p6, B
    227-262, L 1248-72, 1279-90, 1295-
    1321, T 101-129, 1015-55, 1065-97n,
    1077, F p16, L 849, 944, 1329-64
monsters, K 416n, 511n, C 556, W 34-41,
    1029-37, 1043n, 1177, P 181n, 752-
    760, T 521-3n, 1011-2n, 1033, F p12,
    F 143-4, 278-308, 468n, 472-7, 814-

829n, 928, 932-3, 937, E 76-80nn,
    1056-7n, 1104n
mora (battalion), Spartan, destroyed by
    Iphicrates (390), We pp1-2, We 173n
mother, named to prove citizen status, W
    1397n
motherhood, more sacred than fatherhood?,
    C 1444n
mountains:
    and Dionysiac cult, T 992n
    as home of robbers?, F 1344n
    see also under names of particular
        mountains
mourning, A 1024n, C 622, W 480n, F 422-
    7
mule-grooms, evil reputation of, T 491-2n
Munichion (Athenian month, ~ April), B
    1047, F p22 n99
murder, attempted, in comedy, C 1465-6n,
    1475n
music:
    at symposia, K 529-530, C 1355-60, W
        1219, E p14
    competitions in, A 13-16, K 534n*, W
        675n*
    melismas, F 1314, 1349
    modes of, K 989-996*, C 968n*
    of parodied tragic songs, F p17
    old and new, C 966-972*, B 1372-
        1409n*, T 68n, 100n, F 153n*, E
        330n
    oriental, T 120-2, 1160-1225n
    Orthian melody, K 1279
    "prostitutes' songs", F 1301
    "watchman's song", C 721n
    work songs, C 1358, F 1297
musical instruments:
    aulos (reed-pipes, "flute"), A 16n*,
        554n, 681n, 862n, 1227n, K 9, 532-
        3n, C 313, W 8n, 581-2, 1219, 1368-
        70, 1477, P 531, 952, B 667d, 672n,
        857n, 858, 1764n, T 991n, 1175-88,
        1197n, F 154, 311n, 312-3, 513,
        1302, 1317, E 255n, 943n; see
        also piper
    bagpipes(?), L 1242*, 1245
    castanets, K 522n, C 260n, 448n, F
        1305-6n; potsherds used as, F 1305-
        22
    drum, W 8n, 119 L 3, 388, T 991n

stringed instruments, A 13-14n, 16n, 1227n, K 522, 532*, 534n, 989-990, 1277n, C 1355, 1357, W 574n*, 951n, 959, 989, 1278, B 11n, 219, 766n, 771-2n, 858n, 1764n, T 68n, 95d, 101d, 120-6, 137-8, 161-2n, 315, 327, 805n, 1160d, 1175n, 1217, F 229-234, 1282-95, 1304-5, E 739n, We 291, 297

syrinx (pan-pipes), L 2n, F 230n

trumpet, C 165, P 1240-9, F 966, 1042

mutilation, as (barbaric) punishment, We 859n

Mycale, battle of (479), W 1093n, 1098-9n, B 798n

Mycalessus (Boeotia), massacre at (413), B 798n

Mycenae, A 433n

Mycenaean art, B 515n

Mycenaean dialect, F 1144-5n

Myrmecium (Crimea), C 1468n

myrtle-branch, held while singing at symposium, C 1364, W 1222n, 1243n, P 1154, L 632n

Mysia (Asia Minor), A 430n, 439, 497-8n, 541n, C 922

Mysteries, Eleusinian, A 665-6n, C 302-4*, W 377-8n, 831n, 1363, P 420, B 284n, 1073n*, T 101-2n, F 154-9, 289-296n, 319n, 320n, 887, 1032n, 1033n, 1500-27n, 1528-33n, We p5, p11, We 1013-5

adapted, not reproduced, in *Frogs*, F 320n, 323-459n

Aeschylus accused of divulging, F 886n*

Athena and, F 378n

ethical code taught at, F 145-153n, 456-9

herald of, B 876n, F 1437n

highest grade of initiation in, F 745n

initiates of, in Critias' *Peirithous*, F 464n

murderers excluded from, F 354-371n, 456-8n, 1032n

old clothes worn at, F 404-6n, We 845

open to women and slaves, F 157n

opening proclamation (*prorrhēsis*), F 354-371n, 369n

pig sacrifice at, A 747, 764, P 375, F 338n

priests of, *see* hierophant, dāidouchos

procession to Eleusis, T 1147n, F p19, F 313-4n, 323-353n, 324n, 396-7n, 401-2n, 416-439n, 1422n, We 1013-5

profanations of (415), A 88n, K 242-3n*, C 109n, W 1187n, 1268-9n, B 766-7n, 1297n*, L 390-7n, 489n, F p19, F 1422n, 1512n

the Greekless excluded from, F 354-371n, 355n

see also gephyrismos *and* Chorus (j) *in Index II*

Mysteries, Lesser, We 845n

mystery-cults, other, C p3*, C 140n, 254-262n, 302n, W 8n, 9n, 831n, P 277-8*, L 254-387n*, F 357, 1032, We 327n; *see also* Orphism

myth:

and morality, C 904-6n, 1048n, 1080-1n

comedies based on, We p1

providing comic themes, F pp9-11, p18

rationalized, T 11-18nn, E 1029n

Mytilene (Lesbos), A 193n, 793n, K 834-5, 1030n, 1044n, C 1358n, W 523n, 1232-5n, B 1021n, L p1 n6, T 161-2n, F p3 n17, E 644-5n

names:

altered for metrical reasons, F 1512n, E 644-5n

Ar. sometimes careless with, C 65n, W 78n

delayed mention of, A 406n

etymological plays on, A 500n, T 804-9

generational alternation of, C 65, W 1250n, B 280-4

implying gratitude to a god, We p12

internally contradictory, C 67n*

mention of, dangerous when evil beings listening, F 297-300

of Boeotian origin?, L 6n

of hunting dogs, B 1204n

of ships, K 1309n, B 1204n

of topical/political relevance (in real life), B 153-4n

parental dispute over, C 60-67

reflecting parent's wishes for child, C 63n, 65n

significant, A 609-612n, K p3, K 1258n, 1309n, C36n, 88n, 434n, 450n, 792n, W 133-4, 836n, 1201n, 1250n, P 62n, 314n, 1142n, B 1n, 2n, 1329n, L 321n, 838n, E p26, E 1n, We 332n(?)

stock, associated with particular ethnicities, A 861n

stock, for chorus-members, A 609-612n, W 230-3nn, L 254-9nn

stock, for cooks, We 1n

stock, for old men, L 304n, E 293n, 311n, 372n, We pp20-21, We 22n, 332n

stock, for slaves, A 243n, 273n, C 1485n, W 1n, 433n, 828n, P 1138n, 1146n*, B 656n, L 908n, T 270n, 728n, F 1n, 730n, 1345n, E 867-8n, We 1n

stock, for women, C 678n, W 1397n, L 70n, T 373-4n, 803n, E 41-42n

stock, for young men, L 355n

suggestive, for courtesans, B 161n

used as obscene metonyms, E 97n

used in third-person self-reference, W 1396-7, L 365n

variant forms of, for same person, B 1311n

wrongly conferred on anonymous characters, A 395n, T 1n

navy, Athenian, A 95-97*, 162-3, 544-554, 648, 918-925, K 542-4, 554, 555n, 564n, 599-603, 761-2, 812n, 912-3n, 1019n, 1063-79, 1182, 1185, 1300-15, 1351-3, 1366-8, C 869n, W 343, 909n, 1093-7, 1119n, 1189n, 1234, P 348n, 459-472n, 477n, 1234n, B 108, 147n, 879n, 1203-4nn, 1540, L 57-59nn, 64n, 173, 431-2n, 674-5, 804n, T pp1-2, p3, T 804, 837, F pp1-4, p5*, p11, p13, p16, p17, F 48-50, 52-53n, 197n, 362-4, 693-702, 705n, 1071-6, 1422n, 1435-66n, 1442-50n, 1463-6nn, 1531-2n, E p4, p5, p6, p7 n35, p9 n42, p18, E 102n, 197-8, 201-3nn, 366n, 825n, 835n, We p2, We 130-197n, 172, 174n, 176n, 550n; see also Athens (political and legal institutions: trierarchs), Paralus, Salaminia, and under names of naval battles

navy, Peloponnesian, P 477n, F pp4-7*, p13, F 365

navy, Persian, in Corinthian War, E pp2-3, p6, E 197n, 201n, 202n, 825n, We p1, p4, We 173n

Naxos (Cyclades), W 355, F 659n

Naxos (Sicily), B p4

"necessity", as governing power in Presocratic thought, C 377n

necromancy, B 1553-64, F p10 n45, F 1266n

necrophilia, P 891n, F 66-67

Nemea, battle of (394), E p2, E 195-6nn, 199n, 202-3n, We p4 n15, We 550n

Nemean Games, W 1191n

neōkoros, see sacristan

Nephelococcygia, see Cloudcuckooville

Nēsteiā, penultimate day of Thesmophoria, B 1519-20n, T 80n

New Moon, C 1179-95n, 1191, 1195, 1196

as market day, K 43, W 171

festivities at, A 999

rituals at, W 96n, F 366n*

Newcastle, carrying coals to, B 301n

Nicene Creed, B 699n

nicknames, W 151n, 324n, 325n, 342n, 421n, 459n, 462n, 1183-4n, 1221n, 1501n, P 289n, 928n, B 17-18n, 153-4n, 161n, 281-2n, 521n, 763n, 766n, 790n, 822-3n, 1283-4n, 1291-9, 1490-3n, L 63n, T 168n, 170n, 291n, 380n, 861n, F 22n, E 77n, 186n*, We 176n

given ironically, F 55n

night-stools, B 1495d, 1552

nightmare-demons, W 1038-9nn, E 639-640n

Nile, River, C 272, T 855-7

barges on, L 45n

summer flooding of, T 856-7nn

Nineveh (Assyria), B 1021n

Nisaea (Megarid), A 760n, P 246n, 481n, L 1170n

nome (type of lyric poem), P 291n*

nomos (law/custom), disdained, C 1040, 1075n, 1400, 1420-6, 1432n

Notium, battle of (407/6), F 1422n, 1512n

nouveaux riches, W 1309n, B 798n

nudity:

artificial male, L 662-3, 797-804, 1019-20

artificial female, A p28 n85, A 765-835, 1198-1234, K 1389-1408*, W 1326-85, P 868-908, L 686-7, 821-8, 1114-87, T 1181-1201, 1210-4, E 1138n, 1150n

in gymnastics, origin of, E p17

in ritual, C 988-9nn, L 645

of criminal undergoing *apotympanismos*, T 939n

public male, regular at Athens, We 168n

shameful for old men, L 1020n, 1024n, T 939n

theatrical, defined, L 662n, T 641n

voyeuristic references to, C 973-8, 1507n, W 578

see also hair (pubic), sexy mutes, undressing

number, grammatical, inconsistencies in, W 552-572n, 727n, 908n, 975-6n, P 745n, B 415n, L 204n, 549-550n, 696n

nurses. C 1380n, L 958, T 299n, 515n, 609, 691n, F 1305-6n, E 915n

Nysa, Mt, where Dionysus was nursed, L 1283, T 992-3n, F 215

oaths. A 148n, 308, 309n, 860n, 905n, K 298, 424-8, 1239, C 83-84, 91, 108, 245-9*, 351n, 395-402, 1227-9, 1232-5*, 1236n, W 846n, 1046, 1396n, P 214n, 446n, 973n, B 194*, 289n, 438-447, 630, 632n, 705, 864n, 1608-13, L p4, L 51n, 181-239, 403n, 513n, 700-1n, 841n, 903, 914-5, 1175n, 1182n, 1185, 1238, 1273n, 1287n, T 269-276, 359, 383n, 766-8n, F 150, 275, 304-6, 586-9, E 43-45, 105n, 346n, 603, 823-5, 1160, We 61, 396n, 725, 904n, 1069n

and gender, P 214n, L 917n*, F 503n, E 155-9, 160n, 189-192, 558n, We 764n, 1006n

Euripides and, T 275-6, F 101-2, 1469-71

of Council members, E 444n

of Helen's suitors, L 191-2n

quasi- (no god invoked), W 83n, B 520-1, F 1374n, We 396n

self-contradictory, B 1237

taken over sacrificial victim, L 186-197

see also Athens, political and legal institutions (lawcourts: juror's oath; oath of allegiance) *and* gods (swear by themselves)

obeisance, ritual, K 156, We 771-3

obesity, A 88n, 1002n, K 958n, C 353-4n, W 16n, 19n, 822n, 1142n, P 446n, B 289n, 876n, 1475n, T 605n, F 200, We 560, 1037n; *see also* padding

Oblivion, Plain of, *see* Lethe

Odomanti, a Thracian tribe, A 156-8, 164

Odrysae, a Thracian tribe, A 134n, B 1529n

Oenoe (Corinthia), p2 n7

Oenophyta, battle of (457), L 801n, T 806-7n, E 303n

offerings, non-animal:

bread and cakes, T 285, We p12 n60, We 138, 660-1, 680, 1115, 1121, 1126, 1142

"consecration" of, by burning, We 681n

figs, We 1122

grains, B 565-6, 621-6

hair, F 1126-8n

honey, We 1121

laurel, We 1114

meal, P 1040n

myrtle, We 1126n

vegetables, P 923-4n, We 19, p20, We 1197-8

see also incense, libations

offstage singing, C 275-290*, B 202*, 209-222

oikistēs (founder of a colony), B 521n

oil, olive, A 1029n*, C 56, W 252n, E 63; *see also* food

pits for storage of, E 154n

oil-flasks (*lēkythoi*), T 139, 556n

Old-and-New Day (last day of month), C 1134, 1178-1200, 1222

oligarchy, *see* Four Hundred, Thirty

olive-branch, laid on altar in token of supplication, L 1139-40n

ololygē (ritual ululation), K 617, P 97, B 222n, 783n, L 240, T 129, 276n

Olophyxus (Chalcidice), B 1042

Olympia (Elis), K 247n, W 1382, 1387, P 605n, B 510n, 1121n, L 1131, We 185n, 583n

Olympic Games, A 615n, A (end)n, K 534n*, C 69n, W 1187n, 1191n, P 342n, 523n, 876n, L 679n, 1129-32n, E 834n, We p18, We 550n, 583-9

Olympus (mountain, or name for heaven), A 530, C 270, 366, 817-8, B 578, 582-3n, 606, 778n, 780, 867, 1230n, 1231, 1372, 1731, T 331-2, 960, 1068-9, We p6

Olynthus (Chalcidice), B 172n*

omens, A 171n, K 639n, 640n, C 579-586, 1129n, W 17n, P 1026n, 1053-5nn*, B 275n, 358n, 593-6nn, 716-722, 1118n, L 205, 398n, 597, F 196n, 1276n, 1289, E 791-3, We 63, 1181

ōmophagiā (eating raw flesh) in Dionysiac worship, F 357n

onomatopoeia, A 1035n, L 295n, T 45-48, 245n, F 249n, 1285n, We 17n, 291, 297, 895; see also animal noises, bird calls

onyx, C 332

"Openmouthenians", nickname mocking Athenians' gullibility, K 1263

Opuntian Locris, B 152, 153-4n

Opus (Locris), B 152n

oracle-mongers, see Hierocles, Oracle-monger in Index II

oracles, A 430n, K 61, 109-143, 153, 177, 194-211, 220, 797, 818, 961-972, 997-1097*, 1230-48, W 158-161, 380n, 799-804, P 1063-1100, B 276n, 619n, 716n, 724-5n, 959-991, L 767-780, F 1033, 1184-5, 1212n, 1266n, 1319, 1431n, We p9, We 8n, 9, 32-55, 212-3

about "the first person you meet", We 41-43n

adynata (impossibilities) in, P 1076, 1083, 1086, 1112, 1114

alleged post eventum fabrication of, P 1085, B 963-5

metre of, K 197-201n

regarding duration of Peloponnesian War, P 1049n

responses of, written down by inquirers, B 982n

see also Ammon, Delphi, Dodona

orators, verbal blunders by, E 22-23n, 356n

orchēstrā, A p14*, L 288n, T 658n, 689-758n, F 180d, 193n, 296d, 441n, E 496n, 504n, 1152n

Orchomenus (Boeotia), E p4

order of performance, draw for, E 1-18n, 1155-62n, 1158-62

Oreus (Euboea), P 1047, 1126n

Orneae (Argolid), B 399

Oropus (on Attic-Boeotian border), T p3, We 701-2n

orphans, presentation of arms to, B 1360-6

Orphic poems, B 685-702n*, F 52-53n, 311n, 1032n

Orphism, B 685-702nn*, F 52-53n, 311n, 1032n*, We 327n

Orthian melody, A 16

Ortygia, birthplace of Leto, B 870n

Ototyxus (fictitious city of "Howl-in-Agony"), B 1043n

Ozolian Locris, B 152n

padding, in comic costume, A p15, F 200n, E 935n; see also obesity

paeans, K 407, 1318, P 453, 555, B 857n, 1763, L 1291, We p11

Paeonia, imaginary(?) festival, A 1213

Pagasae (Phrygia), We 521n

paintings, A 854n, 992, L 678-9, F 1061n, We 385n

novelty, We 602n

Paitoi (Thracian tribe), E 987n

Palaeologi, last Byzantine imperial dynasty, A p18

Palaescepsis (Troad), B 493n

Palladium (Trojan image of Athena), W 351n, E 1029n

pallakai (unmarried wives), A 527n, W 1353

Pallene (Chalcidice), W 210n, B 824n

Pamphylia (S. Asia Minor), F 970n, E 202-3n, We 550n

Panactum (Boeotia/Attica), P 466n

Panathenaea (festival), K 566*, 656n, 1180, C 28n, 69n, 386, 969-971n*, 988, W 544n, 1203-4n, P 418, B p1 n3, B 826-836n, 827n, 1296n*, 1551n, L 632n, 642n, 646n, 1189-94n, T 395*, 811-2n, 1136-7n, F 153n, 1037n, 1087-8n, 1089-98, E 730-745n, We p29 n118

Pangaeum, Mt (Thrace), A 156n
Panhellenes, P p.xviii, P 302
panhellenism, *see* Greece (common welfare of)
panic fear, E 1068-9n
pannychides (all-night celebrations), L 2n, 409n, 447n, T 795-6n, 1136-7n, F 313-4n, 371, 446
"pantomime" animals, F 35-37n
Paphlagonia (N. Asia Minor), K p3, K 6, C 581n
Paphos (Cyprus), L 556, 833
papyri. A pp16-17, p34, K p5*, C p5*, C 229n*, W p.xx*, P p.xxii*, B p8*, L p8, T p14, F p30*, E p38, We p34, We 321/2n, 689n, 958/9n, 967-9n
parabasis, A p10, p11, A 377n, 626-718*, 1143n, K 498-610, C p4, C 510-626, W 1009-1121, P 729-818, B p5, B 676-800, T p3, p11, T 785-845, F p10 n45, p11 n49, pp13-14, p21, F 354-371n, 674-737, 1442-50n, E p24, p25, We p31
   passage reminiscent of, F 354-371, E 1153n, 1154-62
   second, A p10*, A 971-999(?), K 1264-1315, C 1113-30*, W 1265-91, P 1127-90*, B 1058-1117, T p11, F p10 n45
   substitute for, L 614-705
   use of first person plural in, B 789n*
paradise, for the blessed dead, F 155n, 326n
paraklausithyron, E 952-975n; see also *exclusus amator*
Paralus, Athenian state trireme, A 1158n, B 147n, 1204, 1569n, L 58-59n, F p5, F 1071-3
parasites/spongers, C 686n, W 74n, 326n, 1221n, 1267n, 1318n, 1408n, B 284n, 1296n, We p7, We 975-1024
paraskēnia, see *skēnē* (wings of)
parasol-bearer, in processions, B 1551n, E 734n, 737n
parasols, K 1348, B 1470-81n*, 1494d, 1508-12, 1550-1, 1553n, T 823, 829
parenthood, redefinition of
   by Praxagora, E pp13-14, p16, E 635-650, 1042n
   in Plato's *Republic*, E p14, p16, E 635-643nn, 1042n

parents:
   both named to prove citizen status, W 1397n
   duties towards, A 817n, C 860-4, 994-5, 998-9, 1444n, W 69n, 478n, B 757-9n, 1353-9, 1360n
   imprisoned, C 904-6, W 69-70, 1442-9, 1467n
   prosecution of, C 1413-4n
   violence against, C 911n, 1040n, 1321-1451, W p.xviii*, W 398-402, 1038-9nn*, 1133-4, 1397n, 1467n, B 757-9, 1337n, 1347-52, 1364, 1529n, F 149-150, 274, 773, 1185n, E p13, p14, E 638-643, 1042n, We 487-618n
   violence by, W p.xviii; *see also* corporal punishment
Parnassus, Mt, A 434n, C 603, W 1414n, F 1057, 1212
parodoi (entrance-passages in theatre), *see* *eisodoi*
parodos (entry of chorus), A p9*, C 275-328*, F p18, F 323-459n, 354-371n, 1528-33n, E 729/730n, We p23, p24, We 253-321n, 290-321n
   in tragedy, F 914-5n
   retains some significance even in New Comedy, We 321/2n
   song corresponding to, accompanying *exit* of chorus, E p23, E 285-310n
Paros, W 1189, P 1298-9n
partheneia (songs for maiden choruses), B 919, L 1296-1315n
parties, *see* symposia
parts, distribution of, E pp31-32, We p27
patronage, C 528-9n
patronymics, A 118, 1131, F 429n, 631n
Paupers, *see* Penestae
pawning goods, L 113-4n, E 755, We 450-1
peace:
   and return to the countryside, A 32-36, 266-7, K 805-6, 1388-95, P 545-600, 1318, L 1173
   internally, leads to power externally, L 1289n
   negotiations for (404), F p22, F 541n
   never coherently argued against in Ar., L 484n

not a realistic possibility in 411, L p3, L
    1055, We p20 n85
not an impossibility in 405, F 1531-2n
permanent, hardly to be hoped for, L 49-
    50n
spurned by Athens (425-422), A 45-58,
    K 794-6, P 215-9, 637-8, 665-7
spurned by Athens (410-406), T 805n, F
    pp6-7, p14, F 678n, 715-6n, 1531-2n
spurned by Athens (392-391), E pp3-4,
    p6, p7, E 71n, 200-3nn, We 550n
Peace of Antalcidas (387), E p4, p15 n63, E
    102n, We pp3-4, We 176n
Peace of Callias (c.448), B 284n
Peace of Nicias (421), A p27 n62, A 566n,
    K 6n, 1377n, 1388-9n, W 240n, P
    pp.xv-xvi, P 304n, 342n, 466n, 928n,
    B 126n, 188-9n, L 513-4, E 203n
    Athenian annotation to (419/8), L 513n
peine forte et dure, F 621n
Peiraeus. A p27 n61, K 327n, 815, 857n,
    885, 1246n*, 1366-7n, P 165, B 227-
    262n*, 496n, L p1, F p1, p5, p22
    n99, F 139-140n, 722n, 1167-8n,
    1422n
    agoranomoi for, W 1407n
    Asclepieum, W 123n*, We p11, p12
        n60, p26, We 411n, 662n
    Beetle Harbour, P 145
    Cornmarket Colonnade, A 548
    dockyard, A 552, 918-925, K 238
    Great Harbour, see §Beetle Harbour
    Harbour of Cantharus, see §Beetle
        Harbour
    Long Colonnade, see §Cornmarket
        Colonnade
    market commissioners for, A 723n
    refortification of (begun 393), E p2, We
        p2
    Salamis ferry, E 1087n
    temple of Zeus Soter, We p26, We
        1175n
    tomb of Themistocles, K 819n, E 1107n
Peisistratidae, dynasty of tyrants at Athens,
    W 490n
Pelasgi, a people of early Greece, B 832n
Pellene (Achaea), B 1073n*, 1421, L 996n,
    F 320n
"Peloponnesian War" (431-404), A p13,
    p32, K 123n, P p.xv

origins of, A 524-539*, P 603-627
outbreak of, P 435-6n, 990n
"Peloponnesian War, First" (459-446), P
    507n, E 293n
Peloponnesians (= Sparta and allies), A
    p32, A 620, 623, 720, K 279, 597n,
    818n, P 611-3nn, 632-3nn, L p1 n8,
    p2 n13, L 33-34, 75, 1180-1, F pp1-
    2, E 197-8n; see also navy
    (Peloponnesian) and Sparta
peltasts, A 160, L 563n
"Peltingham", see Attica, demes and
    localities ("Ballene")
Penestae (Paupers), serf class in Thessaly,
    W 1272-4
penis:
    desirable shape for, T 516n
    desirable size for, C 1014
    family likeness detected in, T 515-6
    man dragged along by, L 1119, E 1020
peplos (Panathenaic robe), K 566n, 1180, B
    827, L 642n
Percote (Troad), B 493n
perfumes, K 1332, C 51, P 169, 526, 862, L
    47, 938-947, T 494n, E 524-6, 841,
    1032n, 1112-26n, 1117, We 529n,
    811
Pergamum, library of, P p.xix, We p30
Perioikoi, unenfranchised class in Laconia,
    P 625n, L 1137-44n
perjury, see oaths
Persia, A p5, A 61-125, 647, 709n, K 84n,
    371n, 478, 967n, 1089n, C 521-3n,
    1458-61n, W 98n, 236-7n, 345n,
    499n, 502n, P 108, 411-3nn, 928n,
    1008n, B p5 n18, B 284n, 483-7,
    836n, 1028n, L p1, pp2-3, L 50n,
    619n, 1133n, 1144n, 1189n, 1289n, T
    p2, p3, T 331-351n, 337, 365, 1143-
    4n, F pp4-7, F 791n, 938, 1422n, E
    pp1-4, p6, E 71n, 102n, 195-6n, 202-
    3n, 356n, 602n, We p1, pp3-4, p7
    n29, We 170n, 176n, 178n, 550n,
    859n, 1002n
    royal succession in, F pp5-6
    see also navy (Persian)
Persian dance, T 1175n
Persian language, pseudo-, A 100, B 1615n
Persian melodies, T 1175

Persian War, A 614n, K 84n, 123n, 781, 812n, 814n, 1040n, 1325n, 1334n, 1350-3n, W 12, 220n, 1078-1101, P 289n, 623n, 1070n, B 278n, 962n, 1074-5n, L p3, L 254-387n*, 318n, 653, 759n, 1133n, 1144n, 1247n, 1248-61, 1262n, 1289n, F 694n, 1296-7n, E 293n, 1089n, We p2 n7, We 327n, 561n
  as golden age, K p3
  see also Artemisium, Athens (sack of), Attica (Marathon, Salamis), Eurymedon, Mycale, Plataea, Thermopylae
personifications, A 989n, K 1300-15*, 1389-95, C 112n, 889-1112, P 221-728, 842-906, 923-1126, L 1114-88, T 1056-97, E 974n, We 80n, 237-244n
  of enemy peoples, P 214n
  of towns/countries, in comedy, L 87n
"persuasion":
  Aeschylus, Euripides and, F 1442-50n
  elastic significance of, T 1171n
pessimism, in Ar., K p2, We p20
pettoi (group of backgammon-like games), E 987-8*
phallus:
  absence of, remarked upon, A 826n, W 823n, T 142
  as weapon, L 553n
  colour of, C 639, T 644
  in comic costume (†erect), A p15*, A 346n*, 592, 826n, 1121*, †1216, C 538, 676n, W 823n, 1062d, 1342-4, 1349n, P 142d, †1351, B p6*, †L p4*, †L 831-1013, †991n, †1072-1188, †1182n, T p7, p9, T 62, 239, 643-8, 1114, †1187-8, 1210d, †E p22, †p32, E 470d, †969n, †978d, We p27, We 267n, 295n
  in other ritual, A 243, 259-260, 263n*
  in representations of Pan, L 998n
  in satyric costume, T 157n
  objects reminiscent of, A 1053n, L p4, L 947n, E 150n
  on Hermae, C 1478n, L 1094n
  treated as a person, L 956n
  see also circumcision, satyrs
phallus-bird, L 723-5n

Phanae (harbour at Chios), B 1694n
phantom, taken to Troy instead of Helen, T 850n
pharmakos (human ritual "scapegoat"), K 1405n, L 646-7n, F 733
Pharsalus (Thessaly), W 459n, 1271
Phasis (= Poti, Georgia), A 726n, C 1130n, B 68
Pherae (Thessaly), W 1238-9n
Phibalian figs, A 802
Philippi (Macedonia), W 1019-20n
philosophers, K 1085n, C passim, We 942-3n
  dislike fresh air, C 198-9, 1497n
  dislike washing, C 837, B 1553n, 1554
  pale complexions of, C 94n, 103*, 120, 503-4, 515-6n, 718, 1017, 1112, 1171, 1497n, W 1408n, 1413, B 1296n
philosophos, first use of term in poetry, E 571n
philosophy:
  a rich man's attitude to, E 426n
  treated as mystery-cult, C 140-3, 254-262n, 302n, 463-5n*, 824n
philotēsiā (cup of friendship), A 985n, L 203
Phlegra (scene of battle of Gods and Giants), B 553n, 824-5
phlyax vases, T p12 n74
Phocis, K 1271-3n, B 188-9n, F 1056-7n, E p2 n6, E 303n
  conquered by Athens (457), L 801n
Phoenicia, A 112n, P 1174n, B 504-6, We 267n
  chorus from, use a Semitic poetic device?, T 138n
  ships from, promised to Peloponnesians, T p3 n15
phrontistērion, see Reflectory
Phrygia (N.W. Asia Minor), K 9n, W 8n, 9n, 433n, 1183-4n, 1309, P 291n, 1146n, B 493, 523n, 657n, 762, 763n, 873n, 1244, L 558n, T 101-129n, 121, 728n, F 1331-63n, 1345n, E 1068-9n, We 287n, 521n
Phthia, homeland of Achilles, F 1263, E 330n
physis (nature) in sophistic argument:

contrasted with *nomos* (law/custom), C 1075, 1078, 1432n
contrasted with *nous* (intelligence/rationality), B 371n
Pillars of Heracles (Strait of Gibraltar), C 271n, F 475n
pimps/panders/procurers, K 1069n, W 1028n, 1353n, P 848-850, L 723-5n, 957n, 1270n, T 1176-1200, F 1079, E 693-701n, We 149n
piper, theatrical, P 952n, B p6, B 214d, 223d, 226n, 268-292n*, 672n*, 851d, 857-8nn*, 859d, 1196n, 1403n*, L 1242n, T 121-2n, 1160-75n, F 1263d, 1264-77n, 1282n, E 891; *see also* musical instruments (*aulos*, bagpipes)
harness of (*phorbeia*), W 582, B 672n*, 673-4n, 861
piracy, B 1427, F 204n, We 521n
Pisa (Elis), F 1232
Pitcher Feast, *see* Choes
plagiarism, comic dramatists accused of, K 526-8n*, 864-7n, 1225n, C p2 n3, C 553-9; *see also* collaboration
plague at Athens (430-426), P 213n, E 183-4n, We p10 n48
Plataea (Boeotia):
    battle of (479), L 801n, 1143n, F 1027-8nn, E 303n
    citizens of, given Athenian citizen rights, F 694n
    destruction of (373), We 147n
pledge, binding force of, We p16 n74; *see also* handclasp
pledges, deposited when services supplied on credit, T 1195n, 1196-7
ploughing, ritual, L 397n
poet, social responsibilities of, A 500, 633-658, F pp15-17*, F 686-7, 954-979, 1008-88
poetry, discussion and criticism of:
    comedy, K 507-550, C 518-562
    other, C 1355-78, F pp14-17, F 71-107, 757-1533
poetry, inevitably reflects author's personality, T 164-170
poisoning, P 1014n*, T 430
polar expressions, We 233n
polis in sense of "region", P 251n, L 32n

politicians (as a class), sexual preferences of, K 423-8, 878-880, C 1092-3; *see also* homosexuality
pollution, religious, W 654n, P 968-9nn, T 654n, 721-2n, We 69-70n
    spiritual, F 355
polypragmosyne(inquisitiveness, meddlesomeness), B 471n, We 931
poneria, as characteristic of comic heroes, E p26
Poseideon (Athenian month, ~ December), A 202n
posterity, appeals to judgement of, C 562n*, F 705
Pot Feast, *see* Chytroi
potash, T 537n
Potidaea (Chalcidice), A 538n, K 438, C 415-6n, P 622n
poverty, W 239n, B 605n, 1410n, E pp18-22, E 408-426, 566, 605, 801n, We pp4-5, p8
    abolished?, We pp13-20, We 430, 434, 463-6, 496-7, 604-618, 864-5
    distinguished from "destitution", We 548-554
    economically necessary?, We 507-534
    extreme, miseries of, We 535-547
    of people, advantageous to demagogues, W 703-712
    satirized, A 615n, 854n, 855n, K 1264-73, C 675n, W 787n, 1301n, P 446n, 740n, B 284n, 289n, T 949n, We 800n
    see also Poverty *in Index II*
Prasiae (Laconia), P 242
prayer, A 247-252, 405n, 567n, K 763n, C 264-274, 356n, W 160n, 389-394, 438-440, 556-7n, 846n, 869-886, 1001-2, P p.xvii, P 435-455, 974-1016*, 1320-8, B 622-4, 809-811n, 864-888, L 203-4, 317-8, 833-4, 1262-72, T p2, T 286-291, 295-371, 312-330n*, 972-3, 977-1000, 1143-59, F 297n, 871n, 872-3, 885-894, 1126-8n, 1462n, E 128-130n, 140-1, 171-2, 369-371, 882-3, We 134, 1124-5n
pregnancy:
    faked, T 502-3

illicit, suspected from facial pallor, T 406n
suggested exercise regime for, F 942n
ten months as normal duration of, T 741-2n
Presocratics, C 377n; see also under names of individual philosophers in Index II
priestesses, W 9n, 157n, T 295n, 758-9, F 1273-4n; see also Critylla, Lysimache, Theano in Index II
of Athena Nike, L p5 n31*, L 70n
of Athena Polias, L p5, L 554n, 642n, 759n, 1273*, E p27 n101
Trojan, in Agathon's lyric, T 101-129
priests, A 1087, P 53n, 296-8n, 1056n, 1060n, 1705n, F 297, E 366n, We p22, We 669-670n, 676-681, 687, 1110n, 1143n; see also Priest in Index II
naturalized citizens debarred from being, F 694n
staff carried by, B 893n*
prisoners, treatment of, W 897n
prisoners of war:
Athenian decree ordering mutilation of, F 1512n
Athenian, massacred, after Aegospotami, F 1512n, E 644-5n
privies, T 485n
processions, religious, A 241-279, C 308, W 1005n, P 397, 523n, F 180n, 1037, 1528-33n, E 730-745n, We p17, p23, We 1194-1209; see also chariots, Panathenaea
in honour of Aeschylus, F 1517-8n
procrastination, Athenian (414-411), L 57n
producer, see didaskalos
prologue:
in comedy, A p9
in tragedy, F 946-7, 1119-1250
Prometheia (festival), F 131n
property, private, abolition of:
by Praxagora, E pp12-13, pp19-22
forgotten, E pp21-22*
in Plato's Republic, E p13*, p14, p16, p19 n77
prophets, see Bacis, Cassandra, Glanis, Pythia, Sibylla, Theonoe in Index II
Propontis (Sea of Marmara), K 67n

prosodia (processional odes), K 1264-6n, B 854
prostatēs tou dēmou (populist political leader), K 1128n
prostitutes, see sex-sellers
protagonist, A p15
protenthai, see Tasters
prothesis (laying-out of corpse), B 474n, L 611n
proverbs, A 717-8n, 846n, K 1057n, 1119-20n, W 191n, 447n, 725-6n, 1431n, B 516n, F 186n, 736-7n, 970n, 991n, 1459n, E 109n, 385n, 554n, 1029n, We 149n, 203n, 273-4n, 549n, 1002n, 1151n
proxenoi, B 1021, T 576n, 602
Ptolemies, royal dynasty of Hellenistic Egypt, C 109n
punt-pole, used by Charon, F 180n
purification rites, W 118*, P 151n*, L 757n, 912n, 913, T 654n, E 128, We p10
Pyanopsia (festival), K 729n, W 398-9n, We 1054n
Pyanopsion (Athenian month, ~ October), A 146n, B 1519-20n, T p10, T 67-68n, 80n, 558n, 834n, E 223n, We 627n
Pylos (Messenia), K p2, p3, K 1n, 55, 76, 355, 358n, 702, 742, 797n, 846, 1005, 1054n, 1058-60, 1079n, 1167, 1172, 1201, 1204n, 1330n, W 970n, 1183-4n, P 215n, 219, 665, 928n, 1084n, L 104, 466n, 513n, 1162-6, F 764n
and other places of same name, K 1057n
prisoners taken at, K 394n, 792-3n, 795n, C 186, W 44n, P p.xv, P 479-480
Pyramids, B 1130n, 1145n
pyrrhic dance, C 988n, 989n, B 1169n, F 153
Pythagoreans, C 140n, 219n, P 832-3n*
massacre of, at Croton, 1484-5n
Pythian Games, A 13-14n, K 534n*, W 675n*, 1191n, B 188-9n, L 1129-32n
Pytho, see Delphi
gods of, addressed collectively, B 868n, T 332-3

quince, used as aromatic, W 1056*
Qumran community, E 665n
quotations, meaningless, A 541n, 1188n, C
    595n, W 308n, 757n, 1482-4n, P
    528n, B 1247n, T 693n, 1015

raconteurial skills, W 1174-1207, 1258-61,
    1394, 1399-1405, 1409-11, 1427-31,
    1435-40, 1446-8
rainbow, B 1222
rape, A 273-5, W 769n, P 889-890, 1339n,
    B 15-16n, 1253-6*, L p4, L 162-6,
    225-8, 503n, T 60-62n, 547n*, F
    683-4n, 1081n, 1475n, E p22 n81, E
    467-8n
    false accusation of, T 498n, F 1043n
    homosexual, T 59-62, F 57n
    in New Comedy, T p11 n70
    of man by woman, E 465-470, We 1092
razors, storage of, T 220n
reading, silent, K 122n*
reciprocity, We 93-94n, 979n, 1029
recognition scenes, K 1232-52n, T 871-919,
    F 754n
recognizability of prominent persons, T
    189n
Red Sea (= Indian Ocean), K 1088, B 145
redistribution of land, C 205n, We p19
reeds, used in making lyres, F 234n
Reflectory (phrontistērion), Socrates'
    school, C 91n, 95, 128, 142, 181,
    266n, 380n, 1144, 1347n, 1473n,
    1487
refugees in Athens (405/4?), E 243
rehearsals, P 804-6n, B 1403n, E p20
    for Assembly meeting, E p11
rejuvenation, A 993-9, K p2, K 908*,
    1321*, 1386n, P p.xvii, P 336, 860-1,
    L 364n, 667-670, F p18, F 345-8, E
    p13 n60, p21, p32, We 771d; see also
    generations (inversion of), virility
relativism, ethical, F 1475n
religion, absent from Praxagora's society, E
    p28 n104
rennet, E 404n, We 719n
repeated phrases, in successive lines, B
    114-6, E 221-8, 773-6, 799-803, 862-
    4, 1155-7
restaging of Frogs, F pp21-23, F 678n, 686-
    705n; see also revision of script

resurrection, F pp9-10, p11 n49, p18, F
    499n, 1082n, 1406n, 1517-8n, 1528-
    9, E 1073, We pp8-9
retailers, P 1210n; prejudice against, We
    1063n, 1156n
retirement from headship of household, W
    69n
revenge, extra-legal, We 524n; see also
    adultery (unofficial punishments for)
revision, posthumous:
    of Euripidean dramas, F 1206-8n
    of Wealth?, We p31 n126
revision of script by Ar.:
    after failure of Clouds, C p2*, pp3-4*, C
        518-562n, 546n, 624n, 888-9nn*,
        1113-30n*, 1437-9n, 1465-6n
    for local restaging of Wealth, We pp30-
        31, We 115n, 119n
    for restaging of Frogs, F p17, pp21-23,
        F 1132-5n, 1251-60, 1431, 1435-
        66n*, 1437-53, 1512n, E 644-5n
    of Wealth, after twenty years?, We
        pp31-33, We 115n, 119n
    shortly before performance?, W
        1283/4n, B 1072n*, T p1 n2, pp2-3,
        F p12 n54, pp20-21, F 71-88n, 786-
        795n, 1515-6n, E 1-18n
rewards, offered when public property
    stolen, P 699n
Rhegium (Italy), L 1141n, T 161-2n
Rheneia, island off Delos, B 870n
rhetoric:
    in Euripidean drama, P 534n, T p4*, F
        775, 826-9, 894
    revealing comic blunders in, W 565n,
        666-7n; see also denunciation,
        diplomacy (technique), self-
        condemnation
    teaching of, C p2, C 98-99, 112-5, 239,
        244-5, 252n, 317-321, 417n, 429-
        475, 874-5, 1038-82, 1105-11, 1311-
        8, 1399-1404, B 1701n, F 1114n
Rhodes, L p1 nn4,6, p2*, L 57n, 270n, 944,
    T 804n, F p22, F 455n, We p7
ribbons:
    as emblem of victory, F 393n
    draped on corpses, L 603n, E 1032n
    worn on head at joyful occasions, L
        603n, E 1032n
riddles, W 20-23, B 1296n*, We 602n

ring, We 1036
  as emblem of office, K 947-959
  as mark of wealth, C 332n, E 632
  magical, We 883-5
  used to sweep insect out of eye, L 1027-
    32
river-gods, B 691n, 701-2n, T 855n
river-nymphs, T 855n
road-junctions, sacred to Hecate, F 366n,
    1361-2n, We 594n
role-playing, T pp7-9*
  by dramatist while composing, T 101-
    129, 148-172
role-swapping, F p13, F 494-673, 495n,
    694n
ropemaking, P 36-37, F 1297
rowing, F 180n, 190n, 197-205, 208n, 209-
    268n, 269n

Sacae (people of Central Asia), B 31n
Sacred War, Second (ca.448-6), B 556n
Sacred War, Third (357-347), B 556n
Sacred Way (Athens-Delphi), B 188-9n
sacrifices, A 237-279, 784-794, K 654-662,
    1140, 1320, C 620, W 82n, 844n, P
    p.xvi, p.xvii, P 374-5n, 387, 396,
    422, 925-1126, B 43n, 190-3, 518-
    9n, 584n, 848-1057, 1118, 1231-7,
    1266-8, 1559, L 84, 179, 1063, 1129-
    32n, T 693-5n, F 798n, 1032n, 1241-
    2, E p28 n104, E 782n, We p10, p16,
    p22, We 133, 134n, 137-8, 143, 819-
    820, 1114-6, 1128, 1130, 1138,
    1177-83
  appurtenances of, P 947-962, B 850, E
    732n
  before battle, L 1262n
  burning of, L 238n, We 681n
  collection of blood, T 754n
  comic topos of skinny victim, B 901-2n
  gender and colour of victims, F 847n
  hairs cut from victim's head, P 973n
  human, C 257, B 1529n, E 1056-7n
  of three species (trittoiai), We 820n
  often fails to propitiate the god, We
    1124-5n
  parodied in "slaying" of wineskin, T
    753-9
  portions of, reserved for the god, We
    1128n

prohibitions on taking meat out of
    precincts, We 1138n
  transferred from gods to birds, B 562-
    570, 1236-7, 1516-20
  victim's "consent" to, P 960n, B 959n
  weighing of victim, F 798n
  whole-burnt, C 408n
  see also meat (offal), offerings, omens,
    slaughter
sacrilege, C 995n, W 394*, 845, 1446-7n, B
    1372-1409n, 1529n, T 773n, We
    476n; see also Athens, political and
    legal institutions (prosecutions for
    impiety), Hermae, Mysteries, temple-
    robbery
sacristan (neōkoros) of a sanctuary, We
    669-670n
Saioi (Thracian tribe), P 1298
Saïs (Egypt), E 999n
Salaminia (state trireme), B 147, 1204, L
    58-59n, F 1071n
sales-talk, P 1224-5n, B 156*
Samos, A 846n, K 763n, W 566n, 1007n, P
    129n, 363n, 681n, B 471n, L p2*, L
    103, 421-2n, 582n, T 161-2n, 840n, F
    570n, 696n, 1072n, 1422n, E 202-3n,
    We 550n, 1002n
  revolt of (440), W 283
Samothrace, P 278-9*
Sardinia, W 700, B 172n*
Sardis, capital of Lydia, A 68-69n, 112, W
    1139, P 1174, E p4
  conference at (392), E p3, p6, E 102n,
    We 176n
  conference at (387/6), We p4
Saronic Gulf, W 122n, T 647-8n
satraps, B p5 n18, B 1028n, L p1, L 1133n,
    F 1422n, E pp1-4, We p1, pp3-4; see
    also Amorges, Ariobarzanes,
    Pharnabazus, Pharnaces, Pissuthnes,
    Struthas, Tiribazus, Tissaphernes in
    Index II
satyr-drama, T 157
  imitated, P 296-8n*, B 1253-4n*, F 184
satyrs, B p6*, L 723-5n, 982n, F p11, F
    429n, E 470n, We 295n
scales (weighing), P 1246-9, F 797, 814d,
    1365-1410
Scamander, River (Troad), T 864, F 924-
    7n, 928, We 1005n

scatology, A 104n, K 358*, 721n, 1057n, C 173-4, 295, 411n, 1384-90, W 604, 1183-4n, P p.xvi, P 99-101, 138-9, 151-3, 157-8, 162-176, 790, 928n, 1228-39, 1359n, B 790-2*, 822-3n, 1054, 1117, 1552n, F 7-10, 146, 273-4n, 295, 366, 1075, E 311-373, 595-6, 647n, We 313; see also defaecation, scatophagy

scatophagy, P 1-42, 48, 724, E 595, 647n, We 305, 706n, 1185n

sceptre:
of kings, B 510
of Zeus, B p3, B 480, 510n, 635, 1535, 1600, 1605-25n, 1626, 1631

schools:
advanced, C 94-99, 132-517, 626-1114, 1144-70
elementary, K 985-996, 1235, C 916n, 961-978
gifts to teachers at, C 1146-7

science, confused with magic, C 205n

Scione (Chalcidice), W p.xvi, W 62n, 210, 288n, B 1274-5n, F p5, F 694n

Scira (festival), T 658n*, 834, E p12 n50, E 18, 22-23n, 59

Scirophorion (Athenian month, ~ June), C 984n, T 834n, E 18n, We 1175n

Scyros, K 1312n, E p3, p4, E 110n, We p4, We 627n

Scythia(ns), A 40n, 704*, 707n, 710n, W 592n, B 941, 1700n, L 184, 447n, 451, 455, T 1017, 1026, 1112, 1116, 1121, 1182, 1186, 1218ff.n*, F 608n, 680-1n, E p16 n69, E 143n; see also Archer(s) in Index II

sea-power, Athens advised to concentrate on, A 648, P 501-2, F 1465

sea-urchins, L 1168-9n

seals, W 585, B 1213, L 1198-9
counterfeiting, T 424-5
on doors, T 415, 424-8

seasons, in the dramatic fiction, T 67-68n

seduction, as crime, B 558n; see also adultery

seers, C 332, W 52n, P 1044n

Sélestat (France), A p19*

self-blinding, F 1195

self-condemnation, by comic villains, K 296, 1252, C 359n, W 927-8n, B 1423, 1452; see also denunciation

self-contained scene, E p21, We p24 n100

selfishness, E pp18-22, E 182n, 187n, 197-8n, 202-3nn, 207-8, 306-7n, 366n, 396-7n, 746-876, We p21

semantics, C 361n, B 692n

Seriphos (Cyclades), A 542, T 1101n

serpents, see animals (snake)

Seven against Thebes, P 1270n, 1290n

Seven Sages, W 1410n

sex, heterosexual, A 265, 270-5, 787, 795-6, 994-9, 1051-66, 1147-8, K 1391, C 178n, P p.xvi, P 341, 711, 867, 873-4n, 890n*, 897n, 904n, 1339n, 1348n, B 669, F 740; see also adultery, rape
across the slavery line, forbidden by Praxagora, E p13, E 721-4
anal, see buggery
as bribe, L 861n
as metaphor for artist's relationship with art, K 517, F 94-95n
between half-siblings, whether incestuous, E p14 n62
boycotted, in Lysistrata, L pp3-4, L 124, 146-166, 212-232, 551-4, 698n, 715-780, 829-1013, 1174-81, E p9
can't wait for end of play, T p9, T 1160-1225n, 1193-8, 1210-1
communal, E p13, p16 n69, pp21-22, E 613-634
compulsory, for men, E pp21-22, E 465-472
death during, F 965n, E 97n, 1030-4n
deprivation of, due to war, L 99-110,. 591-7
deprivation of, hits Spartans harder than Athenians, L 1148n, 1171n
fantasies of, L 973-9, E p22, p32
forbidden in sanctuaries, L 754-5n, 910-1, 1182, T 930n; prohibition broken, T 488-9
in daytime, W 500n*
in street, T 489n
instructional manuals on, F 1327-8n
marital, alternatives to, for men, L 1092n*

naval fighting as metaphor for, L 673n, F 48n, 430n

oral, E 470n; *see also* cunnilingus, fellatio

physical pain due to deprivation of, L 962n

positions for, W 501, P 896n, 900n, L 60n, 229n, 231-2, 619n, 677-8, 773, T 153, 489, E 8-11, 265, We 152, 306n

Praxagora's regulations for, E p13, p15, E 615-634, 701-9n, 877-1111

prepubertal, T 479-480

presented as religious duty, L 898n

privileged access to, for older men, E p13, p32, E 625-634, 702-9, 1138n

wife smiles on husband's extra-marital, E p22, p32, E 1137-8

with a barbarian male, soon over?, T 1210n

with respectable woman, must be in private, L 907n

sex-sellers[5], A 524-9*, 537, 551, 1091, 1093*, 1148, 1198-1221, K 167n*, 532-3n*, 765n, 1246, 1277n*, 1285, 1400, 1403, C 996-7, W p.xviii, W 500-2, 739, 1032n, 1245-7n, 1283, P 165, 440, 523n*, 755n, 849n, B 161n, 1261n, L 337-8n, 673n, 1237n, T p9, T 98n, 153n, 346, 489n, 805n, 840n, 1114n, 1160-1225n, 1172n, F 289-296n, 411n, 513-6, 519-520, 544, 678n, 1306n, 1327-8n, E p8 n36, p25 n95, E 22-23n, 385n, 470n, 611n, 614n, 617n*, 693-701n, 721n, 943n, 993n, 1029n, 1034n, 1037-97n, 1101n, 1106*, 1117n, 1150n, 1161, We pp6-7 n27, pp15-16, We 130-197n, 149-152, 179n, 243, 303n, 305n, 959n, 1082n; *see also* Dancing-girls, Dardanis, Fawn, Old Woman (h), Peace-terms *in Index II*

abolished by Praxagora, E p13, E 718-720

citizen women behaving like, E p25 n95, E 617n*, 693-701n, 877-1111n, 952-975n, 1106n, 1166-7n

justice towards, not thought essential,

We 1003n

male, A 79, 603n, K 167n*, 732n*, 1242, W 1187n, P 11, 1236-7n, T 35n, 50n, 173-4n, 258n, F 148, E 97n, 112-3n, 365n, We 153-5

prices for, T 1195n, E 614n

sexual orientations, origin of, E 112-3n

sexy mutes, A p15 n85, P p.xvii*; *see also* Dancing-girl(s), Dardanis, Fawn, Fullfruit, Girls (b,c), Peace-terms, Princess, Reconciliation, Showtime *in Index II*

Shadefeet (Skiapodes), fabulous African(?) tribe, B 1470-81n*, 1553

shadow-stick, for telling time, E 652

shamateurism, sexual, We 153-9

shaving, T 33n, 191, 215-235, 903, 1043, E 65

shewbread, We 678n

shield, throwing away, P 1186, 1298-1301, T 822-3n, 827-9, E 670-1; *see also* Athens, political and legal institutions (prosecutions), *and* Cleonymus *in Index II*

ship-cart, in Dionysiac cult, F 180n

shipbuilding, A 552-3, K 1185n*, 1310n*, B 1157, We 513

ships and seafaring, A 505n, K 430-441, 756-760, 830, P 36-37n, 140-5, 277-8n, 341n, 458n, 1177n, 1306n*, B 586n, 594-8, 648n, 711, 718, 800n, 1203n, 1273n, 1395n, T 877n, 882n, F 121n, 180n, 704n, 933, 999-1003, 1220n, 1318, E 109n, We 1093n; *see also* boats (as stage-property), diseases and ailments (seasickness), navy, piracy

shoemakers, supposed effeminacy of, E 385-7

short stature, despised, F 708-9n, E 629n

shouting, contest in, F 190n, 209-268n, 250-268

siblings, mating of, in Plato's *Republic*, E p14 n62

Sicels, B p4

Sicily:
and banqueting, W 911n
as locale for witty stories, W 1259n

Athenian allies in, W 700n, 924-5n, 965n

Athenian embassies to, K 1377n

Athenian expedition to (427-424), A 606n, K 1303n, W 240n, 924-5n, 965n, P 250n

Athenian expedition to (415-413), A 159n, 566n, 920n, K 1n, 6n, W 924-5n, P 304n, 420n, 1031n, B pp4-5, B 145-7n, 363n, 619n, 720n, 879n, 994n, 997n, 1297n*, 1576n, L p1, L 57n, 391-7, 421-2n, 517n, 524n, 582n, 590n, 593n, 1133n, F p1, p2, F 1039n, 1422n, We p29, We 179n

cheese of, W 838, 896-7, 911, P 250-1

comedy in, A p8*

performances of Athenian drama in, T 390-1n, F p7 n35

"ruler of", complimentary designation of Dionysius I, B 1372-1409n, We 550n

Sicyon, K 1n, B 968

Sidon (Phoenicia), W 220, F 1225

sieges, security precautions during, B 1212-6n*

siesta, W 500n*, P 290n

Sigeum (Troad), L 1150-6n

silence:
    "Aeschylean", W 741n, F p20, F 830n, 832-9, 911-926, 1019d, 1020n, 1132-5n, 1170d, 1410-1n, 1461n
    chorus sing loudly about, T 660n
    enjoined upon nature, in hymns, T 43-50n
    for dramatic effect, W 741-2, 944-7
    of mute performer, attention drawn to, W 944-7, E p31 n118
    of statue, attention drawn to, P 657-9
    ritual call for, A 237n, K 1316, C 263, 297n, W 868n, P 96n, 434, B 959, T 39-40, 295, F 354
    significant breaking of, We 217n

Simois, River (Troad), T 110

singers, professional, in comedy, B p6, B 202n

single mothers, C 530-1, L 139n, T 558n

Sinope (N. Asia Minor), A 566n

Siphae (Boeotia), K 1n

Siwa (Egypt), B 619n

skēnē, A p14, P 923n, L p4, L 1n, T 658n, We p26 n107

doors and imaginary houses in, A p14, A 395n, K 1326n, C 91n, W 152n, 1482-4n, P p.xvii, P 224, 726n, B 849n, E pp28-30, E 327-356n, 564n, 876/7n, 877-1111n, 1114n

entrances from, L 184n

fictive identity of, ignored, T 726n, 930n

fictive identity of, temporarily left obscure, We 53-54n

passage down side of, P 235-6n

position of window in, E 327-356n, 877-1111n

roof of, A 399n, B 202*, 266*, 268-292n*

shadow of, E 496n

wings of, T 1082-9n, 1092n

see also windows

Skiapodes, see Shadefeet

skin colour, T 31n, 246n, 574n, 856-7n, E p32, E 62, 699; see also philosophers (pale complexions of), women (pale complexions of)

skin of sacrificial victim, P 1122-3n, T 758-9, We 1175n

skolia (symposiac songs), A 532n, 980, 1093, C 684n, W 1222-49, B 1416n, T 528n, F 1302, E 938-945n, We pp5-6, p7
    Admetus, W 1238-9, L 1237n
    Cleitagora, C 684n, W 1245-7, L 1237
    Harmodius, A 980, 1093, W 1225-7*, L 632n
    Telamon, L 1237

skytalē:
    Spartan message-stick, L 991n
    Spartan walking-stick, B 1283n, L 991-2

slaughter, sacrificial:
    always kept offstage, P 1018-22, B 1057, L 190n
    technical term for?, B 1563n

slave-market, F 1235n

slave-ownership, how widespread, E 593n

slavery, evidence for principled critiques of, We 6-7n

slavery, "natural", We 461-3n

slaves:
    addressed deferentially, T 64n
    addressing masters disrespectfully, We 46n
    and alcoholic drink, K 85-108, L 427

and novel/foreign cults, W 9, L 388n

as intermediaries in love affairs, L 340-1, 558(?), T 340-2, F 1079n

as major characters in comedy, We p24; see also Carion, Xanthias (e) in Index II

as overseers of other slaves, K 1-7, 43-70, F 1510-4n

beaten without cause, W 1296, 1307, 1325, P 255n, F 812-3n

born in household, W 768n

clothing of, W 443-7, L 1151n

comic, often resemble their masters, L 1222n

conditions attached to manumission of, We 149n, 1003n

dramatic identity of, forgotten, B 434n

eligible for initiation at Eleusis, F 157n, 159n

enlisted as rowers (406), F p2, F 33n, 191n

ethnic origins of, We 1n

excluded from Thesmophoria?, T 294n

female, sexually available, A 270-5, W 769n, P 1138, L 503n, E 721n

freed, see freed(wo)men

given voice, in Euripidean tragedy, F 949

hair styles appropriate to, B 806n, 911n, L 1222n, T 838n

hired labourers equated with, W 681n, 686n, 712n

households too poor to possess, C 133n, W 248n, 301n, E 593n, We 224n

households with large numbers of, W 433n*

households with one child slave, We 823n

how Greeks might become, We 521n

in New Comedy, We n24

justice towards, not thought essential, We 1003n

life without, We 224n, 524-6

luxurious life for, in ideal comic world, P 1002n, We 816-8

newly-bought, how welcomed, We 768-9n

"not to be trusted", We 273-4n

offered freedom and citizenship (406), F p2, F 33n, 191n, 693-6

petty delinquencies of, W 768, 828, P 14n, F 743-753; see also §stealing by

politicians etc. accused of having been, W 1187n, B 760n, T 805n, E 932n

presented as familiar with politics, We 170-9n

prices for, We 157n

procurement of, We 518-524

public, L 435-6*; see also Archer(s) in Index II

punished by chaining, W 435, F 1510-4n, We 276

punished by deprivation of food, W 435, E 468-9n, 665n

punished by hanging up alive, We 312n

punished by sending to mill etc., F 1510-4n

punished by tattooing, L 331n, F 1510-4n

punished by wearing wooden collar, W 897n, P 14n

rations for, E 424n

retaining mentality of a free man, We pp24-25, We 6-7n, 824n, 876n

role of, in comic utopias, E p12, p13 n56, p17, E 651, 721-4, 873n, We 461-3n

runaway, C 7n, P 451, B 760, L 331n, F 720n

servus callidus, P 742n, We 273-4n

servus currens, P 743-742n, T 3n

status of, ignored for sake of joke, K 320n, W 500n

stealing by, A 273, W 449, L 184n, We 27, 318-321, 1139-40

tax on sale of, E 1006-7n

trade in, C 749n, B 1427n, F 1235n, We 179n, 461-3n, 518-521

turning tables on their master, F p13, F 503-673

see also corporal punishment, torture, and Slave(s) in Index II

sleep, on stage, C 1-80, W 1-135, 230-395, T 1136-75

sleight-of-hand, F 1296-7

slops, emptied into street, A 616, W 259-261n

smoke, used to repel insects, W 456-460n

smuggling, A 522n

Social War (357-355), We 180n

social-contract theory, C 1421-2n
socialism, E p13*, E 665n, 673-4n
soliloquies, A 1-42, 480-8, C 126-132n*,
    1131-45, 1476-85, L 865-9, T 765-
    784, E 746-752, 872-6, 1098-1111,
    1112-26n, We 1-17, 335-342
    action suspended during, E 1098-1111n
songs:
    contest of, E 882-923, 942-5n
    fashions in, K 529-530, B 1300-3
sophistic argument, T 5-21, F 25-32n
sophists, A p6, C pp2-3*, C 112-5n, 898n,
    1308-9n, W 1069n, B 284n, 371n, T
    p7, F 428n, 771n, 970n, 1114n,
    1491-2n, 1496-8n, E 810n
    ethics of, C 902n, 903n, 1038-40n,
    1060n, 1075n
    Euripides and, T p4*, F p16 n71
    fees of, C 876n
    semantic development of term, C 331n
sōphrosynē (modesty, self-control), C
    1060n, 1063n, 1067n, We 563n
soul (psūkhē), term associated with
    Socrates, C 94n, 415n, B 1555n
Soviet Union, E 665n
Sparta(ns), A p5, p33, A 52, 131, 175,
    193n, 194n, 224-233, 304-316, 338-
    9, 356, 369, 482, 509-514, 536, 541,
    603n, 647, 665-6n, 982n*, K p2, K
    1n, 55, 327n, 394n, 465n, 467, 471n,
    668, 742, 792-3n, 794-5n, 797n,
    812n, 846n, 849n, 1008, 1053,
    1054n, 1085n, 1271-3n, 1330n,
    1332n, C 7n, 67n, 186, 214-6, 248n,
    521-3n, 553n, W 44n, W pp.xv-xvi,
    98n, 210n, 236-7n, 240n, 282n, 288n,
    345n, 466n, 475-7nn, 502n, 1098-9n,
    1158-65, 1183-4n, P p.xv, p.xvii,
    p.xix, P 212-9, 245, 261n, 274, 282-
    4, 285n, 303n, 395n, 435-6n, 466n,
    475n, 478-480, 609n, 619-620n, 622-
    631, 667n, 701, 928n, 993-4n, 1189-
    90n, B pp4-5, B 38n, 126n, 149n,
    284n, 399n, 619n*, 737n, 1012-3,
    1427n, 1569n, L pp1-2, p4, L 77n,
    104n, 169n, 244n, 276, 490n, 513n,
    620, 621n, 628, 629n, 723-5n, 801n,
    1129-32n, 1223-41, 1287n, 1296-
    1315, T 860, 919, 1147n, F p1, p10
    n4, F 694n, 791n, 965n, 1072n,
        1422n, E pp1-6, p15 n63, p17, E 97n,
        195-6n, 202-3nn, 237n, 248n, 303n,
        356, 810n, We pp1-4, p32, We 174n,
        382-3n,   550n;   see   also
        Peloponnesians, and Herald (d),
        Lampito, Spartan Delegates, Spartan
        Women in Index II
    alliance with Persia (411-404), L p3, L
        1133n, T p3, F pp4-7
    alliance with Persia (387), E p4
    and Athens, treated as a single entity, L
        900n, 1097-8n, 1179n
    Athenian expedition in support of
        (ca.462), L 1138-44
    Athenian tyranny overthrown by (510),
        L 1150-6
    attempt to restore Athenian tyranny
        (ca.506), L 619n
    calendar of, C 615-6n
    communal meals at, E p16*
    conference at (392/1), E pp3-4, p6, E
        71n, 102n, 200-3nn, 356n, We 176n
    habits/fashions of, imitated by some
        Athenians, W 476-7n, B 1281-3
    intervention in support of Athenian
        oligarchy (508/7), L 273-282
    invincibility of, on land, disproved, We
        p2
    once Athens' ally, L p3, L 1247-61
    peasantry of, fictitious, P 625n, L 1174n
    property freely borrowable at, E p16*
    rejected as name for bird-city, B 813-6
    saves Athens from destruction (404), F
        p5 n25
    wife-sharing at, E p16*, E 613n
    see also gerousia, Helots, mora, skytalē
Spartolus, battle of (429), P 395n*, B
    1556n
speakers, identification of, A 395n, K 1-9*,
    274n, 1204n, 1254-6n, C 394n, 740-
    5n, 761-3n, 1105n, 1497n, W 74-84n,
    152n, 461-2n, 903-4n, 1226-7*,
    1263ff*, 1364-5n, P 38-49n, 258n,
    433-457n, 459-472n, 473-483n, 508-
    511n, 549n, 550-5*, 924-936*, 948-
    9n, 978-986*, 1039-41n, 1059n,
    1124-6n, 1210n, 1258n, 1329-59n, B
    1-161n*, 95-96n, 267n, 302-4n, 386-
    7n, 442-3n, 448-450n, 577-8n, 638-
    640n, 644-5n, 809-836n, 833n, 1313-

22n, 1615n, 1691-2n, 1726-30n, 1743-7n, L 69-253*, 77n, 107-110*, 133-5n, 191-208n, 830n, 970-9n, 982ff.n, 1108-11n, 1273-90ṅ*, T p8 n47, T 31n, 32n, 129-130n, 252-263n, 295n, 380n, 571-654n, 610n, 625n, 638*, 928n, 1056-97n*, 1094n, F 184n, 189n, 311-5nn, 414-5n, 644-5n, 1018-9n, 1021n, 1130-6nn, 1162n, 1175-6n, 1177n, 1205n, 1323n, 1393n, 1418n, 1424n, 1427-32n, 1435-66n*, 1442-50n, 1448n, E 30-284n, 53n, 132-168n, 189-213n, 241-2n, 279-284n, 328n, 330n, 348-350n, 356n, 381n, 382n, 583-729n, 603n, 609-610n, 631-4n, 719-720n, 778-9n, 918-927n, 1074-97n, 1127-8n, 1138n, 1166-7nn, We 65n, 99n, 160-8n, 170-9n, 505n, 580n, 824n, 840n, 926-934n, 964n, 1081n, 1088n, 1172n

speech defects, C 862, 870n, 872-3, W 44-45
speechwriters, C 467-475n, W 1270n
Spercheius, River, B 569n, F 1383, We 937n
Sphacteria (island off Messenia), K 1n, 6n, 54-57n, 186n, 281n, 392n, 575n, 792-3n, 846n, 1053n, 1056n, W p.xv, W 44n, P p.xv, P 219, F 764n, 1074n: see also Pylos
spirits, speaking through mediums, W 1019-20n
spongers, see parasites
sponges:
    used to clean anus, T 248n, F 482-7
    used to cool burns, T 247n
sport:
    boxing, W 526-7n, 1503n, F p11, F 792n, 1268n
    chariot-racing, A 615n, K 247n, 556-8, 603n, C 15, 25-27, 28, 31, 69n, 107, 122n, 1264-5, 1272, 1300n*, 1302, 1401, 1406-7, W 1050, 1427-9, P 901-4, B 1443, F 827n, 995n, 1232-3n, 1403n; see also animals (horse)
    cock-fighting, A 166n, 484n, K 492-7, C

889n*, W 147n, B 70-71, 285n, 352n, 834-5n, 1297n, F 861n, E 291n, We 1037n
    horse-racing, P 899-900, F 827n
    hunting, K 1382, W 369n, 1202-3, P 1178n, L 789-791, F 1358n, 1359n, We 157
        of birds, W 208n, B 62, 194n, 525-8, 1083, 1087
    pankration (free-style fighting), W 1190-5, 1383-5, P 897, B 441-3n*
    pentathlon, W 1206-7n
    quail-fighting, W 147n, P 788n, B 1297n
    quail-tapping, P 788n, B 1298-9, We 1037n
    ship racing, K 560n
    wrestling, A 571n, 710n, K 388n, 490-2, 571n, 841-2, 1238, C 179, 417n, 602n, 1047n, 1356n, W 526-7n, 1025, P 34, 896a, 897n, L 1082-4*, F p11, F 469n, 729, 775n, 792n, 957n, 1070, 1200n, E 259-260n
    see also athletes, Isthmian Games, Nemean Games, Olympic Games, Pythian Games
squandering of inherited property, T 819-820n
squaring the circle, B 1005
stage-platform, A p14, E 496n, 1152n
    ascent to, W 1341-4, L 288n, F 180d, 269-270dd, 296d
stage-struck, state of being, in the young, B 1444-5
stage business[6], A 864d*, K 107-8d*, 697d*, C 1-18*, 53-55*, 270-3n*, 541-2, 1104d*, 1494d*, W 7-8d*, 179-190dd*, 188n*, 423n, 757n, 819n, 990-9dd*, 1412d*, P 956-962dd*, B 227-262n*, 363*, 981n, 1001d*, 1336n, L 634n, T 245n, 572n, 743n, 1082-9n, 1092n, E 47n, 504n, 1051-70n, We 64n, 935n; see also asides, costumes and properties, ekkyklēma, entrances, and exits, gestures, knocks on doors, mēkhanē, torches, windows
stage directions, in Greek text, A 112, 114,

---

6   Since almost all the bracketed stage directions would be relevant to this entry, they are specifically listed only if they are amplified, modified or otherwise discussed in the Addenda.

B 222, T 129-130, 276n, F 1263n
stage movements, in Euripidean tragedy, F
    942n
staircases, W 1342n
Star of Dawning, see Venus
stars and constellations, W 22-23n, P 832-
    841*
    Andromeda, P 832-3n*
    Arcturus, F 1190n
    Bootes, P 832-3n*
    Cassiepeia, P 832-3n*
    Cepheus, P 832-3n*
    Cetus, P 832-3n*
    Hyades, P 832-3n*, L 254-387n*
    Orion, P 832-3n
    Perseus, P 832-3n*
    Pleiades, P 832-3n, B 710n, 711n, T 67-
        68n
    Sirius, W 1032n, P 755n
    Ursa Major, P 832-3n*
    Virgo, P 832-3n
stasis (civil strife), B 1014, 1427n, T 788n,
    F 354-371n, 359; see also civil war
statue(s):
    beautiful woman mistaken for, T 1106n
    fixed in position by pouring molten lead,
        E 1110n
    gilding of, E 826n
    metal crescents on, B 1114-7*
    Peace represented as, P p.xvii*, p.xx
        n16, P 524n
    turns head, P 682n
stature, and social class, W 522-3n
Stenia (festival), T 834
steward (tamiās) of a household, K 947-
    959, W 613
stewards (rhabdoukhoi) in theatre, P 734
stillbirth, T 339-340n
stones, used as toilet-paper, P 1230n, E
    372d, We 817-8
stoning:
    as method of mob justice, A 236, 280-
        356, C 1508, F 778
    of bad actors, F 778n
    of the insane, W 1491n, B 524-5, F 778n
    ritual, F 733n
stool-bearer (diphrophoros), in Panathenaic
    procession, B 1296n*, 1552, E 734
stools, portable, K 1384n; see also stool-
    bearer

strigils, T 556n*, 557n*
style, terminology of, F 940-4n
Strymon, River (Thrace), A 156n
Stymphalus, Lake (Arcadia), F 1266n
Styx (underworld river), F 470
suicide, K 80-84*, C 780, W 298n, 522-3*,
    756-7, 758-9n, T 1054, F 120-135,
    1050-1, 1478n, 1504-9, E 644-5n
sundials, B 997-8nn; see also shadow-stick
supplication, A 414n, K 445-6n, 1272n, P
    133n, 1113, L 1138-41, T 180, 689-
    758n, 721-2n, 751, We 382-5
surnames, English, derived from birds, B
    1291n
surrender, typical terms for, L 277-8n
Susa, capital of Persia, A 68-69n
Sybaris (S. Italy), W 1259, 1427, 1435,
    1438, W 344
sykophantai, see informers
Syme, battle of (412/1), T p1, T 804n*
symposia, A 524-5n*, 551n, 982n, K 277n,
    888-9, W 1005, 1208-49, P 770,
    1131-58, B 507n*, L 208n, 632n,
    1125-38, T 137n, 457-8n, 633n,
    1178n, 1195n, E 840n, 841-2n, We
    85n, 190-2n
    conversational skills at, W 1174-1207,
        1320-1; see also comparison game
    group-financed, A 1211n
    guests bringing own food to, A 1086n,
        1211n
    prizes at, T 94n
    professional invitees to, W 1318n; see
        also parasites
    singing/recitations at, K 529-530, C
        1355-72*, P 1266-1304, E 678-680;
        see also skolia
    women's equivalent to, T 796n
synaesthesia, B 1716n, T 1041n, F 637n
synoecism, B 172n*
synonyms, pedantic distinctions between, F
    1167-8n, 1181n, We 548n
Syracuse (Sicily), A 606n, 920n, K 1n,
    1303n, P 250n, 1031n, B p4, p5, B
    363n, 619n, 639n, 926-7n, 1297n*,
    1372-1409n, 1576n, L 57n, F 1331-
    63n, E p4, E 246n, 330n, 825n, We
    p3, p31 n128, We 149n, 290-321n,
    550n
Syria, P 1146n

syrmaiā (Egyptian laxative), P 1254, L 857
Syros (Cyclades), P 363n

table, holy, in temples, We 678, 1128n, 1143n
tables, portable, for dining, A 1159n, F 518
tacking, when sailing against wind, F 1076-7n*
Taenarum, Cape (Laconia), A 510, F 187
Tanagra (Boeotia), W 234n
tapestries, W 1215n
Tartarus, lowest region of the underworld, C 192, B 693, 698, F 475n, We p7
Tartessus (SW Spain), F 475
Tasters (*protenthai*), C 1198-1200
tattooing, W 1296n, B 760, L 332, F 503n, 1511
Tauri (Scythians of the Crimea), L 447n, E 1056-7n
Tauropolia (festival), L 447n
tautology, F 1152-76
taverns and tavern-keepers, B 1292, L 466, T 347, 737, E 154-5, We 435-6
"tax-farmer", as term of abuse, K 248*
tax-farming syndicates, F 367n, E 102n, We 176n
Taÿgetum, Mt (Laconia), L 117, 118n, 1296
teachers:
 gifts to, C 1147
 more honoured than parents, C 871n, 1467
 regarded as infallible, C 1432n
teeth, loss of, W 165, We 266, 1057-9
teeth, permanent, age of eruption, F 418n
teeth, threat to knock out, L 688-690n, F 548, 572-3
"Telamon" (symposiac song), L 1237
temple-robbery, W 845n, 1447, B 1585-6n, T 489n, We 30n, 356-8, 359n; *see also* sacrilege
temples:
 divine co-residents (*synnāoi*) in, We p22 n91

used as public conveniences, We pp16-17, We 1184
Ten, the (short-lived oligarchic regime, 403), E 456-7n
Tenedos, We p3 n10
tenement houses, K 1001, B 997n, T 273, F 1343n
Tenos (Cyclades), We 718
Teos (Ionia), L p1 n4, T 161
terrorism, T p3, T 1143-4n
testicles:
 of sacrificial victim, L 186n
 threats against, K 772, L 363, 694-5n, We 312, 955-6
textual emendations, new[7], A 731*, 1094, 1108-18*, 1182, K 271*, 370-3*, C 156, 439*, 661, 953, 995, 1005-8*, 1119*, 1169, 1310, 1371, W 147, 407*, 536, 1449, P 246*, 300*, 303, 402*, 549, 566, 749*, 832*, 896a, 1023, B 241, 535-8*, 586*, 868, 924, 993, 994, 1040, 1395, L 264, 507, 564, 623, 644-5, 723, 763, 1063-4, 1174, 1284, 1295, T 5, 140, 164, 306, 400, 583, 729, 981-2*, 987, 994, 1013, 1018-9, 1089, 1114, 1198, 1215, F 182, 216, 341, 819, 1028, 1305, 1437-53*, 1438, 1448, E 78, 307, 560, 628, 735, 848, 897, 898, 921-2, 963, 1165-6, 1171, 1173, 1182, We 632
thallophoroi (olive-branch bearers), in Panathenaic procession, W 544, E 743n
Thargelia (festival), K 1405n, B 126n, 971n, L 646-7n, F 733n
Thargelion (Athenian month, ~ May), T p3 n21
Thasos, A 671, P 1298-9n, B 798n, L 196, E 1119, We 1021
Thebes (Boeotia), A 418-9n, 860n, 862, 868, 905n, 911, 1082n, K 238, 901n*, P p.xv, p.xvi, p.xvii, P 214n, 951n, 1270n, L 2n, 697, T 485n,

---

7 This entry lists all and only the passages in which I have either printed or suggested an emendation of which, so far as I know, I am the originator (though some of them had appeared in print elsewhere before they appeared in the volumes of this edition). It does not include passages where my intervention has consisted only in transferring words from one speaker to another, or in changes of punctuation.

996n, F p5 n25, F 694n, 965n, 1021n, 1023, 1167-8n, 1193n, 1225-6n. 1286n, E p1, E 97n, 202-3n; *see also* Boeotia, *and* Ismenia, Ismenias, Theban *in Index II*

Athenian alliance with (378), E 248n

Athens' ally in Corinthian War, E pp2-4, p5. E 193n, 200n, 202-3nn, We p1, p4, We 550n

theft. impossible in communist society, E 667

theogony. B 685-702

Thera. We 925n

Therapne (Laconia), L 1314n

Thermopylae. C 624n, L 1131, F 1383n
  battle of (480), W 1084n, L 1247-72n, 1251n, 1254-61

Thesea (festival), We 627

Thesmophoria (festival), W 831n, P 151n, B 1519, T p7, pp10-12, T 67-68n, 79, 101-2n, 138n, 182, 277-8n, 295n, 312-330n*, 359n, 375-6, 457n, 626-9. 658n*, 747n, 834n, 947-9, 984n, 1150-2, 1231n, E p28, E 18n, 155n, 223. 332n, 443, We 1006n
  even infant males debarred from?, T 717n
  see also Athens, places and buildings (Thesmophorium), Calligeneia, *Mesē, Nēsteiā*

Thessaly. A 434n, 872n, C 686n, W 74n. 459n. 1245-7, 1273, 1414n, L 1150-6nn, 1152, 1168-9n, We 521, 524n
  as home of kidnappers, C 749n
  as home of witches, C 749

thirteen, as round number, P 990n

Thirty. rulers of Athens in 404-403, A 11n, C 104n, W 157n, 987-8n, 1270n*, 1408n, B 1296n, L 103n, 593n, T 170n, F p10 nn46,47, p21 n97, p22, F 541n, 965n, 967n, 1506n, E p1, E 97n. 183-4n, 202-3n, 243n, 456-7n, 802n. We p30, We 147n, 550n. 1146n

Thirty Years' Peace (446/5), A 194n, K 1388-9n

Thrace. Thracians. A 134n. 136, 138, 154, 155, 170, 172, 967n, K p3, W p.xv, W 1n, 42n, P 1298-9n, B 15-16n, 108n, 276n, 303*, 484n, 670n, 710n,

769-784n, 798n, 1179n, 1369n, 1522-3n, 1529n, 1702-3n, L 563-4, T 134-5n, F p1, F 681, 683-4n, 730n, 963n, 1533n, E 987n, 1029n, We p3, We 1n
  Greek cities on coast of, A 602, W 210n, 288, 475n, P p.xv, P 282n, 283, 640n, B p5, B 1369, 1569n, L 103

thrēnoi (laments), F 1303

throat-clearing, by public speakers, T 381

thunderbolt, C 395-407, W 1032-5n, P 42n, 369n, 376n, 755-8n, B p3, B 553n, 576, 1242n, 1538, 1653n, 1714, 1747, 1749-50, 1751-3n, 1760-1n, L 1285n, T 1050-1n, We p9, We 125, 210n, 1189-90n

Thurii (S. Italy), K 327n, C 332, 521-3n*, B 521n, We 84n

thyme, beverage made from, P 1169

thymelē (altar in orchestra), T 689-758n, 748n

thyrsus (bacchic wand), L 1313, F 1211

time intervals reckoned inclusively, P 876n, 990n, L 881n, T p1, T 741-2n, We 584n

time of action, imaginary:
  beginning before dawn, C 1-3, W 2, 216, 365-6, T 1065n, E 1-21, 105
  ending with/after evening meal, A 1085-6, W 1326ff, 1478, P 1192, E 834-1183

time of day, terms for telling, B 1500

Tiryns (Argolid), F 1043n

titles for plays:
  announced in advance?, E 17n
  choice of, F p12 n55
  homonymous, We p28 n113
  of Aeschylus, sometimes not authentic, F 1021n
  when produced in connected suites, F 1124n

toasts to a beloved, L 856-7n

toddlers, diet of, L 881n, T 692n

tomb-robbers, F 1149

tongue of sacrificial victim, P 1060, 1109, B 1704-5, We 1110n

Tongue-to-Belly Men (Englottogastores), B 1470-81n*, 1694-1705*

torch-races, W 1203-4, F 131, 1089-98

torches:

as attribute of drunken reveller, W 1326-85. L 1217ff, E 50n, 692, 938d, 978n, 1111d, We 1041, 1201n
as attribute of Furies, We 425
at weddings, C 1129n, P 1317, We 425n
in concluding scenes of comedies, C 1484-5n, 1490, 1494, W 1326-85, P 1317, L 1217ff, F p18, F 1524-5, 1528-33n, E 1149d, 1150, We 1194-5
in ritual, C 604n, W 1372-3nn, T 101, 280, 655n, 1150, F 313, 323d, 340, 350, 1212, 1361-2, 1517-8n, 1525n
in slapstick, C 543, W 1330-1, L 1217-22, T 238n, 917, We 1052
sold at wine-shops, E 50n
symbolizing joy, T 101
tornado, Aeschylus imaged as, F 824n
Torone (Chalcidice), F p5
torture, P 452, 746n, B 1081n, L 846
methods of, F 618-622, We 875
of citizens, prohibited, A 220n, P 452n, L 489n, F 629n, We 824n
of non-citizens or slaves, in investigations, A 1093n*, We 824n, 859n, 875
of slaves, in litigation, C 620, F 615-673, We p16 n74, We 875n
offer of slave for, conditional, F 618-625
see also Athens, political and legal institutions (challenges)
town planning, K 327n, B 992-1009*
toyboys, We 975-1096, 1200-3
toys, C 864, W 295-6, B 1461
for pet birds, W 129-130n
made by children, C 878-881
tradesmen, profiting by others' misery, E p19, E 412-426
tradesmen-politicians, A 846n, K p3 n1*, K 44-47, 129-143, 315-8, 739-740, 892*, 1304n, 1315, C 551n, 581n, 1065, W 38n, 1007n, P 270, 648, 669n, 690, 753, B 440-1n, 798, T 805n, F 678n, 709-713, E 252-3, We 175
Tragasae (Troad), name exploited for puns, A 808, 853
tragedy:
costumes in, A 410-479, W 1313n, L 1190n, T p7 n42, F 1061-7

emotional impact of, F p15*
how to save, F p1, pp7-9
imitating comedy?, B 213-4n, T p5 n32
in fourth century, F pp8-9
in school curriculum, F 868n
light variety of (Euripides, 414-412), T 848-850nn
lyrics in, F 1248-1364
revivals of, F 868n
scripts of, as reading texts, F 52-53
with freely invented plot, T 29n, F 83n
transmigration of souls, see metempsychosis
trappings, for horses in processions, L 1189
tray-bearers (skaphēphoroi), in Panathenaic procession, E 739n, 742n
trays (tēliai, pinakes) used by market traders, W 1388d, B 14, We 1037n
neck-ring attached to, We 1037n
treason, W 845n, P 363n, B 766-7, 768n, 1585-6n, L 103n, T 331-351n, 346n, 363-6, F p13, p22, F 354-371n, 362, 953n, 1512n, E 644-5n, We 30n; see also Athens, political and legal institutions (prosecutions)
treasure, buried, B 599-602
treaties, A 308n, W 240n, B 632n, T 295-311n; see also Peace of Callias, Peace of Nicias, Thirty Years' Peace
trees, B 1476n
ash, B 742
date-palm, B 590n*
fabulous, B 1473-81
fig, P 558, 598, 627-9*, B 590*, T 1114n; latex of, E 404n
kermes-oak, F 859
linden, B 1377
maple, A 181
mastic, We 720n
oak, A 180, C 402, W 383, 877, B 479-480n, L 118n, T 114
oleaster, B 240, 621, We 269n, 586, 592
olive, A 998, C 1005, 1124, W 252n, 450, P 578, B 617, 995n
wins Attica for Athena, T 318-9n
pine, F 966n; see also torches
poplar, C 1007
Triballi (Thracian tribe), B 1529-33; see also Triballian God in Index II

Athenian "hellfire club" named after, B 1529n

tribute paid by "allies", A 6n, 88n, 505, 643, K 1019n, 1034n, 1070-1n, W 44n, 520n, 657, 660n, 684-5n, 700n, 707, 1100, 1115, P 621, B 191-3n, F p4 n19, We 1192n
replaced by import/export tax, F p4 n19, F 363n
states exempt from, B 879n

Tricca (Thessaly), We p8, p9

trident, K 839, C 566

Triphylia (W. Peloponnese), B 149n

Triton, River (Libya), L 347n

Tritonis, Lake (Libya), K 1189n, C 989n, L 347n

Troad, A 430n, L 723-5n, F p11

trophy (victory monument), T 697, We 453n; see also Attica, demes and localities (Marathon)

Troy (and Trojan War), A 424n, 430n, C 622n, 891n, 1484-5n*, W 351n, P 724n, B 1104n, 1639n, 1757n, L 155-6n, T 101-129nn, 466-519n, 769-770n, 788n, 850n, 864-5n, 901, F p20, F 666n, 924-7n, 928n, 933n, 963n, 1041n, 1276n, 1286n, 1289n, 1291-2n, 1317-8n, 1451n, E 1029n, We p8, p12 n55

Trozen (Argolid), F 194n

truce, Athenian-Boeotian (421), P 466n, B 188-9n

truce, one-year (423), C 7n, W pp.xv-xvi, W 62n

tug of war, E 877-1111n, 1074-1111

twilight, duration of, E 312n

"Twisted Harbour", see Cyllene

tyrannicide, rewards for, K 449n*, 786n*, B 1074-5

tyranny:
Alcibiades suspected of aiming at, F 1432n
as political smear, K 447-9, 1043n, W 417, 464-474, 488-507, 1232-5n, B 1074-5n, L 619, 630-1, T 1143-4n
at Syracuse, E 246n, We 550n
fear of, in 411, T p2, p3, T 338-9, 1143-4

in archaic Athens, A 980n, K 445-6n, 448n*, 449n, 786n, W 1225n, P 642n, L 619n, E 943n
opponents of, automatically classified as democrats, L 664*
Thrasybulus accused of plotting, We 550n
women powerful under?, E p8 n39

Uncaring River (in underworld), F 186n

underworld, see Hades
"scientific" investigation of, C 188, 192

undressing:
by a character, L 920-950, 1093n, T 1181
by chorus, A 627, L p5 n25, p6 n32, L 614-5, 636-7, 661-2, 686-7, T 656
forcible, T 636-642, We 926-936
of condemned criminals, T 939-940
of slave to be flogged, F 641
ritual, L 645
to fight, L 615n, T 568-9
to work in fields, L 1173
see also dressing, nudity

Unwritten Laws, F 145-153n, 456-8n

urination, W 807, 810, 858n, 935-940, P 49n, 1266, 1268-94*, L 402, T 611-618, F 95, E 640n, 832; see also chamber-pots
simulated, on stage, E 369n

urine, offered to Hermes as drink, We 1133n

utopias, P 1314n, B p2*, E p8, pp12-22, E 673-4n, We p6; see also communism

vaginal secretion, K 1285n, P 716n, L 197n, 1061-4n, E 845n; see also cunnilingus

variants, authorial, C 1176(?), 1437-9(?), P 744(?), 896b(?), T 12n(?), F p23; see also revision

vase-paintings relevant to Ar., B 510n, 1615n
Berlin Heracles (Berlin F3046 [lost]), F 1-20n, E 833n
Berlin Horsemen (Berlin F 1697), K p4, F 35-37n
Getty Birds (Malibu, J. Paul Getty Museum 82.AE.83), C 889n*, B p6*

Paris satyr lekythos (Louvre CA 1730), F 32n
Würzburg Telephus (Martin von Wagner Museum H5697), T p12, T 232n*, 734n, 754-7nn
vegetarianism, F 1032n, 1356n
vehicles, on stage, B 1720*, F 963n
ventriloquism, W 1019-20
Venus (planet), P 836-7
Viagra: comedy as good as, E p22
victory, in dramatic competition, references to. A 1224n, K 546-550, 592n, 1253n, C 561-2, 1115-30, B 445-7, 1102-17, L 1291-4, T 972n, 1231n, F 297n, 392-3, E p25, E 1181n, 1182
victory-odes, C 1356n
vine branches, in funerary ritual, E 1031
vines, A 233, 512, 987, 995, 997, W 326, 1291*, P 62n, 190, 267n, 308, 520n, 557, 568, 597, 612, 912, 1146-7, 1162-5, 1197*, B 588, F 92n, 1320
virility, regained by old men, A 993-9, 1198-1221, K 1388-91, W 739-740n, B 1256, F 345-9n, E p22
voice, grammatical (active/middle/passive), P 291n, T 1179n, 1198n*, 1214n, F 1160n
voice, pitch of, T 39-62n, 101-129n; see also falsetto
volcanic phenomena, L 299-300n
vomiting, A 584-7, C 906-7, F 11
voodoo dolls, F 295n
votive tablets, T 773-784
vows, K 660-1n, B 1618-25, L 1262n, We 937n

walking-sticks, A 448, C 217d, W 32, 727n, 1296, L 357n, F 717, E 74-78, 150, 276-7, 327-356n, 509, 543-6
wall-hangings, F 938n
war, not abolished in Praxagora's new world, E 678-9n
warships, see navy
washing soda, F 711-2
water, lustral, P 969n, B 850, 863n, 898, L 1129-30
water flung at performers, P 969-972*, L 381-5, 400-2, 469-470
water-drinkers, disdained, K 89, 349
water-supply of Athens, K 814n, B 997n

"we" for "I", T 183, 195-6
wealth:
  as prerequisite and as objective, We 130-197n, 168n
  assumed to be usually ill-gotten, E 603n, We p5, p13, pp18-19, We 28-38, 48-50, 87-92, 107-9, 219, 352-390, 502-4, 774-7
  insatiability of desire for, E 608n, We 188-197
  miraculous profusion of, We 802-820
  ostentatious display of, T 840-1nn; see also conspicuous consumption
  private, estimated total of, We 195n
  redistributed according to desert, We pp13-20, p22, We 95-98, 217n, 221, 386-8, 475, 490-506, 751-6, 779-781, 822-958
"visible" and "invisible", E 601-2n
weaning, L 19n
weather, C 1117-30, W 260-5, 771-4, P 1141, 1157-8, B 1501-2, 1594; see also meteorology
weddings, A 1047-66, C 1128, P p.xvi, p.xvii, P 843-4, 859, 868-870, 976, 1192, 1206, 1316-59, B 132, 161n, 494-8n, 1689-93, 1706-65, T 795n, E 1030-4nn, We 529n.
  carriage used at, B 1738-40n*
  couple showered with sweetmeats, We 768-9n
  food associated with, P 869n, We 999n
  shutting of bridal chamber, E 1104n
  songs at, P 856-867n, 1329-59, B 1728-42, T 1034
weighing of verses, F 797, 1365-1410
weights, see measures
wells, E 1002-4
"Whitefeet", Athenian anti-tyrant faction (ca.513)?, L 664*
widows, T 345n, 446n, 605n, F 1331-63n, E 877-1111n
wife who is simultaneously a mistress, P 849n
wigs, worn by street prostitutes, T 258n
windows, K 1254, C 723-6*, 1497d, 1506d, W 131-2n, 156d, 173d, 316d, 317n, 379, 395d, 400d, 402d, E p29, p30 n111, E 327d, 356n, 877-1111n, 884-936, 949-968*

winds, A 876-7n, K 430, 437, C 624-5n, W
    265, 1124, L 324n, F 999-1000n,
    1002-3
capable of impregnating birds, B 695n
wine, K 1317n, P 520n*, 535, 576, 703,
    886*, 916, 1103n, 159n, 1323, 1354,
    F 22n, 357n, 511, 1320-1n, E 44-45,
    140n, 307n, 606, 841, 1112-26n, We
    644
avoided by some orators, K 349, C 417n
boiled (siraion), W 878, E 1174
brings success in life, K 91-94
cheap, T 743*
Chian, E 1139
"flower-scented", F 1150n, We 807n
free samples offered in taverns, E 49n
from second pressing, E 634n
love of, associated with (other) virtues,
    W 80n*
mixed with seawater, F 204n
mixtures with water[8], T 743n, We 853n
    (1:1) A 354n, We 1132
    (3:2) K 1187-9
    (3:1) T 743n, We 1132n
neat, A 75n, K 85, 105, 354-5, W 525,
    1217n, P 300n, E 137n, 1123
pits for storage of, E 154n
Pramnian, K 107
sapros, P 554n
sour, A 352n
straining of, We 1087n
Thasian, L 196, E 1118-24, We 1021
see also drunkenness, symposia, women
    (and alcoholic drink)
wineskin-hopping (askōliasmos), We 1129n
witchcraft, C 749-750*, T 534
Withering Stone, underworld landmark, F
    194
wives of well-known men made to look like
    them?, E 51n
"Wolf-feet", Athenian anti-tyrant faction
    (ca.513)?, L 664*
women[9]:
    accused of murder and poisoning, T
        430n, 466-519n*, 560-3
    alleged conservatism of, E p11, E 215-

228
and alcoholic drink, L 114, 184n, 195-
    206, 395, 466, T p7, T 347-8, 393,
    418n, 420, 630-2, 733-761, 795n,
    840n, E p9, p12, p27, E 14-15, 44-
    45n, 132-6, 146, 153-7, 227, 1118-
    24, We 645, 737, 972
and child-rearing, E 654n
and clothes-making, B 831n, L 519,
    535n, 567-586, 729-739, 896-7, T
    821-2, E pp12-13, p15, p17, E 89-93,
    215-8, 654, We 533n
and noisy/orgiastic cults, W 9n, L 1-3,
    387-396
and superstition, W 64n
as breadwinners, in comedy, E p9, E 461
as "deceivers", E p11, E 237-8
as managers of the home, L 495, F 983-
    8n*, E 14-15n, 211-2, 236n, 547n,
    599-600
as soldiers, in comedy, E pp9-10, p17
    n74
as tavern-keepers, T 347, We 435
assembly of, T 84, 90, 277-8, 292-570
"bad influence on each other", L 891n
bodies of, viewed and commented on, L
    78-92, 1136, 1148, 1158, 1162-72;
    see also breasts, nudity, sexy mutes
carrying objects on head, T 284n, E 222,
    We 1198
"chatterboxes", T 393, E 120
"courage not to be expected from", E
    519n
"dangerous when out of house", L 16n,
    E 325-6, 336-8
did not cook meat, F 505-511n
domestic responsibilities of, L 16-19
double plot by, in Lysistrata, L pp3-4
"enjoy rough sex", C 1070
Euripides and, L 283, 368-9, T pp4-6, T
    82-91, 181-2, 331-351n, 336-8, 363-
    4n, 377-550, 584-591, 649-650,
    1160-70, F p16 n71, F 1043-52
expected (in theory) not to go out, T
    790n
expected to be unintelligent, L 1124n

---

8   The numerical ratios are given in the form (water:wine), as is normally done in Greek
sources.

9   In this entry, quotation marks enclose opinions about women, expressed by characters in
the plays and probably in most cases widely held by contemporary male Athenians.

expected to keep silent, L 356, 361, 442, 507-528, 649-650, F 951n, E pp8-9, E 570n

festivals held exclusively by, T p10, T 130n, 834-5; see also Adonia, Scira, Stenia, Thesmophoria

"fussy about food", P 28n

given voice, in Euripidean tragedy, F 949-950

"good at raising income", E 236, 441-2

heroines lack stereotypical vices of, E p26

"idleness" of, L 260-1n

implicitly excluded from the human race, T 683n, 787n

"incapable of rational thought", E 110n

ineligible to be witnesses, W 1413n

'key role of, in Athenian religion, L 638-648, T p11, E 215-228n

lending and borrowing among, E p19, E 446-451*

limit on right to make contracts, T 842n, E 1024-5n

linguistic usages distinctive of, L 970-9n, E 149n, 189-213n, 215-228n, We 706n; see also gender (grammatical), oaths (and gender)

living in manless households, E 877-111n

locked up, T 414-7

"lustfulness" of, L 2n, 23-25, 125-139, 404-419, 715-780, T 392, E p12, pp21-22*, E 228, 877-1111, We p25 n104; see also adultery

"must not be allowed to defeat men", L 450n

names of, not normally uttered in public, L p5, L 1086n, E 51n, E 727n

"not responsible for war", A 1062n

old and young, comparative desirability of, E 893-905

older, may de facto control household, T 345n, 842n

pale complexions of, K 1277n*, B 668n, T 31n, E 64n, 126-7, 385-7, 428

peeping out of doors/windows, P 979-985, T 797-9, E p5, p29, p30, E 924, 930

physical abuse of, L 162, 357, 360-1, 364, 366, 503-5, 516, 519-520, 635,

799, E 467-8n, 994-7n, We 1013-5; see also rape

punished by deprivation of food?, E 468-9n, 665n

refuse to curse other women, T 367n

"regrettably indispensable", L 1039n

reluctant to appear before strange men, T 903n

segregation of, T 789-799

serve community as mothers, L 589-590, 651

sexual freedom for, E p13

Spartan, physical fitness of, L 79-82

"spend household money for private purposes", E 226n

taking initiative, in tragedy, E p26 n97

"thievishness" of, T 418-428, 556-7, 558n, 812-3, E p12, E 14-15

treated as co-owners of family property, L 894

unmarried, plight of, L 593n

use or threaten violence, L 363-7, 435-465, 505, 636, 656-7, 682-695, 704-5, 798, 821-3, T 536-570, E 259-260, 1054-1111

virtuous, in Euripides, T 547-8n

visiting friends, L 700-2, T 795-6, E 348-9

warriors, L 454n; see also Amazons in Index II

"wickedness" of, L 12, 253, 260-1, 369, 968-972, T p7, T 394, 473-5, 549-550, 787

work of, in Praxagora's new society, E pp12-13

working, A 457n, C 555n*, W 35n, P 812n, L 457-8, F p1, F 549-578n, 565n, 840, 858, E 302n, 877-1111n, We 426-7; see also §as tavern-keepers, and Garland-seller, Innkeeper, Myrtia, Plathane in Index II

see also adultery, child substitution, marriage, pannychides, sex-sellers

wood, toughest kinds of, A 180n

Wooden Horse of Troy, B 1128*, T 101-129n

wool, processing of, L 574-586

wool-sellers, sharp practice by, F 1386-7

word, longest in Greek language, E p25, E 1169-75

word-play, A 36n, 176n, 179n, 188n, 234n, 270n, 321n, 589n, 606n, 628n*, 682n, 700n, 701n, 724n, 726n, 739n, 751n, 759n, 808n, 826n, 832n, 835n, 850n, 853n, 866n, 917n, 987n, 1071n, 1082n, 1093n, 1131n, 1134-5n, 1151n, 1210-1n, K 21-23n, 34n, 54-57n, 59n, 78n, 79n, 215n, 262n, 279n, 371n, 449n, 454-6n, 464n, 491n, 529n, 547n, 615n, 759n, 859n, 901n, 919n, 954n, 996n, 1053n*, 1061n, 1182n, 1263n, 1332n, 1391n, C 24n, 30n, 53-55*, 74n, 94n, 156n, 166n, 225-6n, 296n, 394n, 398n, 480n, 503n, 545n, 651n, 654n, 710n, 730n*, 1156n, 1162n*, 1356n, 1507n, W 15-19n, 17n, 27n, 40-41n, 145n, 155n, 185n, 186n, 193n, 195n, 308n, 328-331n, 353n, 380n, 399n, 401n, 418n, 438n, 502n, 572n, 573n, 589n, 769n, 771-2n, 795n, 821n, 823n, 895n, 918n, 939n, 1032n, 1038n, 1082n, 1087n*, 1131-2n, 1148n, 1194-5n, 1283n, 1307n, 1353n, 1465n*, 1501n, 1513n, 1534n, P 17-18n, 42n, 82n, 117n, 123n, 242n, 251n, 279n*, 300n, 376-8n, 432n, 440n, 453n, 616-8n, 643n, 678n, 684n, 896-904nn, 908n, 926n, 964-7n, 969n, 1014n, 1236-7n, 1270-1n, 1286n, 1293n, B 28n, 149n, 179-184n, 276n, 299-300nn, 341n, 374n, 399n, 484n, 489n, 507n, 569n, 696n, 765n, 815-6n, 868n, 911n, 915n, 935n, 1179n, 1204n, 1213n, 1287n, 1289n, 1346n*, 1379n, 1474-5n, 1477n, 1479n, 1511n, 1530n, 1548n, 1555n, 1557-8n, 1673n, 1682n, 1694n, 1699n, 1701-3n*, L 23-24n, 60n, 64n, 87-88nn, 90n, 110n, 114n, 158n, 299-300n, 413n, 417n, 419n, 488n, 549n, 578n, 584n, 739-740n, 749-750n, 771n, 834n, 847n, 852n, 943n, 980n*, 995n, 996nn, 1061-4n, 1078n, 1085n, 1113n, 1162-3nn, 1164n, 1166n, 1168-70nn, T 5-7n, 27n, 50n, 57n, 60-62n, 153n, 172n, 204n, 232n, 248n, 531n, 567n, 575n, 605n, 620n, 629n, 647-8n, 741-2n, 746n, 760n, 761n, 804n, 813n, 845n, 912n, 1033n, 1102-3n, 1215n, F 26n, 84n, 85n, 105n, 121n, 122n, 134n, 184n, 194n, 204n, 257n, 258-9n, 265n, 295n, 338n, 339n, 387-8n, 405n, 414-5n, 418n, 425n, 427n, 429n, 439n, 477n, 520n, 629n, 710-3n, 735n, 740n, 799n, 852n, 855n, 862n, 942n, 970n, 1045n, 1053-6nn, 1143n, 1280n, 1308n, 1323n, 1327-8n, 1394n, 1453n*, 1478n, E p10 n44, E 1n, 22-23n, 38n, 45n, 49n, 104n, 119-120n, 150n, 186n*, 256-7nn, 259-260n, 284n, 306-7n, 317n, 330n, 356n, 382n, 507n, 612n, 624nn, 648n, 686-7n, 719-720nn, 729n, 732n, 767n, 845n, 846n, 907n, 916n, 971n, 979n, 980n, 982-6n, 990n, 1021n, 1048n, 1101n, 1153n, We p25, We 33-34n, 130-197n, 176n, 178n, 278n, 306n, 312n, 453n, 649-652n, 946n, 1102n, 1129n, 1206n

work, abolished for men in Praxagora's society, E 654n

work-basket, carried by women, L 535n, T p7 n41, T 822, E 87d, 125n

wreaths, see garlands

writing, mythical inventor of, T 769-770n, F 1451n

writing, on stage, T 776-784

xenēlasiai (Spartan expulsions of foreigners), P 624n, B 38n, 1013

Zacynthus, L 394

Zancle (Sicily), afterwards Messene, L 1141n

Zoroastrianism, P 411n

www.ingramcontent.com/pod-product-compliance
Lightning Source LLC
Chambersburg PA
CBHW071110100726
47908CB00008B/2331